ARK OF EMPIRE

Ark of Empire

THE AMERICAN FRONTIER

1784–1803

❧

DALE VAN EVERY

WILLIAM MORROW AND COMPANY

NEW YORK, 1963

Contents

MAPS

Foreword

ARK OF EMPIRE is a chapter in the new winning of the West which Dale Van Every is giving us, but it is more. It is a chapter, and a crucially important chapter, in the history of American nationalism. That history is usually written from the vantage—or disadvantage—point of Philadelphia or New York or Washington; Mr. Van Every writes it from the vantage point of the Ohio and the Mississippi.

How did it happen, after all, that the United States became a single nation, spanning a continent, instead of a dozen or a score of nations? We take American nationalism for granted, but should not. Almost everywhere else on the globe nationalism has meant fragmentation—in Latin America, for example, in the nineteenth century, in much of Europe, in the new Africa and Asia. In the twentieth century almost alone in the United States it has meant unification. Yet when Britain reluctantly recognized American independence in 1783 the auspices for successful nationalism were by no means promising, and it was not only the next five or six years that were "critical"; the whole period from 1783 to 1815 was critical. The Earl of Sheffield, no enemy of America, observed in 1783 that Congress could never hope to maintain its authority over "the distant and boundless regions" of the West; Turgot was persuaded that the forces of disintegration were more powerful than the forces of integration, and the somewhat mordant Dean Tucker, in England, dismissed the American experiment as chimerical:

> As to the future grandeur of America, and its being a rising empire under one head . . . it is one of the idlest and most visionary notions that ever was conceived, even by writers of romance. When those immense regions beyond the back settlements are taken into account, they form the highest probability that the Americans never can be united into one compact empire under any species of government whatever. Their fate seems to be—a disunited people till the end of time.

What were the threats to the new nation, and how did the nation surmount them? That is really the theme of *Ark of Empire*. The first threat, the most elementary, is also the most familiar: the weakness of the Confederation. It is fashionable now to argue that this weakness has been exaggerated, and that the critical period was not really so critical. Those who are content to observe the neatness and prosperity of Connecticut or the bountiful fields of Pennsylvania come easily to that conclusion, and so, too, those who confine their attention to political and constitutional developments, and who observe, rightly enough, that the Articles of Confederation were adequate for many purposes and that most of the States were putting their houses in order. But there can be no doubt that observant contemporaries thought the period critical, indeed; there can be no doubt that men of the Western Waters—the heroes (and sometimes the villains) of Mr. Van Every's volumes—thought the period not only critical but desperate, and were, often enough, ready to give up altogether.

The second threat was precisely in the West—in the vastness of territory which the new nation was expected to administer and to defend. The new United States emerged as the largest of Western nations, and by successive acquisitions of land continued to occupy that difficult position. We tend now to consider territory an advantage. The eighteenth century looked upon it as a grave disadvantage, particularly for a republic. Indeed, the philosophers and statesmen of the Old World agreed that it was impossible for a republic to be large—either the republic would fail or it would of necessity become an empire. And how, after all, was the new and feeble nation to govern a territory as large as most of Western Europe? A nation run by a handful of clerks, and an army of less than one thousand soldiers and men! As the greatest of our historians, Henry Adams, wrote of the America of 1800:

> No prudent person dared to act on the certainty that when settled, government could comprehend the whole; and when the day of separation should arrive, and America should have her Prussia, Austria and Italy, as she already had her England, France and Spain, what else could follow but a return to the old conditions of local jealousies, wars and corruptions, which had made a slaughter house of Europe?

What else, indeed?

That was what the men of the Western Waters were asking, all through the critical years of the eighties and the nineties. Could government at Philadelphia really exercise control over so vast a territory? Could it set up a proper land system, create efficient administration, provide defense against Indians and against the British, the Spaniards and—as it turned out—the French?

To many, East and West alike, the outlook was bleak, if not desperate. Some Eastern statesmen, like John Jay, were prepared to sacrifice the West for more immediate advantages of commerce or of politics. Others, like Jefferson, looked with equanimity upon the prospect of Western independence. "We think we see their happiness in their union, and we wish it," he wrote. "Events may prove it otherwise, and if they see their interest in separating, why should we take sides with our Atlantic rather than our Mississippi descendants? It is the elder and the younger son differing." Washington, the most farsighted and statesmanlike of those who concerned themselves with the problem of the West, often despaired. He had known the West since, as a young man, he explored the forks of the Ohio; he had known its problems and its possibilities as Commander in Chief during the Revolution; he knew it again as President, and did more to keep it safely within the Union than any other.

As for the men of the Western Waters, they were quite prepared, most of them, to set up on their own, with or without the aid of Spain, of France, even of Britain. What they wanted was land; what they wanted was protection against the Indians; what they wanted was stable government. The land they could win for themselves—unless governments back East interfered with land titles, as they so commonly did. The governments, too, they could provide for themselves, and there is no more impressive chapter in our political history than that which tells how these rude frontiersmen went about setting up constitutions and governments on the basis of the right principles and the right precedents. Yet here again the States were constantly interfering—striking down the new state of Franklin, threatening the independence of the settlements in Kentucky or in Tennessee, interfering and making demands, but doing little else. Certainly neither the States nor the Confederation, nor—for a long time—the new United States under the Constitution, did anything to protect the frontiersmen against the Indians.

There is no more hackneyed story in our history than this story of Indian warfare; it is a tribute not only to Mr. Van Every's literary but also to his interpretive skill that he has managed to give it fresh color and fresh meaning. He has brought home to us as no writer since Theodore Roosevelt the strength, the tenacity, the cunning and often the nobility of the Indians of this trans-Appalachian West. He has paid tribute to great Indian leaders like Joseph Brant and the fantastic McGillivray, to their courage and their statesmanship. He even persuades us to look at the invasion of the West from the point of view of the Indian. And he makes clear what we so easily forget, that in alliance with the Spaniards to the south and the British to the north, the Indians came very close to winning their war against the frontiersmen.

That was the fourth element in the equation of American nationalism and the West—the Spaniards and the British. We tend to think of the "struggle for a continent" as something that ended on the Plains of Abraham, or perhaps, at very latest, on the fields of Yorktown. Not at all. The struggle for a continent continued unabated to 1815. The British quickly regretted their decision to surrender the West, and defiantly clung to the Northwest posts and with them control of the fur trade of the West. The Spaniards had never really been allies; now they were prepared to become enemies. They wanted to consolidate their position in the Mississippi Valley—our West, but we must remember, their East—and they hoped to control most of the territory west of the Appalachians and south of the Ohio. Both the British and the Spaniards were prepared to subsidize the Indians to do their fighting for them; both were prepared to subvert the American frontiersmen—who were, often enough, quite ready to be subverted.

These were the problems that glared and glowered upon the new nation: feebleness at home, economic and military instability, defenseless frontiers, Indian warfare and a continuation of something like a cold war with Britain and with Spain. How could the new nation overcome these dangers; how could it solve these problems?

How it did so is the story Mr. Van Every has to tell. There were three major ingredients in the solution. The first and perhaps the most important was the Westerner himself—the courage, the tenacity, the ruthlessness, the ambition, of the men of the Western Waters. And we should add, the numbers. That was what proved decisive in the end—the sheer weight of numbers. The second ingredient was in a broad way political. It was the establishment, between 1787 and 1789, of a stable government under the leadership and guidance of the man who best understood the West, George Washington. It was the enactment of that farsighted and statesmanlike plan, the Northwest Ordinance, which guaranteed equality to the West. It was the provision—tardy and still inadequate—of military defense for the West, the defense symbolized by Wayne at Fallen Timbers.

As for the third ingredient, that was perhaps a matter of good fortune rather than good planning. The Revolution, which burst out in 1789, quickly engulfed the whole of Western Europe—and Britain as well. The British, the Spaniards, soon had other things to think about than the Northwest posts, or employing the Creek Indians against frontiersmen. When the British commandant closed the gates of Fort Miami on his stricken Indian allies after Fallen Timbers, that act was symbolic of the passing of British power south of the Lakes; when the British signed the Jay Treaty, giving up the Northwest posts, that act was dictated as much by European considerations as by American. Not for the first time, and certainly not for the last, Europe's troubles meant American immunity.

The struggle for a continent continued for two decades after Fallen Timbers. France entered the scene briefly under Napoleon, and the long struggle reached another of its many climacterics with the purchase of Louisiana and the elimination of France. Britain re-entered the scene, again, with depredations on American commerce, and eventually with a war which threatened the very existence of the United States. Then came the grand climacteric: the Battle of New Orleans. With that the West was really won; with that Europe decided to leave America alone; with that the era of colonialism, which had lasted since 1607, came to an end, and the era of independent nationalism began.

HENRY STEELE COMMAGER

ARK OF EMPIRE

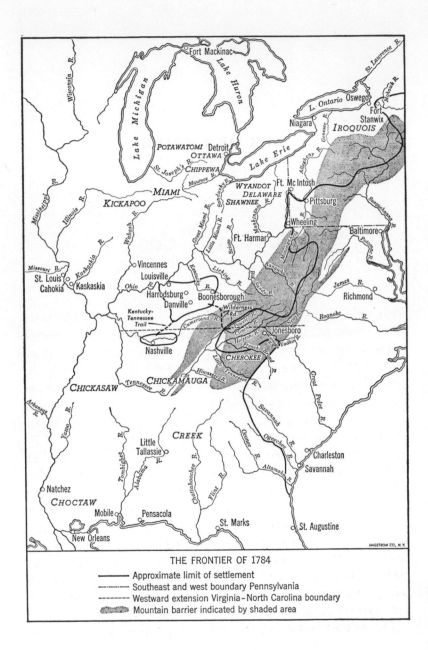

THE FRONTIER OF 1784

——— Approximate limit of settlement
—·—·— Southeast and west boundary Pennsylvania
-------- Westward extension Virginia-North Carolina boundary
░░░░ Mountain barrier indicated by shaded area

I

❦

A New Nation

That fall of 1784 was exceptionally cold and wet. The mountain barrier between the Valley of Virginia and the Ohio, 200 rugged miles to the westward, was wrapped in clouds and drenched by rain. Over its successive ridges struggled a traveler, following no path but his own purpose. On these trackless slopes even the buffalo traces had become choked with brush since the reduction of the former herds by the past quarter century's continued hunting. When, at intervals in a creek bottom, he came upon an isolated backwoodsman's cabin, he inquired not the easiest way but the hardest. The streams between the ridges, offering the only routes out of the region used by the few inhabitants, all, like the mountains, ran north and south. Still, undeterred by the weather or the heights, the traveler kept inexorably to his east-west course, scaling ridge after ridge, sleeping on the ground in the rain, rising each gray and dripping dawn to assail the next mountain. He was more explorer than traveler. There was no record that any man had ever persisted in taking this way before. Yet he kept on with a determination that indicated his purpose was relentless, even desperate.

The weather-beaten pilgrim was George Washington. He was

a man with a problem. As so often with him, it was his country's problem. Only a few months before, in a series of dramatic and moving farewells to his soldiers, his officers, and Congress, he had relinquished command of the Continental Army. The great task of achieving independence had been completed and he had gratefully returned to the personal satisfactions of Mount Vernon. But now, before the end of the first year of peace, he was recognizing his share of responsibility for meeting another and possibly greater task. The nation for which he had won freedom was already drifting toward a collapse certain to deny it every benefit of that freedom.

Among a host of perils, disunion was the basic threat devouring hopes which a twelvemonth before had seemed so fair. The echoes of the victory celebrations had scarcely died away before it had become apparent that the new United States was united in name only. The states' impulse to co-operate, enlivened during the Revolution by the struggle against a common enemy, had swiftly cooled when peace had removed the danger from without. The new nation had begun at once to appear much less a nation than a chance grouping of thirteen separate and competitive ex-colonies strung out along as many hundred miles of seaboard. Those in the north were set so far apart from those in the south that many weeks were required for the exchange of so much as a message. In geographical and commercial environment the two extremes differed as much as Sweden and Sicily. Each of the greater states, Virginia, Pennsylvania, New York, and Massachusetts, was firmly convinced that its own interests were only to be successfully protected at the expense of the interests of its rivals. All the lesser were suspiciously determined to resist any interference by their more powerful neighbors. The great experiment which, when given inspired expression in the Declaration of Independence, had electrified the world seemed already a failure. Among the country's alarmed leaders none perceived the deadliness of the danger more clearly than Washington. As commander in chief during the Revolution he had had perpetually to deal with interstate rivalries and jealousies. By the seven-year-long miracle of his personal exertion, resolution, and patience he had kept the Continental Army in the field until victory was won. No man was in a position therefore to be so keenly aware that now far more bitter rivalries and jealousies were imperiling that victory.

His most effective public virtue was the hardheaded, no-nonsense point of view of a practical businessman. His constant instinct was to face facts. In contemplating his country's problem his thinking was as rational as the addition of a column of figures. He had only to begin with the realization that disaster was only to be averted if the present trend toward disunion was reversed, to come to the realization that this could only be achieved by establishing in people's minds an important national interest in which all the states might share. Such a common cause, equally appealing to all, was not readily evident among coastal communities which considered themselves committed by location to inescapable competition with one another. Washington, however, was able to distinguish one common interest which stood outside every state's local prejudices and which could in the future become of dominating importance: the west.

By a providential diplomatic accident during the negotiation of the recent peace treaty, a vast expanse of the western wilderness beyond the mountains had been ceded by Great Britain to the United States. The English design had been to embarrass, at what seemed in London slight cost, England's traditional enemies, France and Spain, but a much underestimated concurrent development had invested the maneuver with another immeasurably greater consequence. Just before and during the Revolution some thousands of American settlers had found scattered lodgments there. To these they still clung after having survived unparalleled dangers and horrors during the war. Their isolated communities were separated by months of perilous travel from the centers of population in the east, and few people on the seaboard regarded possession of that distant region, for the most part occupied only by wild animals and wild Indians, in any other light than as a national liability. Washington had a longer view. Most of his youth had been spent on the frontier, he had won his military reputation on the frontier, and his intense interest in the frontier had never wavered. He was convinced that the west was bound to develop rapidly and that if retained by the United States it could instead become a tremendous national asset. One of the immediate advantages was an opportunity to underwrite the otherwise impossible compensation promised by every state to its veterans, and another was to reduce the national debt by the sale of western lands. In his opinion what was primarily required was an improvement in the means of communication between the seaboard and the Ohio. Such a trade route could provide a tie holding not only the west to the east but the thirteen states to each other. In any event, whatever was to be done had to be done at once. In both east and west the fatal drift toward disunion was accelerating.

Washington's second most effective public virtue was his willingness to devote his own time and effort to his country's need. Aware of the extreme urgency of the need to understand the western problem, which was at the heart of the national problem, he determined to investigate its many ramifications for himself. On September 1, 1784, nine months from the day the last English troopship had cleared New York harbor and eight months and eight days from the moment he had resigned his commission as commander in chief, he forsook the comforts of Mount Vernon and set out for the Ohio. His primary purpose, as he described it in his diary, was to obtain "a knowledge of facts—coming at the temper and disposition of the Western Inhabitants—and making reflections thereon, which, otherwise, must have been as wild, incohert, or perhaps as foreign from the truth, as the inconsistency of the reports which I had received even from those to whom most credit seemed due, generally were."

On his way west he took the barely passable road slanting northwestward over the mountains from the Potomac to the Forks of the Ohio which he had himself built exactly thirty years before but which had always been called Braddock's Road in somewhat unsympathetic memory of the English general who had come to so memorable a disaster at the end of it. It was upon his return that he circled through the steeper mountains to the south in search of a more direct route between the west and Virginia. In both his wars he had lost every important battle except the last one. It was so now with this undertaking. He had intended while in the west to inspect his own lands on the Kanawha but was forced to realize the Indian danger made this an unacceptable risk.[1] He was equally unsuccessful in his search for a wholly Virginia way west. Commercially effective transportation in the eighteenth century required a route over the greater portion of which carriage by water was possible. His days of climbing the rain-swept mountains eventually established the bleak reality that there existed no practicable way directly westward from Virginia. But he was so little discouraged by these successive disappointments that he wrote in his diary, "I am well pleased with my journey." For he had been seeking facts and facts he had found. His every conviction of the national importance of the west and the urgency of the need to hit upon some means to hold it had been confirmed.

Upon his return he set down in great detail in his diary his reflections upon the situation in the west in relation to the national situation. In the privacy of this daily journal he was able with complete candor to record his view of the dangers threatening the survival of his country in the first year of peace. With respect to the interrelation of conditions on both sides of the mountains he was the best informed man of his times. Events of the next twenty years were to demonstrate how amazingly accurate was his judgment. So malignant did the nation's ills appear to him that he was prepared to consider cures very nearly as harsh.

The first result of his laborious exploration had been to crush any lingering hope that there might exist an all-Virginia route westward. The Potomac-Monongahela route, roughly the old Braddock Road, was, he was forced to admit, "*much* the shortest" route from the Ohio and the Great Lakes "to the tidewater of the Atlantic." This

---

[1] Washington's western lands to which through the years he had gained title by the purchase of the rights of fellow veterans of the French and Indian War, by locations selected for him by his western agent, William Crawford, and by allocations entered in his name by early Kentucky surveyors, aggregated 40,000 acres.

raised the specter of interstate rivalry, the central difficulty that in 1784 appalled every thoughtful American. The route lay largely in Pennsylvania, a companion state to which he, as a Virginian, referred as though it were a foreign country. It was a route, he wrote, "not under our control; being subject to a power whose interest is opposed to the extension of their navigation, as it would be the inevitable means of withdrawing from Philadelphia all the trade of that part of its western territory which lyes beyond Laurel Hill."[2]

Yet he considered the case for trade with the west so urgent that he could bring himself to advocate using the very disunion which he so deeply deplored as a club to compel union. There was, he did not hesitate to point out, a mounting threat which could be expected to deter Pennsylvania interference with Virginia-bound commerce. "Any attempt of that government to restrain it," he wrote, "I am equally well persuaded wd. cause a seperation of their territory; there being sensible men among them who have it in contemplation at this moment." By "sensible men" he meant the discontented settlers in that portion of Pennsylvania west of the mountains, many of whom were Virginians who had always resented Pennsylvania's jurisdiction and were therefore the more impatient with their economic disadvantages. Having thus envisioned the possibility of resorting, if necessary, to the incitement of secession in western Pennsylvania, he proceeded, as was his custom when he had reached a decision, immediately to action. He wrote Governor Benjamin Harrison of Virginia proposing that Maryland and Virginia co-operate in the joint enterprise of river dredging and canal construction indicated. To expedite consideration he himself went to Annapolis as Virginia's representative. So pressing was his interest that he did not even return to spend Christmas at Mount Vernon with his family. Stirred to swift action by his advocacy, within weeks the legislatures of both states had approved the project, and in February of 1785 the Potomac Company was formed to undertake the improvement of

---

[2] In 1758 Washington had been involved in a furious Virginia-Pennsylvania dispute over this same question of rival routes west. Cf. Dale Van Every, *Forth to the Wilderness*, p. 91.

the Potomac-Monongahela-Ohio route, with or without Pennsylvania's acquiescence.

Washington had no compunctions about this aggressive precipitancy. This was, in his estimation, no moment to temporize. In his mind the issue was the far greater question of national survival. Again and again in 1784 in his journal and in his letters to Harrison and others he emphasized his conviction that American retention of the west was in the gravest doubt while at the same time it represented the one hope for the preservation of the union: "The Ohio River embraces this Commonwealth from its Northern almost to its Southern limits. It is now our western boundary & lyes nearly parallel to our exterior, and thickest settled Country . . . The Western Settlers have no other means of coming to us but by long land transportation and unimproved Roads. A combination of circumstances make the present conjuncture more favorable than any other to fix the trade of the Western Country to our Markets . . . The way is plain, and the expence, comparatively speaking deserves not a thought, so great would be the prize. The Western Inhabitants would, I am persuaded meet us half way rather than be *driven* into the arms of, or be in any wise dependent upon, foreigners; the consequence of which would be, a seperation, or a War. The way to avoid both, happily for us, is easy, and dictated by our clearest interest. It is to open a wide door, and make a smooth way for the produce of that Country to pass to our Markets before the trade may get into another channel . . . No well informed Mind need be told, that the flanks and rear of the United territory are possessed by other powers, and formidable ones, too—nor how necessary it is to apply the cement of interest to bind all parts of it together, by one indissoluble band—particularly the middle States with the Country immediately back of them—for what ties let me ask, should we have upon those people; and how entirely unconnected shod. we be with them if the Spaniards on their right or great Britain on their left, instead of throwing stumbling blocks in their way as they now do; should invite their trade and seek alliances with them? What, when they get strength, which will be sooner than is generally imagined (from the emigration of Foreigners who can have no predeliction for us, as well as the removal [west] of our own Citizens) may be the consequence of their having formed such connections and alliances; requires no uncommon foresight to predict. The Western Settlers— from my own observation—stand as it were on a pivot—the touch of a feather would turn them away."

Washington had devoted all of the first years of his public life to opening the first way west. He was now at fifty-two embarked upon an even more dedicated devotion of all of his last years to holding the west. But no other easterner realized as clearly as did he that all depended on what he had termed "the temper and disposition" of the westerners themselves. During the years immediately following 1784 every conceivable circumstance was to conspire to break the tenuous bonds linking them to the infant new nation. An examination of some of the circumstances which inclined them instead to an instinctive groping recognition of their real mission as the chief architects of the country's prodigious growth is a principal object of this book.

II

༜

Congress Proposes

In 1784 the national government had all but ceased to function. Under the Articles of Confederation Congress had no power to raise money or raise an army or to take any significant action except with the express concurrence of nine of the states. Even its own members were paid by the states from which they came. The most routine clerical expense could be met only by appeals for voluntary contributions from the several states. It was expected to give special attention to foreign affairs but its judgment in this field, too, was subject to the veto power of the states. Most of the distinguished men who had served in Congress during the Revolution no longer chose to waste their time in what had become little more than a debating society. Most states after the war's end were represented, if at all, by nonentities. So slight was the general interest in its deliberations that for long periods in 1784 its sessions were stultified by the lack of a quorum. This enfeebled Congress, with authority only to supplicate, constituted all there was to the central government. There was no independent executive department. Every power to decide or to act was reserved to the states.

There was one exception to this rule, one responsibility most states were happy to delegate to Congress. This was the problem of dealing with the Indians ranged along the country's entire western frontier. That this was also the most threatening difficulty confronting the new nation was undoubtedly a blessing in disguise inasmuch as the imperative necessity to make some effort to cope with it kept the breath of life in a national government which had otherwise seemed at the point of expiring.

Indian antagonism had not diminished with the cessation of hostilities between the United States and Great Britain. The basic Indian military tactic of dependence on surprise hit-and-run raids had represented the major Indian menace even during the larger campaigns of the open state of war. During the Revolution it had cost the lives of thousands of border inhabitants. Though Indian invasions in force had ceased at the war's end the raids were continuing on a scale only slightly less deadly. The deaths of more than 200 frontier people had been reported during the first year after the proclamation of peace. All Indians had been quick to perceive that the treaty between the two distant white governments had in no way alleviated their principal grievance, the constant encroachment of white settlement.

This Indian antagonism, everywhere bitter, presented its most critical aspect in the region northwest of the Ohio inhabited by an allied group of peculiarly belligerent nations whose perpetual readiness to strike had been demonstrated by their aggressive participation in every border war since white men had first ventured to cross the mountains. New York and Virginia had for a time nursed rival claims to the area: New York's based on its theoretical inheritance of early Iroquois conquests, and Virginia's on its interpretation of its original charter which had been given some added substance by George Rogers Clark's conquests during the Revolution. Neither, however, was longer eager to become involved in a solitary collision with the defiant Ohio Indians and both made haste to cede their claims to the national government. Connecticut and Massachusetts, each of which had obscure claims to strips of territory extending indefinitely westward, prepared to follow their example.[1] Thus Con-

---

[1] Virginia reserved certain tracts across from Louisville and on the Scioto for eventual grant to veterans, as did Connecticut on the Cuyahoga.

gress, as its first peacetime responsibility, was thrust headlong into this arena of unique and unlimited hazard.

Aside from the basic difficulty of Indian belligerence, many other perplexities were peculiar to the region northwest of the Ohio. By the terms of the Proclamation of 1763, as amended by the Treaty of Fort Stanwix of 1768 and reaffirmed by the Quebec Act of 1774, the area had by British decree been denied to white settlement and reserved for Indian occupancy. In the Treaty of Pittsburgh of 1775 the Americans had pledged their observance of the Ohio line. British officials were now busily advising their former Indian allies that none of this had been altered by the recent treaty of peace ending the Revolution and that they might count on continued British support in any assertion of their rights. Next there were the French communities at Detroit, Vincennes, Kaskaskia, and Cahokia occupied by inhabitants who had formerly been French subjects. They had long been friends of the Indians and yet their interests had to be carefully considered. France had been American patron and ally during the Revolution and was still the only friend of the United States among the great powers. Then there was the awkward circumstance that the area represented the only inch of American soil not claimed by one or the other of the states and thus with inhabitants, whether Indian, French, or American, who were not theoretically under the jurisdiction of any one of the state governments. Upon Congress, for all the strict limitations upon its powers in its own sphere, there had therefore descended the obligation to contrive some sort of local government to fill this void. And, finally, there was the most ominous difficulty of all. The British army which had readily evacuated the seaboard was still garrisoning the former British forts on the Great Lakes where its continued presence was encouraging every Indian impulse to resist.

Congress assailed the many-headed dragon represented by these myriad difficulties with a curious bravado. It is perhaps a political axiom that the more limited the responsibilities of any bureaucracy the more avid it is to seize upon any opportunity to expand them. Indian affairs offering the one area in which it was permitted freely to function, Congress plunged at the problem with doctrinaire abandon. In committee rooms of the itinerant capital, first New York, then Annapolis, then Philadelphia, members ardently debated the formulation of a national Indian policy. The result of these deliberations, conducted in an atmosphere so detached from the bristling realities of the wilderness, was the adoption of a program of precipitate and aggressive expansion altogether out of proportion to any power of Congress to implement. By the Ordinance of 1783 the Indians were pronounced subjects solely dependent on the generosity of the United States and declared to occupy the status of defeated enemies who by their hostility during the Revolution had forfeited whatever rights they might formerly have claimed. Any shadow of Indian title to their ancestral lands was specifically denounced and their continued occupancy ruled subject to the pleasure of the United States. As a preliminary measure a line was designated along the Miami and Maumee rivers behind which the Indians were directed immediately to retire. The Indian right of occupancy in the territory to be vacated had never before been questioned; it comprised most of the present state of Ohio in which no white settlements had as yet been established. The Indians who for the past thirty years had in a series of violent wars fiercely resisted each advance of the white frontier were now called upon docilely to acquiesce in an advance of two hundred miles at a single bound and as a part of the process to abandon the towns and hunting grounds of what they regarded their native lands. American commissioners were appointed with instructions to acquaint the various Indian nations with what henceforth would be required of them.

So intoxicated had Congress become with its freedom of action in this one area in which it had been given license to legislate by the original thirteen states of which it was a creature that it soared to the heights of proposing the formation of new states in this so soon to be Americanized area northwest of the Ohio. This was an innovation in confederation thinking, and the startling proposition excited sharp discussion and many objections in the capitals of the existing states. But meanwhile by the Ordinance of 1784, in the enactment of which Thomas Jefferson had taken a leading part on the eve of his departure to become Minister to France, ten future governments were envisaged in the immense region stretching from the Forks of the Ohio to the headwaters of the Mississippi. Throughout this enormous area, in which not so much as a single American village as yet existed, whenever the number of white inhabitants in any district reached the number of 20,000, Congress provided that they might appeal for acceptance into the confederation as new and separate states. As some indication of how far Congressional imagination had strayed beyond the realities of the present to the fantasies of the future, the ten new states were to be named Sylvania, Michigania, Chersonesus, Assenisipia, Metropotamia, Illinoia, Saratoga, Polypotamia, Pelispia, and Washington. Most more earthbound Americans, realizing the visionary program dealt with a remote and unforeseeable future, lost interest in the subject and for all practical purposes the Ordinance was soon forgotten. Nevertheless, it remained the greatest contribution of the first peacetime Congress to the nation's advancement. There had in it been momentarily and dimly glimpsed the great cornerstone upon which the growth of the country was most to depend—the doctrine of the progressive admission of new and equal states.

For all its enterprise Congress was hampered that spring of 1784 by one most embarrassing restraint. If the Indians were to be at all impressed by these sweeping American edicts and if the British posts on the Lakes were meanwhile to be occupied by American garrisons, some sort of military force was required. But Congress had none at its disposal. The Continental Army had been disbanded at the end of the Revolution and every state was adamantly opposed to the recreation of any semblance of a federal army. In the light of sad experiences during the last two wars a professional military class was regarded as anathema. The institution of a "standing army" was considered a threat to every citizen's liberty, a menace to the independence of every state, and a certain prelude to tyranny. However, under the pressures of emergency and necessity Congress proved sufficiently nimble-witted to contrive a makeshift substitute. The states most directly interested in the pacification of the northwest were beseeched to furnish contingents of their militia for temporary Congressional use. By an enactment of June 3, 1784, it was "resolved, that it be and and it is hereby recommended" that Connecticut furnish 165 men, New York 165, New Jersey 110, and Pennsylvania 260. Lieutenant Colonel Josiah Harmar of Pennsylvania, as senior officer and commander of the largest state contingent, was by general consent given over-all command. As acting commander in chief of the only body of semifederal troops in existence he was thereafter commonly called General Harmar while he, without specific authority from Congress, usually referred to the multistate militia under his charge as the First American Regiment.

All this had Congress proposed. But these buoyant congressional resolves to expedite American occupation of the west were brutally repulsed by every successive encounter with the actual situation there. The swiftly rising thunderheads of opposition, soon visible along the entire western horizon, revealed the existence of forces with which debates and votes were not enough to cope. To Indian resistance, in itself a sufficiently dire deterrent, was being added the resistance of the two world powers, Great Britain and Spain, whose interests in North America were in direct conflict with those of the United States.

In the north at general conferences in September of 1783 at Sandusky and in the summer of 1784 at Niagara the Indians had been striving to perfect a more closely knit confederation in order to present a united front to American aggression. They were encouraged by English advice and sympathy to continue to regard the Ohio as the Indian boundary across which American settlement must never be permitted to advance. American commissioners who the year before had been permitted to address the Indians at distant Detroit were now being prevented by the same English commanders from meeting with Indians at so much nearer Niagara. This assumption of Indian guardianship was given substance by British military control of the principal avenues of wilderness communication in the northwest and by the influence of English traders and agents in Indian councils. Under this renewed British patronage Indian resistance to American demands continued to stiffen. Even though it might no longer be official British policy openly to arm the Indians the result had been the same. English trading interests, with representatives in every Indian town, were fully able to supply Indian military needs. Before the year was out it had become painfully apparent that any attempt to require the Indians immediately to hand over the Ohio country would without question bring on a general Indian war.

Upon this foreground hazard was piled an even more disconcerting development in the background. There were increasing indications that war with the Indians meant war also with Great Britain. When, in July of 1783, Washington had sent Baron von Steuben to arrange for the transfer to American custody, under the terms of the peace treaty, of the British forts at Oswego, Niagara, Detroit, and Mackinac, Governor General Frederick Haldimand had put him off with the explanation that he had not as yet been officially notified of the treaty's ratification. It was by now becoming apparent that it had become British intention to hold them indefinitely. On June 14, 1784, while Congress was occupied with naming new states in the northwest and mustering Harmar's little army, Haldimand had been instructed by the cabinet to maintain strategic control of the region by retaining possession of the forts. London had almost immediately repented the excessive generosity of the hasty cession of the northwest to the United States. Whatever value had been then seen in inserting a wedge between France and the United States during the peace parleys had already been gained. More pressing concerns dictated a reconsideration. The fur trade, always politically influential, had raised vehement objections to the surrender of its most valuable territory. With vivid memories of the horrors of Pontiac's War, colonial officials feared that if abandoned to American aggression the infuriated Indians might vent their vengeance as rigorously on the Canadian as on the American frontier. As a final and possibly more compelling urge, England's conscience had been increasingly troubled by reflection on the callous betrayal of her Indian allies at the peace table. Moved by such second thoughts the government had determined to hold the posts as a reassurance to the Indians and as a bar to the American advance in the northwest. There was a ready excuse for this flagrant breach of the peace treaty inasmuch as every American state had as flagrantly breached it with regard to the stipulated compensation due Loyalists and British creditors.

Equally ominous developments had become apparent in the south where Indian opposition was likewise receiving strong encouragement from a foreign power. On June 1, 1784, Spain concluded at Pensacola a treaty with the Creek, most numerous of all Indian nations, undertaking to supply and arm them and to support their resistance to American encroachment. This move to stimulate the anti-American sentiments of the Indians of the southwest was only one phase of Spanish determination to reassert the Spanish claim to the entire west which, even though vigorously supported by France, had been adroitly circumvented by the American and British peace commissioners. During the Revolution Spain had captured every British base in the west south of Detroit but by the peace treaty had been ceded only East and West Florida. Though these military and diplomatic developments had sufficiently disposed of one potential aggressor there remained the sharper Spanish apprehension of the threat to Spanish dominion posed by the far more pushing aggressiveness of the American frontiersman. Great Britain had shrewdly accentuated this conflict of interests between her two former enemies by ceding to the United States all territory in the west as far south as the 31st parallel, near the outskirts of Mobile. Spain's indignant refusal to recognize this cession had been given added emphasis by a persisting refusal even to recognize the independence of the United States. Driving the point home, Spain had not only refused to give up Natchez, a predominantly English-speaking community 50 miles north of the parallel, but, through French intermediaries, had formally notified the United States that Spain asserted possession of the entire east bank of the Mississippi as far north as the Ohio and of all other territory south of the Tennessee and west of the Flint River, in what is now central Georgia. Spanish commanders proceeded presently to the establishment of new forts and garrisons in the disputed area and continued efforts to encourage the resident Indians to resist any American attempt to occupy it.

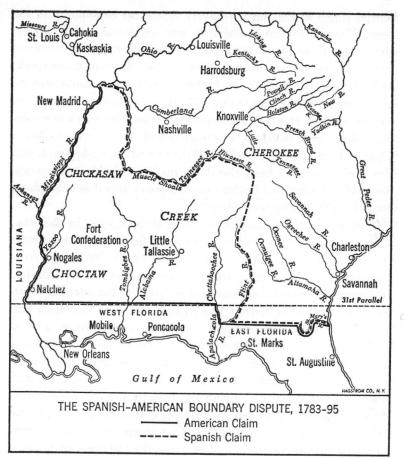

THE SPANISH-AMERICAN BOUNDARY DISPUTE, 1783-95
———— American Claim
– – – – – Spanish Claim

Spain recognized the American claim in Pinckney's Treaty, 1795. American land companies took advantage of the interim uncertainty by attempting to promote their Muscle Shoals, Yazoo and Natchez projects throughout the period that the dispute remained unresolved.

These manifestations of Spain's hostility were climaxed June 14, 1784, by the event which appeared then to dominate every other event in the west for many years to come. The Mississippi was declared closed to any other than Spanish navigation. This was a nearly mortal clutch at the throat of every American community in the west. The one surplus available to any settlement to offer in exchange for those manufactured articles upon which its continued growth depended was in such farm produce as corn, wheat, pork, and tobacco. These made for bulky cargoes which could only be transported over the intervening 200-mile wide mountain barrier to eastern markets at a cost which denied profit. The west's one commercial recourse, therefore, was to ship with the current down the Ohio and the Mississippi to New Orleans and thence by sea. It was this outlet that had been closed by the Spanish blockade in announced and calculated furtherance of a policy aimed at establishing control of the Mississippi Valley.

Confronted by this sudden eruption of opposition in the west, Congress was helpless. To these appeals to force there was no force at hand with which to counter. In December the first ragged company of Harmar's tiny army trudged into Pittsburgh. Before the last company had crossed the mountains in late 1785 the one-year enlistments of the earlier arrivals had expired. Between desertions and refusals to reenlist his command at no time approached the authorized strength of 700 and at most times hovered nearer 300. This was not a force able to make any pretense of moving upon the Spanish at Natchez, or of marching through the wilderness upon the British posts on the Lakes, or of giving the Indians any other impression than of American weakness. Its first and for many months its only field operation was directed not against Indians, or British, or Spaniards, but against American settlers. Since the Delaware withdrawal northward in 1781, a considerable number of astonishingly hardy land seekers, so determined to establish prior rights to choice sites that they were willing to accept the greater risk, had occupied locations on the Indian side of the upper Ohio. By direction of Congress, Harmar's soldiers drove them back across the river and burned their cabins to discourage their return.[2]

[2] Twenty years before, British soldiers under Colonel Henry Bouquet had burned out the first settlers to cross the same Proclamation Line, then running along the crest of the mountains instead of along the Ohio, in a similar effort to avert an earlier Indian war.

The first attempt to formulate a national policy to accelerate American occupation of the west thus ended in total frustration. Made each month more aware of the limitations upon its own capacity to act, Congress for three years took no further initiative other than repeatedly to prohibit American settlement across the Ohio and to define the type of surveys to be made once the region did become available for settlement. By far the most significant consequence of this governmental debacle was that the frontier people beyond the mountains were left, armed only with their own scant resources and guided only by their own impulses, to cope, unaided and unsupported, with the enormous dangers threatening them on every side. These were a people, however, who had long been accustomed to the realization that their survival depended entirely upon their own efforts. In crossing the mountains that separated them by so great a distance from their fellow countrymen in the east in order to seize upon new homes in the midst of a far and hostile wilderness they had become hardened to hazards. They were ready for this new ordeal. If now they were beset by perils that were so much more complex than any they had known before, including even the growth of a doubt that they longer owed allegiance to their distant and impotent government, they were never dismayed when obliged to make any decision, however harsh. It was to be a fearful test but among the many and diverse impulses it stirred in them there was never one to suspect that they need feel unequal to it.

III

The Frontier of 1784

The few thousand Americans west of the mountains upon whom so large a share of responsibility for their country's destiny had descended were a unique people. Their like had never been seen before nor has ever been since. They were as distinct from their fellow Americans as they were from the alien enemies with whom they were confronted. They had emerged from the ordinary population as suddenly as might invaders from another clime and almost as suddenly they were to merge again with the general citizenry of the republic. During their brief ascendancy they dominated every crisis with which they were beset. As befits conquerors, their most striking characteristic was an assurance of their innate superiority to any antagonist.

Some evidence of their inexhaustible vitality may be gained by a glance at the timetable of the westward movement. In the first 158 years after Jamestown, settlement had spread to New River, 220 miles to the westward. In that year, 1766, the emergent frontier people gave first evidence of their new-found enterprise by making their first intrusions beyond the mountains. From that moment, without regard for land-company designs, restraints of their own governments, Indian resistance, or the opposition of foreign powers, they kept on westward. Always it was the inhabitants of the then frontier who were first to reach the next frontier. It was only nine years before they had established Harrodsburg 220 miles farther west. They were briefly delayed by the protracted border war of the Revolution and its aftermath, but it still was only another 23 years before Daniel Boone had resettled on the Missouri another 350 miles farther west. Ahead of them now stretched a totally unfamiliar world of treeless plains, repellent deserts, snow-peaked mountains, and endless distances. Yet it was only 45 more years before, in 1843, the first settlers' wagons were rolling into Oregon 1800 more miles on westward. From Jamestown to New River the advance of settlement had been at the rate of a little over a mile a year. After the frontier people had come on the scene the westward surge became 33 miles a year.

Any recapitulation of their brief history cannot fail to pay tribute to their extraordinary services to their country but can only add to the central mystery of their emergence. Theirs is a success story without parallel but it is that only in retrospect. Few then glimpsed the meaning to the nation of the successes they were achieving. Their calamities were at the time much more apparent. As a people they were born of disaster, lived through disaster, thrived on disaster. Their original appearance as a decisive factor in the nation's development could no more have been accounted for then than it can now in any other light than as an outright miracle. For year after year from 1754 to 1764 the then frontier east of the mountains had been devastated from end to end by the Indian inroads of the French War and Pontiac's War. The border inhabitants were not then the self-willed aggressors of their later years. They were helpless victims, dying by the thousands. Most were unarmed. Many were recent immigrants from Europe. All had been driven to the cheaper land along the edge of the wilderness by the pressures of poverty. Through all those years their only defense was despair. They fled in panic, cowered to await rescue by soldiers, felt no impulse to resist. They suffered until they could endure no more. Then came the moment when suddenly they straightened to face the wilderness and next to plunge into it. Such was their birth as a distinct people. A more sudden and complete transition cannot be found outside mythology.

From that moment their ventures became exploits and their exploits triumphs. They crossed the mountains at what then seemed impossible odds at the last moment before the outbreak of the Revolution must otherwise have made American possession of the west impossible for a generation, perhaps forever. Having hastily erected their few stockades, they withstood during the Revolution a British-Indian onslaught from which for seven terrible years there was no surcease. It was their inexplicable resolve to hold on which gave meaning at the war's end to the British impulse to confound France and Spain by bestowing the west upon the United States. Without the actual presence of the defiant settlers this must have been a senseless gesture. Had the scattered American settlements instead been abandoned under those unceasing attacks, the area must have been occupied by Spanish garrisons with the same celerity with which during the war Spanish military power had carried every British strong point on the Mississippi and the Gulf. It had been this achievement of the frontier people that had presented the new United States with the chance, still a most uncertain chance in 1784, to inherit the west.

However heroic had been these feats during the ten years preceding 1784 and however immense were to be their consequences, the average frontiersman was no paladin. As a person he was rude, uncouth, violent, greedy, cynical, and brutal. He was a poor workman, a bad farmer, and a disorderly citizen. His favorite diversions were drinking and physical competitions. His love of fighting for its own sake inclined him when his enemies were out of reach to turn with equal gusto on his friends. His scorn of authority extended to disrespect for his own elected officers and made him a completely undependable soldier. His own extreme self-will led him to conclude all men were governed primarily by self-interest. Much of his personal conduct was marked by a barbarity to rival any Indian's. He decorated his buckskins with beads and fringe, wore a breechclout, took scalps, and in his callous aping of savage behavior recoiled only at painting his face and burning prisoners.

These turbulent propensities, which must have been considered vices in more civilized surroundings, in the wilderness became virtues that increased the chance of his survival and made possible his achievements. Softer, milder, and more reasonable men could not so well have withstood the shocks to which the frontiersman was subjected daily. He had, of course, many genuine virtues, including the greatest, fortitude. Of all his assets by far the most effective in his struggle to survive was his phenomenal adaptability, the characteristic which more than any other marked him as a unique type. Most of the earlier comers were experienced backwoodsmen, but the later comers took to the wilderness almost as readily. The newly arrived settler was plunged into an alien and infinitely demanding environment in which he must immediately master strange arts and devices of which he never before had dreamed. He must acquire, not slowly or fumblingly but with quick, complete proficiency, such novel skills as how to identify forest noises, how to track wild animals, how to build a fire in the rain, how to depend on game for his daily food, how to treat the ills of his animals and his children, and, above all else, how to cope with an Indian in that Indian's native woods. He must speedily learn to make his own house, furniture, tools, dishes, shoes, clothes, soap, sugar, hominy, whisky, ham, bacon, salt pork, corned beef, and still find time for the tremendous over-all task of clearing a hole in the primeval forest to make room for his corn patch. And he must meanwhile learn to co-operate with his neighbors in the devising of a political framework for the government of his community upon the immediate successful functioning of which the life and death of all depended. All of these demands he met and he speedily invented new and better ways of meeting most of them, including the expedient of the stockade, swiftly constructed of materials at hand, without the protection of which no settlement could have lasted through its first summer; the design of that extraordinary contrivance, such a craft as had never before been seen on land or sea, the Ohio River flatboat, which became his veritable ark of empire; and a system of local self-government so fiercely self-willed as to exact accommodation from other nations and eventual conformation from his own. His adaptability was so encyclopedic that he did not seem so much to adapt himself to his environment as to adapt his environment to his own needs and wishes. Unlike the Frenchman on the frontier who tended to live like an Indian, or the Spaniard who sought only to subjugate, convert, and govern, or the Englishman who brought his community with him, the pioneer American made over the wilderness into his own image.

Frontiersmen naturally varied from this average type, for better or worse, as much as do people from the norm in any society. All did not become hardened and warwise woodsmen upon whom the existence of the settlement might depend. Among them were weaklings and cowards and scoundrels. Also among them was an occasional natural leader, usually a man of substance and education, whose superior qualifications were so soon recognized by his neighbors that he was more likely than others to be elected a colonel of frontier militia or a delegate to a frontier convention. Some of these emerging leaders were as literate and articulate as their supremely talented counterparts of that genius-sprinkled period east of the mountains. Their capacity to grasp and express the highest political principles is illustrated by passages in the 1785 Petition of the People of Kentucky to the Virginia assembly, renewing the demand for independent statehood:

> Our sequestered situation, from the seat of Government, with the intervention of a mountainous desart of two hundred miles, always dangerous, and passable only at particular seasons, precludes every Idea of a connexion, on Republican principles . . . 'Tis not the ill directed or inconsiderate Zeal of a few, 'tis not the impatience of Power to which ambitious minds are prone, nor yet the baser consideration of Personal Interest, which influence the people of Kentucky; directed by superior motives, they are incapable of cherishing a wish unfounded in justice, and are now impelled by expanding evils, and irremediable grievances, universally seen, felt, and acknowledged, to obey the irristible dictates of selfpreservation, and seek for Happi-

ness, by means honorable to themselves with the consent and by the authority of our Constituents, after the most solemn deliberation being warned of every consequence, which can ensue, for them, for ourselves and for Posterity unborn—do Pray—That an Act may Pass at the ensuing session of Assembly, declaring and acknowledging the Sovereignty & Independence of this district . . . Our application may exhibit a new spectacle in the History & Politics of Mankind—A Sovereign Power; solely intent to bless its People agreeing to a dismemberment of its parts, in order to secure the Happiness of the whole . . . In this Address we have discarded the complimentary style of adulation & insincerity—it becomes Freemen when speaking to Freemen, to imploy the plain, manly unadorned Language of Independence.

Most contemporary observers, however, were agreed in finding little to admire in the more obvious characteristics of the frontier people. Father Pierre Gibault, for one example, who had wholeheartedly welcomed and assisted George Rogers Clark's invasion of the Illinois, was soon given cause to repent his magnanimity when the first American settlers began to crowd into the formerly placid little French communities:

There is no distinction from the greatest to the least except that by force; of the tongue, pernicious, calumniating and slanderous; of crying out very loud, and giving forth all sorts of insults and oaths. Everybody is in poverty, which engenders theft and rapine. Wantoness and drunkeness pass here as elegance and amusements quite in style. Breaking of limbs, murder by means of a dagger, sabre or sword (for he who wills carries one) are common, and pistols and guns are but toys in these regions.

James Seagrove, for another, whose duty it was, as United States Agent to the Creek Nation, to attempt to negotiate a frontier peace, put it more bluntly:

It is to be regretted that the insatiable rage of our frontier brethren for extending their limits cannot be checked and kept within the bounds set for them by the general government. The United States, like most countries, is unfortunate in having the worst of people on her frontiers.

While Brigadier General William Irvine, commander at Pittsburgh at the end of the Revolution, with a frankness possible in a personal letter to his wife, referred to that most important of all frontier communities as:

"The most wretched and miserable vile hole ever man dwelt in."

But it was Baron de Carondelet, Spanish Governor of Louisiana, who without moral reflections came most directly to the essential point—the consequences springing from their being the kind of people they were:

> This prestigious and restless population, continually forcing the Indian nations backward and upon us, is attempting to get possession of all the vast continent which those nations are occupying between the Ohio and Mississippi Rivers and the Gulf of Mexico and the Appalachian Mountains . . . Their method of spreading themselves and their policy are so much to be feared by Spain as are their arms . . . Their wandering spirit and the ease with which those people procure their sustenance and shelter quickly form new settlements. A carbine and a little maize in a sack are enough for an American to wander about in the forests alone for a whole month. With his carbine he kills the wild cattle and deer for food and defends himself from the savages. The maize dampened serves him in lieu of bread. With some tree trunks crossed one above another, in the shape of a square, he raises a house, and even a fort that is impregnable to the savages by crossing a story above the ground floor. The cold does not affright him. When a family tires of one location, it moves to another, and there settles with the same ease . . . If such men succeed in occupying the shores of the Mississippi . . . nothing can prevent them from crossing . . . and penetrating into our provinces on the other side.

It was this freedom of movement which so much disturbed the Spanish governor that most conditioned the behavior of the frontier people. It had made them total pragmatists. Whatever course was discovered effective in producing a desired result was forthwith adopted. Freedom of movement had won that freedom of action that they had come to seek and most to value. Former standards of conduct had been left behind. The new standard judged means only by the ends. If something proved to work it was considered no more than sensible to continue doing it until a better way chanced to be hit upon. The fearful pressures of a hostile environment made hesitations or compunctions preposterous. There was no time to make any other approach to a problem than the most direct one, to measure any undertaking by any other rule than the probability of its achieving its purpose. This made for amazing progress in adapting the wilderness to the needs of the newcomers. If a small raft could sweep one family down-river to Kentucky, then it was obviously sensible to construct one large enough to carry half a dozen families together with their cattle and horses. It also suppressed normal sympathies in a people who had themselves suffered too much to remain sensitive to the pain of others. If Indians had been known to imitate the wails of lost children to lure a boat into a shore-laid ambush, then thereafter it was obviously foolish to attempt to determine whether in a later instance the cries might this time be authentic. There could be no limit, however extreme, to the application of this harsh syllogism. If there was even a chance that the Indian practice of butchering white women and children could be discouraged by the butchery of Indian women and children, then they must never be spared. The end result of this rule of practicality was the fundamental frontier tenet: Nothing must be permitted to curb the advance of settlement. If government attempted to interfere, then government must be disregarded, and if Indians persisted in asserting their prior right to the land, then care must be taken that even a temporary peace was never established to delay the rate at which new land could be acquired.

This pragmatic attitude was notably evident in the extraordinary vitality of the democratic process on the frontier. A new settlement's compelling first task was to get up a stockade before Indians had had time to discover the development and to mount an attack. The need for an organized division of labor became instantly imperative. In addition to the men engaged in the construction others must be assigned to watch the grazing stock, to range the surrounding forests to detect any approach by Indians, and to stand guard at night. Other demands upon community decision were almost as pressing.

The land within and near the stockade was bound to become more valuable than that at a greater distance which made it necessary to allocate this so that all might share equitably in the eventual return from their common labors. To deal with such immediately urgent questions therefore required the institution of local self-government without an hour's delay. The first enterprise of a new settlement was necessarily to meet this challenge by a town meeting, in which all men able to carry a gun had a vote, to decide all issues by majority rule. When a station was being established by a single large land-owner, the majority still ruled since the station could only be main-tained by the willing co-operation of a sufficient number of families to conduct its defense. The first action of the first meeting was the election of a militia commander to supervise that defense. He became a kind of ex-officio mayor, sheriff, and all-purpose representative. The earlier all-Kentucky conventions were meetings of these local militia commanders who had assembled to confer on joint defense measures.

This frontier democracy could not be susceptible to gradual devel-opment. It had to begin functioning at once if the community were to survive. It had to continue to function, literally from day to day by successive meetings and successive votes, since the uninterrupted co-operation of the inhabitants was necessary to assure their common defense. Its driving concern must be for the immediate needs and perils of each local community. There was little room for political theorizing on wider issues. There was less room for sentimental attachment to the states from which the inhabitants had migrated, and least of all to the distant, shadowy, newly created central govern-ment of the United States.

Realizing how difficult distance made Virginia's participation in their defense, the people of Kentucky were soon compelled by the multiple dangers with which they were confronted to demand sepa-ration. Similar movements were as soon under way among the Penn-sylvanians and North Carolinians who had found new and more precarious homes west of the mountains. What the westerners re-quired of government was not jurisdiction so much as protection, and this it was becoming increasingly evident in 1784 they could expect only from a government of their own. To people whose survival had for so many years depended solely on their own decisions and exertions it was not a long step from demanding separation from their parent states to beginning seriously to debate the conceivable future advantages of an arrangement with Spain, Great Britain, or France compared to the known present disadvantages of adherence to the United States. As practicing pragmatists they expected government to work. For people in their situation it had to be made to work.

The physical limits of the frontier in 1784 were still much the same as during the fearful tumult of the Revolution. The line marking the outer edge of settlement still ran from the central Mohawk in eastern New York southeastward to the corner of New Jersey, westward across the mountains to the upper bend of the Ohio, south along the Ohio to a little below Wheeling, southeastward and then southwestward among the higher Appalachians to the headwaters of the Savannah, and finally southeastward to the Atlantic in southern Georgia. Two hundred miles to the west of the westernmost portions of this main frontier line were the isolated islands of settlement on the Kentucky and the Cumberland. The western bulge of the frontier was therefore a salient thrust far into the wilderness. Defensively it presented every military disadvantage common to a salient. The main concentrations of Indian power were adjacent to its shoulders, both in the north and in the south, and particularly threatened its only lines of communication with the east, the Ohio River in the north and the Wilderness Road in the south. The first settlers had not assumed this peculiarly exposed position of their own volition. They had been forced into it by the shifting pressures of Indian resistance. Only between the Ohio and the Cumberland had the wilderness had no Indian occupants. That supremely attractive region had become a kind of Indian no-man's land as a result of nearly a century of intertribal wars between Northern and Southern Indians. It had been of this curious circumstance that the original settlers had taken advantage in their daring dash for Kentucky in 1775.

Across this immense area west of the mountains were scattered some 70,000 white inhabitants, of whom nearly two thirds lived in the more thickly settled districts along the Monongahela and the east bank of the upper Ohio in southwestern Pennsylvania. A people who moved about so frequently were not easy to count and anything like an accurate census was impossible. Even the military reports of local militia commanders on the number of men on their muster rolls were studded with references to the fact that the number varied widely from month to month. In the spring of 1784 the population of Kentucky probably approximated 12,000, the Holston 10,000, and the Cumberland 2000. All lived in or near stockaded stations. The larger settlements were towns in name only. Louisville had less than 300 inhabitants, Pittsburgh's population had reached only 376 in 1790, and Nashville had in 1785 but two houses outside the original stockades. More striking than these sparsely settled areas were the intervening expanses of totally unoccupied wilderness. Along the more than 600 miles of the Ohio from the outskirts of Wheeling to the Falls at Louisville both banks of the Ohio were still uninhabited on account of the Indian danger. Between Kentucky and the Holston stretched 200 miles of pack trail winding over mountains in which Indians were as free to roam as in any of the centuries before. The total number of these Indians, however, did not greatly exceed the white population. Most contemporary estimates made by English and Spanish officials charged with supervision of Indian affairs placed the population of all Indian nations between the Great Lakes, the Mississippi, and the Gulf at around 100,000.

The external pressures which had forced the frontier line into so awkward a configuration had been in nowise reduced by the restoration of international peace in 1784. If anything they had been increased. In the north the Shawnee, Wyandot, Delaware, and Mingo who had provided the spearheads of British-Indian attack during the Revolution remained as bitterly determined to resist, while to this group of belligerently hostile nations had been added the Miami who had been neutral during most of the war. The same British bases on the Lakes were continuing to supply Indian military needs.

The same English agents residing among the Indians, officials as well as traders, were continuing to promote and encourage their resistance. If in the north the situation had not been improved by peace, in the south it had taken a decided turn for the worse. Spain, formerly a friend, was now an enemy. British patronage of Indian resistance had been succeeded by Spanish patronage. The Spaniards were to prove less adept at making use of Indian hostility but, on the other hand, Spain's opposition to American occupation of the Mississippi Valley was given the added weight of a fully determined national policy. In addition to encouraging Indian resistance and imposing commercial restrictions, Spanish governors did not hesitate to interfere in the internal affairs of the settlements by resorting to bribery, espionage, and conspiracy. These pressures in both the north and the south constituted deterrents to American expansion so formidable that the outer line of settlement advanced but little during the next ten years.

However, in spite of all that was known about this complex of difficulties and dangers in the west very many people were moved to accept the risk. The overwhelmingly most significant event influencing the frontier of 1784, in the long run far overshadowing in importance either the British retention of the Lake posts or the Spanish closure of the Mississippi, was that year's sudden increase in migration. Before the summer was over the population of both islands of settlement on the Kentucky and the Cumberland had doubled.

This was the fourth great pulse in the westward movement. The first had been the transmountain rush toward the Forks of the Ohio after the first Treaty of Fort Stanwix, the second the reach for Kentucky after the victory over the Shawnee at Point Pleasant in 1774, and the third the mid-Revolution surge after Clark's Illinois conquests. This 1784 wave had been precipitated by the proclamation of peace and Great Britain's cession of the west, giving rise to the same misapprehension as in the earlier instances that wilderness dangers had materially lessened. This wave, however, continued year after year, without intermission, and in 1788 and again in 1795 with explosive increases in the rate of the movement.

The earlier migrations had been largely composed of the frontier people themselves, men, women, and children already accustomed to the wilderness. In the first two the inhabitants of the then frontier had seized possession of new locations much farther west where they had continued to deal with the same problems they had been facing before. In the third, residents on the Monongahela or the Holston had tended to sell their partially improved holdings to newcomers from east of the mountains in order themselves to press on to the Kentucky or the Cumberland. The renewed urge to find the new land had been almost incidental. The stronger urge had been to seek more complete freedom, to enjoy better hunting, to welcome new hazards, to be first in a new country. Perhaps the strongest impulse of all had been the mere impulse to yield once more to the tempta-tion to make another move, to enjoy the sensation that freedom of movement had become a birthright. These were men in whom this impulse persisted until they had also crossed the Mississippi and then the Rockies.

But this fourth migration of 1784 took on a different cast. For the first time it included a considerable proportion of easterners who had had little or no wilderness experience and whose sole interest was land. With many of these it was no more a devotion to land for its own sake than was the case with the genuine frontiersmen. They were not intent upon a permanent residence devoted to a gradual increase in value incident to continued cultivation, development, and improvement. The great hope was for a quick fortune. The great attraction was the happy possibility of gaining title to a tract that might be presently sold at a handsome profit. The urge to get rich was as deeply imbedded in the American consciousness then as it has remained since. The returns from industry and commerce were slow and laborious and in any event beyond the reach of men without capital. Land in the west appeared to be the one conceivable road to fortune open to any man.

The greater proportion of this eastern contingent, however, were farmers or farm workers or veterans with land rights who had de-cided to make a permanent move west for the sake of getting a new start in life. The routes west available to such a migrant family of 1784 were the same as in 1775 when the first settlers had sought new homes in Kentucky. The hardships and dangers had not diminished. The same two enormous obstructions still intervened. There was first the mountain barrier to be surmounted, and then the wide belt of uninhabited, Indian-infested wilderness to be traversed before the wider opportunities envisaged on the Kentucky or the Cumberland were to be attained. The easterner who contemplated making so fearful an attempt had first to decide whether to take the land route in the south or the river route in the north. In either instance the distance, time, and labor involved made the journey an awesome undertaking even were the attending dangers ignored.

If he elected to take the southern route and started from anywhere in the general region of the country's then center of population near Baltimore, he had more than 450 miles of primitive wagon road to cover before reaching the mountains at the foot of the Valley of Virginia. Gaining the Holston frontier he had to leave behind his wagon and all his effects too bulky to pack on a horse or the backs of himself and his family. For ahead of him now stretched the 200 miles of tortuous mountain trail so singularly misnamed the Wilderness Road. He had already been two months on the way and was still two weeks from Kentucky and three from the Cumberland. It did not take him long to realize how painfully justified was the reputation long since gained by this terrifying path. Following it he scaled ridge after ridge, dropped into cane-choked gorges, forded rushing torrents, camped on ground that seemed always frozen, rain-soaked or wind-swept. In venturing into this craggy and thicketed fastness he had as an ultimate cause for dismay also subjected himself and his family to constant and mortal danger. During 1784 more than a hundred such wayfarers as he were killed on the Wilderness Road. He might not have considered himself a frontiersman when he had set out from his former home but if he survived to reach Whitley's Station, Kentucky's easternmost settlement, he must by then surely have realized he had begun to become one.

If the incipient mover possessed more stock and property to take

with him and could afford the cost of a flatboat, he was more likely
to choose the northern route. The two hundred odd miles over the
mountains were barely passable by wagon. The two military roads,
Braddock's and Forbes', had been in existence for nearly 30 years
during all of which period they had steadily deteriorated. Almost
from hour to hour the 1784 user was obliged to struggle with mired
and overturned wagons. If the weather proved unusually favorable
he made Redstone or Pittsburgh in three to four weeks. Here he
competed with the bids of fellow movers for the procurement of a
boat of a size to meet his needs. The going price in 1784 for a flatboat big enough to carry a family, a wagon, and four horses was $40
but soared with the demand and especially when a fall in the river
level made an immediate departure of the anxiously competing
bidders imperative. When at last loaded and drifting with the current down the Ohio he might have thought his troubles were over.
They were only beginning. In essence a flatboat was no more than
an oversize raft with a pen for stock at one end and a shed for shelter
from the weather at the other. Its movements were totally dependent
on the vagaries of the current. The navigation of no craft could
become so constant an aggravation. There could be no mudbank
upon which it did not lodge, no eddy in which it did not spin, no
backwater in which it did not stall. Meanwhile the Indian danger
was intermittent but real. The most uneventful passage could be
interrupted at any instant by the sudden blood-curdling pounce. In
Indian estimation a lumbering family flatboat with the large proportion of noncombatants in its crew and its cargo of horses and tools
was a supremely attractive prize. Wallowing on down-river through
hundreds of miles of uninhabited forest the mover was obsessed by a
final depressant. Even were he inclined to turn back it was now too
late. The river ran but the one way. To whatever fate awaited him
somewhere ahead he was now inexorably committed. To all this he
was subjected during the three weeks and 400 miles of his seemingly
endless passage to the mouth of Limestone Creek, the present Maysville, the usual debarkation point for Kentucky.

In 1784 conditions on the Wilderness Road had not changed since

Boone had first opened the trail in 1775. The only change for the next ten years was for the worse. The trail remained as onerous while the Indian danger became greater in the early 1790's than it had been in the 1770's or 80's. The tens of thousands of people who used it were repeating every hardship and hazard of Boone's original venture. The route did not become safe until after the general Indian peace of 1795 and was not made passable for wagons until 1796. During this same period, on the other hand, there were tremendous changes on the other great migration route in the north. Shipbuilding developed at such a rate on the upper Ohio that by 1792 seagoing ships were sliding from the ways at Pittsburgh. Of far more consequence to the westward movement was the invention of the Ohio River flatboat and its continual enlargement until it became a floating community.

There is no clear record of the discovery of the peculiar advantages of the flatboat as a craft capable of transporting large cargoes and large numbers of people downstream. Early references to it indicate that it came into use the first year after the Revolution. Originally it seems to have been an enlarged adaptation of the flat-bottomed scow, commonly called a bateau, which had long been in use on western waters for the transport of military and traders' stores. The bateau's size and capacity had been limited by regard for the need to propel it upstream as well as down. Having once hit upon the flatboat principle that all that counted was capacity inasmuch as there was never to be a need for a return upriver, the size of the novel device increased rapidly. As early as 1786 a traffic census kept by Harmar's officers established that the average cargo of 323 boats counted was 18 people and 13 head of stock and that two out of three included at least one wagon. A flatboat big enough to carry five or six families was more difficult to navigate but this disadvantage was far overbalanced by the enormous advantage of a greater number of defenders against Indian attack.

There is striking evidence in contemporary references to Simon Kenton's venture in 1783 of how early came at least one instance of a flatboat of great size.[1] After twelve years of wilderness experience, which had included service with Clark, a particularly painful captivity, and innumerable frontier defense exploits, Kenton returned to Bull Run, Virginia, to escort his family and some of their neighbors to Kentucky. On Kenton's order the craft built for him at the Boat Yard on the Monongahela was large enough to carry 41 people and 19 horses. In this party, presumably a typical sample of the post-Revolutionary westward movement, were 36 whites: 12 men, 7 women, and 17 children, and 5 negroes: 1 man, 2 women, and 2 children. All were family groups, or their slaves, except two unattached men who were listed as "went to visit Kentucky." This Kenton passenger list casts a revealing gleam upon the character and composition of the sudden population surge in 1784. It was the migration of a people, comparable to the historic movements of Germanic and Slavic tribes into Europe. Development of the flatboat, more than any other factor, made this mass movement possible. It had become a migration not of individuals or even of families but of entire communities. Due to the flatboat, people seeking new homes could take with them their tools, stores, household effects, and livestock. The lowly raft had become an ark sweeping a whole people into possession of an empire.[2]

The torrent of newcomers beginning to pour into Kentucky in 1784 increased the number of defenders but brought with them few other advantages discernible to the settlers already established there. Among the influx were needed craftsmen, artisans, doctors, teachers, and ministers but also politicians, land agents, and, above all, a host of lawyers. Before the bemused pioneers had realized what was developing the more sophisticated newcomers had assumed political control. In the Kentucky convention of 1785 Benjamin Logan

[1] Most unhappily, no contemporary journals of this Ohio River migration, paralleling the hundreds of daily journals kept by participants in the later covered-wagon crossing of the plains, seem to have been preserved. Conceivably the flatboat people were kept too busy to keep diaries.

[2] The flatboats were abandoned upon disembarkation, usually on the beach at Limestone, where they accumulated in such numbers that even the material of which they were constructed was regarded as valueless. In 1789 Fort Washington at recently established Cincinnati was largely constructed of salvaged flatboat timbers.

was the only delegate representing the generation who had defended Kentucky during the Revolution.

So strong was the wilderness-molded personality of the earlier settlers, however, and so compelling the influence of so demanding an environment that the newcomers were soon hardly to be distinguished by manners, dress, deportment, or social and political attitudes from their hard-bitten forerunners. They found the same relish in complete personal freedom, hated all Indians with the same fury, began to suspect all easterners with the same bitterness. Within days of their arrival they had totally accepted the fundamental western conviction that the west's every hope depended solely upon actions and decisions taken by westerners. Without having had the attributes stamped upon them by years of sufferings they had themselves become frontier people.

This conjunction of sympathies and interests was nevertheless accompanied by one conflict of extreme malignancy. Many of the newcomers had come armed with claims to land based on veterans' rights, or the purchase of such rights, land-company grants, earlier surveys, and other legalistic formulas. The land laws of Virginia and North Carolina, the states asserting jurisdiction over the Holston, Kentucky, and Cumberland frontier districts, had been drafted by politicians with a far more intent regard for the favor of eastern voters and investors than the rights of western settlers. As a result, with the return of peace the west was swept by an avalanche of title disputes, eviction notices, and legal dispossessions. The earliest pioneer who years before had braved every wilderness danger to choose a piece of land and then for years had fought to hold it was forced now to realize that this long struggle had still not made him its owner. Most of the men who had come to Kentucky in the desperate years of the 1775–1779 period were left landless by these legal processes. Under these displacement pressures they were forced to seek new locations on the outer fringe of settlement where they continued to constitute the frontier's first and most perilous line of defense. Their disillusionment could not have been more eloquently described than in the words of the 1784 Petition of the Inhabitants of Kentucky to the General Assembly of Virginia:

> Your petitioners . . . are like to be overwhelmed in Litigation; which will not only create discords amongst us, but ruin hundreds of poor Families, who being opprest and stript of almost their whole Substance by the Indians, have not the Means of defraying the Expences of a Law Suit . . . Such of your Honourable House as have not been Eye Witnesses can form no Idea of the Distresses which many of your petitioners have suffered for a Series of Years from the cruel and vindictive Hand of the Savages; and now on the back of these Distresses to be compelled into a Court of Judicature, by those who are endeavoring to avail themselves of our poverty and that Ignorance of the Law which was unavoidable in our remote Situation, will complete our Ruin: If we prosecute our Claim the last Cow and Horse must be sold to maintain the Suit; or if we decline the Contest, the Land upon which we had Hopes of supporting ourselves and Families in peace during the Remainder of our Lives will be wrested from us.

This array of many troubles threatening the frontier people, dangers within and without, dangers awaiting them and pursuing them, was more than matched by the array of even greater threats oppressing their Indian enemies. The white inhabitants of the west were challenged by the opposition of world powers and confused by the treachery of their parent states, but the Indians had every occasion to fear that they were being made the foredoomed catspaw of their powerful patrons and that at the onrushing crisis they would again be betrayed as they had been so often before. The whites could be inspirited by the memory that in their own lifetime they had advanced their border hundreds of miles but the Indians had only the memory of generations of retreat. Against the whites' assumption that eventually they must surely prevail was the Indians' consciousness that they were making their last stand to survive as a free people.

On both sides of the frontier the individual in his isolated and forest-shrouded community was quite unable to comprehend the endless complexities of his situation. He could identify and confront his nearer enemies but he was denied by the lack of communication any clear knowledge of what forces might be gathering in the distance against him. On both sides there was the same excruciating need for the guidance of informed and far-sighted leaders. In response to the urgency of this need the year 1784 was bringing into new prominence a number of extraordinary men who had been prepared by the harshest experience to face the most dangerous decisions and who were endowed with the natural leader's disposition to welcome responsibility. Five stood out. They were Joseph Brant, the great Mohawk who had been the Indians' heroic champion throughout the murderous border campaigns of the Revolution and upon whose shoulders was now descending the principal burden of averting his people's final fate; Alexander McGillivray, the curiously talented "King" of the Creek Republic whose Machiavellian skill as a diplomat preserved his nation's independence so long as he lived; James Robertson, the most representative of all pioneers who himself had founded two of the most memorable of all settlements and who remained for thirty years the foremost defender of the outermost border; John Sevier, the darling and beau ideal of all frontiersmen whose singularly active career was marked by so many astounding victories in every sort of cause; and James Wilkinson, one of the more incredible figures in all history, the perpetual schemer against his country who nevertheless planted his country's flag at Natchez and New Orleans, who served as Commander in Chief of the Army of the United States under four presidents while at the same time serving as secret agent of Spain, England, and France. The course of events in the west in their time was given its chief direction by the aspirations, conflicts, successes, and failures of these five remarkable men.

IV

༂

Brant

At the end of the Revolution Joseph Brant was forty-one. In its every aspect his life had presented extreme departures from the normal. The variety of his experiences had been fantastic. Among them had been achievements rare in a man of his age of any race. For an Indian they had been unprecedented. Born in a wigwam, by the time he was fifteen he had made himself as much at home in the white world as in his native forest. Thereafter his distinctions had ranged from the startled approbation of his teachers to his translations of the scriptures, from his lionization by London society to his ravaging the American border from New York to Kentucky. During the war he had been the one English field commander who had known victories. He could count many of England's most famous men his personal friends. He had won recognition, by his fellow Indians, by British governors, and by his American enemies, as the champion of his race. Even in his private life there had been deep satisfactions. His beautiful young third wife, Catherine, had just borne him a son.

For him, therefore, the taste of defeat was bitter indeed. The loss of the war meant to him far more than the end of British rule over the former thirteen colonies. It meant the end of the world as he had known it. Every cause to which he was devoted had been stricken by the British surrender. Every member of his family, including his beloved sister, Molly, who for so many years had been the celebrated chatelaine of Johnson Hall, had been made a homeless wanderer. The frontier principality established by Sir William Johnson, in whose fabulous household he had spent his youth, had been extirpated. The Tory landowners who had been his neighbors and associates had been driven into impoverished exile. His own people, the Mohawk, once the most feared and still the most warlike of all Indians, had been deprived for all time of their storied homeland. The entire country of the Iroquois had been devastated and that proudest of Indian nations forced into beggared dependence on English charity.

As though these many calamities had not been enough to endure, there had fallen one more blow which for Brant was the most grievous of all. He had never ceased to consider himself an Indian but he had also come to consider himself an Englishman. When the war had broken out he had unhesitatingly taken the English side and had taken his trusting Mohawk with him. Due to him they had sacrificed their every present and future prospect. His and their loyalty to the King had been proved on innumerable fields. He had felt honored to wear the red coat of an English colonel. He would limp for the rest of his days from the wounds he had sustained. He had exhorted the other Iroquois, advised them that England was their faithful friend, himself led them again and again to battle. He had extended his campaigning to the far Ohio in order to inspire the western Indians to greater exertions in England's behalf. Impressed by his example, every Indian nation of the Great Lakes–Ohio region had become England's active ally. Yet the moment the war had ended all this had been forgotten. In the peace treaty there was no reference to Indian services, no mention of their rights. Instead, Great Britain had expressly ceded to the United States the whole territory in which they lived, and they had been abandoned to defend themselves as best they might against whatever demands the Americans might now make upon them.

Brant was at first stunned and then outraged by this callous betrayal. But personal resentment was a luxury he could not afford. The dangers now threatening all Indians were far more desperate than they ever before had been. From the victorious Americans, justifiably infuriated by Indian atrocities during the war, they could expect no consideration. Yet any effort to resist American intentions required a military supply system which could only be provided through the same British channels as in the past. Swallowing his wrath and pride, he earnestly besought renewed British support.

Extracting Governor Frederick Haldimand's promise to allot lands in Canada to the refugee Mohawk and to continue to feed the other Iroquois at Niagara, Brant rushed west to confer with the western Indians. With his grasp of the Anglo-American as well as the Indian situation he could see with terrible clarity that the one Indian hope rested on proving able to present a united front. The extent of British aid and the rate of American aggression would alike be governed by the resolution with which Indians undertook their own defense. Every great Indian disaster of the past, including notably the last and greatest, the Shawnee defeat in 1774 which had opened Kentucky to the Americans, had been a direct consequence of Indian disunity. Even the self-centered Iroquois were beginning to appreciate this fundamental truth. The fallacy of their age-old policy of sacrificing the interests of other Indians to gain an apparent Iroquois advantage had by now been disastrously demonstrated. Their survival was at stake, too.

Delegates from 35 nations assembled at Sandusky in September, 1783, in a conference, promoted by the anxious Iroquois, to consider their common danger and plan their common defense. The Iroquois had long been accustomed to the deference of world powers and had therefore been the more astounded by the British betrayal. The western Indians were equally enraged but to them betrayal was a familiar story. Just 20 years before they had been left in the lurch in exactly the same fashion by their then French ally. Then their fury had led to Pontiac's War which had cost 3000 English lives. Uppermost among the second thoughts on the peace treaty already beginning to trouble the British government was a sudden appreciation of the need to avert another such catastrophe. As a result Haldimand had approved the conference and it was addressed by Sir John Johnson, the King's Indian Superintendent who was at the moment harboring the hope that he might be about to succeed Haldimand as Governor General, and by Alexander McKee, the western representative of the Indian Department who for the next 15 years was to be the actual administrator of Britain's Indian policy. It was their task at the conference to soothe Indian resentment, to stave off a general Indian war in which Great Britain as well as the United States must become involved, and yet to hold Indian friendship in order to maintain the Indian barrier to block the advance of American settlement toward the Great Lakes. This they managed with some success. They advised the Indians to cease their provocative raids on the American frontier but meanwhile to hold themselves in readiness to defend their lands. They assured them that the peace treaty had in no sense extinguished their title to those lands. They implied that if the Indians proved sufficiently determined to defend their rights they could count on British support. Indians had long since learned to suspect white men's assurances, but there was tangible evidence to lend some credence to the Johnson-McKee assertions. There were still British garrisons in the Lake posts, British commanders were still distributing food, and English traders were still supplying powder and lead. The conferees listened, pondered, and embarked upon endless discussions among themselves.

All hinged on the matter of title to the land. This was a principle Indians had from their first contact with white men been unable to grasp and after centuries of unhappy experience were still unable to grasp. In Indian estimation the Creator had provided the land for the good of man and had stocked it with fruits and game for the free use of all men. Indian nations had been accustomed to assert hunting rights in certain areas adjacent to their towns and to fight with rivals over these assertions, but any presumption to own the land itself remained as incomprehensible as to claim ownership of the air, the sunlight or the rain. The countless times in the past various Indian nations had been obliged under white pressure to "sell" portions of the land over which traditionally they had exercised such rights had been regarded as transactions merely relinquishing those rights.[1] Each time they had withdrawn deeper into the wilderness to observe with mystified horror the ensuing consequences of the white man's practice of destroying the forest along with all of the earth's other natural attributes and of his even more revolting practice of parceling it out among individual private "owners."

If they were unable to comprehend ownership of land by an individual residing on it, they were even less able to comprehend the assertion of ownership termed "sovereignty" over limitless expanses of the continent by strange nations situated beyond the ocean at so immense a distance that their rulers had never been able so much as to set foot on their new dominions. The same lakes and rivers and mountains and forests and prairies surrounded him, brightened by the same sun, shadowed by the same clouds, but the Indian was expected to realize that henceforth he might roam and hunt and live in this land he had always known only by the sufferance of those remote and mysterious princes. The principle of international law upon which this assertion of sovereignty was based remained for the Indian an insoluble riddle. Prompted by it, from the first appearance of white men on the continent European nations had claimed possession by virtue of "discovery." No early explorer standing on the bank of a newly sighted river hesitated to claim for his king all territory drained by it. The royal charters of early English colonies on the Atlantic seacoast described their western boundaries as the western ocean. The first semblance of white occupation was considered a confirmation of this right of possession by discovery. No species of right was attached to occupancy for the last hundred generations by the Indian inhabitants. Under prevailing international law only the

[1] The Iroquois, as a result of seventeenth century conquests, often dealt in the usage rights of vassal peoples, thus repeatedly selling to Pennsylvania land actually occupied and used by the Delaware or Shawnee.

Christian nations of Europe were considered capable of asserting legitimate sovereignty over any territory anywhere in the world. Indian resistance to this white assertion of possession was therefore not considered a conflict between legitimate belligerents but an insurrection of traitorous subjects. Soon all North America had been claimed by various European nations, chiefly Spain, France, and England but also Holland and Sweden, including distant regions never penetrated by any explorer or visited by the most widely wandering trader. The Indian residents were considered as natural a part of this possession as the soil, the rocks, the trees, or the wild animals. In the instance of transfers of sovereignty, as with Holland's cession of New York to England in 1674 or France's enormous cessions to Spain and England in 1763, dominion over the Indians occupying the territory involved was considered to have been passed by the same stroke of the pen from one European nation to another. It was to this view that Pontiac took so furious, and for a time successful, exception. At no time had Indians understood or recognized it. They had been physically forced to accept it, as they were presently to continue to be by the United States, by white military superiority made more speedily effective by Indian failure to unite.

In the case of the region between the Ohio and the Great Lakes, however, from which most of the delegates to the Sandusky conference had come,[2] the principle had been so limited and defined that it had been made more nearly comprehensible even to the most ordinary Indian mind. By the Proclamation of 1763 all land west of the mountains had been reserved for Indian use and occupancy. At the 1768 Treaty of Fort Stanwix this line had been adjusted with formal Indian consent to make the Ohio River a permanent boundary between white and Indian country with future white settlement limited to the area south and southeast of it. The validity of this demarcation had been drummed into the Indian consciousness at subsequent conferences with British authorities and restated at the general conference with Revolutionary American representatives at Pittsburgh

[2] There were also a few delegates from nations as distant as the Sioux, Creek, and Cherokee.

in 1775. These were developments the more easily grasped because a majority of the delegates at Sandusky had also participated in the proceedings at Fort Stanwix and Pittsburgh. They clung to the notion that in making concessions then they had received in exchange confirmation of the Ohio boundary. By the same British authority which had negotiated the Stanwix treaty and the peace treaty ending the Revolution they were now being assured that the latter had not abridged their rights under the former. McKee and Johnson made the most of Indian eagerness to believe this. The atmosphere of crisis in which the conference had gathered began to dissipate as the formerly disturbed delegates began to feel that they were after all not in so much jeopardy as they had feared.

As the conference droned on, its deliberations impeded by the loquacity of Indian oratory and the need to intercept every speech into so many languages, Brant was increasingly discouraged. He suspected that the implied promises of British support being made by Johnson and McKee were not backed by any genuine determination of the British government. Even the intention to continue to hold the Lake posts was subject to the whim of ministers in far off London with little knowledge of and less interest in this obscure border of the empire in the depths of the North American wilderness. He knew that the words of the chiefs proclaiming so vociferously their devotion to the ideal of Indian confederation were as hollow. No more than before were most of them prepared to risk his or his nation's comfort for the common good. Most discouraging of all was the temper of the ordinary Indian at the conference. The Indian as an individual had by 1783 lost much of his former vitality, more of his one-time integrity, and most of his original insistence upon personal freedom. Indian moral fiber, the factor upon which the survival of any people most depends, had sadly frayed.

This was a deterioration in Indian character which had set in with his first contacts three centuries before with European traders coasting along the Atlantic shore. White men's weapons and implements had from that moment needed only to be handled to become an irresistible attraction. Possession of a gun so fundamentally expanded the capacities of a hunter or warrior that to acquire one became an obsession. An appetite for all trade goods had swiftly followed. Possession of metal tools, cloth garments, manufactured ornaments came to measure an Indian's status in his community. Instead of maintaining his self-respect by hunting to feed his family he catered to it by hunting to purchase a ruffled shirt or a silver brooch. Terrible prices were exacted. Drunkenness became a racial vice. The Indian who had spent a winter trapping with the intention of buying a gun was easily diverted by a trader's counteroffer of a jug of rum to the exchange of his furs for a week-long debauch. A higher price was disease. Ills to which the Indian had never before been exposed became epidemics that had soon reduced the total Indian population to a fraction of its former number.[3] The highest of all prices was the loss of independence. Trade goods were only to be obtained from white men, whether Spaniard, Frenchman, or Englishman, and the Indian became necessarily dependent upon his only source of supply. He became less and less the fierce free wanderer, guided by strong religious instincts and immemorial tribal conventions, and more and more a hunter for hire, influenced by white manners, vices, and values. Through seeking trade advantages to improve its military position with respect to its rivals, his nation became a pawn manipulated by European powers. His personal freedom of action became hopelessly limited. The indomitable Pontiac was forced to sue for peace not by the might of the English army but by his people's dependence upon English trade.

This long, slow deterioration of Indian character had been accelerated by the past 20 years of almost continuous war during which the normal Indian way of life had been so much disrupted. Hundreds and thousands of Indians had spent season after season camped about first French and then English forts, waiting for another issue of rum or flour, waiting to be told by white commanders upon what

---

[3] The Indians of the seacoast began to die off after their first white contacts. There is some evidence that the process spread rapidly into the interior. The communal labor required to construct the hundreds of immense mounds dotting the eastern Mississippi Valley would seem to indicate an earlier Indian population many times more numerous than when the first white men viewed them.

project they were expected next to embark. That arrogant insistence upon individual freedom in thought and action which had originally been the Indian's chief attribute had been fatally weakened and replaced by an absurd inclination to ape the white man's attitudes while accepting his judgments.

Many phases of this Indian degeneration were evident at Sandusky. But there were also evident elements of Indian strength. The average delegate had become much more sophisticated than he had been even a generation before. He had attended conferences at Montreal, Albany, Philadelphia, Charleston. He knew more about the white man than the white man did about him. This sophistication was accompanied by a new confidence. During the same past 20 years of conflict the average warrior had been constantly exercised in all the arts of war. He had taken part in more raids, campaigns, and battles than he could count. So much experience with combat had made him a battle-tested veteran. His successes had been so often repeated as to convince him that man for man he was the white man's superior. In the bizarre tactics of stealth and surprise that marked forest warfare he considered himself the master, his white antagonist still the tyro. He was aware that in total population the Americans outnumbered the nearer Indians by more than thirty to one but he was also aware that, were all the nations represented at the conference to take the field at once, they could muster more than 10,000 warriors. No white army so numerous had ever appeared on the border. In all the endless talk at Sandusky there were few expressions of fear that Indian resistance might be crushed were the Americans to elect to resort to force.

The conference ended in the usual round of carouses. Delegates who had been filled with wrath and foreboding at the outset had been mollified and reassured. It had been generally accepted that with British garrisons still in the Lake posts the Americans represented no great threat to the Indian position. The need for confederation had been universally acclaimed but no emergency had become so apparent as to require immediate and definite steps. The conference adjourned with the agreement, on Brant's urgent motion, to reassemble the next summer at Niagara.

The delegates had scarcely dispersed before the enormity of the demands the Americans were to make was revealed. By the Act of October 15, 1783, Congress not only repudiated the Ohio boundary but called upon the western Indians forthwith to withdraw beyond the Miami. Meanwhile the state of New York, whose embittered people had suffered so fearfully from Indian inroads during the war, was proposing the total expulsion from the state of all Iroquois except some of the Oneida and Tuscarora who had been friendly or neutral. The Iroquois protest was startled but so resolute that New York in turn was startled. Washington, still commander in chief, and New York's Major General Philip Schuyler counseled caution. The Continental Army was disbanding and no other military force was available. If the Iroquois were pressed to the point of resistance the presence of British garrisons at Oswego and Niagara in the Iroquois country made British involvement in the war almost certain. New York reconsidered the expulsion demand.

But Brant was under no illusions. He knew the white pressures were certain to persist and the war of nerves to continue. With his wide acquaintance with the white world he understood as did no other Indian the overwhelming superiority of the white man's power. Aside from the tremendous advantages of political oragnization and industrial capacity numbers alone doomed Indian defense. To subsist by hunting an Indian community of a hundred families required the use of an area capable of supporting 10,000 white families. Nothing could be more certain than that such a disparity in numbers could not indefinitely fail to prove decisive and that the westward spread of white settlement must eventually prevail. In Brant's view the one chance of survival remaining open to Indians lay in themselves learning to become farmers and herdsmen and artisans. He was so advising his Mohawk. But a transition so complete in the Indian way of life required time. To gain time the white advance must be retarded while Indians struggled to adapt themselves to their new situation. All still came back to the necessity of a united front. Without it the separate Indian nations must topple like a row of dominoes.

He had already taken the position from which he was never to retreat. There could be no valid negotiations, he maintained, between Indians and any one state or between the United States and any one Indian nation. The basic Indian right to survive as a people was an indivisible right which must be so affected by any local surrender that other Indians must be driven to take counteraction against the surrender. A satisfactory peace settlement could only therefore be realized by a general agreement between Congress representing all the states and the Indian confederation representing all Indians. There could be no disputing the proposition that this procedure offered the sole hope of continued peace, but two seemingly insuperable difficulties lay in the way. Congress had no control over the states. And the Indian confederation did not yet exist.

Of these companion infirmities, the Indian was the first to become deplorably apparent. The western delegations reassembled at Niagara in late August of 1784 but became impatient when the American commissioners with whom they were to treat were delayed by various preliminaries. Most of the westerners drifted home to prepare for their winter hunting, leaving the Iroquois to confront the Americans alone. They were summoned to Fort Stanwix where the commissioners opened the conference with a stern reading of the terms of the British-American peace treaty which had ceded their country to the United States. "You are a subdued people," they reminded the Iroquois. "We shall now, therefore, declare to you the condition on which alone you can be received into the peace and protection of the United States." Indian resistance was to persist with increasing success for the next ten years, but at the moment the distraught Iroquois could see little room for any such hope. Brant had withdrawn from the conference after it had become apparent that it was not to be the negotiation with all Indians upon which he had insisted. The Iroquois made a half-hearted effort to gain American recognition of the old Stanwix line but the most influential chief, Cornplanter, of their most numerous nation, the Seneca, had come to the conclusion that their one recourse was to seek an accommodation. All of his fellow delegates were almost as bitterly conscious that they had been abandoned by their western allies and remained uncertain of British support. At the second Treaty of Fort Stanwix, October 22, 1784, the Iroquois ceded to the United States their ancient territorial claims north of the Ohio as at the first treaty there in 1768 they had ceded to England their claims south of the river. The American commissioners were concerned only with that western region, Congress having no jurisdiction over the nearer Iroquois homeland in New York and Pennsylvania. They therefore withdrew while New York and Pennsylvania commissioners descended upon the dispirited Iroquois with demands which would reduce the Iroquois living space by more than half.

The congressional commissioners had meanwhile rushed west to Fort McIntosh to which they summoned the western Indians who actually occupied the Ohio country to which the long discounted Iroquois claims had already been ceded. Partially accredited delegations representing the more pacifist factions of the Wyandot, Delaware, Chippewa, and Ottawa, put in a nervous appearance. They were shocked by the same reading of the peace treaty and the same assertion of unlimited American dominion. In the Treaty of Fort McIntosh, January 2, 1785, the bewildered delegates who had attended signed away the claims of their nations to most of what is now the state of Ohio. At Sandusky the year before every Indian nation had vowed to enter into no agreements to which the confederation was not a party. At the first tests of Indian resolution at Stanwix and McIntosh the Indian dream of a united front had ended in the reality of an Indian debacle.

So far it had been Indian weakness that had been made manifest. But already a comparable American weakness was becoming evident. The arrival on the Ohio of the first tattered companies of Harmar's little army testified to how feeble was the force Congress could actually command. A total lack of funds inhibited every congressional purpose. Dissension among the states had become a public spectacle. The American confederation was proving no more suc-

cessful than the Indian. These signs of American impotence were
not lost on Brant. There might still be time to restore the Indian
position. What was most required was a more solid assurance of
British support. He determined to make another journey to England
to attempt to stir a livelier interest in the Indian cause among his
many influential English friends.

Indicative of how generally understood was the significance of his
mission was the manner in which his arrival at Salisbury in December of 1785 was described in the London press:

> Monday last, Colonel Joseph Brant, the celebrated King of the Mo-
> hawks, arrived in this city from America, and after dining with
> Colonel De Peister, at the headquarters here, proceeded immediately
> on his journey to London. This extraordinary personage is said to
> have presided at the late grand Congress of confederate chiefs of the
> Indian nations in America, and to be by them appointed to the con-
> duct and chief command in the war which they now meditate against
> the United States of America. He took his departure for England im-
> mediately as that assembly broke up; and it is conjectured that his
> embassy to the British Court is of great importance.

His second English visit was an even greater triumph than had
been his first. He became the sensation of the London season. The
variety of his costumes which ranged from tailored broadcloth to
feathered cloaks and headdresses, the equal ease with which he
wore sword or tomahawk, powdered hair or scalp lock, the alternat-
ing civility and arrogance of his demeanor, the sense of humor
which delighted in signalizing with a sudden war whoop his pres-
entation to any other exotic visitor, such as a Persian or a Moor, the
apparent earnestness of his interest in religious affairs, the dwelling
by his companions-at-arms on anecdotes of his bloodstained exploits
during the late war—all these contrasting facets of his personality
made his visit a principal topic of conversation. Among the old
friends who welcomed him were Sir Guy Carleton, Lord Rawdon,
Sir Charles Stuart, the Duke of Northumberland, the Earl of War-
wick, James Boswell, George Romney, Charles Fox, and the Bishop

of London. The Prince of Wales became his frequent companion, and he was repeatedly entertained by the King and Queen.

He was not in London, however, merely to enjoy London society. On January 4, 1786, he was presenting the Indian case to Lord Sydney, the Colonial Secretary, reminding him of their "sufferings, losses, and being drove from that country which their forefathers long enjoyed in consequence of their faithful attachment to the King and the zeal they manifested in supporting the cause of His country against the rebellious subjects in America." With reference to the British betrayal he bluntly said, "We could not believe it possible such firm friends and allies could be so neglected by a nation remarkable for its honor and glory, whom we had served with so much zeal and fidelity." He concluded by coming with brutal candor to the main point upon which all else hinged: "We desire to know whether we are to be considered as His Majesty's faithful allies, and have that support and countenance such as old and true friends expect."

To this direct question Sydney found it most difficult to frame an answer. Consultations with his colleagues gave him little help. The British conscience had been disturbed by the abandonment of their Indian allies, now dramatized by Brant's visit. On the other hand there was, both in and out of government, a general disinclination to be reminded of the late unpleasantness in North America. After every war English foreign policy has stranded on the same shoal. A peace-loving people have always so welcomed peace that they seemed determined to forget even the objectives for which they had recently fought. After earth-shaking victories in the Seven Years' War, the immediate English drift toward disengagement from North American responsibilities had resulted within a dozen years in the loss of most of what had then been won. Having ignominiously lost this more recent war, there was even less inclination to face up to a frontier issue that nevertheless remained as formidable as in Braddock's time. Not until April 6, 1786, did Sydney contrive an answer. It was as vague and indecisive as his government's policy was uncertain. After referring to Brant's expression of "the desire of the confederacy to be informed what assistance they might expect from this country in case they should be engaged in disputes with the Americans relative to their lands" his reply was:

> His Majesty . . . shall at all times be ready to attend to their future welfare; and . . . he shall be anxious, upon every occasion wherein their happiness may be concerned, to give them such further testimony of his royal favor and countenance, as can, consistently with a due regard to the national faith, and the honor and dignity of his crown, be afforded them. His Majesty recommends to his Indian allies to continue united in their councils, and that their measures may be conducted with temper and moderation; from which, added to a peaceable demeanor on their part, they must experience many essential benefits, and be most likely to secure to themselves the possession of those rights and privileges which their ancestors have heretofore enjoyed.

As a bolster to Indian hopes of British support Sydney's careful statement of his government's position was far from satisfactory. Yet it referred to the Indians as "allies" and strongly approved Brant's effort to organize an Indian confederation. Since success in achieving a united front must inevitably lead to a general war with the United States, there was an implied promise that Britain would when that moment came assist the Indians. Essentially the British position appeared to be that if the Indians sufficiently helped themselves they might conceivably expect British help. The eventual dimensions of British aid were a calculation for the future. For the present Brant had received British encouragement to persist in his confederation program.

While in Europe he even gave some attention to the possible future attitude of France. It had long since been demonstrated how deeply involved were Indian fortunes in the enigmatic game of international power politics. Within his lifetime immense portions of North America had been handed about among France, Spain, Britain, and, finally, the United States. There was every likelihood that with future shifts in the European balance of power France might return to the continent. The white population of the St.

Lawrence, the Great Lakes, and the lower Mississippi was still predominantly French. The interest of France was clearly worth cultivating. His reputation gained him a warm official reception during his brief Paris visit that spring. What he learned is uncertain and in any event unimportant since the ministers with whom he conferred were about to pass from power with the fall of the monarchy, and France's next intrusion on the American scene was to be under the Republic and the Empire. In that last quarter of the eighteenth century the white world was being disrupted by upheavals as convulsive as those confounding the Indian world.

Brant set out on his return home to grapple with problems that had been little clarified by what he had learned abroad. It was a very long way from the streets of Paris to the great Indian encampment at Hurontown on the Detroit River. During a journey reminiscent of George Croghan's historic travels in the course of comparable missions, he traversed nearly 5000 miles of ocean, lakes, and rivers by ship, bateau, and canoe to reach his destination in time to preside in December 1786 over the most significant Indian conference so far. This year the delegates were ready for something more than talk. There was no longer any doubt in the mind of the most heedless Indian of the immediate and imperative necessity of a functioning confederation.

Upon his return Brant had found every frontier tension more acute. The effect of the first two American attempts to pacify Indians had been greatly to aggravate them. Salt had been rubbed into those two wounds when Shawnee delegates had been summoned to Fort Finney where on January 31, 1786, their delegates were obliged to sign away Shawnee claims to the territory east of the Miami, thus completing the process initiated at Fort Stanwix and continued at Fort McIntosh. The United States had gained in theory an Indian undertaking to withdraw from the major portion of their homeland along the northwest frontier. The forced negotiations had in reality left the incensed occupants more than ever determined to resist.

In every Indian nation there was an impatient faction advocating immediate war. These extremists had no need to win over their more moderate fellows to their own aggressive views. To make war inevitable they needed only to resort to the simple device of themselves secretly embarking on independent raids upon the American frontier. In 1786 the number of these raids swiftly multiplied.[4] Young warriors anxious to win a reputation were prone to join these irregular parties. Others sought loot, especially horses. In the early months of 1786 more than 500 horses were reported taken in the Limestone area alone. Ohio flatboats were another favorite target. The white border was tormented from end to end. Georgia settlements were harassed by the Creek and Cumberland's by the Chickamauga. In one 1786 Wilderness Road attack on an immigrant party 21 were killed and 5 women carried off. One band of Cherokee elected to camp semipermanently north of the Ohio in a location from which they might more conveniently strike at the Kentucky frontier. The ostensibly still peaceful Delaware, Wyandot, Shawnee, and Miami were unable and perhaps none too eager to restrain the secret participation in these continuing depredations of any of their warriors who so chose.

Congress, having embarked prematurely on a policy of aggression, was powerless to take any further steps to advance it. Harmar's soldiers were too few to guard adequately their own supply boats. He was plagued by the continued desertion of his seldom paid, poorly fed, and scarcely clothed men and able at most to furnish small detachments to guard the government surveyors of the Seven Ranges across the Ohio from Wheeling and to continue the practice of burning out settlers who had ventured to locate illegally north of the river. Any thought of offensive action was out of the question. Even defensively his army was in no faintest sense a shield to the frontier. Exasperated beyond endurance, the Kentuckians in the fall once more took matters into their own hands. Colonel Benjamin Logan with 750 volunteers crossed the Ohio, made a six-day forced march through the wilderness, surprised the Shawnee, and on

---

[4] On April 6, 1786, Colonel William Christian, who had commanded regiments and armies during his twenty years of distinguished servce as frontier defender, was killed in one of these raids. Colonel John Donelson, cofounder of Tennessee, died in another.

October 6, 1786, burned their two principal towns, Machacheck and Wapatomica. He brought back 40 Shawnee prisoners to be held as hostages for the return of white captives. The Shawnee for the past two years had been somewhat less guilty of frontier depredations than had other Indians and felt that at the Fort Finney treaty they had shown remarkable restraint. The chief result of Logan's expedition was therefore once more to commit this most bellicose of all Indian nations to implacable hostility.

The Hurontown conference assembled in an atmosphere of furious resentment and restored determination. Apprehension of renewed general war was no longer so disturbing as it had seemed in 1784. It had become evident that actually the war had never ceased. White or Indian families who had perished in defense of their homes during this presumed peace were as dead as any who had died during the Revolution. Hundreds of raiding parties had successfully returned with scalps, loot, captives, and horses. In the face of these extreme provocations the American government had as yet made no effort to protect its people or to retaliate against the offenders. To enforce its extravagant demands the United States had been able to raise no more than a shadow army. The Indians' chief enemy was still, as always before, the settlers. With them Indians had always felt able to cope.

Brant addressed the conference with a fervor recalling Pontiac's historic call to arms 20 years before:

> Before Christian Nations Visited this Continent we were the Sole Lords of the Soil . . . What is the reason why we are not Still in possession of our forefathers birth Rights? . . . because they wanted that Unanimity which we now So Strongly and Repeatedly recommend to you . . . Let us have a Just sense of our own Value and if after that the Great Spirit wills that other Colours Should Subdue us, let it be so, we then Cannot reproach our Selves for Misconduct . . . The Interests of Any One Nation Should be the Interests of us all, the Welfare of the one Should be the Welfare of all the others.

Inspired to a new sense of unity, the conference denounced the recent treaties of Stanwix, McIntosh, and Finney as without validity on the grounds that (a) they had been negotiated with separate nations instead of the confederation, (b) the Indian signers had been without authority to cede territory, and (c) the Indian concessions had been exacted under duress. Under Brant's supervision the conference drafted an address to Congress, December 18, 1786, which was signed not by individual delegates but by the eleven nations represented, the Iroquois, Wyandot, Delaware, Shawnee, Ottawa, Chippewa, Potawatomi, Miami, Wea, and Piankashaw. This letter was a remarkable document as an indication of the degree of diplomatic sagacity of which the Indians were intermittently capable. It made its principal point with the statement that it was a message to the Congress of the United States from "the *United Indian Nations,* at their Confederate Council." After a preamble stating "it is now more than three years since peace was made between the King of Great Britain and you but we, the Indians, were disappointed, finding ourselves not included in that peace," the address expressed the hope that there might be "a reconciliation and friendship with a set of people born on the same continent with ourselves," asserted "that the quarrel between us was not of our making" and declared that the first step toward improving relations was recognition of the principle that it was "indispensably necessary that any cession of our lands should be made in the most public manner, and by the united voice of the confederacy; holding all partial treaties as void and of no effect." The message then came to its concrete and all-important proposal: "Let us have a treaty with you early in the spring; let us pursue reasonable steps; let us meet half ways . . . let us pursue such steps as become upright and honest men." And it closed with the stern warning: "If fresh ruptures ensue, we . . . shall most assuredly, with our united force, be obliged to defend those rights and privileges which have been transmitted to us by our ancestors."

Even so faint a gesture toward peace displeased the stubborn Shawnee. Brant adroitly countered the Shawnee objection by commissioning them to deliver the address to the Americans, thus making them directly responsible were war precipitated. British authorities were also disturbed by the possibility the Indian barrier might weaken. The British attitude on the Indian boundary question had noticeably hardened since Sydney's gingerly statements. After the Hurontown conference Brant was in effect reproved for having left a door open to further negotiation. Sir John Johnson, presumably with the approval of Carleton, now Lord Dorchester, who had resumed his former governorship of Canada, was writing Brant, March 22, 1787:

> Your conduct, I hope, for your own sake, will always be such as to justify the good opinion that has been entertained of you by your friends the English, and such as will merit the continuance of their friendship. I hope in all your decisions you will conduct yourselves with prudence and moderation, having always an eye to the friendship that has so long subsisted between you and King's subjects, upon whom alone you can and ought to depend. You have no reason to fear any breach of promise on the part of the King . . . Do not suffer bad men or evil advisers to lead you astray; everything that is reasonable and consistent with the friendship that ought to be preserved between us will be done for you all. Do not suffer an idea to hold a place in your mind, that it will be for your interests to sit still and see the Americans attempt the posts. It is for your sakes chiefly, if not entirely, that we hold them. If you become indifferent about them, they may perhaps be given up; what security would you then have? You would be left at the mercy of a people whose blood calls aloud for revenge; whereas, by supporting them, you encourage us to hold them.

So soon after the Indians had been delivered to American rule by the peace treaty were British authorities reasserting suzerainty over them. Further light on developing British policy was cast by Major Robert Matthews, Dorchester's military secretary newly appointed to command at Detroit, in writing Brant, May 27, 1787:

> I shall begin by informing you of what his Excellency, Lord Dorchester, desired I would . . . he cannot begin a war with the Americans, because some of their people encroach and make depredations upon parts of the Indian country; but they must see it is his Lord-

ship's intention to defend the posts; and that while these are preserved, the Indians must find great security therefrom, and consequently the Americans greater difficulty in taking possession of their
lands; but should they once become masters of the posts, they will
surround the Indians, and accomplish their purpose with little trouble.
From a consideration of all which, it therefore remains for the Indians
to decide what is most for their own interest . . . In your letter to me,
you seem apprehensive that the English are not very anxious about
the defence of the posts. You will soon be satisfied that they have
nothing more at heart, provided that it continues to be the wish of
the Indians, and that they remain firm in doing *their* part of the
business, by preventing the Americans from coming into their country, and consequently from marching to the posts.

Thus was Brant made ever more piercingly aware of how extreme were the handicaps under which he labored. For the sake of
his people's genuine interests he must continue to struggle to avoid
a full-scale war with the Americans which he realized the Indians
must, whatever preliminary successes they might win, eventually
lose. At the same time he was obliged to seem to conform to
British demands that Indians resist American demands, since if
deprived of British patronage the Indian cause must immediately
collapse. Meanwhile, he could exert but imperfect control over his
own followers, could not prevent factions among them from continuing their irregular attacks on the American frontier, could
never be sure that anything approaching a majority of Indians could
be persuaded to hold long to any course. He was as uncertain of the
sincerity or permanence of British support. No statesman could face
a greater task than was his in undertaking to assure the survival
of his people. Few statesmen have ever been confronted by difficulties more intricate or disheartening.

The Hurontown address was outwardly a defiance but in a deeper
sense a peace overture. The seeds of conciliation Brant had hoped
to sow bore no fruit. The sullen Shawnee delayed for months trans-
mission of the address. Under renewed insistence from the Wyandot
and Delaware it was finally delivered at Fort Pitt in June of the

following year. It was not until July 23, 1787, that Secretary of War Henry Knox wrote Brant a noncommittal acknowledgment of its receipt, and many more months before Congress, engrossed by the proceedings of the Constitutional convention, gave it consideration.

The Indian council, with Brant again presiding, reassembled on the Maumee in the fall of 1787 to await the American reply. None came. The delegates dispersed to concern themselves with their winter hunting. Again the feeling of crisis and emergency had dissipated. Congress on October 22nd finally instructed Arthur St. Clair, newly appointed governor of the newly proclaimed Northwest Territory, "carefully to examine into the real temper" of the Indians and to "do everything that is right and proper" to re-establish "peace and harmony" with them. But the creaking governmental machinery of the United States under the Confederation was grinding to a stop. The old congress was marking time while states debated ratification of the new constitution and the public anxiously awaited the verdict. St. Clair did not reach the Ohio until July 9, 1788, and it was another six months before the peace conference proposed by the Hurontown address actually convened.

The long delay was fatal to Brant's hope to negotiate a settlement which might sufficiently protect the interests of both parties to avert a war. Among the virtues inherent in the Indian character, patience and foresight were among the least. The zeal which had marked the impulse toward union at Hurontown had waned. Indians were as inclined to forget last year's dangers as last year's weather and even less inclined to prepare for next year's new dangers. When at last they confronted the Americans at the council table their resolve to present a united front had during the long interval so diminished that Brant declined to participate. But British pressures upon the Indians to refuse American demands had not diminished. Nor had those demands. Nor had Indian resentment. War had become a certainty.

V

McGillivray

Many far more noted nations have had a shorter and less eventful history than the Creek. The dramatic course of their career as a free people was distinguished by the perpetual efforts of alien powers to possess their fertile homeland. This exceptionally pleasing country embraced most of the present states of Georgia and Alabama. Their devoted defense of it obliged them to cope, often simultaneously, with the designs, maneuvers, and aggressions of Spain, England, France, and, eventually, the United States. They were the first Indians north of the Gulf to experience attack by white men and almost the last Indian nation west of the Mississippi to succumb. For a full three hundred years their resistance proved sufficient. They had had their first notice of the approach of the strange race from beyond the ocean with word of Ponce de Leon's 1514 cruise in search of his fountain of youth. Not until 1814 was their nation at last overthrown by the implacable Andrew Jackson at the head of an army of American frontiersmen.

These three centuries were marked by constantly recurring crisis. The maintenance of Creek independence required the development in their untutored forest councils of a foreign policy as complex as any ever contrived by the Medicis or the Borgias. The threats to which they were exposed began early and never abated. In 1528 the first white men appeared on their border. Panfilo Narvaez' 600 soldiers were equipped with armor, firearms, and horses, all fearsome novelties to aborigines until then totally ignorant of the world beyond their horizon. The inhabitants nevertheless forthwith established the tradition of resistance that was thereafter to save them so long. Assailed by armor-piercing arrows shot by bowmen too elusive to be met by cavalry countercharges and meanwhile wasted by starvation and disease, the broken-spirited intruders were rendered unable even to regain their ships.[1] In 1540 a more redoubtable Spaniard, Hernando de Soto, forced his way through the Creek country, repulsing their attacks in a series of desperately fought battles, chaining captives to carry his baggage, and depleting Indian granaries to feed his army. But he kept on like a passing storm to continue his doomed search for cities of gold. His more enduring threat to the Creek was his returned followers' glowing accounts of their country that whetted the interest of many later intruders. In 1565 Spain by the foundation of St. Augustine became a permanent and dangerous neighbor, though Creek vigilance kept Spanish posts and missions confined largely to the inlets and islands of the seacoast. In 1670 a new and greater threat appeared with England's establishment of Charleston. Creek foreign policy made the best of the presence of two white enemies by continuing to play them against each other. Creek ability to resist was meanwhile increased by the readiness of English traders to supply them with arms. In 1699 France established Mobile, and the Creek nation became a small buffer state closely encircled by the three greatest world powers, each hostile to the other but each therefore the more determined to absorb the intervening Creek country. For a time the Creek found safety in their neighbors' rivalries, but at length it

---

[1] The only four known survivors of the expedition achieved under the leadership of Cabeza de Vaca that outstanding overland journey to the Gulf of California which became the first transcontinental crossing north of the Rio Grande and the last within the present limits of the United States until Lewis and Clark in 1805.

became evident that greater security lay in accepting an alliance with one or the other. The Spaniards had nothing to offer. The Creek preferred English trade goods but felt more confidence in French professions of friendship. In 1717, the year before the foundation of New Orleans, the French by Creek invitation established Fort Toulouse in the heart of the Creek country, near the present Montgomery, Alabama. For the next generation the Creek were able to take advantage of French military and political patronage and at the same time of English willingness to continue trade. By the trade competition they maintained their arms supply and as a result their independence.

Their comfortable situation was suddenly and profoundly altered by the expulsion of France from North America. In the great land cessions of 1763 both the French and the Spaniards were removed from Creek borders and their nation entirely enclosed by English territory. Their worst fears were soon quieted, however, as the moderation of English intentions was revealed. By England's institution of the Proclamation Line they were protected from settler encroachment and under the vigorous administration of John Stuart, England's southern Indian Superintendent, their trade was regulated and their privileges respected. Grateful for English consideration, they became England's ardent allies during the Revolution. At the war's end their situation took another violent turn, this one by far the most threatening of any they had experienced in all their long familiarity with peril. By this new treaty their great friend, England, was replaced on one border by their old enemy, Spain, and on the other by a new enemy, the most dangerous with which they had ever been confronted, the United States. It was against a background of memories of so many former dangers and in full realization of this desperate new crisis that the Creek turned for leadership in 1783 to a sickly youth of twenty-four, Alexander McGillivray.

For all his exceptional attainments, McGillivray was a curiously representative product of his people's past. While fiercely resisting military invasion by white men, the Creek had for generations welcomed social and commercial relationships with individual white men. Intermarriage with white officers and traders had long been an accepted feature of Creek society. In every important Creek town white traders had been accepted as permanent and leading citizens who were peculiarly influential by reason of their acquaintance with white skills and accomplishments and who in the course of time founded prominent and often ruling Creek families. Increasing Creek familiarity with white manners, dress, weapons, and tools had led most observers to credit them with having come well along the road to civilization. As one evidence of these progressive tendencies McGillivray's birthplace at Little Tallasie in the center of the Creek country was a plantation house surrounded by the gardens, orchards, and cultivated fields of an estate stocked with some dozens of Negro slaves and herds of cattle and horses.

His maternal grandfather was a French commander of Fort Toulouse who in 1722 married a high-ranking Creek woman of the powerful Wind Clan. His mother, Sehoy Marchand, was celebrated in all contemporary accounts for her beauty. His Scot father, Lachlan McGillivray, had come to Charleston in 1738, the same year William Johnson reached the new world, and, like Johnson, had soon by his activities as an Indian trader acquired one of the great early American fortunes. Among Lachlan McGillivray's enterprises in the Creek country was courting and winning of Sehoy and begetting Alexander, as well as a number of daughters reputedly as beautiful as their mother.

At the age of fourteen Alexander was taken to Charleston where, in an exact parallel to the career of Brant, he was subjected to a white man's education. He was tutored by his cousin, Farquhar McGillivray, and served for a time as apprentice in a Savannah counting house to acquaint him with commercial affairs. His schooling lasted only three years but in so brief a period his penmanship developed a beautifully rounded legibility and he learned to express himself in English with remarkable power and clarity. He was, after all, three quarters white and aided by his father's wealth and influence must in the normal course of events have found a permanent place in the white world. His every prospect was altered, however, by the outbreak of the Revolution. Lachlan, a rabid loyalist, suffered the confiscation of his immense seaboard properties and retreated to his native Scotland to spend the rest of his days. Alexander chose, instead, to return to his mother's people. British authorities, sensing his usefulness, commissioned him colonel and made him their commissary to the Creek. He served his English friends well, dispatching Creek war parties to supplement Tory ravaging of Georgia and South Carolina and himself leading a Creek army in a vain attempt to save the British garrison of Pensacola from Spanish conquest.

His gradual acceptance by the Creek as their paramount leader was not due to heredity, rank,[2] formal election, or his prowess as a warrior; it was based primarily upon his ability to write. This enabled him to present the Creek point of view to friend and enemy alike in a fashion which commanded attention. His long series of reasoned and cogent letters to the representatives of foreign powers became Creek weapons more efficacious than had been the showers of armor-piercing arrows that had routed Narvaez. They were state papers in every sense of the word for they were the forceful expressions of the coherent policies of a statesman who was sagacious, ruthless, and whenever necessary unscrupulous. Though his principal reliance was upon his own intelligence and throughout his short life his physical activity was impaired by gout, rheumatism, and headaches, his leadership was never passive. His final step to political supremacy over his own nation was the suppression of his chief Creek rivals by the timely execution of their white advisors, and when the moment came he did not hesitate to commit his nation to war.

At the end of the Revolution the Creek population approximated 20,000, living in some 50 towns and speaking 6 languages. Their warriors, usually referred to in white records of the time as "gunmen," numbered perhaps 5500. Actual Creek military power fell short of this figure, however, since each town was notoriously

2 His Creek name was Hoboi-Hili-Miko, meaning The Good Child King.

self-centered and seldom could as many as a thousand fighting men be mustered at any one time for any national purpose. Some 300 white traders or white men who had married Creek women were semipermanent residents. Though McGillivray's wealth was far above the Creek average, many of their chiefs lived in substantial homes and owned slaves and herds. The Creek had been in contact with the white world for so long that they had developed an un-Indian sense of possessiveness with respect to land and they were therefore the more disturbed that the United States was claiming the eastern two-thirds of their country and Spain the western two-thirds. It was of this overlapping of American and Spanish claims that McGillivray took instant advantage.

Among the many threats to Creek survival in 1783 two stood out above all others. If they were to maintain the arms they required for defense they must find a source of supply for the trade goods formerly furnished by the English and if they were to hold their country at all they must find a way to resist the encroachment of white settlement. Their southern neighbor, Spain, was unable to offer trade but, on the other hand, presented no settlement threat. Their eastern neighbor, the United States, was prepared to offer trade goods but that advantage was offset by the immensely greater disadvantage that any sort of friendly relations with the Americans must inevitably result in the loss of land to them. How voracious was this American appetite for land was immediately revealed in 1783. Congress declared Indians defeated enemies and demanded their withdrawal to make way for settlement. Bringing the threat nearer home to the Creek, North Carolina on August 17th declared all Indian land extending as far west as the Mississippi open to settlement. Then Georgia, frantically impatient to extend a settlement line which at no point reached farther westward than 40 miles from the Atlantic or the Savannah River, pressed a demand for a wide swath of Creek territory between the Ogeechee and Oconee rivers which was granted in the Treaty of Augusta on November 1 by a minority delegation of Creek chiefs who were political opponents of McGillivray.

McGillivray denounced the Augusta treaty on the grounds the Creek signers had not been authorized representatives of the Creek nation, denied that the Creek were subject to the United States, and countered American aggressiveness with a bid for an alliance with Spain. The moment he had heard of England's formal cession of the Floridas to Spain he was writing, January 1, 1784, Arturo O'Neill, Spanish commander at Pensacola:

As the Floridas are Confirmed to the Crown of Spain by the Peace I solicit in behalf of the Creek Nations his Majestys most Gracious Protection for themselves and Country, as is by them claimed and now held in actual possession. If in the event of War Brittain has been Compell'd to withdraw its protection from us, She has no right to transfer us with their former possessions to any power whatever contrary to our Inclination and Interest. We Certainly as a free Nation have a right to chuse our protector and on our Search what power is so fitting as the Master of the Floridas . . . I beg to offer to Your Excellencys Consideration what I have now written. If it shoud meet with approbation the Crown of Spain will Gain & Secure a powerful barrier in these parts against the ambitious and encroaching Americans.

Having been assured by O'Neill of Spanish interest in his proposal, McGillivray on March 28, 1784, addressed himself directly to Estevan Miro, Spanish governor of Louisiana:

It is necessary for me to Inform you that I am a Native of this Nation & of rank in it. At the commencement of the American Rebellion, I entered the British Service & after a long Contest of faithful Services we have at the Close been most Shamefully deserted as well as every other people that has relied on their honor & Fidelity For the good of my Country I have Sacrificed my all & it is a duty incumbent upon me in this Critical Situation to exert myself for their Interest. The protection of a great Monarch is to be preferred to that of a distracted Republic.

The burden of McGillivray's letter to Miro was devoted to his proposal that, inasmuch as Spanish commercial capacities were unable to fill Creek trade needs, the English firm of Panton, Leslie and

Company be granted Spanish permission to fill them. William Panton was an old friend and his firm represented the only remaining link with those former English associations which McGillivray had always valued so highly. But the personal relationship with Panton was merely a happy coincidence. McGillivray attached far more importance to the assurance of a supply source safe from American interference than he did to any of the military advantages of the Spanish alliance. Miro demurred for a time. To sanction English commercial enterprise within the borders of his province was offensive to every Spanish imperial tradition. But McGillivray continued to insist and Miro yielded, a step at a time. The Creek leader was securing a more favorable trading position than any ever before enjoyed by an Indian nation. He was assured of an arms supply without there being imposed along with it by the supplier any limitation upon his freedom of action. It was upon this unique advantage that his entire policy, so long successful, was based.

At the June 1, 1784, Treaty of Pensacola, Spain appointed McGillivray Creek commissary and undertook to defend all Creek territory within the area claimed by Spain, west of the Flint and south of the Tennessee rivers, against American aggression. Georgia, impressed by the threat of Spanish intentions and aware of its own limited resources, informed McGillivray in November no attempt to settle the disputed Oconee region would be made. He was now free to face the general menace of American encroachment, both present and future. In a memorial of July 10, 1785, to the King of Spain on behalf of the Chiefs of the Creek, Chickasaw, and Cherokee nations, which amounted to a declaration of Indian independence for the information of all states, nations, powers, and parties concerned, he wrote:

> We Cheifs and Warriors of the Creek Chickesaw and Cherokee Nations, do hereby in the most solemn manner protest against any title claim or demand the American Congress may set up for or against our lands, Settlements, and hunting Grounds in Consequence of the Said treaty of peace between the King of Great Brittain and

the States of America declaring that as we were not partys, so we are determined to pay no attention to the Manner in which the British Negotiators has drawn out the Lines of the Lands in question Ceded to the States of America—it being a Notorious fact known to the Americans, known to every person who is in any ways conversant in, or acquainted with American affairs, that his Brittannick Majesty was never possessed either by session purchase or by right of Conquest of our Territorys and which the Said treaty gives away . . . The Americans altho' sensible of the Injustice done to us on this occasion in consequence of this pretended claim have divided our territorys into countys and Sate themselves down on our land, as if they were their own. Witness the Large Settlement called Cumberland and others on the Mississippi which with the late attempts on the Occonnee Lands are all encroachments on our hunting Grounds. We have repeatedly warned the States of Carolina and Georgia to desist from these Encroachments . . . To these remonstrances we have received friendly talks and replys it is true but while they are addressing us by the flattering appellations of Friends and Brothers they are Stripping us of our natural rights by depriving us of that inheritance which belonged to our ancestors and hath descended from them to us Since the beginning of time.

The memorial closed with an appeal for increased Spanish aid. This was forthcoming, but in the meantime Congress had appointed commissioners to negotiate with the southern Indians in the same fashion as with the northern Indians. Their authority was dubious since all territory south of the Ohio was claimed by one or another of the states and was therefore outside the jurisdiction of Congress. To please the Spaniards McGillivray refused to meet with these congressional emissaries, but the passing Indian interest in negotiation enabled Georgia at Galphinton, November 17, 1785, to extract from two anti-McGillivray Creek subchiefs another ostensible cession of the Oconee strip. In venturing to intervene in southern Indian affairs Congress had hoped to preserve border peace by more clearly defining Indian rights and by restraining settler encroachments. This however was a policy Congress had no means to carry out and one contrary to the several southern states' local land designs. Even had the national policy enjoyed state support the normal aggressiveness of individual American frontiersmen could not have been discouraged. Everywhere they were continuing to push into previously unsettled areas.

Having assured his supply lines, arranged an alliance with Spain, and gained the promise of support from his Indian neighbors, Mc-Gillivray was ready to deal by force with the trespassers. Nothing so long distinguished border history as the endless repetition of this one phenomenon—the sudden outbreak of another Indian war. Even when the event had been anticipated the actuality seemed always a surprise, a development born of obscure and unfathomable Indian impulse, an enterprise as unpremeditated by the Indians as unforeseen by their victims. The eruption of the Creek war in 1786 is given a greater interest, therefore, by the opportunity to examine for once the processes leading to Indian decision. The Indian commander in chief himself has clearly recorded every step in his own words. As he reported to O'Neill March 28, 1786:

> I had Issued orders to all the Chiefs of this Nation to meet in Convention . . . My Motives for assembling the Chiefs was to deliberate upon the Conduct of the Americans toward this Nation . . . we observe with much concern that the americans are not at all disposed to Comply with our Just & peaceable remonstrances against their Usurping & settling our hunting Grounds . . . Under such Circumstances we cannot be quiet Spectators. We the Chiefs of the Nation have come to a resolution in this last general meeting to take arms in our defence & repel those Invaders of our Lands, to drive them from their encroachments & fix them within their own proper limits.

There is the equally unusual opportunity to follow the succeeding course of events from the Indian viewpoint. On May 1, 1786, he was reporting directly to Miro on the progress of the war:

> Ever Since the Congress of Pensacola in 1784 we have observed with much discontent the rapid encroachment made upon our Lands, by the Americans in every quarter that we possess . . . To prevent future evil being the general policy of all Nations, it was our duty to

check the Americans in time before they got too Strong for us to contest with them. The advice I had thus given to the Chiefs, they unanimously resolved to adopt. I then Issued orders & Instructions needfull for the occasion & directed them to Collect a Sufficient Number of Warriors & to Set out without loss of time & to traverse all that part of the Country in dispute & whenever they found any American Settlers to drive them off . . . Parties of Warriors Set out in every direction to wherever the Americans were Settled, & where they were forming new establishments. The Oconee Lands were the first visited & cleard of the Settlers. Other parties went on the Cherokee river to a place called the Muscle Shoals where we were informed the Americans were forming a New Settlement but the Indians found at that place only a few working utensils & some preparations for buildings & which they destroyed. Cumberland being an old establishment & the Inhabitants numerous the party that went against it could not drive them Intirely off but the Indians forced them to retire & take Shelter in their Strong Holds when they ravaged & destroyed the plantations & out places which has much Interrupted their cultivation for this Year. Operations of this Nature must in Time cause them to abandon that encroachment.

McGillivray's war was not marked by the hit-and-miss outrages characteristic of most Indian outbreaks. He had embarked upon it in the furtherance of a carefully calculated policy. He knew how disinclined were the impoverished American governments, both state and national, to raise armies to protect the intrusions of settlers and land companies into the Indian country, but he knew as well that on the other hand any outright Indian invasion of long populated American territory was certain to draw such a vigorous response as had crushed the Cherokee in 1776. Therefore he fought a strictly limited war. His warriors were cautioned to confine their attacks to settlements in territory he regarded as Indian. From time to time he called off his raiders and occasionally he offered truces which lasted until there were new settler aggressions. So adroit was his balanced policy of the alternate application of force and restraint that not once during his ten years of Creek leadership was there an American invasion of his country by any official military force mustered by the United States or any of the states.

In spite of the skill and prudence of his undertakings his Spanish allies became alarmed. Spanish authorities had been taught to dread the aggressiveness of American frontiersmen by the Revolutionary exploits of George Rogers Clark and James Willing, and their apprehensiveness had been sharpened by all they had observed since. Concerned lest McGillivray's activities arouse an American frontier counteraction that might endanger Spanish interests that were more important than their system of Indian alliances, Miro drastically reduced Creek military aid. McGillivray remained unmoved. By threatening to turn for supplies to the British in the Bahamas or even to some arrangement with the Americans he forced Spanish toleration of his policies.

These continued to prevail. He was unable to dislodge the Cumberland settlers but these were on the extreme periphery of the Creek sphere of influence. All nearer Creek borders were held inviolate. To achieve this defense of the Creek homeland was a task involving incredible ramifications. He had continually first to take into account the intrigues of rival Creek chiefs, the schemes of competing English traders, the timidities of Spanish policy, the irresponsibilities of allied Indian nations, the designs of land companies, the idiosyncrasies of settlers, and the totally unrelated conduct of Indian affairs by the states of Georgia, North Carolina, and South Carolina, as well as by the irregular authorities of Franklin, Cumberland, and Kentucky, before he could begin to deal with his major problem, a workable solution of differences with the United States.

Through this maze of difficulties he steered an ingenious course. While he lived his people were kept safe. No other great Indian leader, not Brant or Pontiac, Philip or Powhatan, had ever approached his success. His major victories were not won by leading his warriors into battle. They had been gained while seated, pen in hand at his desk in the quiet seclusion of his study in the rambling old plantation house at Little Tallasie. The advantages he had sought for his country he had achieved after the manner of more modern statesmen by the psychological effect of the long series of diplomatic notes he composed and dispatched. With unerring judgment he wrote the right letters at the right time to the right people. Spain and the United States, Georgia and Cumberland, friends and enemies alike, were managed like pieces on a chessboard. Seldom has there been a more striking demonstration that the pen can be mightier than the sword.

VI

&

Robertson

Of all the indomitable figures whose achievements made memorable the first generation of the westward movement James Robertson was the most representative of the peculiar genius of the frontier people. That extraordinary vitality which was their chief attribute was marvelously manifest in him. His whole life was spent on the most advanced and exposed of all frontiers. Throughout the quarter century between the first settler violation of the Proclamation Line and the end of the great Indian wars in 1795 he knew no day not committed to the survival of himself, his family, and his neighbors, no relief from any danger to which a settler could be subject. Though he also was militia commander, Indian agent, magistrate, assemblyman, senator, convention delegate, and acknowledged leader of his district, he was primarily a settler. He was himself the first to visit a new site, the first to undertake the planting of a first crop, the first to labor on the construction of a first stockade, and from first to last stood always, rifle in hand, in the first line of the settlement's defense. From his boyhood he was never even momentarily free of such arduous concerns until he died at the age of seventy-two while engaged in a negotiation with the Chickasaw.

No reference to his personal career can be so brief as not to seem a recapitulation of the history of the frontier of his time. His, as did no other single career, exemplified every stage of that unique and historic phenomenon, the establishment and development of an original transmountain settlement. No other achievement contributed so vitally to the nation's advancement as did success in this communal effort, and no other man contributed by his own direct action so much to that success. Other frontier leaders won more military and political acclaim, but none participated so continuously and so intimately in the daily labors and vicissitudes of a settler's existence. It was his hands that were always on plow handle or gunstock, his arms that swung the ax to make a clearing or build a stockade, his eyes that peered from loophole or thicket, his example that heartened his fellow venturers, his head that was bowed as violent death struck again and again in his family.

He was born in Virginia in 1742, but his parents soon moved to the then frontier on the Yadkin in North Carolina where his acquaintance with his neighbor, Daniel Boone, ripened into a lifelong friendship. Boone's accounts of his long hunts in that fabulous far country beyond the mountains stirred in Robertson a resolve to possess for himself a place in it. This was an excitement, as with so many others who in their youth had listened to such accounts, which was never to diminish.

In 1769 Robertson was among the earliest settlers on the Watauga during the sudden westward surge that followed the Treaty of Fort Stanwix.[1] These first Wataugans had deliberately invaded territory in which their right of occupancy was denied by Great Britain and the Cherokee, and when they in addition realized that they were outside the acknowledged limits of either Virginia or North Carolina he took the lead in those processes by which they undertook by the institution of the Watauga Association the obliga-

[1] As evidence that even the most redoubtable frontiersman was occasionally subject to human failings, on his way back alone over the mountains to the Yadkin after his first inspection of the Watauga he became lost for 14 days, leading his bride to fear that he had been taken by the Indians.

tions of self-government. In 1774 he commanded a company in Andrew Lewis' frontier army which in battle with the Shawnee at Point Pleasant made possible the settlement of Kentucky. In 1775 he and Boone assisted Richard Henderson at the Sycamore Shoals purchase of Kentucky from the Cherokee which led to the establishment of Boonesborough.

The outbreak of the Cherokee War in 1776 multiplied the demands upon him as a principal leader of the Holston frontier. All inhabitants were rushing to the refuge of their stockades in one of those sudden ingatherings which they so tersely termed "forting." Robertson assumed command of the post at Sycamore Shoals in the first of those station defenses against Indian attack which he was so many times to repeat thereafter. As he described the situation in a letter got off July 20, 1776, to William Russell: "I am sure they will attack this Fort in the Morning. Myself & the other Officers is in good Spirits & will do all we can, I hope we will be able to give them a warm Reception & keep them Out, untill you can assist us with more Men. Farewell James Robertson." The Indians were kept out during a siege that lasted weeks. Amid all the tumult of the Cherokee War that summer, with all the inhabitants of the Holston confined to their stockades, Robertson still found time to suppress a Tory community on the Nolichucky suspected of co-operating with the Indians and to detach one platoon of his company to cross the mountains eastward to aid in the defense of Charleston.

At the conclusion of the Cherokee War he was appointed North Carolina agent to the Cherokee, which gave him an opportunity to broaden his frontier experience, already so extensive, by more than a year's residence among Indians. The great interest of his life, however, was land, and he resigned as agent in order to seek it in a distant region then reputed to be the most favored and known to be the most dangerous of any in the west. Henderson's Transylvania Company had lost its claims to Kentucky when Kentucky had become a Virginia county, and he was resolved to retrieve something from the disaster by establishing a new settlement on the Cumberland in an area to the south he believed to be within the future westward extension of North Carolina's jurisdiction. At his solicitation, Robertson undertook the field direction of this project, as Boone had for Henderson in the foundation of Boonesborough, and was thus embarked upon the achievement which made him famous as the founder of middle Tennessee. From that moment on he was required to grapple in succession with the series of supremely critical questions and decisions awaiting the founders of every new settlement.

First always came the inspection and approval of a prepossessing site. In late 1778 with eight companions he made a 250-mile journey through the wilderness to a point on the southern bend of the Cumberland where Nashville now stands. His conclusion that the region was as superior as had been reported by traders and long hunters led to the first great decision. This was unquestionably the spot for the prospective settlement. He planted a corn crop so that when the first families arrived there would be a harvest awaiting them. The next great question was the matter of title, the desperate importance of which settlers were now beginning to realize. Many of the earliest comers to Kentucky were losing by litigation land that for years they had improved and defended. All depended here on whether the bend of the Cumberland would prove to be in Virginia or North Carolina when the boundary survey upon which Henderson and Dr. Thomas Walker, the great explorer and Jefferson's onetime tutor, were then engaged. Robertson was not inclined to await a verdict which might be indefinitely delayed but was even less inclined to subject the settlers he intended to recruit to future title uncertainties so self-evident. He therefore continued his winter journey to the Illinois to seek an arrangement with George Rogers Clark who had some years before filed a Virginia claim to 3000 acres on the Cumberland. Assured now of some protection under the land laws of whichever state eventually took jurisdiction, he rushed back to the Holston to round up enough settlers to offer some hope that the new settlement, once established, might be held.

In the foundation of any new settlement no component was so critical as the character of its personnel. Every man's life, together with the lives of his wife and children, was as dependent on the constancy of every other man as upon his own. The 256 men Robertson assembled that late summer and fall of 1779 were men he knew and who knew him. They formed as stubborn and hardy a band of pioneers as ever set out westward. They had need to be. The trials they were to undergo were to be more demanding and more protracted than any ever inflicted upon any other new settlement. These trials began at once. Colonel John Donelson, Robertson's associate, who took a quota of the colony, including the women and children and the heavier stores, by boat down the Tennessee and up the Cumberland, suffered a loss to Indians en route of 33 killed or captured.[2] Robertson, circling overland through southern Kentucky with the rest of the men and the stock, suffered incredible hardships in that coldest winter of which there had been any record.

The first and most pressing task of any new settlement was attention to its defense. On the Cumberland a number of stations were hastily erected, each stockade sheltering two to a dozen families. The next was to provide for communal law and order. The boundary survey had by now determined the bend of the Cumberland to be in North Carolina but that state's government, 500 miles to the eastward beyond many ranges of mountains, was too preoccupied with the general demands of the Revolution and the immediate demands of an English invasion to feel responsible for so remote a colony. To fill this political void the settlers met in convention on May 1, 1780, with every man able to carry a gun having an equal say, and on the 13th signed the Cumberland Compact, the essential language of which was:

We are, from our remote situation, utterly destitute of the benefit of the laws of our country . . . so we think it our duty to associate, and hereby form ourselves into one society for the benefit of present and future settlers, and until the full and proper exercise of the laws of our country can be in use, and the powers of government exerted among us: we do most solemnly and sacredly declare and promise

[2] The Donelson voyage is described in Chapter XIV of Dale Van Every, *A Company of Heroes.*

each other, that we will faithfully and punctually adhere to, perform, and abide by this our Association, and at all times, if need be, compel by our united force a due obedience to these our rules and regulations.

Meanwhile the Indian danger, though it had been foreseen, was taking on proportions which had not been anticipated. The Chickasaw, who had proved their martial capacities in many past wars with the French and the Spanish and who were soon to drive the American garrison from Fort Jefferson on the Mississippi, were incensed by this intrusion into what they considered their territory. The Chickamauga, under the fierce leadership of the violently anti-American Dragging Canoe, were pitilessly hostile to all settlers, wherever they might be found. In the early weeks of that summer continued Chickasaw and Chickamauga attacks cost the little colony more than 30 killed. Among the dead was Robertson's oldest son, James. Cumberland was as a result almost at once confronted by the most critical of the many painful decisions that could be demanded of a new settlement, to hold on or to get out. It was too distant to expect aid even from the two nearer frontiers, Kentucky 100 miles to the north or the Holston 200 miles to the east. Kentucky was at the moment desperately beating off the most menacing Indian invasion to which it had ever been subjected. Holston was gathering its forces for an expected Cherokee invasion and for the decisive battle at King's Mountain. As the summer wore on the Indian inroads upon Cumberland became more violent. Left to its own slight resources, the colony's hopes of survival flickered day by day nearer extinction. So proven a frontier veteran as Donelson concluded the situation was impossible and withdrew to Kentucky with his family. Many more than did would have followed his example had they not already lost their horses to the Indians. Flight on foot with their women and children seemed more hazardous than to remain in their isolated stockades. Coming to grips with the necessity to decide, Robertson, addressing a settlers' meeting, put the question with relentless practicality:

Everyone decide for yourselves, and do as you please. As for me, I have come to stay . . . We shall not find a better country. I believe we can do better here, and be safer, than we are likely to be by flight. We have to fight it out here, or fight our way out of here.

Enough of them stayed and fought it out there to keep the settlement in existence. But it was a grim and bitter struggle. At the end of the Revolution there were left but three small stockades and 21 men able to bear arms. Relief, however, was now in sight. Robertson managed at last to negotiate a peace with the Chickasaw. North Carolina determined to offer compensation to her continental soldiers by granting them land on the Cumberland. The county of Davidson was erected and the name of Nashboro changed to Nashville. Robertson, elected a delegate to the North Carolina assembly, threw all of his energies into taking advantage of this opportunity to promote immigration. Groups of land speculators, the most important headed by William Blount, grasped the same opportunity. Robertson welcomed their activities as readily as originally he had Henderson's. Hundreds of new families were soon moving westward. By the end of 1785 the population of Cumberland had increased to 4000 in more than 40 stations.

But the breathing spell proved short. The increase in population added to the number of defenders but also provided more targets for Indian attack. The Chickamauga, chronically embittered by more than a generation of white aggressions, had never ceased their inroads. When in 1786 McGillivray committed his Creek, the combined Indian assault again threatened Cumberland's survival. As was the case with so many other settlements the shocks and trials to which Cumberland was subjected continued until the strain became more than any people could be expected to endure. Robertson was reduced to a desperate attempt to open negotiations with the Creek chieftain.[3] The geographical distribution of Cumberland stations, with all of them strung out along one river valley instead of gathered in a mutually supporting clump as in Kentucky, made

[3] McGillivray was exultantly writing O'Neill, August 12, 1786: "The Cumberland people are begging hard for peace."

defense excessively difficult. All that summer the raids were unremitting. Farming a wilderness clearing was an arduous occupation under any circumstances. When the seasonal pursuits of planting, cultivating, harvesting, and stock tending were being perpetually interrupted by recurrent Indian alarms, each requiring another frantic flight to the sanctuary of a stockade, it became a nearly impossible one. The rush of immigration came to an end. Many of the later arrivals were withdrawing.

McGillivray, with his usual finger on the pulse of events and concerned lest too severe harassment of Cumberland might arouse North Carolina to call up its militia, relaxed Creek depredations in the spring of 1787. But the Chickamauga attacks continued. Many came from Coldwater, a newly established town near Muscle Shoals on the Tennessee, which was being furnished arms by French traders from the Illinois. Grieved by the death of his brother Mark in one of these raids, Robertson determined to strike back. With a force of 130 mounted volunteers he crossed the Tennessee in the night and descended upon Coldwater so swiftly that he took the place by complete surprise. Twenty Indians were killed before they could escape to their canoes. Two French traders and a French woman were also killed during the assault. The goods of 11 other French traders were confiscated. This considerable booty provided a notable acquisition for the impoverished Cumberland settlers.

Six of the fallen Indians, however, had been visiting Creek. McGillivray had by now realized that neither Georgia nor North Carolina had any serious intention of mounting offensives against him to relieve the pressures on their beleaguered settlements. He therefore seized upon the Creek fatalities at Coldwater as an excuse to resume his attacks on Cumberland. Though his Spanish allies were anxiously cautioning him to take greater care to avoid drawing down massive retaliation from the Americans he was imperturbably informing O'Neill on July 10th, "In Consequence of this affair I have Sent off between five & Six hundred warriors under approved leaders to go & ravage the Settlement of Cumberland & destroy their houses & plantations." The renewed Creek-Chickamauga onslaught was the most severe that had yet struck Cumberland. Again the possibility loomed that the settlement might have to be abandoned. Robertson's determination to stay remained nevertheless as unshaken as ever.

He appealed to Governor Samuel Johnston of North Carolina to intercede with Congress in Cumberland's behalf. Johnston took the unsympathetic position that the settlement was suffering no more than any exposed settlement had reason to expect. A comparable lack of sympathy with the plight of western settlers was general in the east. The opinion was almost universally held that settlers were deliberately provoking the Indians and that in any case, by electing to occupy land in the edges of the Indian country, the settlers had invited difficulties which they might at any time escape by a sensible return to more normal regions. Even had Johnston pressed Robertson's appeal upon Congress nothing could have come of it. Congress in 1787 had neither the authority, the means, nor the troops to attempt to defend the territory of either North Carolina or of any of the states.

As 1787 drew to a close Robertson, after striving for eight desperate years to hold Cumberland, was thus faced with the necessity to consider the ultimate decision. It was one likewise confronting every other western settler. The course of events had revealed the stark realities of the situation in which all westerners were entrapped. They were opposed by world powers committed to their suppression or expulsion. Great Britain was blocking their advance at the Ohio. Spain was barring the Mississippi to their commerce. Both were inciting the Indians to destroy their homes and families. In this dire and prolonged emergency Americans in the west had been granted no support by their states or the United States. No settler had long survived except by learning to take advantage of any circumstance that promoted that survival. To most westerners the conclusion was inescapable that having been left to shift for themselves they were obliged to look to their own salvation. They began, almost unconsciously at first, to speculate on the possibility that their woes might be more speedily and certainly relieved by turning to a foreign nation for the protection that they had been denied by their own. England offered the advantage of a common language and religion. Spain offered the greater advantage of comparative weakness plus the Mississippi which provided a commercial outlet to the sea so much more serviceable than the English Great Lakes–St. Lawrence route. Both offered relief from Indian attack were their attitude to shift from hostility to friendliness.

Robertson conceived his great responsibility was to the Cumberland settlement and to the people in it who had suffered so long. He had never hesitated to follow an unbeaten track however remote and unknown the region to which it might lead. He did not hesitate now to embark on a course the end of which was more unpredictable than any upon which he had ever ventured. His first independent excursion into the hazardous realm of international intrigue indicated that he felt driven to resort to almost any expedient. He wrote McGillivray suggesting a combined Cumberland-Creek attack to drive the Spanish from the Gulf coast, an undertaking he maintained could succeed were McGillivray to assemble sufficient supplies through his English contacts. McGillivray was not interested. Robertson then went to the opposite extreme of communicating with Miro, suggesting a possible community of interests between Cumberland and Spain. Miro was definitely interested. In making this approach to Spain Robertson was not acting alone. With the dawn of that supremely critical year, 1788, every other important western leader, without exception, was yielding to the same impulse.

VII

Sevier

Those extraordinary qualities of the frontier people which were first manifest among the border inhabitants of the Valley of Virginia reached their apogee in the Valley's extension of settlement southward along the Holston. It was on the Holston that the frontiersman developed that total self-confidence which made him so phenomenal a success in the face of difficulties as phenomenal. It was there that he rose to that pitch of complete self-expression which enabled him to give free rein to his impulses, as free to those that were outrageous as those that were admirable, and which made him the master of his environment and a predominating influence upon his times. Among these men of the Holston, so ready for action, so scornful of authority, so impatient with restraint, so headstrong and headlong, John Sevier still stood out so vividly as to seem their personification. Every other borderer saw in him the full development of those accomplishments to which he himself most aspired. He could ride, shoot, hunt, fight, talk, play, drink, brawl, court women, breed children, and claim land, all on a grander scale than lesser men. As final touches to his frontier appeal he was hearty, generous, hospitable, and captivatingly gregarious.

Before he was thirty he had become by universal acclaim a leader in a society in which every man was notoriously reluctant to recognize any other man as under any circumstances his superior. The respect, admiration, and affection which he inspired mounted to hero worship. When he took his rifle down and started for his horse the hundreds who sprang instantly to answer his call were ready to follow him anywhere. He led them always to victory. In his more than twenty campaigns he never knew defeat. The public disillusionment that has so often clouded the career of popular favorites did not shadow his. The adulation of his friends, neighbors, and fellow frontiersmen continued to wax and at no time waned. He was elected captain of his militia company the year he arrived on the Holston frontier and 40 years later was representing these same admirers in Congress. In the interim he had been governor of the lost state of Franklin, twice governor of Tennessee, and always the ranking militia commander of his frontier.

He was born September 23, 1745, in the Valley of Virginia of Huguenot parents whose family name had originally been Xavier. After having spent his youth and young manhood on what had until then been the outermost border, at the age of twenty-seven he moved with his own growing family from the Valley to the newer and wilder frontier on the Watauga. Like his fellow Wataugan, Robertson, he participated in the founding of the Watauga Association and in the Sycamore Shoals conference and served in the Shawnee and Cherokee Wars. In 1779 he became colonel of militia and thereafter was perpetually a senior Holston commander. In his three major Indian campaigns during the Revolution, in 1780, 1781, and 1782, he broke Cherokee resistance and burned 31 of their towns, carrying the war so vigorously into the depths of the Indian country as far south as the Coosa River in Georgia that the Holston was almost completely relieved of Indian harassment. In the intervals between these Indian campaigns he led contingents of Holston horsemen eastward over the mountains to King's Mountain in 1780 and to ride with Francis Marion in 1781. As a consequence of his military operations the Holston frontier, unlike all others, was

able to pass from a defensive to an offensive posture during the closing years of the Revolution and to advance its outer line of settlement more than 60 miles southward into the Cherokee country.

To the inhabitants of the frontier the negotiation of peace ending
the Revolution heralded more than the promise of relief from the
seven-year-long struggle for survival. It appeared also to offer sudden
new opportunities beyond every horizon. The unforeseen British
relinquishment of the whole immense region south of the Lakes
seemed to have opened a way to limitless advantage to any man
quick enough to seize upon it. Spain's claim to the west was at first
taken no more seriously than was the chance that the Indians might
continue to resist. Even eastern authorities had seemed for once to
rise to the occasion. Congress declared all Indians disinherited. All
of North Carolina's western lands were declared by its legislature
immediately open to settlement. People on the Pennsylvania and
Kentucky frontiers began crossing the Ohio. Cumberland pushed its
already precarious line of settlements toward the Mississippi at
Chickasaw Bluffs. Nowhere along the border was this impulse to
reach for more land more aggressive than among the irrepressible
residents of the Holston. They had long been accustomed not only to
reach for but to take whatever they wanted. During their twenty-
year advance down the Holston they had repeatedly violated royal
decrees, the proclamations of provincial governors, and the terms of
successive treaties with the Cherokee. Their attention was now
directed not only west toward Kentucky and Cumberland but
southwest to the Mississippi and south to the Gulf.

But that same opportunity apparent at the war's end had given
the individual settler a frontier rival in the quest for western land.
Land companies had again entered the field. For a time it seemed an
unequal contest. The settler, animated by his immemorial assumption that the more distant the land the more certain was it to prove
superior to what he already held, sought a new and possibly larger
family farm. The land company was intent on tracts ranging to
hundreds of thousands and even millions of acres. The settler was
required to make careful preparations for his tremendous move, to

wait upon disposal of his present place, the gathering of his harvest, or the pregnancy of his wife, and then to commit his family to the most violent hardships and dangers. The land company had only to draw lines on a map and then to maneuver a grant through a complacent legislature. It was not, however, a contest the company was destined to win. The settler, defending his actual occupation of the land, eventually prevailed over the speculator as completely as he did over his Indian, French, English, and Spanish opponents.

Land companies had from the beginning of the westward movement played an important, and at times even an honorable, role in the frontier's advance. In 1748 James Patton's land company had founded at Draper's Meadows on New River the first English settlement on western waters. In 1750 and 1751 the first English explorers of Kentucky, Thomas Walker and Christopher Gist, had been representing land companies. Washington's winter journey in 1753 and his first campaign in 1754 had been conducted in co-operation with land-company activities. Throughout the twenty years before the Revolution Franklin had devoted a considerable portion of his great influence to the furtherance of land-company designs. The 1768 Treaty of Fort Stanwix which provided the first great opening to western settlement had been engineered by land companies. Clark's first sight of central Kentucky had been while a land-company surveyor. In those pre-Revolutionary years every land-company project was based on the hope that a grant from the King might be obtained. With the outbreak of the Revolution all such prospects faded. Efforts to enlist congressional sympathies failed. Meanwhile, some thousands of settlers had taken possession of the land the companies had sought.

The first purely American land company had been Henderson's Transylvania Company which had promoted the settlement of Kentucky and then Cumberland. He had had the inspiration to rely not on a royal or governmental grant but upon an ostensible purchase from the Indians. His success had enlightened rival operators to whom the end of the Revolution was now revealing what appeared a speculators' paradise. Title to the whole region extending west-

ward to the Mississippi from the Carolinas and Georgia was confused by the conflicting and overlapping claims of Spain and the
United States, of Georgia, South Carolina, and North Carolina, and
of four Indian nations, the Cherokee, Creek, Choctaw, and Chickasaw. No more fertile field for land-company operations could be
imagined. All that was required to get into business was to take the
first steps toward making a deal with any one of the nine claimants.
In the case of Indian negotiations, arrangements entered into with
the most irresponsible minorities of a nation were sufficient. Most of
the grants secured from state legislatures were as irresponsible. The
land involved was far beyond the state's borders, and no action was
required beyond the acceptance by legislators of stock in the company.

The first major post-Revolutionary land-company operation, the
so-called Muscle Shoals project, typified the process. Leader of the
group undertaking the enterprise was William Blount, then representing North Carolina in Congress and later a United States Senator from Tennessee. His principal associates were Richard Caswell,
six times governor of North Carolina; John Donelson, co-founder of
Cumberland; Joseph Martin, Virginia's agent to the Cherokee and
Patrick Henry's land agent; Griffith Rutherford, North Carolina's
senior militia commander; Wade Hampton, leading figure of South
Carolina's frontier; four members of the Georgia legislature; and
Sevier.

Blount had had advance notice that the current survey of veterans'
bounty lands in Cumberland was showing that the southern bend of
the Tennessee River lay below any westward extension of North
Carolina's southern boundary and therefore within territory claimed
by Georgia or South Carolina. He and his associates recognized the
opportunity to claim land on an even wider scale than North Carolina permitted. They took a number of Georgia politicians into the
company and on February 20, 1784, obtained from the Georgia
legislature an undertaking to form a Georgia county there once an
actual settlement had been established. Blount had meanwhile,
through Martin, promised one Cherokee faction future payment for

Cherokee consent to the transaction. The area in question, however, bordered on Creek and Chickasaw country as well as Cherokee, was more than 200 miles west of Georgia's settlement line, and was claimed by Spain, who was bound to consider any occupation an American invasion. It was in such troubled waters that land companies had delighted to fish since land-company maneuvers had brought on a world war in 1754.

Every land-company design depended on an initial introduction of original settlers of a breed hardy enough to defend the location during the operation's early and more dangerous stages in order to permit the general sale of land to later comers upon which the company's hope of eventual profit was based. Under similar circumstances Henderson had enlisted Boone in Kentucky and then Robertson in Cumberland. It was fulfillment of this need that made Sevier's participation an invaluable adjunct to the Muscle Shoals project. His Holston followers were the hardiest settlers known and, were the proceedings to precipitate a general Indian war, or even a war with Spain, he could take the field at the head of 1500 mounted riflemen who constituted the most formidable military force existing anywhere on the continent.

The seemingly certain success to which so much sagacious preparation had expected to lead was delayed and then disrupted, however, by a totally unexpected collateral development which illustrated the multiplicity of forces keeping the frontier in a state of perpetual confusion throughout the 1780's. The coincidental impulse of the Holston settlers to set up the new state of Franklin necessarily distracted the attention of everyone connected with Muscle Shoals. Sudden as was the final action, it had been long discussed and was a natural outgrowth of the area's physical situation. The Virginia and North Carolina counties on the Holston had far more in common with each other than either had with their parent states. The mountain barrier, cutting them off economically and socially from the east, left them with all the disadvantages of isolation and none of the advantages of independence. It was inevitable that a people so self-reliant should consider themselves better able to manage their own affairs than could distant officials or seaboard legislatures.

The growing inclination to separate was given added impetus by North Carolina's land policy. That state's land laws, to an even greater extent than Virginia's, had for years favored eastern investors at the expense of western settlers. This favoritism had become flagrant at the war's end. In declaring the west open in 1783 the legislature's purpose had not been to encourage settlement so much as to facilitate speculation. Title to hundreds of thousands of acres in the west was within months taken by easterners at the cost of no greater exertion than the maintenance of personal and political contacts with officials, judges, and legislators. The westerners were outraged, but their protests commanded little attention at a seat of government hundreds of miles away beyond the mountains.

The Holston's dissatisfaction was crystallized into action by two provocative events in the spring of 1784. The ruling conservative party lost control of the North Carolina legislature to the radical opposition which thereupon voted a cession of North Carolina's western lands to the United States. At almost the same moment Congress by the Ordinance of 1784 appeared to be inviting the formation of new states in the west. The people of the Holston seized immediately upon this opportunity to make themselves the political masters of their frontier's development. Meeting in convention at Jonesboro in August they voted unanimously to form a new state and called a second convention in December to frame its government.

At the moment of decision in August the way had seemed clear. The proposal to set up a new state had the presumed approbation of existing authority at both state and national levels. But as swiftly as it had in the spring the scene changed again before the year was out, subjecting the new state to the first of these storms which were to beat upon it throughout its short and tumultuous career. By fall the conservative party had recovered control of the North Carolina legislature and the cession to the United States was repealed, thus

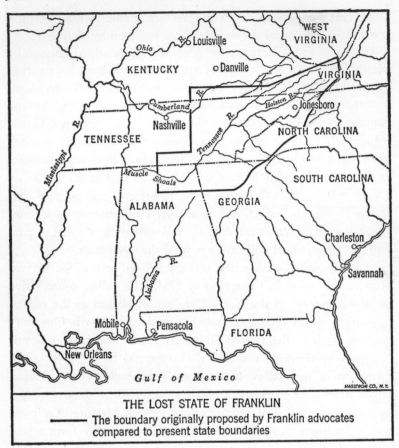

THE LOST STATE OF FRANKLIN
—————— The boundary originally proposed by Franklin advocates
compared to present state boundaries

placing the proponents of independence in Holston's North Carolina counties in a state of insurrection if they persisted. They accepted the challenge. In their December convention they debated North Carolina's disapproval and then went ahead with their program. They selected the name Franklin,[1] elected Sevier governor, adopted a temporary constitution, and got off petitions to North Carolina, Virginia, and Congress demanding recognition as an independent state.

[1] Frankland, signifying the land of free men, had been for a time considered.

This zeal posed Sevier a difficult dilemma. He had not sought the governorship or favored the formation of a new state. The land-company operations upon which he relied to build his personal fortunes could be expected to function much more freely under the laws of North Carolina than under those of a new government dominated by settlers. Yet he hesitated to sacrifice his personal popularity by declining the governorship or by outwardly opposing the new state movement. As the December convention deliberated he managed by the shrewd use of that popularity to have his cake and eat it. He accepted the governorship and at the same time was able to secure the adoption of a temporary constitution incorporating the North Carolina type of land laws which had until that moment been considered a chief incentive for seeking independence. At the 1785 convention there was more debate and enough resistance to the proposal to produce a narrower vote, but again in the definitive constitution Sevier succeeded in fastening upon Franklin a judicial system which fostered the activities of land companies at the expense of the individual settler.

The exercise of his personal influence for this personal purpose was no secret but neither did it notably lessen the regard in which he was held by fellow settlers whose interests he was affecting. It was taken for granted on the frontier that any man worth his salt would reach for as much land as he could possibly hope to get. The acquisition of land was the one means by which any man might aspire to wealth, and it was an American principle as well established then as it has remained since that material advancement should constitute any man's major purpose in life. A man who improved his opportunities by association with politically influential easterners was considered to be exhibiting a diligence and perspicacity more to be admired than deplored. The general frontier acceptance of the assumption that any means to gain land were permissible extended even to land-company designs involving injury to the interests of the individual settler, the corruption of legislatures, and threats to the nation's peace. This curious complacence was a vast disservice to thousands of ordinary settlers but nevertheless represented a dynamic contribution to the westward movement. No land company ever succeeded to the point of making a corporate profit, but land-company activities kept the frontier in a constant ferment of new expectation and new initiative which continually stimulated expansion.

Having put his new governmental house in order, Sevier turned again to the forwarding of the Muscle Shoals enterprise. He encountered little opposition among his Holston followers. The Franklin legislature twice voted to raise an expeditionary force to seize the area whenever he so decided. Blount, the calculating politician, felt that the company's future title might prove more sound were the formal call to arms to come from an established state, such as Georgia, instead of the as yet unrecognized Franklin. When Georgia, startled by McGillivray's bold front, postponed and then evaded issuing such a call, a companion grant to the same region was secured, through the intercession of Wade Hampton, from Georgia's rival claimant, South Carolina, in February 1786. McGillivray's declaration of war that spring instilled in South Carolina a discretion equal to Georgia's and the summons was again delayed.

By this time Franklin had become too disturbed by internal stresses to embark alone upon the crusade. As many political confusions as Sevier had foreseen were inhibiting decision even among a people customarily so decisive. Congress had ignored the petitions for recognition. Under pressures from Patrick Henry, again governor of Virginia, the Virginia Holston counties which had originally initiated the independence movement were withdrawing from the new state. In early 1787 North Carolina began actively reasserting jurisdiction in her section of the Holston. Soon in every county there were two sets of officials, Franklin's and North Carolina's. Among a people so naturally contentious incidents were numerous. Though the district drifted to the brink of civil war there was less direct resistance to North Carolina's attempt to resume jurisdiction than most had anticipated. The sentiment was growing in the northern counties of the Holston that having lost their Virginia neighbors it was no more than sensible to return to North Carolina. Loyalty to

Franklin remained strong only in the southern counties whose residents occupied land south of the Cherokee boundary defined by the 1777 Treaty of Long Island to which Cherokee title had been reaffirmed by the 1785 Treaty of Hopewell between the Cherokee and the United States. There were local fears that these settlements might be obliged to withdraw were outside authority to resume control.

In every other respect it was becoming increasingly clear that establishment of Franklin had as yet promoted no advantage sought by either Sevier or his fellow settlers. On the contrary, for the four critical post-Revolutionary years of 1784 through 1787 the discords and confusions infesting the new state movement had neutralized the energies of the frontier's most aggressive district and most aggressive leader. After careers of uninterrupted success marked by many amazing conquests, both the Holston and Sevier had during these years been reduced to near impotence. By 1787 there also were on every wider horizon fewer signs than ever that the situation might improve. The government of the United States had exerted its feeble powers not to assist but to restrain the advance of the frontier in the southwest. The state governments of North Carolina, South Carolina, and Georgia, spiritlessly shrinking before McGillvray's brazen defiance, could be counted on for little support. The Kentucky and Cumberland frontier districts to the west seemed committed by the economic necessities of the Mississippi closure to seeking some accommodation with Spain.

It seemed to Sevier that more was involved in this impasse with which Franklin was confronted than the frustration of his personal prospects. He could not forget his deeper responsibilities as the acclaimed leader of his frontier. In the 40 years since Stephen Holston had built the first cabin on the headwaters of the river named for him, the Holston frontier had been advanced 180 miles. Its future appeared still to be in a continued advance on down the Tennessee. Sevier was determined that advance should resume. Like Robertson, he felt compelled to any course that promised deliverance.

It was this resolve that, as 1787 drew to a close, was preparing him to resort to James White's intermediation in the opening of conversations with Diego de Gardoqui, Spain's envoy to the United States, and with Spanish governors at Havana and New Orleans, in order to explore the possibility that American settlement of the middle Tennessee might be welcomed were the development to be accompanied by the attachment of an independent Franklin to Spain.

VIII

🎵

Wilkinson

Of all the resolute young men who at the end of the Revolution were making their way west to seek their fortunes none could have been so bent on achieving that feat as James Wilkinson. The fortune he sought, moreover, was one presenting all the dimensions and facets of a rajah's treasure. His preliminary ambitions were to make himself the political master of the west, to attain supreme military rank, and to win historic fame, but his great urge was to make an unlimited amount of money.

The first three goals he reached. As a politician he for years held Kentucky in the hollow of his hand. As a soldier he was commanding general of the Army of the United States under Washington, Adams, Jefferson, and Madison. His fame did not endure but in his own time wherever he appeared upon the scene—whether Lexington, Pittsburgh, Detroit, Mackinac, St. Louis, New Orleans, Richmond, Philadelphia, Vera Cruz, or Mexico City—he became at once the center of public attention and excitement. His one failure was to make enough money. He succeeded in making what other men would have considered a great deal but it was not nearly so much as he craved. It was his desire to get more that drove him to devices that were beyond belief ingenious, fantastic, and unprincipled. There were times during the years he served as brigadier general, high commissioner, territorial governor, and major general when he was simultaneously seeking or accepting money, in addition to the salary paid him by the United States for his full-time services, from friends, associates, and partners, from competing land companies, from smuggling enterprises, from filibustering projects, from bribe proffers of every sort, and from espionage devoted to the interests of France, Spain, and Great Britain.

The primary weapon with which he won his many public successes was his ingratiating personality. Though of slight stature—ordinarily a fatal bar to any bid for leadership on the frontier where physical prowess was so highly regarded—he had a graceful carriage, a pleasing voice, an engaging manner, a frank, handsome countenance, and a way with him as attractive to men as to women. He charmed, almost on sight, whomever he met and it was an inherent charm that won friends and did not pale on long acquaintance. He was so plausible and persuasive that he was able with equal ease to disarm intransigent frontiersmen, embittered political rivals, suspicious business associates, dubious Spanish governors, and anxious American presidents. A great many men who were in all other respects honorable and intelligent became and long remained his doting supporters and in effect his accomplices. He was as articulate with his pen as with his tongue and thus was able to cast the net of his influence over men at any distance whom he may never have met. He was particularly adept at seeding letters, contracts, memorials, petitions, and statutes with eloquent and flowery phrases which concealed while serving his designs.

Had he accepted with good will and at face value the many legitimate rewards showered upon him his career must have attained genuine eminence. But he could never gain one advantage without forthwith prostituting it to an endeavor to gain some other advantage, not always greater. His every personal, financial, political, and military preferment was no sooner won than it was placed on the block, sometimes to go to the highest bidder, but more often to be offered in a kind of raffle which might lead to a chance contact with some distant and hitherto unsuspected patron who might in turn indicate a hitherto undetected road to wider profit. This inordinate craving for more money than could be earned by any direct effort committed him to schemes of such devious and intricate complexity that his efforts were perpetually as compromised materially as they were morally. He was like a juggler striving to keep so many balls in the air that some were bound to fall. All finally fell. Yet for more than thirty years his labyrinthine activities deeply affected not only the course of events in the west but the course of national policy. Occasionally beset by scandals, congressional investigations, military courts martial, and trials for treason, he remained personally unshaken and legally unconvicted. When he died, December 25, 1825, an expatriate in Mexico, he was still diligently seeking the great fortune that had eluded him in his own country. His powers to confuse and persuade had not diminished with age. He had managed to attract for his final schemes the somewhat bewildered but almost awed attention of a succession of Mexican revolutionary governments.[1]

When he came to Kentucky in December 1783, he had never before been west of the Susquehanna, but the exercise of his talents did not require familiarity with his new surroundings. The twin novelties of his flamboyant personality and the worldly nature of his former experiences made him a fascinating figure to the so much less sophisticated frontier. These experiences had been notable if various. At the outbreak of the Revolution he had left medical school to enlist in the Continental Army from his native Maryland. His war record had been outwardly distinguished. He had served with Benedict Arnold at Quebec, as Horatio Gates' adjutant general at Saratoga, and for three years as Washington's clothier general. These services had been interspersed with accomplishments of another sort that had prepared him for the vaster duplicities upon which he was soon to embark. In the Saratoga dispute between Gates and Arnold he had with unconcerned alacrity switched his allegiance from his

[1] While in Mexico he was also serving as agent of the American Bible Society.

former friend and commander, Arnold, to his new friend and commanding general, Gates. Next he had taken a leading part in the
Conway Cabal designed to replace Washington with Gates but in
doing so had talked so freely in his effort to advance his own expectations as to embarrass the conspirators and infuriate Gates. He
was already evidencing an instinctive capacity for intrigue by accepting in swift succession the risk of offending two powerful former
patrons while moving with such mercurial evasiveness that he had
not disillusioned Congress or Washington. This record of consistent
readiness to betray anybody with whom he had dealings was presently to take on outlandish proportions.

Eventful as had been his previous career, he was only twenty-
seven when he disembarked that midwinter day at Louisville. He
was representing a group of Philadelphia merchants, but there were
as yet but three stores in Kentucky and it required no more than a
first glance to realize that frontier merchandising was not a field
offering appropriate scope for his ambitions. Neither was he long in
hitting upon something more promising. On January 17, 1784, only
weeks after his arrival, he was writing the president of Congress
offering advice on the conduct of the current peace negotiations with
the Chickasaw, a nation he had never visited and of which he had
no firsthand knowledge whatever. This was not just a shot in the
dark but the calculating initiation of a project every elaborate detail
of which had been planned on the spur of the moment. This personal advancement program was of no less magnitude than to gain
as speedily as possible political leadership of Kentucky, military command in the west, and control of western Indian relations. These
were unquestionably areas in which success must improve materially
his chances to make much more money, but all three responsibilities
were at the time in the firm grip of George Rogers Clark, the west's
renowned Revolutionary War hero.

Clark had at the war's end been hastily discharged from its military service by an impoverished Virginia desperate to halt demands
on its empty treasury, but he and his soldiers had been voted extensive land grants, Congress had appointed him Indian Commis-

sioner, and he was still regarded in Kentucky with all the confidence and esteem he had earned as the frontier's great champion. To challenge so powerful and seemingly invulnerable a figure appeared a hopelessly irrational venture for a recently arrived young easterner but Wilkinson did not hesitate. In the letter to Congress he had recognized an opportunity to open his campaign. He had been able at Louisville to intercept John Donne, Clark's emissary to the Chickasaw, then en route east with messages to Congress dealing with the pending Chickasaw treaty. Wilkinson read the dispatches and added one of his own calculated to give Congress the impression that it was he more than Clark who was managing the Chickasaw negotiation. This was the first thin, scarcely noticeable entrance of a wedge which, when eventually driven home, alienated Clark for years from his state and his country.

Kentucky in that first year of peace provided a wide range of opportunity for so enterprising an adventurer as Wilkinson. The whole frontier was in a tumult of frustration and dissatisfaction. Instead of relief, peace had brought new dangers and uncertainties. The rush of new settlers filling every community with strangers had added to the confusion. The great uncertainty was title litigation, which was costing many of the oldest settlers possession of the land they had been developing for years. The great danger, growing by the week, was from Indian attack as small packs of warriors sifting among the settlements resumed their wartime burning and killing. Both evils were aggravated by Kentucky's distance from Virginia's seat of government, five weeks travel time away beyond the mountains. The land laws were made and administered by eastern legislators and officials, and sole authority to call up the militia to repulse the Indians was invested in an eastern governor and his council.

As the summer advanced the Indian danger increased, destroying lives along with property until it displaced the title grievance as Kentucky's principal concern.[2] In the fall a report gained circula-

[2] Among many less noted settler deaths in August was that of Walker Daniel, the district's attorney general, who was killed while engaged, in partnership with Wilkinson, in the operation of a saltworks at Bullitt's Lick.

tion that a general Cherokee invasion was imminent. Benjamin Logan, the founder in 1775 of one of Kentucky's first three stations, called an informal meeting of militia officers at Danville, November 7, 1784, to consider the frontier's defense. The stark fact that under Virginia law the people of Kentucky had no authority to call up their own militia even to resist an invasion was faced in all its dismal absurdity. Most Kentuckians had harbored the hope of eventual statehood since the days of the Boonesborough Convention in 1775. The great majority of the men attending the Danville meeting were Virginians, but they realized as clearly as did transplanted Pennsylvanians and Carolinians that the time had come to grasp the nettle. At this council of veteran Indian fighters was born the demand for Kentucky's admission to the union that was to be pressed to the point of near secession before being finally accepted eight long years later. But these custodians of a tormented frontier proceeded initially with deliberate patience and every regard for legality. Their first step was to call for the election in each militia district of delegates popularly empowered to consider the question of separation from Virginia.

This First Kentucky Convention, meeting at Danville, December 27, 1784, elected Colonel William Fleming, the gallant veteran of Point Pleasant, president, and Isaac Shelby, later to become the first governor of Kentucky, chairman.[3] Sentiment, as at the former meeting, was unanimous for separation. But still no precipitate action was taken. Statements of Kentucky's grievances arising from its distance from Virginia's seat of government and protests over the operation of Virginia's land laws were drafted. The statehood question was then again referred to the people for their further consideration and the election of instructed delegates to another convention. The Second Convention met May 23, 1785. Again sentiment for separation was unanimous but, there having been some apparent

---

[3] There has been occasional confusion with regard to the nomenclature of the several Kentucky conventions. Some chroniclers have referred to this as a second convention and others to the next, meeting in May 1785, as the first. This one, meeting in December of 1784, was the first convention whose delegates had been elected by voters who had been aware that they were voting on the question of statehood.

irregularity in the election of several of the delegates, the question
was again returned to the voters, together with an address informing them that the convention had unanimously resolved "that it is
expedient and necessary for this district to be separated from Virginia and established into a sovereign independent state, to be
known as the Commonwealth of Kentucky, and taken into union
with the United States of America." There were as yet no printing
presses in Kentucky. The people were informed of the address by
attaching handwritten copies of it to the gates of stockades and the
doors of cabins in which local justices held court.

On August 8, 1785, the Third Convention met at Danville, its
authority to speak for Kentucky having been three times reaffirmed
by the expressed will of the voters, and this time it drafted by unanimous consent a formal petition to the Virginia legislature demanding Virginia's recognition of Kentucky as a "free, sovereign and
independent republic."[4] This was the first convention to which Wilkinson was a delegate. The facility of his persuasive speaking and
rhetorical writing gained him immediate influence over its deliberations. But there is no evidence that at this time he, any more than
did any of his fellow members, had any faintest thought of
secession from the United States, much less of the possibility of any
future resort to union with Spain or Great Britain. All Kentuckians
were of one mind. They were determined upon gaining recognition as a separate state and admission as an equal into the confederation of the original thirteen. The historic importance of this frontier
movement for independence and equality, initiated at Boonesborough in 1775 and renewed at Danville in 1784, is that henceforth it
persisted until it culminated in the admission of Kentucky in company with Vermont as the vanguard of that ensuing great procession
of new states which made possible the unlimited development of the
United States.

The mature deliberation, repeated consultation of the will of the
people, and regard for all the forms of legality which had so far
marked the new state movement is noteworthy. Some of this was

[4] See p. 24 for a portion of the text of the petition.

undoubtedly due to the circumstance that many of the more influential members of the conventions were recently arrived and
comparatively well-to-do easterners who were inclined by their former associations and their business interests, particularly their land
interests, to maintain amicable relations with Virginia. But the ordinary frontiersmen, all of whom had had repeated opportunities to
vote on the issue, were exhibiting in this instance an equal regard for
legality. They had learned in a hard school the fundamental necessities of self-government. For a great many years the survival of any
station had depended on the individual's subordination to the will
of the majority. Unruly and refractory as was the average frontiersman in most of his attitudes, he had grown to regard at least the
forms of the democratic process with a curious respect.

The conciliatory patience with which Kentucky had conceived
the petition was rewarded by the sympathetic resignation with which
Virginia received it. There was little disposition to attempt to hold
the transmountain counties against their wish. Washington, Jefferson, and Madison were among the Virginia leaders who advised
cultivating Kentucky's good will by cheerfully yielding a freedom
which could in any event not very well be indefinitely denied. On
June 10, 1786, the Virginia assembly voted to recognize Kentucky
as a separate state if another convention elected by the people continued to request it, the separation to take effect when Congress
agreed to admission. Certain provisions were included in the act to
protect the western land rights of Virginians but since these served
also to protect the interests of Kentucky's more substantial pro-
prietors they were acceptable to most members of the conventions.

So far everything in connection with the statehood movement had
progressed with suspicious smoothness. But it had been the west's
experience that nothing ever went smoothly for long. It did not in
this case. The moderation that had characterized the earlier stages of
the demand for statehood suddenly erupted in a fury of resentment
that shook Kentucky's loyalty and threatened the nation's unity. As
with most of the west's crises, the fuse setting off the explosion was
the Indian danger. In 1786 this had increased to a pitch that was

becoming unendurable. General Indian dissatisfaction with the congressional treaties and McGillivray's declaration of war in the south had combined to excite the militant faction in every Indian nation. The Chickamauga and the Miami were the most openly aggressive but adventurous young warriors from every Indian town were slipping away to join in the forays and their return home with captives, horses, and scalps was hailed in their communities with as much acclaim as in the past. There were no organized incursions by large forces of Indians as during the Revolution. Instead the innumerable outrages committed were by smaller parties that struck and withdrew before they could be intercepted. The settlements near the Ohio were most seriously menaced, but Kentucky's eastern and southern frontiers were almost as frequently assailed. The little American colony at Vincennes was threatened with extinction. Attacks on immigrant boats on the Ohio multiplied. The Wilderness Road became passable only to very large armed parties. No one west of the Kanawha, afloat or ashore, was safe. The universal danger was cruelly emphasized in April when two of the most noted of all frontier leaders, William Christian and John Donelson, were among those killed.

General Harmar's national army represented no shield to Kentucky's borders. His 300 men occupied Fort McIntosh at the northern bend of the Ohio, Fort Harmar, at the mouth of the Muskingum, and a temporary post, Fort Finney, at the mouth of the Miami. He was straining his limited manpower to provide detachments to guard Thomas Hutchins, Geographer General, then engaged in the survey of the seven Ranges directed by Congress, and to burn the cabins of illegal settlers north of the Ohio. As in so many former emergencies Kentucky's hopes for relief depended entirely upon Clark.

He had taken no part in the conventions and but little in any of Kentucky's political affairs since the war, having been preoccupied with journeys to Virginia to press his repeatedly rejected appeals that Virginia reimburse him for those personal expenditures connected with his wartime conquests by which he had been bankrupted. He had also been engaged in supervising the survey of lands granted his former soldiers and concerned with his duties as Indian Commissioner. On January 31, 1786, he had extorted from the sullen Shawnee in the Treaty of Fort Finney the agreement to relinquish their lands east of the Miami which they had evaded at the Fort McIntosh conference. The treaty was meaningless in that it was imposed under duress, Clark being the one white commander before whose threats Indians had learned invariably to quail. This treaty, like its recent predecessors, had served to intensify rather than reduce Indian hostility.

As Indian raiders infested Kentucky in ever-increasing numbers, all eyes turned to Clark. As so often before, upon him fell responsibility for Kentucky's defense and, as always before, he proposed an offensive against the Indians as the only adequate defense. He was reminding his fellow Kentuckians that "Scouts and Forts on the Frontiers answer but little purpose and in the end cost more than an Army that would do the Business Effectually at once," and on June 8, 1786, writing Congress his reiteration of the long established strategic principle, "If Detroit was in our possession it might in a great measure silence the Indians." But Congress had neither the disposition nor the resources to consider Detroit an objective. The confederation treasury that June was unable to furnish even the thousand dollars required to ship ammunition to Harmar's midget army. Realizing there was no prospect of support from either Virginia or the United States, Clark recommended that Kentucky raise volunteers, with or without Virginia's consent, to punish at least the Miami who were judged the nation most guilty of the summer's depredations. Most Kentuckians were ready to respond to his call and Governor Henry, grieved by word of the death of his old friend, William Christian, hastily dispatched Virginia's approval of the expedition.

Clark's energetic preparations confronted Wilkinson with a personal crisis. The barrier to his immediate ambitions represented by Clark's already established renown appeared about to be raised, not lowered. Were Clark to win another of the great victories that he

had won so often before, his position must become unassailable and
any rival condemned to remain indefinitely in his shadow. To assure
that no such victory eventuated Wilkinson resorted to shrewdly
schemed devices, each safely dependent on the co-operation of other
men most of whom were possibly unaware of the real purpose for
which their activities were being used. The first step in the design
was to undermine Clark's personal reputation. A number of letters
were received, almost simultaneously, by important figures in Virginia's government and in Congress. All were ostensibly written by
public-spirited westerners but all were filled with florid and lurid
phrases in Wilkinson's unmistakable style. All declared that Clark
had become an irresponsible drunkard totally unfit for command.

There has survived no testimony of anybody directly associated
with Clark that year that he was drinking more in 1786 than he had
at the time of any of his earlier campaigns. He habitually drank, as
did practically every other man on the frontier, but there was no
contemporary reference aside from this sudden spate of letters to his
having turned so suddenly and sensationally to drinking to excess.[5]
The field officers of Kentucky's militia establishment, all of whom
had been in frequent personal contact with Clark, were almost
unanimous in urging him to accept the 1786 command. The veteran
frontier colonels, Benjamin Logan and Levi Todd, both of whom
had had many violent disagreements with Clark in the past, both
strongly urged his selection as commander of the Wabash expedition. There was likewise no contemporary testimony reflecting on
his conduct of the ensuing campaign. Even the returning mutineers,
anxious as they were to excuse their abandonment of the expedition,
made at the time no charge that Clark had upon any occasion been
unable to perform his duties as commander. Nevertheless, the accusing letters, supported presently by the new accusations of insobriety
in the report of the convention's investigating committee of which

[5] John May, for example, though an opponent of Clark's policies, was writing
Patrick Henry, July 14, 1786: "I am of the same opinion of the Rest of this Country.
I have been with him frequently, and I find him as capable of Business as ever, and
should an expedition be carried against the Indians I think his name alone would
be worth half a regiment of men."

Wilkinson was chairman, fixed in the minds of many highly placed easterners the conviction that Clark, with whom most were personally unacquainted, had suddenly become a hopeless inebriate. His reputation was never to recover from the blow. The assumption of his chronic alcoholism came to be generally accepted by eastern public opinion then and by most historians since.[6]

The next step in Wilkinson's design was to interfere directly with Clark's military operations. Many of his political associates willingly lent themselves to this effort, as each angled for higher rank for himself or a protégé or for more profitable supply contracts. Frontier militia were under any circumstances notoriously difficult to handle, with each man certain that he knew how all might be so much better managed. With so skilled a manipulator as Wilkinson behind the scenes, appealing to county rivalries, encouraging the delay of supply shipments by contractors, stirring jealousies among officers, reminding recruits of their legal rights, much could be made of this inherent recalcitrance of frontier troops. Clark had always before been notably capable of exercising personal control over militia, but in his new command there was the added difficulty that a large proportion of his recruits were recently arrived settlers who had never before served under him and many who had never been on any wilderness campaign. There were also honest differences of opinion in Kentucky that summer. Many denied the authority of either Governor Henry or Clark to order militia to march beyond Virginia's borders, and a number of county courts, whether or not sympathetic to Wilkinson's group, so ruled. Many of Clark's officers were at the same time advocating an attack on the so much nearer Shawnee rather than the Miami on the distant upper Wabash.

As a consequence of the politically contrived advantages taken of so many disagreements and diversions, but 1200 of the 3000 Clark had expected assembled in September. The season being late, he nevertheless marched. Logan, his second in command, was sent back to round up the remaining quotas. En route north hundreds more

[6] There is ample evidence that in later years, as his disappointments accumulated, Clark did become a periodic drunkard.

deserted. Whole companies and battalions, together with their officers, mutinously refused to continue the march, alleging an insuffi-
ciency of supplies or disagreeing with the expedition's prospects on
other pretexts. By the time Clark had reached the upper Wabash his
force was too reduced to permit anything decisive against the Miami.
Instead of joining Clark, Logan with the second division had meanwhile embarked, as had John Bowman under similar circumstances
in 1779, on an independent attack on the Shawnee. He burned several of their towns with comparative ease, most of the Shawnee warriors having gone to the Wabash to aid the Miami. Clark was left
with no other recourse than to withdraw to Vincennes where he
established a small garrison. Though the Miami were so relieved by
his failure to press his attack that they readily agreed to treat for
peace in the spring, his campaign as a military operation had been a
fiasco, the first such total failure in his career.

Wilkinson having succeeded in blemishing Clark's reputation and
frustrating his campaign, Clark himself next made the fatal mistake which led to his permanent downfall. To support his Vincennes
garrison, the establishment of which was in itself technically illegal
in the estimation of Virginia and the United States, he confiscated
the goods of three Spanish traders on the grounds that they were
without licenses to operate in American territory, that they had been
supplying the Indians, and that in any event the action was a justified retaliation for the many Spanish confiscations of American
cargoes in transit down the Mississippi. At the same time a rumor
gained currency, apparently with Clark's encouragement, that he
was contemplating the organization of a volunteer expedition to
enforce the claim of the United States to Natchez and to require
Spain to open the Mississippi to American commerce. All Kentucky would have applauded such an undertaking and most Kentuckians would have welcomed an opportunity to participate. This
report was given substance and wide circulation, with Clark's knowledge and apparently with his approval, by a declamatory letter
written from Louisville, December 4, 1786, by the Georgian adventurer, Thomas Green, who had the year before been expelled from

Natchez after an attempt to set up a Georgia county there, in which he made such extravagant assertions as:

> Preparations are now making here (if necessary) to drive the Spaniards from their settlements, at the mouth of the Mississippi. In case we are not countenanced and succored by the United States (if we need it) our allegiance will be thrown off, and some other power applied to. Great Britain stands ready with open arms to receive and support us.

When this letter reached the convention at Danville, Wilkinson instantly perceived that his rival had been delivered altogether into his hands. However popular on the frontier might be any proposal to retaliate against Spanish closure of the Mississippi, most more responsible Kentuckians realized as well as did eastern governors and congressmen how unprepared was either Kentucky, Virginia, or the United States for a war with Spain. The Fourth Convention, called to assemble in September 1786, had been recessing from day to day for lack of a quorum, a majority of the delegates being away on service with Clark and Logan. Wilkinson had no difficulty persuading those members who were present to vote the institution of a committee, with himself as chairman, to investigate Clark's activities. The committee, appointed December 19, 1786, after two days of inquiry got off a report to the government of Virginia, expatiating on Clark's gross misconduct, urging that he be removed from command, and, as a thoughtful footnote, recommending that he be replaced as Indian Commissioner by Wilkinson.

Reaching Richmond on the heels of the recent accusations of drunkenness, the report made an immediate and painful impression on Governor Edmund Randolph and his council. On February 28, 1787, Clark was officially censured, his actions disavowed, and his military authority rescinded. Virginia's congressional delegation was directed to inform Congress of this repudiation and to deliver Virginia's apologies to Gardoqui, Spain's envoy. Congress was as impressed as had been Virginia's council by the need to mollify Spanish indignation at the west's apparently aggressive intentions.

On April 22, 1787, Clark's actions were condemned and on April 24th Harmar was ordered to send troops to dispossess "a body of men who had, in a lawless and unauthorized manner, taken possession of Post Vincennes in defiance of the proclamation and authority of the United States." As recommended by Virginia, Clark and his two associate Indian commissioners were replaced by Wilkinson and two of his.

When this deluge of repudiation descended upon Clark he remained outwardly unmoved. He made no effort to deny the charges that he had contemplated aggressive action against Spain. The man who had once so dramatically conquered the region from which he was now being ejected in disgrace appeared as little disturbed by opposition as he had been then. His conviction that the west's future depended on dislodging Spain from the Mississippi was unshaken. "I respect the State of Virginia," he wrote Randolph. "The information you have received hath already been stained with the blood of your country. Things will prove themselves."

In the three years since he had come as a stranger to the frontier Wilkinson had made himself known to every westerner and in the process had achieved astounding success with each step of the program for advancement he had set himself. His bold and ingenious maneuvers had made him the undisputed political master of Kentucky. In obtaining the Indian commissionership he had gained a position of influence over the future allotment of land grants upon which most contemporary hopes to win fortunes were based. With Clark in eclipse his own rise to military command had been made certain. Nothing seemed now beyond his reach. But, as had always been the west's experience, the totally unexpected was again at hand. The storm of fury, aroused by the policy of the United States as much as that of Spain, which swept the west in the opening months of 1787, altered the attitude of every Kentuckian and posed Wilkinson an entirely new set of problems and opportunities.

The sudden realization that the west was being sold out by the eastern states and their creature, Congress, whipped up the storm. The sense of betrayal was aggravated by the west's political helplessness. Measures affecting the lives and fortunes of all westerners were being voted not by their representatives but by New Englanders, New Yorkers, and Pennsylvanians. As a final occasion for outrage, the west had been denied news of the culminating development for many months. The story, when finally pieced together, was made the more disturbing by having gained circulation in sensational driblets.

In July 1785, the Spanish envoy, Diego de Gardoqui, had reached Philadelphia with instructions from his government to explore the possibility of establishing normal diplomatic relations with the United States, which from the Spanish point of view meant to obtain American acceptance of Spain's territorial claims in the southwest which in turn meant Spain's complete control of both banks of the Mississippi south of the Ohio. As a partial balance to this jolting demand he indicated that he was prepared to offer a commercial treaty granting the United States trading privileges with Spain and the Canary Islands. Congress was unwilling to give up the territory but very much wanted the trade. There was a special advantage in trade with Spain in that Spanish customers were accustomed to pay in gold and silver and nothing could have better served the revival of American enterprise after the war than the infusion of a current of specie into the circulation of depreciated paper money. Chief responsibility for dealing with the difficult Gardoqui fell upon John Jay, Congress' Secretary for Foreign Affairs. Jay had been minister to Spain during the Revolution when he had for two years failed at Madrid to gain even recognition; he found the task of gaining concessions from Spain no simpler in Philadelphia. At last, on August 29, 1786, Congress in secret session approved by a 7 to 5 vote his last-resort proposal to offer American acquiescence in Spain's control of the Mississippi for a period of 25 years in return for trade advantages elsewhere in the world. The vote was not final or decisive since a majority of nine states was required to authorize a treaty, but the vote of seven northern states testified to the attitude toward the west in much of the east, particularly in those states which had no western lands or settlements to consider.

It was this revelation of congressional willingness to sacrifice the interests of the west in order to gain a commercial advantage for the east that raised the frontier storm. News of it came slowly and intermittently, at first as no more than rumors. But the story persisted and became more circumstantial and detailed until in January and February of 1787 the realization spread that it was all too true. The initial secrecy that had shrouded the vote on Jay's proposal gave the maneuver the aspect of a deep and diabolical plot. The entire west was moved to fury and by the usual frontier impulse to strike back. Many westerners had long suspected the east's intentions. Through twelve long years of border war the so much wealthier and more populous east had looked on unmoved while the frontier fought off perpetual Indian attacks. Congress had acquiesced in the British holding the Lake posts and in the Spaniards holding Natchez and in both continuing to promote Indian hostility. The proposal now to continue this acquiescence for twenty-five years was a final confirmation of every suspicion of eastern ill will. There seemed no longer any doubt that eastern lawmakers, merchants, and bankers were bent upon retarding the progress of the west.

Much of the west's suspicion was fully justified. Throughout the northern states and in most of the southern seaboard the opinion was general that development of the west should be delayed until the east was more completely developed. This view was supported by a fear that a prematurely self-sufficient west must inevitably become a separate nation. Jay, who had proved his devotion to expansion during the peace negotiations, was nevertheless of the opinion in 1786 that overrapid settlement west of the mountains "will, unless checked, scatter our resources and in every view enfeeble the nation." Rufus King, the influential New Englander, believed, "Should there be an uninterrupted use of the Mississippi at this time by the citizens of the United States I should consider every emigrant to that country from the Atlantic states as forever lost to the confederacy." Even Washington, for all his frontier interests and sympathies, considered the closure of the Mississippi fortunate in that it served to keep the west more dependent commercially on the United States.

Excitement mounted on the frontier. Public indignation was equally stirred in Pittsburgh and Lexington, Jonesboro and Nashville. Committees of correspondence were organized to exchange news, views, and plans for counteraction. Westerners who had for so long sought separation from their parent eastern states for the first time began angrily and openly to discuss the possible advantages of secession from the United States.

Nowhere in the west was this general resentment so strong as in Kentucky. That the patience with which the statehood movement had been conducted and the tolerance with which Congress's continued neglect to vote admission had been regarded should have been thus penalized intensified Kentucky's ire. The resumption of Indian attacks, undiscouraged by the Clark and Logan campaigns and undeterred by Harmar's feeble dispositions, poured more fuel on the fire of discontent. Though for the first time since he had come to the frontier Wilkinson was remaining in the background, political leaders most closely associated with him actively encouraged and promoted meetings, resolutions, and declarations giving voice to Kentucky's resentment. Providing one final spur to the west's impulse to revolt, Kentucky's first newspaper, *The Kentucke Gazette,* was founded on August 18, 1787. From its first issue it bitterly denied the good faith of the United States and was soon openly advocating secession.

Public opinion rapidly developed support for some sort of action. As early as March 29, 1787 a letter signed by four of Kentucky's most prominent citizens, George Muter, Harry Innes, John Brown, and Benjamin Sebastian, was circulated among all western counties, declaring, "As the inhabitants of this district wish to unite their efforts, to oppose the cession of the navigation of the Mississippi, with those of their brethren residing on the western waters, we hope to see such an exertion made, upon this important occasion, as may convince Congress that the inhabitants of the western country are united in the opposition, and consider themselves entitled to all the privileges of freemen, and those blessings procured by the revolution; and will not tamely submit to an act of oppression." On July 21, 1787, Harry Innes, the district's attorney general, was writing Governor Randolph, "I am decidedly of the opinion that this western country will in a few years Revolt from the Union and endeavor to erect an Independent Government."

Clark would have had no need to be a more adroit politician to have recaptured leadership of Kentucky that summer. The public's agitation provided a clear invitation to resume his former position at the center of western affairs. In popular estimation he had in a matter of months been proved right and his opponents wrong. Had the design to attack Natchez of which he had been accused in 1786 been renewed in 1787 thousands of Kentuckians must have rallied to his standard. That he remained withdrawn from the tumult was variously attributed by his critics to his selfish reluctance to prejudice his claims against Virginia and by his admirers to his unselfish reluctance to lead what would amount to a rebellion against Virginia and the United States. Lacking the focus of resolute leadership the west's anger failed to develop beyond expressions of protest. The members of the Fifth Convention in September, faced with the responsibility of defining Kentucky's position, were embittered but still disposed to cling to their former regard for legality. The demands for separation from Virginia and admission by Congress were renewed, with the added urgency of provisions calling for the drafting of a constitution by the next convention and for fixing December 31, 1788, as the final date after which Kentucky would in any event consider itself a state. Virginia, impressed by the clamor of Kentucky's protests on the Mississippi issue, included a leading Kentuckian, John Brown, in Virginia's congressional delegation so that he might take personal charge of pressing the petition for admission.

Meanwhile, Wilkinson, like Clark, had that turbulent spring taken no outwardly active part in the west's violent reaction to the Jay proposal. He had perceived in the suddenly developing situation a far greater opportunity than the dispatch of indignant protests to Congress. While his successful campaign to displace Clark was still in its earliest stages, his attention had become fixed on a vastly more complex project. He realized that, the way having been cleared to the attainment of his principal preliminary ambitions, the time had arrived to get on with his major purpose. His most rewarding financial enterprise so far had been the establishment, on land he had acquired, of the town of Frankfort which he would presently arrange to have selected as Kentucky's capital. But profits from land, even when expedited by political power, were slow. He was intent on quicker and larger returns. His acquaintance with conditions in the west had by now made it clear that the one truly profitable commercial opportunity available to a westerner lay in taking advantage of the gateway to world trade provided by the Mississippi. This was an advantage dependent upon the favor of Spain. To Wilkinson the obvious way around this difficulty was to win that favor.

His steps to further this purpose were as direct, ruthless, and efficient as in the development of his design to ruin Clark. On December 20, 1786, the first day of his chairmanship of the committee investigating Clark, he wrote Don Francesco Cruzat, Spanish commandant at St. Louis, warning him that Clark contemplated an invasion of Spanish territory. Having testified to his friendliness toward Spain, he next applied to Gardoqui for a passport to visit New Orleans. Gardoqui, reluctant to accord his rival, Miro, the advantage of developing relations with so important a westerner as Wilkinson, refused. But Wilkinson, having established friendly contacts with Manuel Gayosa, commandant at Natchez, as well as Cruzat, confidently launched his venture without a passport or any other assurance that his shipment would not be confiscated as had been so many others.

In June of 1787 he embarked with a cargo of corn and tobacco, leaving behind him a Kentucky seething with resentment against Spain, while he, Kentucky's foremost citizen, prepared to present himself at New Orleans as Spain's great friend. His forecast of his most probable Spanish reception was proved justified in every respect. He was passed through the customs, was cordially welcomed by Governor Miro, and was able to sell his tax-free cargo at a profit of $35,000.

Wilkinson's correct diagnosis of the Spanish attitude had been a product of his shrewd estimate of Spanish fears. Spanish commanders on the lower Mississippi were hagridden by a perpetual dread of attack by American frontiersmen. Western geography left them peculiarly exposed to surprise. Months of labor were required to ascend the Mississippi while it might be descended in a few easy days. Every garrison was obliged to live with the constant thought that any dawn might reveal the spectacle of a river blackened by boatloads of buckskinned riflemen. The animosity that was known to possess Kentucky had made this fearful eventuality seem every month more likely. When instead there appeared on July 2nd this most important of all Kentuckians, with outstretched hand and beaming smile and gracious words, Miro could only regard the event as a special dispensation of providence.

For the next three months Wilkinson was closeted almost daily with the Spanish governor. As Wilkinson continued to talk with his singularly plausible assurance, Miro's delight mounted. He was hearing what he most wanted to hear. The burden of Wilkinson's message was that Kentucky was ready to secede from the United States and set itself up as an independent state which must necessarily be sympathetic to Spain on account of its need for the Mississippi trade outlet. He declared that he was so convinced that this was the inevitable shape of things to come that he proposed to place himself at the head of Kentucky's secessionist movement and thereafter to use his influence to swing all American communities west of the mountains in the direction of an ever-closer attachment to Spain.

As an initial token of the earnestness of his intentions, on August 22, 1787, he took a formal oath of allegiance to the King of Spain. On September 5th, the same day the Fifth Convention was meeting in Danville to renew Kentucky's denunciations of Spain, he completed the draft of a memorial to the King, recommending the course which might most speedily and certainly promote Spanish interests in the west. The most important item in this program was Wilkinson's suggestion that he as an individual be granted exclusive trading rights on the Mississippi. The profits accruing to him as a consequence of this unique ability to ship his cargoes untaxed through New Orleans, he argued, would so excite other Kentuckians that they would join his secessionist movement in such ever-increasing numbers as greatly to hasten the turn of the American west away from the United States and toward Spain. As a second and also useful step, he suggested that he be appointed exclusive agent to promote the establishment of American colonies in Spanish territory, thus providing new bonds of mutual interest between Spain and the American frontier. Miro received these recommendations with enthusiasm and dispatched the memorial to Madrid with his ardent endorsement. There seemed reason for his elation. The aggressiveness of American frontiersmen which had so long presented the gravest threat to Spanish dominion on the Mississippi appeared suddenly and miraculously, thanks to the interposition of this astonishing American, to be on the verge of being transformed into a Spanish bulwark.

Wilkinson's return to Kentucky in February of 1788, after the circuitous journey by sea—Richmond, Pittsburgh, and the Ohio which was then considered a less arduous route by which Kentucky might be reached from New Orleans than a direct ascent of the Mississippi—was a triumph. He appeared with an ornate coach and a retinue of liveried slaves. His oath of allegiance to the Spanish king and the conspiracy hatched with the Spanish governor remained sealed secrets never disclosed in his lifetime. But there was no secret about the profits he had made in New Orleans or the usefulness of the contacts he had made with Spanish authorities there. The mood of Kentucky altered almost overnight. Spain the archenemy began to appear as Spain the potential source of all hope. The west's commercial prospects which had been so stagnant began suddenly to effervesce. Prices doubled and redoubled. Tobacco sold for $2.00 a hundredweight one day and $9.50 the next. The possibility that under Wilkinson's inspired guidance the west's produce might find a world market in New Orleans stirred a burst of optimism as excited as had been the fury of the west's former resentment.

At the outset of that supremely critical year, 1788, Wilkinson conceived that all was going as well for him as he had so adroitly planned. The success of his mysterious trading expedition had confirmed his leadership of an adulatory Kentucky. He had every reason to expect that he could shape Kentucky's destiny in whatever fashion best suited him. He saw himself, as he confided to an intimate, as the "Washington of the West," the great liberator and chief of state of a new and expanding independent republic on the Mississippi. To what extent this new nation might drift into Spain's orbit did not greatly concern him. What did concern him was that there was every prospect that, whatever else developed, the already so happily initiated process of making a huge fortune might indefinitely continue.

IX

℘

Adventure Unlimited

In the estimation of people then alive two attributes of the post-revolutionary west stood out above all others. It was a country that beckoned in that it promised an opportunity for any man to improve his condition. But it was also a country that repelled in that it threatened every sort of disappointment and danger. Some who went west welcomed both prospects. Most who yielded to the urge had with varying degrees of doubt convinced themselves that the hazard was not too great a price to pay for the opportunity.

The most stolid settler who had committed his family to the perils of the Wilderness Road or a flatboat on the Ohio was adding his own distinct eddy of agitation to the general ferment of a society still unformed in a land still wild. There were also, in the midst of the perpetual confusion, a few imaginative egoists led on by aspirations as bold and expansive as any of those harbored by the great frontier leaders who have attracted the closer attention of history. Their careers often cast even sharper and more revealing gleams across a frontier world so many aspects of which are now so difficult to recapture.

One of the more noteworthy of these lesser adventurers was William Augustus Bowles. Any attempt to recount his experiences must make them seem incredible had they been associated with any other environment than the forever astonishing frontier. Born in Maryland, at the outbreak of the Revolution he enlisted in the British army at the age of thirteen. His regiment of Maryland loyalists, after serving several campaigns against Washington, was refitted at Jamaica and in 1777 assigned to the garrison of Pensacola. In spite of his youth he had by 1778 risen to the grade of ensign but at Pensacola he was reduced to the ranks for insubordination. He carried the insubordination a step farther by deserting and taking refuge in the Indian country. There he adopted the Indian way of life, learned the Creek language, made many Creek friends, including McGillivray, and married a daughter of Tom Perryman, an important Creek chief. In 1781 he led a Creek party in the Creek attempt to assist their English friends in defending Pensacola from Spanish attack. Though the arrival of the Indian auxiliaries failed to save the place, Bowles was temporarily reinstated in rank and must have accompanied the surrendered English garrison when it was transported under the capitulation terms to New York, for the next contemporary mention places him there in 1782. He had found employment as a comedian in a theatrical company engaged in entertaining the bored army of occupation and the throngs of Tory refugees. When the British evacuated New York he accompanied the troupe to the Bahamas where so many exiled loyalists were currently finding new sanctuary. Here he made an apparently comfortable living by acting and painting portraits.

His earlier experience with the wilderness, plus his acquaintance with the Creek language and country, drew him eventually, however, into more robust employment. Lord Dunmore, who as the last English governor of Virginia, had busied himself with the promotion of land schemes, Indian wars, Pennsylvania-Virginia boundary disputes, and Dr. John Connolly's plan to organize a Tory-Indian invasion, became Governor of the Bahamas in 1787. He was as interested now in personal profit and official intrigue as he had been then. In a not too silent partnership with the Bahamian firm of Miller and Bonamy, he undertook to claim a share of the Creek trade of which Panton, Leslie and Company had been enjoying a monopoly under the patronage of Spain and McGillivray. Bowles, the onetime soldier and former friend of the Creek, appeared peculiarly suited to take field charge of the venture. The expedition was so scantily stocked with trade goods that his experience as an actor may well have been judged helpful and emergencies might have been foreseen in which even his talent as an artist could also have been considered an asset.

Bowles appeared alone in the Creek country in June of 1788 with a few presents to cultivate Indian favor and support his assertion that he was in a position to furnish an ample supply of the arms needed by the Creek in their war with the Americans. McGillivray, discovering upon investigation that the mysterious stranger was his old friend of Pensacola days, was elated by the apparent windfall. He was having difficulties from which Bowles' assurances, whether they were ever substantiated or not, promised to extricate him. Governor Miro, disturbed lest the vigor of McGillivray's resistance to American settlement precipitate an American invasion of Spanish territory, had recently reduced the supply of arms to the Creek. McGillivray was now able to put pressure on Spanish authorities by threatening to resort, through Bowles, to English support. By the time Bowles had reappeared with his main party in November, McGillivray's Spanish supply line had been reopened and he had lost interest in the Bahamian alternative. Bowles had brought only a fraction of the elaborate arsenal he had advertised, the disillusioned Creek public became less friendly, most of his frightened white followers deserted, and he was forced to take flight. The Creek, however, had by no means seen the last of him.

Accompanying Bowles in his ignominious withdrawal were a number of still loyal Indian followers. On his way through the keys around the southern tip of Florida he sighted a wrecked ship. Among items in the hulk's cargo was a shipment of dress uniforms. The actor in him came immediately to the fore. He took passage with his party on a fishing schooner to Nova Scotia, clad his Indians in the uniforms, was able to convince the British governor at Halifax that he was conducting an important Creek and Cherokee delegation to England, and was sent on across the Atlantic at official expense. In London his luck continued to hold, for a while. His Indian retinue gained him a popular welcome. He could not, moreover, have appeared at a more propitious moment. As a consequence of the Nootka controversy, war with Spain seemed imminent that summer of 1790. With his train of ostensible Indian chiefs and his background of intimate acquaintance with Spain's Florida frontier he attracted governmental attention. Pitt himself, with much of his father's remarkable capacity for estimating local situations in the farthest corners of the globe, repeatedly consulted him with a view to giving him an important part, possibly even as commander, in a contemplated expedition against Florida. But the war scare passed and Pitt's interest turned to other affairs.

His self-confidence further inflated by this brush with the mighty, Bowles returned to the Bahamas where his accounts of his successes at the Empire's capital persuaded Dunmore and the Miller firm to underwrite another trading venture to the Creek country. Upon landing in September of 1791 Bowles proceeded to his father-in-law's town among the Lower Creek where he assembled a small Creek following and proclaimed himself "General and Director of the Nation." In this second descent his undertaking was no less than to displace McGillivray by playing upon the considerable Creek dissatisfaction with McGillivray's recent treaty of peace with the United States. His initial supply of trade goods proving inadequate to support designs of such magnitude, on January 16, 1792, he looted the St. Mark's store of his trading competitor, Panton. McGillivray had not been too concerned by the challenge to his supremacy, had taken no sterner countermeasures than to offer a scornful reward of $300 for Bowles' head, and was soon able to persuade the Spanish to intervene.

Hector de Carondelet, the new Spanish governor of Louisiana, was disturbed by the possibility that Bowles might be representing

British intentions, yet interested by his proclaimed hostility to Americans. He invited him to New Orleans for consultation. Bowles accepted his safe conduct at face value, but once he came under Spanish control he was kept in Spanish custody. For the next five years he remained a Spanish prisoner though he was treated with some deference since there was always the chance Spain might find some use for his personal influence among the Creek. During these years his travels were more extensive than during any other stage of his lifelong odyssey. He was taken first to Havana, then to Madrid, and finally to Manila. While being transported back around the world to Spain in 1797, he contrived to escape to the British colony of Sierra Leone on the coast of Africa. Reaching London he was again received as a public hero.

He was still not finished with the Creek. Since McGillivray's death in 1793 they had had no generally recognized national leader and he proposed to fill the vacuum. In this third descent he contemplated a landing on Florida's northern Gulf coast and expected some supply support from a British government interested in his nuisance value as an irritant to Spanish authority in the area. His modest expedition was shipwrecked, but he struggled ashore and on October 26, 1799, proclaimed the State of Muscogee and its independence of both Spain and the United States. The Creek sympathized with his announced intention of defending their country against encroachment from any quarter but remained sharply divided on his prospects, with the faction doubting his success more numerous than those rallying to his standard. On April 5, 1800, he declared war on Spain and on May 19th captured the Spanish fort at St. Marks. The chagrined Spanish military soon recaptured St. Marks and drove him back into the interior. Governor Vicente Folch of Pensacola offered a reward of $4500 for him dead or alive, but his residue of Indian adherents continued to shelter and defend him. During this last phase of his long and so often renewed effort to make himself the official custodian of Creek independence he appeared to have discounted his British connections and to be earnestly devoted to Creek interests. Nevertheless, most of the Creek, or at any rate the Creek chiefs, held aloof. For nearly three more years he was able to keep his little de facto State of Muscogee in being on the lower Apalachicola. But in 1803, while attending a conference intended to coordinate Indian policy in resisting land cessions, he was seized, in violation of the traditional Indian respect for the immunity of ambassadors, by the Creek faction opposed to him. On the advice of Benjamin Hawkins, American agent to the Creek, he was delivered to Spanish custody. This time Spain took care that he did not again escape. He died in Morro Castle, December 23, 1805.

If the adventures of Bowles illustrated conditions in that borderland between nations occupied by Indians, traders, and soldiers, those of Dr. James White[1] exemplified conditions in that even more obscure borderland between nations occupied by politicians, land speculators, and secret agents. Shortly after removing to North Carolina from Philadelphia, where he had studied both law and medicine, White was elected to the state assembly. Aside from a business association with Blount and an acquaintance with Governor Caswell, his chief qualifications for such immediate preferment appeared to be that he was a Catholic and could speak French. These were accomplishments of little use in an American legislature but conceivably of more in meeting the demands of missions to Havana or New Orleans where his religion and command of the language of diplomacy might prove of considerable service. The timetable of his subsequent movements gives further indication of how thoughtfully planned was the purpose for which he had been recruited.

In December of 1785 the new assemblyman was elected to Congress, by a legislature politically dominated by the Blount-Caswell group. He took his seat on May 2, 1786, and on August 26, during the debate on Jay's Mississippi navigation proposal, called on Gardoqui. The Spanish envoy reported to Madrid that the freshman congressman had assured him that a majority of American frontiersmen had been so disillusioned by the lack of support from their national

[1] Not to be confused with Colonel James White, noted pioneer and founder of Knoxville.

government that they were prepared to secede if by so doing they might gain the use of the Mississippi. There is no certain evidence that White was speaking for his land-company sponsors but he could in any event not yet have known, three days before the vote, of the popular resentment the congressional action would arouse when news of it finally reached the west.

The way had now been prepared for the next step in the enterprise for which he had been selected and was being progressively groomed. On October 6, 1786, he was appointed by Congress Superintendent of Indian Affairs for the Southern Department, the troubled area of the Spanish-American border dispute. He had never been west of the mountains while the other two candidates for the post, Arthur Campbell and Joseph Martin, were border leaders who had had many years of experience with the frontier and with Indians, but the political influence behind White was sufficient to gain him the appointment.

He reached the Creek country in February of 1787 to undertake negotiations with McGillivray of which few of the more pertinent details have been recorded. Of major interest to both was McGillivray's passing impulse to seek recognition of Creek independence as a kind of buffer state between American and Spanish territory, an objective he had discussed with Spanish authorities, but McGillivray was most distinctly not contemplating a free Creek state dominated by American land speculators. He granted a truce during his exploratory conversations with White but soon lost interest in the American agent's proposals and resumed his war against the American frontier. As he wrote on April 18, 1787, to Arturo O'Neill, Governor of Pensacola, White "might as well have not Come into our Nation." It could have been only a coincidence that one of the first incidents of the ensuing resumption of hostilities was McGillivray's premeditated dispatch of the war party that killed Georgia's "commissary" to the Chickasaw, William Davenport, who had had a part in the 1785 attempt to set up the County of Bourbon at Spanish-held Natchez and in 1787 was engaged in the attempted establishment of another land-company project at Chickasaw Bluffs on the Missis-

sippi. In any case, White had not succeeded in modifying McGillivray's determination to resist any form of American demand for
Creek land.

He returned to New York to report somewhat perfunctorily to
Congress on his failure to bring peace to the southwestern frontier.
In January of 1788 he resigned as Indian Superintendent to make
himself available for a more promising attack on the problem of
gaining an opening on the Spanish-American border for the operations of land companies. He had meanwhile also reported, more
confidentially, to Gardoqui, who in his New York station was always avid for firsthand information dealing with conditions in the
distant wilderness area under the jurisdiction of Miro, his fellow
official of whose successes he was perpetually jealous. Gardoqui had
recently been informed of Miro's sensational conversations with
James Wilkinson and was eager to take a hand in this promotion of
secession in the American west which Madrid could be expected to
view with so much favor. With the Spanish envoy's blessing, White
journeyed to Franklin to interview John Sevier and to instigate
Sevier's correspondence with Gardoqui which culminated in Sevier's
offering to lead Franklin from the American into the Spanish camp.
That same spring of 1788 White, at the suggestion of Caswell, was
putting James Robertson, driven frantic by Indian attacks on Cumberland, into touch with both Gardoqui and Miro.

White was now ready for the major throw of the international
dice contemplated from the beginning by the land-company sponsors
in the background for whom he was agent and spokesman. With
passport furnished by Gardoqui he sailed to Havana for conferences with Bernardo de Galvez, the conqueror of British Florida
during the Revolution and now Captain General of Louisiana, Cuba,
and the Floridas, and with visiting Manuel Gayoso, commandant of
Natchez, the most critical point in the disputed Spanish-American
borderland. White went on to New Orleans, arriving there April 15,
1789, to confer with Miro and to acquaint the attentive Spanish governor with all he had learned during his extensive perambulations.
In his conversations with both Galvez and Miro, according to their

reports to Madrid, White had been urging Spanish recognition of Franklin's independence, acquiescence in an extension of Franklin's borders down the Tennessee past Muscle Shoals, and permission for this new Franklin to trade with the outer world by way of the Alabama and the Mississippi. He had not attempted to gloss over how much this was bound to increase the value of land in the area but had indicated that this was an advantage by which sagacious and influential Spaniards might also profit. Both governors had been as gratified as had been Gardoqui by his account of the growth of secession sentiment on the American frontier.

By the time White reached New Orleans, Miro had received his government's reaction to Wilkinson's memorial. Spain's chief minister, José Foridablanca, necessarily more concerned by European problems, had taken a more pessimistic view of the risks involved in meddling with American internal affairs than did his deputies in America. White was told by Miro that Spain would warmly welcome a declaration of independence by the west or any portion of it and that such a secession would be rewarded by trading privileges and other favors. The full significance of these advantages would appear once the secession had actually been proclaimed. But beyond these earnest assurances Miro was not empowered to go. He could promise no direct action by Spain in support of sedition in a nation with which Spain was at peace. The attempt of White's shadowy backers to tinker by backstairs diplomacy with the destiny of a continent had thus led to no more than what they had already known they possessed—Spain's enthusiastic sympathy. The situation remained much what it would have been had he remained in his seat in Congress. The fateful decision was still left for the frontier people to make for themselves.

White had completed his mission and had passed from the notice of history. His efforts had, however, not been totally without effect. He had given a certain coherence to the ramifications of western dissatisfaction and resentment, to the confusions of rumor, misinformation, and hallucination, to the general disorder in the thinking of embittered men who would otherwise have remained longer unaware of how many of their fellows shared their restlessness. Wilkinson had made his own way to the Spanish governor's closet. But it was White who opened for the two other most important western leaders, Sevier and Robertson, lines of communication to Miro and Gardoqui and even McGillivray. He had established a pattern of intrigue which enabled all participants in what came to be called the "Spanish conspiracy" to keep in constant touch with each other and with Spain. The lowliest secession agitator was thereafter aware of Spain's interest in his efforts and certain of his secret dole of Spanish silver. This was no child's game. At issue was the integration or disintegration of the republic. It was an issue finally to be taken in hand by world leaders—by Washington and Napoleon and Jefferson. But White had still had his hour of playing with fire.

Perhaps no man was personally involved in more important events over the whole of the early frontier's most critical period, from before Pontiac's War to after the Louisiana Purchase, than was George Morgan. During his lifetime the states of Kentucky, Tennessee, and Ohio had been admitted, the domain of the United States had been extended all the way to the Pacific Ocean, and more than a million Americans had found homes west of the mountains, but he could remember that when he had first entered the wilderness there had been packs of Indians infesting the shores of the Susquehanna and herds of buffalo splashing through the shallows of the Monongahela. In much of this extraordinary transition he had taken a considerable part.

He was born in Philadelphia February 14, 1743, orphaned at six, and at thirteen apprenticed to Baynton, Wharton & Company, then the most important American firm engaged in the Indian trade. His services in the company were from the beginning active and successful, both in the wilderness and in the home office. In 1764 he married the senior partner's daughter, Mary, and the next year became himself a partner. Meanwhile, in the course of his trading activities he had become a close friend of George Croghan, then the most important and influential of all figures on the Ohio frontier, and had with him been subjected to the many trials of Pontiac's War. In 1765 Morgan's 70-horse pack train, laden with goods intended to support Croghan's efforts to restore peace with the Indians at his Pittsburgh Conference, was despoiled by the Pennsylvania Black Boys, frontiersmen so furiously opposed to supplying the Indians with anything that they objected even when the purpose was pacification. The next year he accompanied Croghan on his memorable journey down the Ohio to negotiate peace with the Indians of Pontiac's Illinois citadel. Morgan had just turned 23 when he embarked in command of 17 batteaux loaded with Baynton, Wharton & Morgan trade goods to establish those trade relations which were indispensable if peace with Indians were ever to be maintained. He had by now abundantly proved his claim to the title of genuine pioneer. He had traveled the Ohio from end to end three years before Daniel Boone had made his famous long hunt, four years before the Watauga settlement had been organized, and nine years before the first permanent white man's habitation had been erected in Kentucky.

The Illinois venture proved profitless. He had encountered the supreme difficulty that was equally to plague American settlement of the west throughout the next generation. Trade moved readily with the current down the Mississippi to the sea and only by the greatest exertion against the current up the Ohio and across the mountains to the western seaboard. But he had also been captivated by a prospect far more alluring than trade. There had opened the sudden possibility that western land might conceivably be acquired in tracts the size of a European state. Formerly the rewards of the wilderness had appeared to be confined to the profits that might be earned by trading with the Indians and many wars had been fought for trade advantage. Henceforth land was to become the great objective the pursuit of which was to bring on many more wars. Morgan was one of the first to become obsessed by that insatiable urge to acquire vast expanses of land in the west which provided a persistent and driving impulse to the more effective westward movement of actual settlers.

In the 1768 Indian conference at Fort Stanwix, the Iroquois were persuaded by their good friends, Sir William Johnson and George Croghan, to make an enormous grant of land, for which they as a nation had no immediate or prospective use, in ostensible compensation to traders for the losses they had sustained during the recent great Indian wars. Morgan rushed home from the Illinois to become secretary of the Indiana Company in which most of the "suffering traders" had pooled their interests. The company was pressing its claim, based on the Iroquois grant, to three and a half million acres between the mountains and the upper Ohio. A necessary first prerequisite was royal affirmation of their title. This was promised, delayed, and again promised, as for six years it seemed repeatedly on the verge of being granted. Meanwhile thousands of individual settlers were rushing illegally into the area. The outbreak of the Revolution brought to an end any hope of the King's approval and, at the same time, a long pause to the settlers' advance. For years the members of the Indiana Company had seemed to have fortune at their fingertips but now everybody concerned was committed, on one side or the other, to the war.

Morgan took the patriot side. His long acquaintance as a trader with the wilderness and the Indians and in particular with the critical upper Ohio frontier led Congress on April 10, 1776, to appoint him Indian agent for the Middle Department. He struggled, for a while successfully, to keep the Shawnee neutral and was able to maintain friendly relations with the Delaware throughout his term of service. No task could have been more difficult or more thankless. Hostile warriors of the very nations with whose chiefs he was treating continued to attack the frontier. Settlers, envenomed against all Indians, denounced his every attempt to promote border peace. The successive murders of the great chiefs, Cornstalk and White Eyes, while they were making peaceful overtures, were stunning blows to his policy. His attempts to influence the conduct of campaigns in ways which in his judgment might least alienate Indians still neutral or friendly led to quarrels with American military commanders. After a stormy three years of striving to keep the peace on a frontier where there could be no peace, he resigned in the spring of 1779 and served through the remainder of the war as a colonel in the eastern armies.

But no wartime exigency had been so extreme as to distract him from his obsessive interest in land. In no Indian negotiation or campaign council did his attention ever stray far from the land possibilities involved. The war could not last forever and to him as an original and confirmed westerner the future and the land were synonymous terms. In Clark's conquests, in designs to attack Detroit, in the shepherding of Indian delegations to Congress, he saw the ultimate disposition of land on the Illinois, the Wabash, or the shores of Lake Erie as an inseparable consideration. During the worst torments to which the frontier of which he was a principal and diligent defender was subjected, his preoccupation with land persisted. At one time his friends, the Delaware, made him a direct grant of six square miles. He had enough regard for his official position to decline for himself but accepted for his children. His concern with the prospects of the Indiana Company remained as constant. During the darkest hours of the war the company, having long since lost any chance of royal approval, repeatedly petitioned American authority for recognition of its enormous claim on the Ohio. Resort was first had to Virginia which, were the Revolution to succeed, must inherit jurisdiction over the area. When Virginia vigorously resisted, appeal was made directly to Congress.

After the war, Morgan returned to his home in Princeton where he became a leading citizen and a trustee of the college. Residence in New Jersey had the additional advantage that its congressional delegation, representing a state with no western lands and therefore more than willing to embarrass states which did have, took an earnest interest in pressing the Indiana Company's case. Congress, however, remained obdurate and by 1784 the expectations of immense fortune so long harbored by the company's members had for all practical purposes come to nothing.[2]

But the hopes of so dedicated a landseeker as Morgan never died.

[2] Residual hopes remained flickeringly alive until 1798 when the United States Supreme Court refused to consider a final appeal.

From his window east of the Delaware his mind's eye could see all the way down the Ohio to the Mississippi. After a petition for a grant of 2,000,000 acres in the new Northwest Territory had been denied by Congress, he approached Gardoqui, in association with Thomas Hutchins, early explorer, fort builder for Henry Bouquet, and more recently Geographer of the United States, with a proposal to establish an American colony on the Spanish side of the Mississippi. Gardoqui was enthusiastic about the project, endorsed the application for a grant of 15,000,000 acres, and advanced the preliminary expedition financial support. On January 3, 1789, Morgan set sail from Pittsburgh with four armed boats and 70 colonists, re-enacting his down-river voyage with Croghan 23 years before. His state of mind accentuates the basic anomaly characteristic of the land fever of the period: Men who were in all other respects devoted to the United States were able to dismiss considerations of loyalty whenever their compulsive anxiety to acquire land was involved. While en route he wrote Washington his judgment on public opinion in Kentucky that year. His survey expressed the point of view of a man whose first concern was his country's welfare. He reported with obvious satisfaction that in his estimation the current seditious agitation in the west was largely the product of a few selfish leaders and that people generally, though deeply disturbed, had not been strongly attracted by either the Spanish conspiracy or Dr. John Connolly's British intrigue. Having thus given voice to his own patriotic sentiments, he then went on to found a colony on foreign territory which, if successful, must prove signally adverse to the interests of the United States.

On the west bank of the Mississippi, just below the mouth of the Ohio, he apportioned land among his followers, named his town site New Madrid, established a species of self-government, and then went on to New Orleans to seek approval of Miro, governor of the territory of which he had elected to become an inhabitant. Meanwhile James Wilkinson, ever alert to undermine a competitor, had written Miro describing Morgan as a man motivated only by "the vilest self-interest." Miro was in any event none too eager to favor a project promoted by his own rival, Gardoqui. He did not abruptly disapprove but he restrained many of the privileges Gardoqui had promised and he deprived Morgan of his chief interest in the enterprise by ruling that he might allot but might not sell land to later settlers. When Miro also sent a Spanish garrison to New Madrid Morgan gave up in disgust and returned to his native country.

None of his land projects had materialized. In this he ran true to type. No major land speculation based primarily on the expectation of private profit ever succeeded. The west was inherited by the individual settler. The significance of the land speculators' efforts lay in the public danger they represented. Most were founded on a readiness to embrace foreign interests at the expense of American interests. The speculator had become so possessed by his glimpsed possibility of enormous profit that he was perpetually prepared to sacrifice any other value to improve his chances. This moral obtuseness in otherwise honorable men is revealed in startling clarity by Morgan's last land design.

On April 16, 1796, eight years after the adoption of the Constitution had given most Americans ample time under Washington's devoted administration fully to realize that they were Americans, he wrote Alexander McKee at Detroit appealing for his assistance in gaining a land grant on the British side of the frontier. He had known McKee well when they were both young traders at Pittsburgh. He had known him better as the Tory whose flight to the British in 1778 had proved the severest blow sustained by his own Indian pacification program. With his lifelong familiarity with the west he could not have failed to realize as clearly as did any harassed settler that during the next seventeen years McKee's instigation, promotion, and personal leadership of Indian attacks had cost the settlements thousands of lives and had made him the most feared and hated of all enemies of the American frontier. Still Morgan was now writing that his "Friendship and Attachment" for McKee had never abated and went on to say:

Mrs. Morgan (who desires to be particularly remembered to you) & all my Family who are at home, are well . . . The frequent Enquiries I have made respecting you, have afforded me singular Satisfaction & More especially as Mr. Allen tells me you continue to enjoy good Health & your usual Share of Activity.

He then came to the point of his letter which was his endeavor to induce McKee to use his influence with British authorities to gain Morgan a grant "or at any rate a purchase of some Miles Square at a Moderate Price." He threw in almost casually the stipulation that "I or my Children or some of them should become a british Subject."

Nothing came of the venture other than to provide another illustration of the ability of the speculator to adopt a separate standard of conduct whenever the acquisition of land was involved. The accompanying anomaly that in most cases his loyalty remained otherwise unaffected was again emphasized by Morgan's last public service. In 1806 when Aaron Burr on his way west confided his plans to Morgan at Morganza, his Chartier Creek estate, the old westerner at once denounced Burr's design in a letter of warning to Jefferson and at his own expense traveled to Richmond to testify against Burr at the latter's trial for treason. Except when his reach for land was concerned Morgan had always been a patriot who had served his country well. Without doubt his greatest service was that, in common with other speculators, all of whom were equally imaginative, articulate, and influential, he had demonstrated so strong a faith in the west's future that the dissemination of the doctrine became a dynamic stimulus to the growth of the west.

It was occasionally possible to become a frontier adventurer without ever venturing near the west. Joel Barlow, all but two years of whose life was devoted to his major interests as poet, clergyman, lawyer, journalist, political agitator, and diplomat, had such an experience. After attending Yale as a divinity student, serving as chaplain in the Continental Army, founding a literary magazine, being admitted to the bar, writing a series of esoteric essays, and publishing the then highly considered epic poem, *The Vision of Columbus,* he accepted employment by the Scioto Land Company and was sent to Paris as its agent to sell land and attract emigrants. There was some doubt that he was aware that the company possessed only an option on the land he had been commissioned to sell and certainly his ignorance of the Ohio wilderness was complete. Among the enticements offered prospective purchasers, whether or not of his own composition, were such descriptions as: "a climate healthy and delightful; scarcely such a thing as frost in winter; a river, called by way of eminence, 'The Beautiful,' abounding in fish of an enormous size; magnificent forests of a tree from which sugar flows, and a shrub which yields candles; venison in abundance; without foxes, wolves, lions or tigers; no taxes to pay, no military enrolments; no quarters to find for soldiers." His sales effort was misleading not so much by reason of his having exaggerated the new country's advantages as by his having withheld from uninformed and credulous inquirers any mention of its equally striking disadvantages. At any rate all was sufficiently in key with the century-old travel classics of the early French travelers, Lahontan, Hennepin, and Marquette, to gain wide acceptance. Many Frenchmen were captivated, disposed of their property, paid five shillings an acre for the Scioto Company's offering, and embarked with their families for this waiting Eden.

When the first 500 French colonists arrived, they were distressed to discover that their promised land on the Ohio was unbroken forest, that the company that had sold it to them had meantime failed amid charges of fraud, and that a general Indian war was convulsing the entire frontier. Totally unsuited to the wilderness, terrified by the Indian danger, unable in their inexperience even to cut down the giant sycamores that covered their holding, they suffered intolerable hardships and attracted the widespread if somewhat ineffective sympathy of the frontier and the country. Many took refuge in the older French communities in the Illinois or at Detroit but a hardy few persisted and somehow the little town of Gallipolis survived. As a curious footnote to the episode, twenty-two years later

Barlow, then serving as American minister to Napoleon, became involved in the terrible winter retreat of the Grand Army from Russia and perished of exposure on the Polish frontier.

Not all lesser adventurers were concerned only with land and fortune. Richard Conner left Maryland in his youth to hunt and trap west of the mountains during the first years of uneasy peace after Pontiac's War. He had embraced the dangers of life in the wilderness not to improve his material prospects but to enjoy that complete freedom of action and movement sought by the typical long hunter. In his wanderings he visited the Shawnee where he met a young white captive, Mary Myers. He purchased her for $200 and made her his wife. They continued to live among the Shawnee since a condition of the sale and marriage contract provided that their first born must remain in the nation and be considered an Indian. In 1774 Richard and Mary were among the white captives given up by the Shawnee under the terms of the Treaty of Fort Charlotte imposed by Lord Dunmore, but the next year they returned to the Indian country to attempt to ransom their son, James, who had been retained by the Shawnee. Visiting the Moravian mission on the Tuscarawas en route, they were so impressed by the work of the missionaries that they thereafter made their home among the Christian Delaware. The former long hunter became an active and zealous member of the wilderness church. In his secret messages to the American commander at Pittsburgh, warning of incipient Indian attacks of which he had been able to gather reports, John Heckewelder, the mission's pastor, occasionally remarked upon Conner's faithful service. His activity during these desperate war years was confined to his mission duties. His one recorded personal contact with larger and more belligerent events was a 1779 encounter with Simon Girty when Girty was passing through the mission towns on one of his many forays against the frontier. The illiterate partisan was in tantalizing possession of written reports from Tory secret agents in Pittsburgh describing American military dispositions the nature of which he as commander of his Indian war party had an intense desire to know. For a moment he considered asking Conner to read the messages to him but, deciding it unsafe to acquaint an American, no matter how kindly and pacifist, with their import, put them back in his pocket and went on with his burning curiosity still unrelieved.

When in 1781 the Moravians were forced into exile by the British and Wyandot, Conner was among the mission leaders taken to Detroit instead of Sandusky and thus he and his family escaped the massacre of the Christian Delaware by Pennsylvania frontiersmen the following spring. After the war they remained near Detroit and eventually became the first white settlers of St. Clair County. His career was significant in that it represented so complete a departure from the rule. He had made the transition from wandering long hunter to substantial settlement founder not only without any participation in violence at any stage but also by way of a religious experience almost unique in an environment so generally irreligious.

More representative of the moral and spiritual outlook of the average frontiersman were the lurid adventures of Lewis Wetzel. He, like Conner, evidenced no interest in the improvement of his own material prospects but, on the other hand, he could not have conceived of lending himself to any slightest effort to make Indian prospects anything other than intolerable. His one devouring ambition was to kill Indians and this urge he satisfied with a success that made him the universal idol of his fellow borderers. In 1769 when he was six his father, John, a native of Switzerland, moved with his family from the South Branch of the Potomac over the mountains to the Monongahela and in 1772 on to Wheeling Creek, so that Lewis grew up on what was in his boyhood the most exposed and violent of all frontiers. In the endlessly repeated Indian attacks of the period, the militia engagements, the expeditions, the various sieges of Wheeling, the innumerable raids, the Wetzel family took a most active part. His father was killed by Indians. Of his four older brothers George was killed and Martin and Jacob captured.[3] Lewis himself was wounded and captured at the age of fourteen but escaped the third night of the raiders' homeward progress after coolly lingering until he had found an opportunity to take from his sleeping captors a pair of moccasins to protect his naked feet and his father's rifle which they had taken when they had taken him.

As he approached manhood his hatred of Indians became a passion. He spent most of his time ranging the wilderness, usually alone, though occasionally with one or two sufficiently rash companions, stalking and hunting Indians as others might bear or buffalo. A number of these imprudent associates were killed, including John Madison, a cousin of the fourth president, but Wetzel was so skilled a woodsman and so crafty a bushfighter that he always came back unscathed. A primary factor in forest combat was the 20 to 30 seconds required for the 23 distinct and successive movements of lips, teeth, and both hands involved in the reloading of a long rifle. Once a combatant had fired he was for that long relatively defenseless and his antagonists were constantly alert for the opportunity to close in upon him during this interval. But Wetzel had taught himself not only to reload with remarkable speed but to reload even while running, an accomplishment which proved fatal to many of his overconfident opponents. In one instance, while being closely pursued he was able almost without breaking his stride to wheel and shoot down three of his pursuers in succession before the others drew off, mystified by a white man's rifle that seemed never to require loading. His urge to kill led him often to trail Indian hunting parties until they had camped for the night when he would spring upon them in the darkness, dispatching with knife and tomahawk his bewildered victims as they started up from sleep. He was vain of his reputation as a killer and became so absorbed in sustaining it that he never married, established a home, or turned to more

[3] Martin's captivity provided a favorite story of the time. After being adopted into the family of the great Shawnee chief, Cornstalk, he remained patiently among the Shawnee until, assuming he was resigned to his lot, they permitted him considerable freedom of movement. He then killed three Indian hunting companions and returned to the settlements in triumph with their scalps.

normal employment. One of his idiosyncrasies was to let his carefully tended hair grow almost to his knees so that by providing so ostentatious a scalp it might represent an additionally taunting challenge to his Indian enemies. The prevalence of the accounts of his exploits eagerly circulated during his time would indicate that the number of Indians he had killed may have ranged toward a hundred.

His most noted feats, however, were considered praiseworthy only by his fellow frontiersmen. He had a special relish for killing Indians in public under circumstances attracting the most attention possible. This involved attacks on prisoners or friendly Indians or emissaries who had come within reach under a flag of truce or other safe conduct. In yielding repeatedly to this impulse he was epitomizing the basic attitude of the frontier. It was the belief of most genuine frontiersmen who had long known, as had their fathers before them, the stresses of border violence that no opportunity must ever be lost to embitter the antagonism between the races so that the conflict might be the more relentlessly waged until the last Indian had been exterminated. Wetzel obeyed this dictate with cruel gusto. During the Coschocton campaign a Delaware chief who had been invited to the American camp under a safe conduct to discuss peace terms was tomahawked by Wetzel while the envoy was standing face to face in conversation with the American commander, Colonel Daniel Brodhead. The militia so heartily approved the act that Brodhead was obliged to forego any idea of punishment. At the Treaty of Fort McIntosh under similar circumstances Wetzel struck down an Indian delegate, though in this instance the victim recovered.

The most celebrated of Wetzel's assassinations, as well as the one that most thoroughly illustrated the temper of the times, occurred during the conference that led to the Treaty of Fort Harmar in 1789. The Indian policy of the United States had been devoted for years to the successful negotiation of that treaty. Governor Arthur St. Clair of the Northwest Territory had after months of diplomatic maneuvering and cajoling persuaded some hundreds of Indian delegates to assemble at Fort Harmar for the conference that represented the last chance to avert the general Indian war that was daily appearing more imminent. So critical and public an arena was to Wetzel an irresistible temptation. Lying in ambush between the Indian camp and the fort, he shot an important Indian delegate, whose adopted white name was George Washington. Harmar, the outraged American commander responsible for maintaining order at the conference, had no difficulty learning the identity of the assassin. Wetzel boasted of his achievement and circumstantial accounts of the incident were received everywhere on the frontier with shouts of approval. Harmar dispatched a detachment of troops to the Mingo Bottom settlement which he was known to frequent to apprehend Wetzel. The angry settlers swarmed in such numbers to defend him that the soldiers withdrew to avoid a pitched battle against overwhelming odds. Wetzel, continuing to move about as freely as ever, was shortly thereafter seized by another military detachment when Harmar heard that he was recklessly spending the night on an island near Fort Harmar. The irate commander ordered him confined in irons in the fort to await hanging. Wetzel persuaded his guard to remove the leg irons so that he might exercise on the edge of the parade ground and forthwith ran off at a speed that outdistanced pursuit. He successfully eluded the search of Harmar's patrols, aided by Indian trackers, by hiding in riverbank thickets until he contrived to get across the Ohio by furtively attracting the attention of a Kentuckian fishing from a canoe. At the first settler's door at which he appealed for help his handcuffs were struck off and he was once more free.

Some weeks later he was drinking in a Maysville tavern when the commander of an army convoy proceeding down-river chanced to recognize him. He was again arrested and again imprisoned, this time in Fort Washington, then under construction at Cincinnati. Some hundreds of aroused frontiersmen, under the leadership of Colonel Henry Lee, Mason County lieutenant and for years a circuit judge, Simon Kenton, Wetzel's frequent Indian-hunting companion, and other border notables, surrounded the army post with furious threats to rescue the prisoner by force. Territorial Judge John Symmes relieved Harmar from his predicament by issuing a writ of *habeas corpus* ordering Wetzel's release. He was never brought to trial for the murder.

After the Treaty of Greenville ending the Indian wars he rapidly faded from public notice. Still somewhat in character, he was once reported in a Spanish prison at the end of a flatboat voyage to New Orleans. He was recruited for the Lewis and Clark party but, failing to conform to its rigid disciplines, was not with the expedition when it embarked from winter camp on its great transcontinental journey. He died obscurely near Natchez in 1808. He might not appear outside his environment an altogether admirable figure, but any attempt to assess the behavior standards of his times must take into account the inescapable fact that he was considered by his neighbors and contemporaries an outstanding public servant.

If Lewis Wetzel vividly personified the virulence of white animosity, Doublehead, the Chickamauga, as truly exemplified Indian implacability. When in 1776 the Creek nation divided—with the peace faction under the famous old chief, Attakullaculla, remaining in their original towns and the war faction under his intransigent son, Dragging Canoe, removing farther down the Tennessee to continue resistance—Doublehead became a wholehearted adherent of the belligerent group. From then on he took a prominent part in Dragging Canoe's incessant raiding of the Holston, Kentucky, and, after 1780, Cumberland settlements. In appearance and deportment he was pre-eminently suited to transfix his victims with that utter terror which was the primary objective of every raid. Stalwart, ugly, pock-marked, he was given to explosive fits of temper dreaded even by his devoted followers. His hatred of whites was stirred to lasting frenzy by the cold-blooded murder in 1788 by a detachment of Sevier's Franklin militia of his brother, Old Tassel, at a moment when that respected and peace-seeking Cherokee head chief had entered the American camp by invitation under a flag of truce to discuss terms. Doublehead's revenge was as fearful as had been Logan's memorable retaliation in 1774. With a pack of only seven warriors he lurked in ambush for weeks along the Cumberland until among other whites he had succeeded in killing were three of the sons of Sevier's brother, Valentine.

His excessive belligerence gained him recognition, after the death of Dragging Canoe in 1792, as a principal war chief of the Chickamauga. At Panton's solicitation he visited Pensacola where he was ceremoniously received and his party supplied with unlimited ammunition as a feature of Carondelet's new policy of encouraging more aggressive Indian action against the American frontier. The United States was at the same time making strenuous efforts to win Chickamauga neutrality. A companion chief, Bloody Fellow, temporarily reconciled to the Americans by a festive visit to Philadelphia, was attempting to assist this peace movement. Doublehead, returning from Pensacola, staged an anti-American war dance around the American flag Bloody Fellow had hoisted over the council house, thus succeeding in demoralizing his rival's effort.

For the next two years he sought by exhortation and example to stimulate the already fiery war spirit of the Chickamauga. Among countless atrocities which faded from frontier memory because they so much resembled their counterparts, one attracted more lasting attention by its exceptional brutality. The small blockhouse of Alexander Cavett, near Knoxville, was occupied by a family of thirteen, only three of whom were men. Assured that their lives would be spared by Doublehead's English-speaking nephew, Bench, the defenders surrendered to the overwhelming number of Indian attackers. No sooner was the gate opened than Doublehead, in one of his frequent wild furies, fell upon and personally tomahawked and scalped the helpless captives.

Other chiefs had been edified by officially conducted trips to Philadelphia to be feted and rewarded as a part of the United States program of Indian pacification. Doublehead long refused the invitation but at last yielded to the temptation to experience the singular distinction. As a counterbalance to the peace gesture he devoted the last four months before setting out for Philadelphia to almost unremitting attacks on Wilderness Road travelers during which his victims included Thomas Ross, first post rider to carry mail overland to Kentucky, two Baptist ministers, Captain William Overall, one of Robertson's original party in the founding of Nashville, and Thomas Sharpe (Big Foot) Spencer, one of the most noted of all frontiersmen. In the latter accomplishment he gained, in addition to so prized a scalp, $1000 in gold which Spencer had received as a recent legacy.

Having registered so forcefully and unmistakably his actual attitude toward frontier peace, he set off cheerfully for Philadelphia, accompanied by a band of his most devoted and murderous followers. There were other more temperate chiefs in the Cherokee delegation but Doublehead, on account of his bloodthirsty reputation, became the center of official attention. Secretary of War Knox received him, along with the others, with every mark of respect and esteem. As a further inducement to make and keep peace the annual allowance paid the Cherokee by the United States was increased from $1500 to $5000. All the chiefs were loaded with presents. For their part the Cherokee agreed to relinquish their claim to the land occupied by the Cumberland settlements. This was hardly an important concession since the area had been formerly ceded in the 1785 Treaty of Hopewell and fourteen years of continuous war had failed to dislodge the settlers. At the close of the conference the visiting Cherokee were addressed by Washington who assured them: "We mean now to bury deep and forever the red hatchet of war. Let us therefore forget past events."

The attentions showered on Doublehead did not end with his Philadelphia entertainment. He and his band were returned to Savannah aboard an American man-of-war. In his custody was the first annual payment of $5000 in goods which as a special favor he had been permitted to draw in advance. Returning home in triumph he divided the proceeds as though they were the loot of an exceptionally successful raiding expedition, taking care to distribute the major portion not to the peace faction but to his own most warlike followers. In his first flush of gratification over his novel experiences and his having met "my father the President" he wrote Governor Blount of the Southwest Territory, October 20, 1794, that he and his warriors were "determined to hold the United States fast by the hand" and "live in peace now like brothers." But the proclivities of a lifetime were not so easily shed and this mood of benevolence soon passed. On November 11, 1794, within a month of his return from the presumably civilizing excursion during which he had visited the cities of the United States and shaken hands with its lawmakers, cabinet ministers, and president, he led a peculiarly atrocious attack on the station of Valentine Sevier from which he had chanced to discover all the men but two were at the moment absent. Among the women, children, and infants butchered, multilated, and thrown into the flames were three more members of the Sevier family.

The general Indian peace of 1795 limited his opportunity to indulge in further barbarities though he continued to dominate Cherokee councils in all their dealings with the national government. In his violent demise in 1807 there was a certain irony. He was shot and axed to death by fellow chiefs in an altercation resulting from their accusations that he had privately profited through the sale of Cherokee lands to the United States.

Of all the lesser adventurers who stirred their own eddies of agitation to add to the general confusion of the frontier scene one possessed a special claim to distinction in that his activities came perilously close to precipitating a world war. Dr. James O'Fallon, who boasted of descent from Irish kings and of having studied medicine at Edinburgh and who was reported to have been at one time a Catholic priest, came to America just before the Revolution to seek his fortune. At the outbreak of war after some apparent indecision he embraced the patriot cause. He was fluent and sociable and among personal contacts in the course of his service were friendly associations with two such contrasting figures as Tom Paine and Anthony Wayne. But the anticipated new world opportunity continued to fail to materialize until in 1789 it suddenly opened to him in breath-taking proportions.

Georgia had unanimously ratified the Constitution and its legislature was eager to cater once more to land companies before the approaching necessity of ceding the state's western land claims to the central government brought such exchanges of mutual benefit to an end. By the Act of December 21, 1789, Georgia sold for five-sixths of a cent per acre 25,000,000 acres of land along the Tennessee and Mississippi rivers to the Tennessee Company, the Virginia Company, and the South Carolina Yazoo Company. The land involved was hundreds of miles west of Georgia's westernmost frontier, was claimed by Spain, and was occupied by Indians. Georgia did not pretend to deny the eventual jurisdiction of the United States over the area or to assert any intention of assuming political or protective responsibility for the proposed colonies. All that had been accomplished by the statutory sale had been to furnish the companies with a quasi-legal excuse to undertake development at their own and their country's risk. Among the more notable speculators interested in the immense ventures were Patrick Henry, William Blount, John Sevier, James Wilkinson, George Morgan, George Rogers Clark, and Baron von Steuben.

Of the three projects the Yazoo was the most ambitious and the most critical. Its enormous tract stretched along the east bank of the Mississippi above the present Vicksburg. This was an area in which American settlement was bound to be vigorously resisted by Spain unless means were discovered to moderate Spanish objections. With this difficulty in view, the company, dominated by the prominent South Carolinians, Alexander Moultrie, Wade Hampton, and Isaac Huger, appointed James O'Fallon general agent. It was assumed that his being a Catholic and an Irishman might facilitate his negotiations with Spanish authorities.

O'Fallon entered upon his duties with vigor and zest. He embarked upon a voluminous correspondence not only with Gardoqui and Miro but also with McGillivray, since Indian complacence was also desirable, at least at the outset. His essential proposal was that Spain approve the settlement of the Yazoo by Americans selected by his company who would thereupon set up a free state independent of the United States. He professed to see a prosperous future for the colony initially as an important center for the Indian trade and the slave trade and soon as a principal depot for the trade of the entire Mississippi Valley. He emphasized that its necessary commercial outlet at New Orleans must inevitably bind it ever closer to Spain. The new state's immediate value to Spain, he argued, was that as a buffer between New Spain and the United States it would constitute a barrier protecting Spanish territory from the American government's territorial pretensions and from the aggressiveness of American frontiersmen. At the same time that he was appealing with so much eloquence to Spanish self-interest he was writing Washington, assuring him that he was merely hoodwinking the Spaniards and that American official approval of the project would result in an important advance of the American frontier into the disputed zone claimed by both nations.

Miro encouraged O'Fallon's feverish correspondence in order to gain further clues to his more probable intentions. But there was little possibility of gaining Spanish sanction of a project so potentially dangerous to the interests of Spain or Spain's Indian allies. O'Fallon became impatient with Spanish ambiguities and began to hint to Miro that no matter how pro-Spanish were his company's intentions he might not be able indefinitely to restrain sympathetic Kentuckians from seizing the Yazoo area by force. He had meanwhile become associated with George Rogers Clark who, still smarting from the frustration of his 1786 Mississippi design and brooding over the more recent Spanish rebuff of his colony proposal, was prepared to organize an assault by irregularly recruited Kentuckians on Natchez and New Orleans. This dovetailed with the ever-enlarging program envisaged by O'Fallon's soaring imagination. The alliance between the two was cemented by the marriage of the middle-aged O'Fallon with Clark's fifteen-year-old youngest sister, Frances.

The threat to international peace inherent in the filibustering project was suddenly raised to lethal proportions by the revelation of the impending war between Spain and Great Britain.[4] Carried away by the prospect that Spanish ability to resist must be compromised by the exigencies of a war with Britain, O'Fallon cut his every friendly tie with Miro and began publicly to support Clark's preparations. He was soon bombarding Miro with thunderous threats that he was gathering an army of ten thousand men to take by force what Spain had now lost the opportunity to concede. It was true enough that many Kentuckians were stirred by a new interest in the proposal, so often previously debated, to drive the Spanish stopper from the Mississippi bottle. Always before, the capture of New Orleans, so easy of achievement by such a leader as Clark with so aggressive a following as he could command, had seemed, on second thought, an empty gesture, since Spain with command of the sea could render the port useless by blockading the mouth of the Mississippi. But now, with the prospect of Britain chasing the Spanish fleet to cover, the project appeared, even to the more thoughtful, as practicable as it had always seemed attractive.

Washington was profoundly alarmed by the possibility that his struggling year-old government could be about to be involved in a three-nation war. He issued a proclamation denouncing the O'Fallon-Clark expedition and calling upon all loyal citizens to refrain from assisting it. But the nation had neither the funds nor the forces to do anything more tangible to diminish the threat. Only great good luck, with some help from Wilkinson, averted the catastrophe.

The Spanish-British storm clouds passed as swiftly as they had gathered. O'Fallon, having burned all his bridges of negotiation with Miro, could only persist nevertheless in the preparations for Clark's Mississippi expedition. At this juncture he was frustrated by Wilkinson, who always knew how to go straight for the jugular vein of any rival. Wilkinson had at first co-operated with the Yazoo

---

[4] Spain, reasserting long claimed territorial rights on the Pacific Coast, had seized the cargoes of English traders in Nootka Sound on Vancouver Island. Great Britain issued an insulting ultimatum and began openly preparing for a war that was only averted in November 1790, when Spain, deprived of the support of her traditional ally, France, by the complications of the French Revolution, was obliged to yield abjectly to British demands.

Company but had been mortified when O'Fallon instead of he had been appointed its director of operations. He had returned to his Spanish allegiance, kept Miro informed of developments, used his Kentucky influence to discourage recruiting, and furnished the company's South Carolina headquarters evidence of certain financial irregularities in which its general agent had become involved. The company's eastern backers had been dismayed by Washington's disapproval and O'Fallon's impetuosities. The charge that he had also wasted the company's money was a sufficient last straw. He was hastily discharged. Deprived of material support the Clark-O'Fallon New Orleans project remained dormant until its later revival under French auspices.

O'Fallon had occupied the center of the western stage for only a few months. But it was a clamorous appearance while it lasted. Of all the bad moments suffered by Washington during the first infinitely troubled months of his administration those caused him by O'Fallon appeared at the time the most excruciating. At issue was entanglement in a war which clearly threatened the loss to the nation of the entire west. The unforeseen escape provided another instance in which providence seemed to be guarding the new republic.

O'Fallon remained in Kentucky, taking an active part in local politics and particularly in the democratic societies' pro-French agitation of the next decade. As his more lasting public service, he fathered two sons by Frances Clark, Benjamin and John, who became important contributors to the development of the trans-Mississippi west.

X

~~~

War in the Dooryard

Governors and congressmen, generals and militia commanders, land companies and speculators, conspirators and adventurers, all played their parts in the westward movement. But it was the role of the individual settler that was decisive. From his readiness to make his home in a wilderness clearing and to stay there with his family in the face of hardships and perils that must have proved intolerable to any other breed of men sprang the extraordinary vitality of the American reach for the midcontinent. Spaniards had been in Florida for 200 years and Frenchmen in Canada for 180 without their grip upon the land becoming much more firm than it had been when they came, but in half a generation the first American settlers to cross the mountains had established a dominion that no challenge could shake. This achievement was the personal triumph of the individual homeseeker. His victory was won against continuously distressing odds that were aggravated by the realization that total disaster was always at hand. For upon every rigor and privation inescapable from existence in the wilderness was superimposed the supreme anxiety of the perpetual Indian threat. During the 20 years after 1774 no settler could fall asleep without his last waking thought being the somber reflection that the next dawn might be the last for himself, his home, and his family. Yet he stayed.

The Indian threat was made the more oppressive by presenting a danger which the victim could never be prepared to avert. By its very nature the long dreaded onslaught came always as a surprise. This was not a conflict shaped by planned campaigns or decided on formal battlefields. The sudden blow fell upon children playing in the dooryard, on a mother bending over her hearth, on a father hoeing his corn. The most difficult to endure of the whole range of apprehensions was the uncertainty. A family might go on for summer after summer, again and again observing smoke in the sky from a neighbor's burning cabin, without ever seeing an Indian. Another family might be destroyed the day of its arrival and a third agonized by repetitions of calamity. There were instances of men marrying and remarrying as they lost a succession of families while they themselves always unaccountably survived. There were more usual instances of women bearing successive broods of children to successive husbands. Few families' fortune was so favorable as to enable them permanently to escape catastrophe. The spectacle of a man dying of natural causes in his bed was regarded with special solemnity because it seemed so uncommon.

Aside from this general law of improbability which seemed to govern any family's likelihood of being spared there was a certain geographical range to the danger. Most Indian war parties preferred to strike quickly and withdraw quickly. Inhabitants of the slightly more thickly populated areas 15 to 20 miles from the outer fringe of settlement in actual contact with the wilderness were in relatively less peril. Those occupying areas a few miles farther away ordinarily needed only to fear the theft of their horses, the killing of their grazing stock, or the ocacsional ambush of an unwary hunter or traveler. These more populous districts, such as the middle Kentucky, the lower Monongahela, and the upper Holston, furnished the bulk of the frontier's militia, most of its appointed and elected officials, and the votes that made its political decisions. There was also in these safer areas a tendency to remain somewhat less exercised by the Indian menace than were the inhabitants of isolated cabins and forest-encompassed clearings where the danger was constant. There was little, in any event, that could have been done to protect this outer fringe of extreme vulnerability. It stretched over distances that could not have been defended by a dozen field armies. The main frontier line extended from the upper bend of the Ohio southward for more than 800 miles across Appalachian ridges and valleys to Georgia. The perimeter of Kentucky faced outward in all directions toward the wilderness over a circumference of 450 miles. The entire Cumberland district, composed of settlements strung out along the river, was exposed.[1] Any family living at any point along these edges of the wilderness lived with the possibility attack might come at any time for the vast extension of the line gave the Indians complete freedom of choice.

This outer line of maximum hazard was in the 1780's still largely held by the original frontier people, members and descendants of the same frontier families who had held the outermost frontier since they had first been subjected east of the mountains to the great Indian attacks of 1755. They had been first to cross the mountains, first to reach the upper Ohio, first to reach for Kentucky. Most had lost possession of the sites they had chosen to later comers armed with more legal claims, veterans' rights, state land warrants, land-company titles. Many would have yielded in any case to the continuing restless urge to keep moving on to newer country and better hunting and greater freedom. The effect was, as western settlement developed, that the original frontier people kept pressing onward and outward into the wilderness and therefore continued to constitute, as they had from the beginning, the frontier's outer line of defense. The movements of the thousands of such obscure frontier families cannot be traced, but the trend was so evident as to be

---

[1] The New York frontier which had been the most troubled of any during the Revolution was comparatively safe afterward. The towns of the Iroquois were so near that their more responsible chiefs feared white retaliation, and the nation was so dependent on British supply that it was obliged to conform to British admonitions to refrain from provocations in this area.

unmistakable. It was illustrated by the fully recorded movements of more historic pioneer families. Daniel Boone moved from the Susquehanna to the Yadkin to the Clinch to the Kentucky to the Missouri. James Robertson moved from the Valley of Virginia to the Yadkin to the Watauga to the Cumberland. William Christian moved from the Valley of Virginia to the New to the Holston, down the Holston with the advancing frontier, and then on the Beargrass in Kentucky. The Zane family, after sustaining all the shocks of the 1750's in the mountains of northwest Virginia, moved to the Ohio to found Wheeling and then kept pressing on northwestward into the Indian country. The Wetzel family moved from the South Branch of the Potomac to the Monongahela to the Ohio. Simon Kenton, after 12 wandering years of astounding adventure in the wilderness, took his Virginia family to the most exposed sector of the Kentucky frontier on the Limestone and then kept on northward across the Ohio. All of these families suffered through the years grievous losses in killed, wounded, and captured. Those less noted could have suffered no less.

The constant menace to which this outer fringe of settlement was exposed was surprise attack by small parties of Indians who had crept undetected into the vicinity. During the 1780's there was seldom occasion to apprehend the massive Indian invasions frequent during the Revolution but more occasion than ever before to fear these lesser but far more numerous Indian raids. All Indian nations except the Creek, the Chickamauga, and the Miami were ostensibly at peace with the United States from 1783 to 1790, but in every one there were many recalcitrant warriors eager to prove their prowess and give rein to their resentment. On either flank of the area of western settlement projecting westward into the Mississippi Valley between the mountains, the Ohio, and the Tennessee were more than a hundred Indian towns. All of them were separated by some hundreds of miles of intervening wilderness from the white border. From any one of them might issue at any time a pack of warriors free to select for attack any isolated cabin or community at any point along the nearly two thousand miles of frontier. This was a perpetual threat against which there could be literally no defense. The frontier family in its lonely clearing could only watch and wait and trust that it might not be the next to attract savage notice.

The practice of raiding had been the fundamental tactic in Indian warfare since long before the white man had come to the continent. After hunting it had always been the Indian male's principal preoccupation. With a few chosen companions, he was accustomed to make tremendous journeys devoted to taking a distant enemy by surprise, to manifesting his superiority over that enemy by the sudden terror excited by his unexpected assault, and to returning with loot, scalps, and captives to prove to his fellow townsmen the success of his undertaking. After white men became the chief enemy the incentive was greater. There was more abundant loot, including horses, the scalps were colorfully variegated, and there was a fiercer hatred to be demonstrated. By the 1780's the raiding technique had become so standardized that each new outrage seemed but a dismal repetition of the thousands that had preceded it. This typical raid was a process that developed in four stages.

The first of these was the approach. A band of warriors, occasionally as few as 5 or 6 and infrequently as many as 15 or 20, moved by a shared impulse to improve their community status, set out from some distant Indian town. They sought a renewed opportunity to exhibit their personal valor while at the same time acquiring wealth and supporting the general Indian cause by striking another blow against the universally hated white enemy. During the first days of their long journey through the wilderness they were apt to take a leisurely and meandering course, to pause often to hunt, to enjoy what amounted to a holiday, and, around the camp fire at night, endlessly to discuss the project they contemplated. As they neared the section of the white frontier they proposed to assail, they began to move more carefully and swiftly. For the last three days of their approach they fasted and practiced other forms of self-denial which they had from boyhood been taught enhanced a warrior's skill, cunning, and courage. On the last day, as they lay in hiding, they stripped to moccasins, breechclout, and weapons and painted on their faces and bodies those designs of red and black, yellow and green, which each considered might create the most fearsome effect. That night they crept with extreme stealth toward the edges of the clearing which could have been selected by chance or as a consequence of some former observation by one of their number.

The next stage was the attack. The approach had been timed to reach their goal at dawn. From their concealment in trees and in the underbrush fringing the clearing they watched as the growing light revealed the relative arrangement of cabin, outhouse, stock-pen, garden, spring, and corn patch. They waited while the members of the family began to emerge to attend to calls of nature and morning chores. They noted with particular attention the movements of the men of the family and what weapons, if any, they had with them. A signal from the raiders' appointed leader, usually a bird or animal call, triggered the attack. The first reverberating volley of gunfire, aimed at the men, was echoed by the eerie wail of the war whoop and followed by an immediate charge. Had the men been felled as intended by the first fire only the women and children remained to sustain the howling rush. The swiftest of the attackers was delegated to strive to reach the cabin doorway before the door could be closed and barred from within. Most of the more frightful barbarities that distinguished raids were committed during the extreme excitement of these first moments of an assault. Anything living and within reach, whether a cow or a grandmother, was struck down, hacked, slashed, and mutilated in that first frenzy. A crying infant was dispatched with as little compunction as a squawking chicken.

The third stage was the gathering of loot. The humblest of a white man's possessions was wildly coveted by Indians. Anything portable was valued. Trinkets and keepsakes were seized upon almost as avidly as weapons, tools, clothing, whisky and food. Women's garments particularly caught Indian fancy and were promptly stripped from their wearers to be wreathed grotesquely about their own greased and painted nakedness. Of all acquisitions horses were the most highly prized, since in addition to their intrinsic value they were immediately useful in transporting the plunder. The most excruciating moment for any surviving victims who had by agility or concealment evaded the first frenzied killing came when they were assembled for the selection of those who were to be carried away as captives. Sturdy young women able to become wigwam drudges and teenage boys suitable for adoption were the types most preferred. Others, older or younger or injured or considered for whatever reason unlikely to endure the homeward journey, were casually tomahawked. Loading their booty on the horses and the backs of the captives, the raiders set off on their march back at a forced pace calculated to outdistance pursuit.[2]

The last stage was the attempted relief. Apprised of the attack by the column of smoke, or, if the victim's location had not been too isolated, by the sound of gunfire, neighbors had hastily assembled an armed relief party. The scene as the rescuers arrived was horridly familiar—the glowing ruins, the sprawl of dismembered and disemboweled dead, the dreadful silence. Often the prospect was unnaturally whitened by a ghostly litter of wind-fluttered feathers scattered by the Indians when they had emptied pillows and featherbeds to carry off the fabric. In case any of the hogs had survived they were already feeding on the bodies. The vengeful pursuit needed to be wary as well as precipitate since there was always the chance that the Indians might be waiting in ambush. Seldom were the raiders overtaken.

All raids were not so successful. Surprise was not always achieved. An alert father could have made it an invariable practice to undertake an investigation of the nearer edges of the forest as his first

[2] The captives were brutally beaten and mistreated en route but the women among them were almost invariably spared the final trial of sexual outrage. Until Indian attitudes had been influenced by long association with whites, a warrior would have considered his purity and therefore his strength fatally impaired by sexual relations with an impure white woman. After she had been adopted and had been taught to practice all essential purification rites, he might take a white captive as wife. This warriors' purification cult was general among forest Indians though much less widely regarded among the plains Indians with whom the frontier came into later contact.

morning duty, or a dog or horse could have caught the scent in time to bark or neigh a warning. Many an indomitable family proved able to hold their beleaguered cabin until help arrived. The thwarted attackers often made desperate efforts to storm the little citadel, to break down the door, to gain an entrance by tearing apart the stick and clay chimney, or to set fire to the outer walls, but when confronted by a resolute resistance they seldom persisted long. Indians much preferred surprised, terrified, or helpless enemies. There were innumerable accounts testifying to how far from terrified or helpless were most women. The frontier woman was accustomed to the use of an ax. In the emergency of an attack she reached for it as instinctively as did her husband for his rifle. There were frequent instances of such women, defending their children or their threshold or their hearth, striking down two and three Indians with that favorite weapon. Boys were taught to shoot as soon as they could lift a rifle. Establishment of the new home had been a family effort and its defense was as much one. Of the many stories of raids in circulation most were of successful defenses. Stories of the more numerous Indian successes only gained currency when the attack had been accompanied by excesses more revolting than usual.

This was a kind of warfare that exerted unique pressures threatening every tie upon which a family or community most depended. In that first stunning moment of an unexpected attack the individual was required to make instant decisions with regard to his most personal loyalties and, in the longer strain of defense or flight, he was compelled to make stark assessments of his deepest impulses. Frontier folklore was perpetually concerned with these inhuman compulsions to make painful decisions. Among stories most often told was of the man in flight with his infant son in his arms who elected to drop the child in order to save his faltering mother. Or of the mother who closed the cabin door against those of her children running toward it from Indians in the yard in order to conserve some chance to save her other children who had already gained the cabin. Or of the hysterical young woman hiding in a thicket who smothered her baby to prevent its crying from betraying her location to searching Indians. This testing of basic sentiments extended even to consideration for the family dog which during a flight to the stockade had to be strangled lest its barking guide pursuing Indians.

History has tended to ignore this continued testing of the frontier people's endurance after the Revolution. During the later 1780's there were no important campaigns, no pitched battles, no obvious turning points, no clearly decisive events. It was a war fought in the dooryard with its apparent consequences no more significant than the extinction of another family which, if it had been governed by more discretion, would never have ventured into a location so insecure. Even the people who had suffered began soon to forget how much they had suffered. After the general Indian peace of 1795 memories of what they had formerly been obliged to endure faded rapidly. A new generation, absorbed in the sudden burgeoning of a new west in which no aspiration seemed impossible, became less and less interested in the reminiscences of their elders. The recent period of perils with which the multitude of newly arrived easterners was unacquainted had already begun to seem almost as distant and unreal as it may now.[3]

The actual prevalence of danger to the inhabitants of the outer frontier during the late 1780's was difficult to estimate then and impossible now. The destruction of another family seldom attracted attention beyond the range of its immediate neighbors. Communications even between adjacent communities were slow and intermittent and over longer distances dependent on letters entrusted to chance travelers. There were few official efforts made to record or compile casualties. In 1790 Harry Innes, United States Judge for the District of Kentucky, in a letter to Secretary of War

---

[3] There was strikingly early evidence of this tendency to forget in the March 9, 1788, letter of General Harmar to the Secretary of War giving his personal estimation of the character of Captain Pipe, the Delaware war chief who only six years before had presided over the unspeakable death by torment of Washington's great friend, Colonel William Crawford. After entertaining Captain Pipe at his headquarters, Harmar came to the conclusion: "He is a manly old fellow, and much more of a gentleman than the generality of these frontier people."

Knox estimated that 1500 Kentuckians had been killed in the six years since the end of the Revolution.[4] The population of Kentucky had by then risen to 73,000, but the majority occupied the more thickly populated central section and the greater part of this casualty total was therefore supplied by the inhabitants of the thinly settled perimeter. The Innes estimate also took no account of the casualties suffered during those years on the upper Ohio, upper Monongahela, Greenbrier, Holston, Cumberland, or Georgia borders. According to most contemporary estimates the annual toll of emigrants and travelers on the Wilderness Road ran to a hundred. There were no such estimates for the flatboat migration on the Ohio. Unlike the Wilderness Road where bodies were left to the observation of later passers, the river swept away the traces of every disaster. The weight of evidence would seem to indicate that the various frontiers and migration routes suffered in the late 1780's a death by violence rate on the order of 450 per year. In view of the limited number of inhabitants of the more exposed areas this must be considered a prevalence of danger on the verge of desperate.

One other and possibly more indicative clue to the casualty rate is provided by the experiences of prominent persons whose adversities were more likely to attract attention and more certain to be recorded or at least remembered. The most prominent figure of any locality was a colonel, the elected official who served as county lieutenant and militia commander. During the 20 years from 1774 to 1794, 37 colonels were listed as killed in action. Even more prominent figures were the outstanding frontier leaders, Daniel Boone, James Robertson, and John Sevier, who were themselves actual settlers and as such subjected to the same range of risk as were their lesser known neighbors. (The scale of risk was in fact weighted in their favor; their families normally resided in strongly garrisoned stockades and most of their military activities were in conjunction with relatively large bodies of militia.) Boone was

---

[4] Reuben T. Durrett, first President of the Filson Club, after a lifelong study of frontier records, concluded that 3600 had been killed in Kentucky during the 20 years after the founding of Boonesborough.

twice wounded and twice captured, two of his sons, James and Israel, were killed, his daughter, Jemima, was captured, and his brother, Squire, wounded. Robertson was twice wounded, once so severely that his death was considered certain, and two of his sons, James and Peyton, and his brother, Mark, were killed. Sevier himself miraculously escaped serious injury during all his vigorous campaigning but his brother, Robert, four of his nephews and two of his nieces were killed, and one of his nieces survived a scalping.

The conclusion becomes unmistakable that no war could have been more real or more bitter than that war in the dooryard. And few could have been more significant. A man fought to save his corn patch and his cabin and the lives of his family. These were great issues to him but a greater issue was at stake. Upon his continued determination to stand fast depended the whole future of the United States.

XI

‽

Resort to Union

That spring of 1787 the divisive forces threatening the United States under the Confederation were very nearly as disruptive as those against which Brant was struggling in his endeavor to maintain his Indian confederation. Brant's great task was to convince ignorant Indians that their one hope as a people lay in recognizing and serving the common good. The better informed citizens of the United States were proving almost as difficult to convince of that same truth. Their central government had been kept weak by design in order to guard the people's newly won rights. The great states had remained determined to reserve control over all important issues affecting their own interests, and the smaller states had continued to envy the power of their larger neighbors. All states had imposed trade restrictions that were discouraging interstate commerce. This insistence upon the localization of political power was heartily supported by public opinion. Men to whom the word liberty had been a battle cry during the Revolution were still making the word the slogan for their resistance to the delegation of political authority beyond the borders of their immediate community. During the six and a half years since Yorktown the same Americans who had fought for the right to govern themselves had thus increasingly demonstrated their apparent unreadiness to take full advantage of the privilege. Their national government was a proven failure. Most European observers in a position to appraise the situation were convinced that the new nation was about to disappear as suddenly as it had appeared. Most Americans capable of political perspective were painfully agreed and realized that the process of dissolution was accelerating. Some grasped at the hope that the nation's independence might still be preserved by the institution of a constitutional monarchy with one of the younger English princes on the throne.

These divisive forces, which on the more populous seaboard had split the Confederation into thirteen competing states while inciting citizens to deprecate all authority, were even more glaringly evident in the distant, detached, and thinly settled region beyond the mountains. The rage stirred in Kentucky by the Mississippi navigation issue had that spring likewise stirred a merciless examination of many other sectional issues. A people who realized their country had so far done nothing for them were beginning to wonder what it was they owed their country. Every most influential western leader was publicly proclaiming his loss of faith in the national government. John Sevier and James Robertson were coming to the conclusion that the one hope for their fellow settlers who were relying on them for guidance was to look elsewhere for succor. George Rogers Clark, brutally repudiated by the state and nation he had served so notably, was coming to the belief that it was his duty to save his fellow westerners without regard for either Virginia or the United States. James Wilkinson was already on his way to New Orleans to offer to sell his country to the King of Spain. Every Spanish official in the new world was confidently expecting the imminent drop of the American west into Spain's lap. Sir Guy Carleton, now Lord Dorchester, recently returned to the governorship of Canada, was reporting to London that the west had become so disillusioned with its national government that public opinion was ready for a reunion with Great Britain and was asking his government's approval of whatever measures seemed indicated to take fullest advantage of the trend.

Thus, that spring of 1787, the twelfth since Lexington and Concord and the fifth since British concession of American independence, the union of the United States under the Confederation was ingloriously collapsing in both east and west. No nation, young or old, could have been confronted by perils more clearly mortal from which there seemed less hope of escape. It was a graver testing of a people's instinct to survive as a people than was to come in 1861 when the nation's political structure had been solidified by its acceptance by three generations of its citizens. The preservation of the union in 1787 could not have been gained by a struggle, however deadly. Only a miracle could have sufficed.

Then, when the need became desperate, the miracle was brought to pass by a people innately aware of which freedoms may be yielded and which must never be. The opportunity for it was supplied by the dynasty of great Virginia leaders which since 1754 had played so significant a role in every American crisis. Washington was a determined advocate of a stronger federal union. In this view he was supported in principle by every other important Virginian except Patrick Henry, the radical and doctrinaire libertarian. Virginia had taken the initiative the year before by proposing a convention at Annapolis to consider the reduction of interstate trade restrictions but most states had ignored the call. Virginia renewed the proposal and on February 3, 1787, Congress grudgingly approved a convention to meet in Philadelphia May 14, 1787, to consider amendments to the Articles of Confederation. Most states were still so dubious that it was May 28th before the arrival of the ninth state delegation permitted decisive deliberation.

Except for the absences of Thomas Jefferson, minister to France, and John Adams, minister to England, the majestic roll of the nation's founding fathers was well represented at that memorable gathering: George Washington, Benjamin Franklin, James Madison, Alexander Hamilton, Edmund Randolph, Rufus King, Roger Sherman, Gouverneur Morris, George Mason, John Rutledge, Robert

Morris, James Wilson, and others who as principal rebels and spokesmen for their communities in earlier crises had never hesitated to make the hardest decisions.[1] With such men assembled to take earnest counsel together, it presently became apparent that all might not yet be lost. The American people, for all their recent display of heedless contentiousness, were being proved by these their chosen representatives to possess that measure of political understanding most required if democracy is successfully to function—a readiness to consider and to accept reasonable compromises between opposing views. Hammering out such compromises by patient deliberation, the convention turned away from the old Confederation and began its shaping of a new form of government for the nation by regarding the United States no longer as a federal league of independent states but instead as a union of the people of equal states.

While these momentous proceedings were under way in Philadelphia, a coincidental development second in historic importance only to the drafting of the Constitution was taking shape in Congress, meeting that summer in New York. At the point of expiration and after years of ineffectuality this last Congress under the Confederation was by one final and spasmodic burst of energy erecting one of the major pillars of constitutional doctrine upon which the future of the United States was most to depend.

Since the end of the Revolution, Congress had been haunted by its obligation to contrive some form of government for the area northwest of the Ohio. There could be no escape from the grating reminder that as the one area outside the bounds of any state it was the one area subject to the direct jurisdiction of Congress. Year after year Congress had shrunk from the responsibility. The region

1 The continuity of leadership was far from complete, however. Of the more prominent delegates among the 38 signers of the Constitution (Washington, as presiding officer, did not sign, and Randolph and Mason declined to sign), only Rutledge and Sherman had been members of the First Continental Congress, and only Franklin, Wilson, Sherman, and Robert Morris had been signers of the Declaration of Independence. Among the Constitution's signers who were also members of the 1787 Congress were King and Madison.

was a wilderness guarded by British garrisons and occupied by hostile Indian nations. Its sole white inhabitants resided in a few scattered French communities. These were formidable problems which it had seemed useless to expect a congress without either power or funds to solve. After so many years of procrastination, Congress was finally spurred to sudden and decisive attempt at a solution in midsummer of 1787 by the interposition of the most unlikely and least public-minded of agencies, a land company.

By its earlier passage of the Ordinance of 1784 Congress had hoped to reduce the national debt by the sale of federal lands. British and Indian opposition and the objection of some states had made the ordinance a dead letter almost as soon as it had been passed, and there had been minimal returns to the treasury from the venture. Thomas Hutchins had made a preliminary survey of a narrow belt of federal land along the west bank of the upper Ohio but due to the continuing Indian danger there had been few buyers. The only actual settlers had been squatters who, having entered the area without buying land, had been ordered evicted by a frustrated Congress. In the spring of 1787 Congress made another routine gesture toward dealing with the apparently still insoluble problem. A committee reported a draft of a new ordinance to regulate eventual settlement, but on May 10th action on the report was postponed indefinitely. Congress was dismally aware of its own approaching demise. If the Philadelphia convention succeeded in restoring the union, this Congress would be superseded by another better adapted to a stronger national government. If it did not succeed there would be no national government.

Meanwhile, a group of more resolute private citizens had been taking more aggressive action. New England had been denied by its geographical location an opportunity to take any direct interest in settlement beyond the mountains. But a way had now been hit upon that would permit New Englanders to participate in the westward movement. Three Revolutionary generals, Rufus Putnam and Benjamin Tupper of Massachusetts, and Samuel Parsons of Connecticut, had for the past year been promoting a disposition among their fellow veterans to purchase western land from the national government by offering as payment the much depreciated certificates that had been issued to them in lieu of pay by that government. The proposal caught on and, on March 8, 1787, the New Ohio Company was organized in Boston to undertake a large-scale settlement by New Englanders, primarily veterans, in the Ohio country. The Reverend Manasseh Cutler, a Massachusetts doctor of divinity almost as well versed in law, medicine, politics, and science, was dispatched to New York to conduct the necessary negotiations with Congress.

Cutler proved impressive and persuasive not only as a negotiator but as an advisor. Congress turned out to be suddenly and unexpectedly willing to listen to his counsel as well as to his proposition. Many members were also delegates to the constitutional convention and there had been much running back and forth between the two cities. The exciting stir of new determination and new hope animating the convention's deliberations had been transmitted to the somnolent proceedings of Congress. New England members who had tolerated their southern colleagues' western interests only in return for an equivalent toleration of their own fishing and commercial interests were now taking the lead in advocating this new expansion project. Most effective of all in capturing congressional attention was the prospect after so many profitless years of making so considerable a land sale. Cutler was talking in terms of millions of acres. This meant a possible retirement of a sizable fraction of the national debt. To a Congress so long inactivated by the lack of funds no prospect could have seemed more attractive. This conjunction of favorable influences produced a decisiveness of which Congress had been incapable since its heroic mid-Revolutionary days. Cutler arrived in New York on July 5th. On July 9th a new committtee was instructed to draft a plan of government for the national territory northwest of the Ohio into which Cutler proposed to introduce settlers. Four days later the Ordinance of 1787 was adopted by the unanimous vote of eight states.

For all its haste Congress had composed a remarkably compre-

hensive document establishing precedents as fundamental as those
in the Constitution then under construction. It had established a government for a wilderness where government had never before
existed. For the first time authority to govern a portion of the
people of the United States had been vested not in the government
of a state but in the government of the union of the states. Also
for the first time the great doctrine of the admission of new states
had been firmly implanted as a permanent and principal covenant in
that union. Most significant of all, the people of the several states
had been given that common and mutual interest which Washington in 1784 had considered a necessity were the union to endure.
It had at last been made apparent that the people of Massachusetts
or Connecticut could have the same interest in the projection of
the United States westward into the Mississippi Valley as had the
people of Virginia or the Carolinas.

The Ordinance enacted July 13th dealt with a wider range of
definitions of political power than did the Constitution which was
signed the following September 17th and not ratified by the decisive ninth state until June 21st of the following year. It broke into
radically new constitutional ground with its assumption that the
national government, even under the Confederation, possessed inherent powers never hitherto contemplated. The area northwest of
the Ohio ceded to the United States by Great Britain and by the
several states with former claims to portions of it was designated
the Northwest Territory of the United States. Executive authority
in its government was vested in a Governor and a Secretary, and
judicial authority in three federal judges. This in itself represented
a tremendous constitutional development for there were no such
delegations of direct authority to the national government under the
Confederation. Provision was made for the future erection and admission of five new states, the eventual Ohio, Indiana, Illinois,
Michigan, and Wisconsin. Progress toward that goal was clearly
defined. When the settlement of a frontier district gained a population of 5000 the settlers were authorized to elect their own territorial assembly with a nonvoting delegate in Congress, and when

such a territory gained 60,000 inhabitants it was authorized to organize a state government and apply for admission to the union as a free and equal member. In those four crowded July days Congress had been inspired as though by a vision of the future growth of the United States to open and guard the way to that stupendous achievement.

But the drafters of the great Ordinance did not limit their efforts to a mere general outline of the American west that was to be. They attended also to every detail. Provision was made for the conveyance of property, the freedom of navigation, the qualification of voters, and the organization of counties. A complete and specific bill of rights was included. Freedom of religion was guaranteed. Land was set aside to support public education. On the initiative of Virginia, future limitations were placed on slavery. In sum, the Ordinance made it possible for any American who henceforth sought a new home in the wilderness northwest of the Ohio to feel confident that he might remain an American whose every American right and privilege was surely protected under a local government as responsible to him as had been the one he had left.

Credit for authorship of the Ordinance has been much disputed. It was largely the work of otherwise unknown men. Richard Henry Lee of Virginia and Rufus King of Massachusetts were the only nationally prominent figures connected with the accomplishment. Lee was a member of the second committee, and King took a personal interest in many of the cloakroom conferences. Nominally most responsible for the resolution were Nathan Dane of Massachusetts, chairman of the first committee and member of the second, and Edward Harrington of Virginia, chairman of the second committee which reported it in its final form. Manasseh Cutler took an active advisory and admonitory part in many of the committee discussions and used his influence to secure the inclusion in the Ordinance of a number of provisions that resembled similar articles in the recently adopted new constitution of Massachusetts. Jefferson, though in far off Paris that summer, has often been considered originally responsible on account of his having taken a leading part in drafting the earlier Ordinance of 1784 in which was also envisaged, though more dimly, the admission of new states in the west.[2] In any event there was credit enough to give every member of Congress his due. The resolution appeared to have been given its final shape by committee discussion so earnest that it resulted in a meeting of many minds. The atmosphere had suddenly become so electric that July, in both New York and Philadelphia, that even the most ordinary men became capable of rising to extraordinary heights.

Not the last among the consequences of Congress' sensationally unexpected activity was the effect on the Philadelphia convention. Opponents of a strong union were disconcerted and proponents heartened by the startling news. If a lethargic Congress could awaken to stare so boldly into the future, then surely the most dubious were obliged to admit a new and fresher wind must be beginning to blow through national council halls. Waverers were converted and action expedited. On July 24th a committee was instructed to draft that general convergence of views that was to become the constitution. Its report was received on August 6th. On September 17th the Constitution was adopted by the unanimous vote of the 11 states present.[3] As Washington recorded the day in his diary: "The business being thus closed, the Members adjourned to the City Tavern, dined together and took a cordial leave of each other; after which I returned to my lodgings . . . and retired to meditate on the momentous work which had been executed."

Meanwhile Congress was absorbed in a less inspirational task. Though it had been the New Ohio Company's practical proposal to buy land that had precipitated congressional adoption of the notable Ordinance, succeeding negotiation of the land sale itself proceeded on a much less exalted level. While offering advice on the form of government to be established in the wilderness, Cutler had loftily

[2] For example, the antislavery article in 1787 used the identical phraseology proposed by Jefferson in 1784. Many Virginians of this generation were morally opposed to slavery.

[3] The New York delegation, except for Alexander Hamilton, had withdrawn from the convention, and Rhode Island had declined to attend.

urged that New England settlers were only to be attracted were they sufficiently assured that they would continue to enjoy that high-principled democracy to which they had so long been accustomed. But when the time came to talk dollars and cents he changed to the hat of shrewd and grasping businessmen. He entered into an arrangement with William Duer, secretary of the Board of the Treasury, the congressional agency empowered to conduct land sales, whereby the proposal to purchase was increased to 5,000,000 acres. Of this acreage the Ohio Company would take 1,500,000 for its own settlement project while subcontracting the other 3,500,000 to the Scioto Land Company, a group of speculators headed by Duer which included members of Congress, various officials, prominent businessmen, and others whose public position would not otherwise have permitted them to participate in the direct acceptance of private benefits from Congress. The grant, which was in the form of graduated options to buy, ranged from a price per acre of 66⅔ cents down to 8 cents. Congress balked for a time at the terms but acquiesced when confronted by Cutler's threat to withdraw his offer altogether. There had been presented, however, another striking example of the range of forces contributing to the success of the westward movement. Though by far the greatest contribution was the readiness of the individual settler to endure what was demanded of him, the driving urgencies of profit-seeking free enterprise brought to bear a strong secondary influence. For the immense service about to be rendered to national expansion by New England settlers there would have been no opportunity at so early a date had it not been for the selfish scheming of a pack of land speculators.

Cutler was as successful in influencing the selection of personnel to administer the Northwest Territory. The President of Congress, Arthur St. Clair of Pennsylvania, was appointed Governor. Though not his original preference, Cutler, after several conversations with the candidate, approved the appointment. William Sargent, the Secretary, and Samuel Parsons, one of the three judges, were principal stockholders in the Ohio Company. Having so well accomplished every purpose for which he had been commissioned, Cutler

returned home. Preparations were at once initiated, under the vigorous supervision of Rufus Putnam, to establish New England's first
colony in the west. No white settlement had so far been attempted
on the Indian side of the Ohio. These New Englanders proposed
forthwith to plant one there.

Monumental as were the declarations of new constitutional
principles embodied in the enactment of the Ordinance by Congress and the adoption of the Constitution by the convention, both
still remained only declarations of intent. They were so far no more
than proposals addressed to the attention of the American people.
Congress had no power to implement its decree. The convention
could only hope that its labors might receive the eventual sanction
of an aroused public opinion.

That same July that Congress was voting a future government for
the wilderness and selling 5,000,000 of its forested acres, it received
Brant's long delayed letter announcing the position taken by the
great Indian council at Hurontown the previous December.[4] The
letter offered a conference between the Indian confederation and
the United States to consider their many differences but demanded
the immediate cessation of surveys and threatened war were there
to be an attempt to advance American settlement across the Ohio.
Congress paid little attention to the message. Brant was reassem-
bling the Indian council on the Maumee to consider the reply expected from Congress to the Indian overture. But no word came
because no word had been sent. On October 22nd Congress instructed St. Clair to neglect no "opportunity that may offer of ex-
tinguishing the Indian rights to the westward, as far as the river
Mississippi." Congressional irrationality must have been chiefly due
to congressional inability to take any practical steps to deal with
the situation. The most uninformed member must have been aware
of the gravity of the Indian threat. Only five years had passed
since the Indians had been ravaging the American border from
New York to Georgia. The same Indians were still proclaiming
their defiance and demonstrating their continued hostility by almost

[4] See page 57.

daily raids against the more exposed sections of the frontier. The same British garrisons which had formerly supported their attacks were still occupying their posts in the heart of the northwest Indian country. Congress by encouraging an advance of settlement into this explosive area had made certain an Indian war that threatened to involve England, and yet had given no thought to the necessary preparations for waging that war. In the southwest where Spanish garrisons had replaced English a similar danger loomed. A noble plan for a potential future had been outlined. It was the grim realities of the present that had still to be confronted.

From Philadelphia the newly inspirited delegates to the convention hurried homeward to their states to preach the new gospel. They found people neither so ready to welcome the prospect of stronger union nor so impressed by the alternate threat of complete disunion as had been expected. Public opinion did not rally as swiftly as had been hoped. The Constitution's opponents were violent and vociferous. Many patriots who had been active and single-purposed during the Revolution were now as active and single-purposed in their objections to a stronger central government. State leaders and entrenched local political cliques took sharp exception to the proposed diminishment of their importance. Soon it became evident how scant was the hope that every state would accept the Constitution. Soon thereafter it became as evident that there was no assurance that even the nine states necessary for the establishment of the new government would ratify.

There was even less assurance that during this anarchic interim the rebelliously dissatisfied west might not continue its drift away from the nation until it had passed beyond recall. At the very moment western leaders were beginning to extend feelers toward Spain the national government had been rendered totally helpless by the need to await the verdict on ratification. The impulses toward a stronger union voiced at Philadelphia and New York had stirred few new hopes on the Kentucky, the Cumberland, or the Holston. The west which had received no support from a weak central government expected little more from a stronger central government than a possibly greater inclination to meddle in western affairs. What the west wanted was its own government, not more government on the seaboard. Kentucky and Franklin were far more impressed by congressional refusal to admit them as states than they were by the Ordinance or the Constitution. For the Ordinance there was some approval of the sort always given any anti-Indian development. But there was also wry notice of the fact that Congress which had been so slow to serve the interests of the west had been so quick to serve New England interests and of the companion fact that the Indian war Congress was inviting promised to become one that Kentuckians would be obliged to fight. All in all, there had been little in the frontier's first reaction to the drafting of the Ordinance and the Constitution to improve the chance that the west's ties to the nation might continue to hold.

The year 1787, which in midsummer had glittered with so many great new expectations, therefore closed upon uncertainties more terrifying than those upon which it had opened. Not only the preservation of the west but the survival of the nation remained in doubt. On every quarter glared fearful dangers, issues that demanded vital decisions which represented at best a choice among evils—the trans-Ohio venture, Indian defiance, British hostility, the Spanish intrigue, the ratification ordeal. Every American's destiny was in suspense. The coming year, 1788, was to be the year of crisis—the gravest with which the United States has ever been confronted.

XII

❧

1788

In the most unrestrained melodrama more harrowing suspense could not be contrived than marked the events of this momentous year. We who are permitted to reflect now on how happily all turned out may regard the hazardous sequence of those events with complacence, but for anxious citizens then who were not blessed with that foreknowledge the suspense sharpened until it seemed unbearable. The dedicated advocates of a stronger union were dismayed by the swiftly rising tide of resistance to the proposed constitution. Had they been as fully aware of the opportunity offered Spanish and British territorial designs during those same desperate months by the mounting secession sentiment in the west, they must have been even more deeply disturbed. The national dimensions of the threat were appalling. While the east was resisting union, the west was preparing to abandon the country altogether.

The year opened with a flare of hope that soon proved premature. By January 9th five states, Delaware, Pennsylvania, New Jersey, Georgia, and Connecticut, had ratified without reservations. But from then on doubts and difficulties multiplied. The Massachusetts convention, after nearly a month of violent disputation in which many patriots denounced the Constitution as a fatal threat to personal liberty, made its February 7th ratification contingent on the acceptance by a second national convention of a long list of amendments. Maryland ratified on April 28th and South Carolina on May 23rd. But here the roll call of states came to a nerve-shattering pause. Eight had accepted the Constitution but nine were required before any attempt to organize a new national government could be undertaken. North Carolina was known to be opposed. Virginia and New York were becoming every day more doubtful with the influential figures of Patrick Henry and Governor Clinton leading the opposition. A union that failed to include either of these two great states was foredoomed.

In the west the skies were even darker. No outstanding western leader advocated ratification.[1] The average westerner was much too involved in nearer and seemingly far more vital problems to become greatly concerned with the issue. He had ceased to expect help or even sympathy from the national government, and continued disappointment had reduced toward the vanishing point any sentimental attachment to it he may once have felt. What he most wanted was to be permitted to handle his own affairs in his own way, particularly in connection with his determination to get on with the dispossession and extermination of Indians. In the election of delegates to the various state conventions this attitude was made abundantly clear. In the Pennsylvania convention the frontier delegates from west of the mountains voted 7 to 2 against ratification. In the Virginia convention the Kentucky delegates voted 11 to 3 against. In the North Carolina convention every transmountain county but one opposed ratification.

As a corollary to this suspicious resistance to a stronger union the

[1] William Blount of North Carolina, soon to become an important westerner and already widely influential in the west on account of his land-company interests, favored ratification. He had been a member of the 1787 Congress and of the Constitutional Convention. The New Ohio Company's success in gaining preferential treatment from Congress had led him to conclude that land speculation might enjoy wider opportunity under a stronger central government. He eventually persuaded Robertson to share his views.

proposal to withdraw from it entirely was being discussed with increasing bitterness. The whole west was seething with incipient revolt. The ordinary settler was almost completely uninformed of current developments in the seats of government in his own country and totally unaware of what designs concerning him might be being considered by the even more distant governments of Spain, France, and Great Britain.[2] He was therefore the more ready to accept the guidance of those presumably better informed public figures who had long been neighbors he knew, respected, and trusted. In that supremely critical year, every prominent western leader was advocating some form of secession from the United States even though all fully realized an independent Kentucky, Franklin, or Cumberland must necessarily soon afterward accept an alternative association with Spain or Great Britain.

Wilkinson, reaching Richmond upon his return from negotiating his compact with Miro in New Orleans, was disagreeably astonished to learn of the drafting of the Constitution. Realizing how much a stronger central government might impede the development of his Spanish intrigue, he hurried on to Kentucky where, from the moment of his arrival on February 4th, he devoted all of his extraordinary ingenuity to agitating against ratification and to preparing the minds of his Kentucky adherents for consideration of his secession program. The instant rise in prices precipitated by news of his commercial success in New Orleans gained him an attentive hearing. The embittered Clark, after long brooding over his wrongs, had felt driven to a renunciation of the allegiance he had formerly valued so highly and served so valiantly. On March 15, 1788, he wrote Gardoqui stating his personal conviction "that no property or person is safe under a government so weak and infirm as that of the United States." He requested permission to found an American colony on Spanish territory and offered, if his petition was granted, to become

2 John Brown, recently arrived to take his seat as the Kentucky member of Virginia's delegation to Congress, was writing from New York to George Muter in Kentucky, July 10, 1788: "I have found it almost impossible to transmit a letter to Kentucky, as there is scarcely any communication between this place and that country."

a Spanish subject. Sevier's Franklin troubles culminated February 27, 1788, in an armed conflict with North Carolina adherents under John Tipton in which three men were killed. This humiliating altercation with some of his own former followers, added to the continued refusal of North Carolina and Congress to recognize the State of Franklin, made Sevier the more ready to listen to Dr. James White's proposal that he seek the support of Spain. Eight years of unremitting Indian attack on Cumberland had also driven Robertson that spring to the desperate expedient of suggesting to his chief enemy, McGillivray, that they join forces either in alliance with England against Spain or with Spain against the United States. Thus, of the four men whose long-established reputations enabled them most powerfully to influence western public opinion not one was hesitating to use his standing to turn that opinion away from the United States.

The significance of this tide of dissatisfaction sweeping the west was not lost on Spain or Great Britain and their officials in North America bestirred themselves to take advantage of it. Dorchester entered into a discreet exploratory correspondence with various receptive Americans in New York, Philadelphia, Pittsburgh, and Kentucky. In the east as well as the west there were that year thoughtful and reputable men who had been led by the ineffectuality of the Confederation to the conclusion that American future welfare might be better assured by a return as an autonomous commonwealth to the fold of the British Empire. Dr. John Connolly, who had twice failed to foment a pro-British uprising on the frontier during the Revolution, was meanwhile dispatched to Detroit to organize another attempt. Dorchester's estimate of the reality of the opportunity was supported by the fact that the westward migration during and just after the Revolution had included so high a proportion of dispossessed Tories whose English sympathies could be considered still active. What he could offer western Americans was British military and naval assistance in clearing the Spanish impediment to their navigation of the Mississippi.

What Spain could offer was the reverse of the same coin—Spanish permission to use the Mississippi in return for the west's association with Spain. On April 18, 1788, Gardoqui was writing Sevier: "His Majesty is very favorably inclined to give the inhabitants of that region [Franklin] all the protection that they ask for." Sevier was too occupied at the moment with preparations for an Indian campaign to do more immediately than to give a general encouragement to Gardoqui's emissary, James White, but a similar overture drew a quicker response from the even harder pressed Robertson. McGillivray wrote Governor O'Neill of Pensacola April 25, 1788, that a delegation from Cumberland had informed him that "they woud become Subjects to the King & that Cumberland & Kentucke were determined to free themselves from a dependence on Congress, as that body coud not or woud not protect their persons & property nor encourage their Commerce." Wilkinson had already had his bid accepted and upon his arrival in Kentucky began immediately to take advantage of his personal understanding with Miro by getting off for New Orleans a number of flatboats loaded with tobacco, hams, butter, and tallow in order to prove to his fellow Kentuckians how profitable could be relations with Spain.

For the east the terrible suspense came to an end just before the 12th celebration of the Declaration of Independence. On June 21st New Hampshire ratified and as the ninth state won thereby the distinction of bringing the Constitution into force. On June 25th Virginia ratified by a bare majority of ten. And on July 25th New York, the last of the big states, ratified by the excruciatingly close vote of 30 to 27.

The news that there was a new United States under a new Constitution providing for a stronger national government reached Kentucky July 12th. A young lawyer on his way west, Andrew Jackson, brought the word to Cumberland. But for all the rejoicing it had occasioned in the east it was not news that brought westerners any relief from their suspense. No settler's present plight had been eased nor was he aware that his future prospects had brightened. To the people of western Pennsylvania, Franklin, Kentucky, and Cumberland the new union appeared of possible benefit to easterners but to offer little basis for new expectations west of the mountains. Jackson, as one indication of the prevalent state of public opinion, lost no time adopting a point of view completely and narrowly western. He had scarcely arrived in Nashville before he was participating in the local Spanish intrigue.[3] For Kentuckians the more significant news from the east that summer was that Congress had again refused to admit Kentucky as a state.

What concerned most westerners more than political developments in the east or the devious maneuvers of their own leaders was the stunning increase in the Indian danger. Depredations in 1788 were becoming more numerous, more persistent, and more deadly than during the worst years of the Revolution. The increase in the west's population since the Revolution had served rather to weaken than to strengthen the frontier's defensibility. It had resulted in an expansion of the perimeters of Kentucky and Cumberland that had greatly increased the number of inhabitants occupying those outlying fringes of settlements most exposed to Indian attack. The line of these isolated farms and communities facing outward upon the wilderness had been lengthened by hundreds of miles. War parties from distant Indian towns on the upper Wabash or Maumee were able to cross the Ohio and descend at will upon any point along Kentucky's long northern and eastern borders. Creek and Chickamauga parties from the south were able to strike as freely at Cumberland and at Kentucky's and Franklin's southern borders. The settler who had just lost his home or his family or who had just witnessed such a loss by his nearest neighbor was in no mood to theorize about political or constitutional principles. Were it to be made certain to him that Spain or Great Britain might afford him protection from this continuing torment, he would have considered it totally irrational to reject the offer. His own country had already been proved unable to protect him. In all the long years since the first settler had crossed the mountains the westerner had had always to fight his own battles.

[3] Jackson long remained a rabid westerner who regarded unlimited expansion as the west's overriding objective to be pursued at whatever sacrifice of other considerations. As late as 1806 he was an active supporter of Aaron Burr's project and in 1807 at Burr's trial for treason was his most aggressive defender.

The tiny federal garrisons presently stationed at Fort Harmar at the mouth of the Muskingum, Fort Steuben at Louisville, and Fort Knox at Vincennes, were too weak even to protect their own communications. During the summer of 1788 four of their supply convoys were disrupted by Indian attack.

Of the many outrages perpetrated that spring two in May attracted special frontier attention, not so much by the number of casualties involved as by the degree of Indian perfidy practiced. In the one a minor Cherokee chief, Slim Tom, so long considered peaceful as to be regarded as harmless, called at the cabin of John Kirk, near the present Knoxville, where he had often been befriended and fed. Noting that Kirk and his grown son were absent, he returned with a number of companions and butchered the eleven women and children of the family. That same week Colonel James Brown was on his way down the Tennessee with his large family en route to establish a settlement near Nashville. His boat's loopholed bulwarks, mounted swivel gun, and well-armed crew appeared too strong, as he had foreseen, to invite attack while running the gauntlet of the Chickamauga towns. Instead, a number of prominent Chickamauga hailed the travelers with gestures of friendliness and professions of a wish to trade. When Brown incautiously permitted them to approach they whipped weapons from beneath their blankets and overwhelmed the defenders. Brown, two grown sons, and the five men of the crew were killed. His wife, two younger sons, three daughters, and a Negro woman were taken captive.[4] The twin betrayals of white willingness to fraternize stirred frontier hatred of Indians to a new pitch of fury.

As always in the long and frightful history of frontier warfare, outrage bred outrage. North Carolina had instructed the state's Indian agent, Joseph Martin, to continue his attempts to negotiate improved relations with the Cherokee and had ordered militia com-

---

[4] Mrs. Brown and her daughter, Elizabeth, were ransomed by McGillivray and returned to their relatives in North Carolina. Her son Joseph was later exchanged and guided the combined Kentucky-Cumberland expedition which finally destroyed the Chickamauga towns in September 1794.

manders to refrain in the meantime from offensive action. But Sevier, considering neither himself nor his followers bound by any North Carolina injunction, issued a call for volunteers and embarked upon another of those devastations of the Indian country the Cherokee had for so long learned to dread. His attack was as usual directed against those nearer towns which were more peaceably inclined than those more distant. One of them, however, was Chilhowie, the residence of Slim Tom, murderer of the Kirk family. Major James Hubbard, commander of one of the Sevier's battalions, prevailed upon a group of chiefs to discuss terms with him under a flag of truce. The envoys were led by Old Tassel, head chief of the Cherokee, who had been as long noted as an earnest advocate of peace as had Hubbard been noted as an inveterate Indian fighter. When the Cherokee delegation had entered the Indian house in Chilhowie in which the meeting was ostensibly to be conducted, Hubbard ordered his soldier to block the exits and handed John Kirk, Jr., a tomahawk with the suggestion that the opportunity had arrived to avenge his mother and sisters. Kirk axed the five defenseless ambassadors. Sevier, who was not present, was responsible only in the sense that he had organized the unauthorized expedition. Virginia, North Carolina, and federal authorities denounced the act as a provocation bound to disrupt the already precarious peace negotiations. Governor Johnston of North Carolina issued a warrant for Sevier's arrest under a charge of treason. Even on the frontier, where any blow struck at any Indian was usually applauded, there was disapproval of the murder of the widely respected Old Tassel.

The majority of the main Cherokee nation had subscribed to their fallen leader's peace policy. After his death hundreds of warriors rushed to arms to join their Chickamauga cousins and McGillivray's Creek in a renewed assault on the southern frontier.[5] No outlying

---

[5] Tecumseh, the future successor to Brant and Pontiac as the paramount Indian leader, was visiting his widowed Cherokee mother and participated in a number of these attacks. In one his older brother, Cheeskau, was killed by a schoolboy, Hugh Rogan, during an assault on a log schoolhouse at the outset of which the schoolmaster, George Hamilton, was shot through a chink between the logs while leading the children in song.

settlement from the Watauga through southeastern Kentucky to the western Cumberland was safe. The Holston was confronted by a graver danger than it had known since the great Cherokee invasion of 1776. Among those killed in Cumberland were Colonel Anthony Bledsoe, after Robertson that frontier's most notable leader, and Robertson's son, Peyton. Among principal stations assaulted or besieged were Bledsoe's, Sherrill's, and White's (later Knoxville). Gillespie's was taken and Harman's abandoned.

The Indian offensive obliged North Carolina to sanction some action. Joseph Martin, who had been appointed brigadier general of the state's western militia in the place of Sevier, was instructed to raise whatever force was necessary to restore the situation. But the prolonged dissensions that had accompanied the effort to establish the state of Franklin had demoralized the Holston, formerly the most belligerent and self-reliant of all frontiers. Men who had always before rallied militantly against any threat were now divided, morose, suspicious, unsure of each other's constancy. Many resented Martin's displacement of Sevier. Others considered that his earlier advocacy of a peace policy made him untrustworthy as a commander.[6] The effort to stem the Indian onslaught met serious reverses. Captain John Fain, leading a reconnoitering expedition across the Little Tennessee in an endeavor to learn Indian intentions, was routed near Settico with a loss of 16 killed. In August, Martin assembled a force of nearly 500 men at White's Station for the purpose of striking at the Chickamauga towns, which had so long been the fountainhead of Indian hostility. These were the same mounted riflemen who throughout the Revolution had been irresistible, but in 1788 their morale was no longer the same. When three of their captains were killed in a first brush with the Chickamauga on the slopes of Lookout Mountain, they so completely lost confidence both in their commander and in themselves that Martin was forced to

6 Martin had from his youth been an active and aggressive frontiersman, had in 1769 been one of the first settlers on the Holston frontier, and had for many years been Patrick Henry's friend, associate, and land agent. But he had also often served Virginia and North Carolina as Indian agent and peace commissioner and had married Betsy Ward, daughter of the great Cherokee chieftainess, Nancy Ward.

acquiesce in a headlong retreat. The triumphant Indians redoubled their attacks on the frontier.

Sevier, who had not been permitted even to accompany Martin's expedition, raised a party of volunteers in time to save Sherrill's Station. With his volunteer following increased to 172 and two of his sons as company commanders he thereupon made one of his inimitable dashes into the heart of the Cherokee mountains, driving as far south as the Hiwassee where he burned a number of their towns, including two of their oldest, Ustally and Cootacloohee. But the Cherokee gathered with unexpected belligerence in such overwhelming numbers that he was forced to make a withdrawal as hasty as had been his advance.

To Sevier this near failure was a final disappointment. The Franklin statehood movement was by now in its death throes, with a great majority of the inhabitants sullenly accepting the inevitability of their return to North Carolina's jurisdiction and only those settlers occupying lands in violation of treaties still determined to gain independence. Sevier, rendered for once unwary by an unaccustomed resort to the bottle to forget his many troubles, was arrested October 10th by his old enemy, Tipton, and carried across the mountains in irons. The Indians, flushed by their recent successes and encouraged by the seeming fall of Sevier, sensed the possibility of a victory so decisive that it might at last actually turn back the long advance of the frontier. Upwards of 2000 Cherokee and Chickamauga were joined by 1000 Creek and, separating into small packs, deluged the southern border with a storm of raids. Though the attacks were scattered and unco-ordinated the number of assailants made this eruption one of the more formidable threats to which any frontier had ever been subjected.

During this year when the west was being more plagued by Indian hostility than in any other since the Revolution the national government's Indian policy was as little calculated as its policy of acquiescence in the British and Spanish barriers to counter the west's drift toward secession. There was in this Indian policy a curious ambivalence so irrational as to seem incoherent. In the north, where the Indian menace was made so much more dangerous by the efficacy of the English supply system, Congress continued to insist on immediate territorial cessions certain to provoke general Indian war. In the south, where Indian resistance was handicapped by the uncertainties and timidities of Spanish support, Congress continued to placate the Creek and Cherokee with concessions and favors extended at the expense of settler interests. The two diametrically opposed attitudes had one attribute in common. Both were certain to aggravate western resentment by increasing the pressures of Indian hostility which the frontier was committed to sustain without national aid.

St. Clair at last arrived at Fort Harmar July 9, 1788, to assume his responsibilities as governor of the new Northwest Territory. His first and principal duty was to negotiate the consent of the Indian nations occupying it to a rapid, progressive opening of the region to American settlement. Congress had voted $20,000 to meet the expenses of holding a general Indian conference and to make a token payment for the relinquished land. St. Clair was not long in realizing how insistent were most Indians upon maintenance of the old Ohio boundary, but Congress, hounded by the three land companies proposing to develop their 5,000,000 acres of congressional grants north of the Ohio, continued to insist that he demand the entire area extending to the Miami, the Maumee, and Lake Erie that had been included in the earlier disputed cessions at the Treaties of Forts Stanwix, McIntosh, and Finney. St. Clair dutifully began attempting to persuade the Indians to attend a general conference, reminding them that they had themselves suggested in Brant's address to Congress of 1786 such a meeting to settle outstanding differences.

In August of 1788 Brant for the fourth time since the Revolution came west to reanimate and give guidance to the Indian confederation on the establishment and maintenance of which he had labored so diligently. In the stagnant interval since the firm resolution manifest at the 1786 council Indian union had sadly weakened. At the Maumee council of 1788 opinion was so divided that the Indian confederation fell into complete disarray. Brant himself was so well aware of the realities of international power that he urged conceding something to American demands by giving up a limited area east of the Muskingum which was in any event already within the sphere of American military control. War must be avoided, he argued, for it would become a war the Indians were bound eventually to lose unless they were saved by British intervention, a prospect in which he had little confidence. The large pacifist faction at the council advocated compliance with all American demands and acceptance of whatever presents, payments, and other benefits might be available. The Shawnee and Miami, on the other hand, refused to enter into any negotiations with the Americans and declared their resolve to fight for the Ohio boundary. As the acrimonious discussion continued, Brant's moderation program was denounced by both parties. The peace faction accused him of serving British interests, and the war faction of hoping to curry American favor. Unable to re-establish an Indian united front, Brant eventually advised against Indian attendance at the American conference and himself declined to attend. Since he was unable to speak for all Indians, he was unwilling to compromise his basic contention that only in Indian union was there any hope for Indian survival.

After months of dogged negotiations St. Clair finally assembled at Fort Harmar in mid-December variously accredited delegations representing varying segments of the Seneca, Delaware, Wyandot, Potawatomi, Chippewa, Ottawa, and Sauk. The two most belligerent nations of the region, the Miami and Shawnee, did not attend, and the only important Indian leader present was Brant's Iroquois rival, Cornplanter, the Seneca. Cornplanter haughtily reminded the western Indians that the Iroquois had ceded the northwest to the United States at Fort Stanwix in 1784 and that it was not for them now to question the matter. He supported St. Clair's principal demands and was specifically critical of Brant's efforts to promote Indian unity. "I now tell you," he declared, "that I take Brant & set him down in his chair at home . . . he shall no more run About amongst the Nations disturbing them and causing trouble." Though St. Clair and Cornplanter dominated the conference there ensued

some weeks of argument during which the bewildered and brow-
beaten delegates continued to voice pained protests regarding the
extent of the American demands. St. Clair, however, continued to
insist and was able to dictate the terms of the Treaty of Fort
Harmar, finally signed January 9, 1789, which reaffirmed the earlier
cessions opening to American occupation the greater part of the
present state of Ohio. He conceived that he had won a great victory
in having succeeded in dividing the Indians while fulfilling the letter

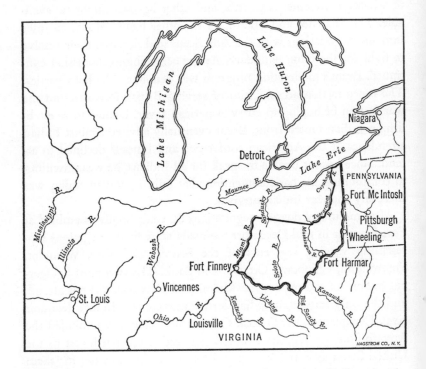

Black line denotes territory demanded of the western Indians in the
treaties of Stanwix, McIntosh, Finney and Harmar. The Continental
Congress assumed no authority to deal with Indians except in areas
outside the bounds of existing states. Long continued Indian insistence
upon the Ohio River boundary was based on their conception of their
occupational rights as originally defined in the King's Proclamation of
1763.

of his territorial instructions. What he had actually achieved was a four-year war on one future field of which he as commander was to meet the most ignominious defeat ever suffered by American arms.

In the south, Congress' conduct of Indian affairs led to equally unpromising developments. After Dr. James White's report of his failure to negotiate peace with McGillivray and his own resignation, Congress, on February 29, 1788, appointed Richard Winn, also of North Carolina, Indian Agent for the Southern Department with instructions to make renewed efforts to achieve peace with the Creek and Cherokee. Winn found McGillivray even more difficult than had White for the sagacious Creek had realized that Bowles' timely arrival had assured him improved Spanish support. The Cherokee, formerly anxious for peace, had been made almost unapproachable by their fury over the murder of Old Tassel. Disconcerted by Winn's reports, Congress on July 15th inquired of Secretary of War Knox what federal force he judged would be required to enforce peace in the southwest. In his reply of July 26th, Knox reported that on account of the "union, leadership and strength" of the Creek he could advise no less than an army of 2800 with artillery and cavalry which would cost a minimum of $450,000 for the first nine months of service. Congress, stupefied by an estimate so much beyond its resources, thereupon resorted to the other extreme of total appeasement with a proclamation September 1st calling upon the inhabitants of the southern frontier to cease aggravating the Indians and to withdraw from Indian lands. The proclamation was accompanied by a resolution of the same date directing Knox "to have a sufficient number of troops in the service of the United States in readiness to march from the Ohio to the protection of the Cherokees, whenever congress shall direct the same; and that he take measures for obtaining information of the best routes for troops to march from the Ohio to Chota, and for dispersing among all the white inhabitants settled upon or in the vicinity of the hunting grounds secured to the Cherokees by the treaty concluded between them and the United States, November 28th, 1785 [Treaty of Hopewell]." The resolution was an absurdly unrealistic gesture which could not conceivably be implemented by troops too few to be sure of holding the northern forts in which they were quartered and represented only an expression of congressional ill temper. It did nothing to improve relations between the United States and the Indians who were absorbed that fall in inflicting as much damage as they could manage on their primary enemy, the settlers. Its one effect was further to poison relations between those settlers and the national government with which they were already so dissatisfied. Men struggling to defend their homes and families were hardly to be gratified by the gratuitous announcement that were federal troops ever to be sent to their frontier they would be sent with orders to defend the Indians.

The miseries and horrors incident to the great acceleration in Indian depredations provided a fertile seedbed for the growth of the secession movement in the west. Every development that summer and fall suggested that events might be rushing toward a crisis. In August, North Carolina, still claiming jurisdiction over Franklin and Cumberland, declined to ratify the Constitution while readily acceding to Robertson's request that Cumberland be henceforth designated the District of Miro as a flaunted demonstration of his and his fellow settlers' Spanish predilection. Andrew Jackson's first public office in the west which he was in time to dominate was to become Attorney General of an administrative area named in honor of a Spanish governor with whom he was already in correspondence. White was on his way to impress upon Spanish authorities at Havana and New Orleans how widespread was the desire of frontier Americans to turn toward Spain. The three most prominent figures on the southwest frontier were currently giving striking support to White's assertions. On September 2nd, Robertson was writing McGillivray that in his frank opinion the west must ultimately join whatever nation controlled the Mississippi. On September 17th, Sevier in a letter delivered in person by his son James was writing Gardoqui: "The people of this region have come to realize truly upon what part of the world and upon which nation their future happiness and security depend, and they immediately infer that their interest and prosperity depend entirely upon the protection and liberality of your government." On November 8th, Joseph Martin was writing McGillivray, "I hope to do honor to any part of the world I settle in, and am determined to leave the United States, for reasons that I can assign to you when we meet, but durst not trust to paper."

In this mounting crisis the issue hinged on the action of Kentucky. Were its great preponderance of the west's population[7] to move toward secession, it must carry with it Franklin and Cumberland and possibly western Pennsylvania as well. Whatever was to be its decision Kentucky was face to face with the necessity of making it. Its Sixth Convention was scheduled to assemble July 28th.

Gardoqui in New York and Miro in New Orleans were striving, each according to his own lights, to abet the hoped for secession of the west. Gardoqui had rebuffed Clark's colonization offer, to avoid antagonizing Wilkinson, but was warmly encouraging George Morgan's similar scheme with which Wilkinson was almost as dissatisfied. Gardoqui was also cultivating John Brown, Kentucky's newly arrived member of Virginia's congressional delegation.[8] According to Brown's confidential letter of July 10, 1788, to trusted Kentucky friends, George Muter and Samuel MacDowell, the gist of Gardoqui's proposal was his assurance "in the most explicit terms that if Kentucky will declare her independence, and empower some proper person to negotiate with him, that he has authority, and will engage to open the navigation of the Mississippi . . . But that this privilege never can be extended to them while part of the United States."

Miro was poring over Wilkinson's request that he be furnished a slush fund of $18,700 which if distributed judiciously among 21 Kentucky "notables" of his selection would, Wilkinson asserted, unquestionably bring about early secession. Among those on his list

---

[7] Kentucky's population had by contemporary estimate passed the 60,000 mark by midsummer of 1788.

[8] Brown came of distinguished frontier lineage. His mother was a daughter of William Preston who on New River had been among the earliest of transmountain settlers and as Fincastle surveyor more responsible than any other man for the opening of Kentucky in 1773–74.

characterized by Wilkinson as "confidential friends who support my plans" were Harry Innes, Attorney General, John Brown, member of Congress, and Caleb Wallace and Benjamin Sebastian, district judges. Among those described by Wilkinson as favoring "separation from Virginia and an amicable agreement with Spain" were Benjamin Logan, famous pioneer, and Isaac Shelby, later the first governor of Kentucky.[9]

Members assembling for the opening of the Sixth Convention were immediately infuriated by the coincidental arrival of news that Congress had again, this time indefinitely, postponed consideration of Kentucky's admission. The brutal increase in Indian attacks during the last months had further strained Kentucky's forbearance. The convention therefore met in an atmosphere offering every opportunity to the advocates of secession. If the smoldering movement were ever to be kindled into a blaze then the time was surely at hand. What did transpire has been disputed ever since. As in most conventions the more important decisions were reached not in public sessions but in private conversations and secret caucuses. By the time questions came to a recorded vote they were carried unanimously as a consequence of predetermined agreements. What may have led to the achievement of these agreements led in turn to an historic controversy among Kentucky writers of Kentucky history that persisted for generations. A whole literature grew up dealing with disputed interpretations of what had actually occurred in those backstairs conferences at the two conventions that summer and fall at Danville. To it many participants, their sons and their grandsons, have contributed acrimonious volumes.[10] One party to this literary controversy fiercely maintained that with the exception of Wilkinson and possibly Sebastian no single Kentucky leader ever swerved even for a moment from his loyalty to the United States. The other as

[9] Miro was sufficiently impressed by Wilkinson's bribery prospectus to recommend to Madrid that the money be made available, and in 1789 Wilkinson was advanced $7000 as a private loan to use as he saw fit.

[10] Humphrey Marshall was the most partisan accuser in his two-volume *History of Kentucky*, Frankfort, 1824. A reasoned rebuttal may be found in Temple Bodley's introduction to the Filson Club reprint of *Littell's Political Transactions*, Louisville, 1926.

fiercely asserted that an entire clique of Kentucky's most prominent citizens was engaged in a cunning and diabolical conspiracy to snatch Kentucky from the arms of the United States and cast it into the arms of Spain.

The controversy gained heat as the years passed by the failure of the disputants to distinguish between the meaning of loyalty to the union after it had functioned successfully under the administration of half a dozen presidents, and the meaning of loyalty in 1788. In 1788 the Constitution was being violently opposed in conventions in Boston, Richmond, and New York by national leaders of greater experience and renown than any member of any Kentucky convention. As a political institution the government of the United States was still an experiment. Any man's patriotism was measured not by his devotion to the rule of an American central government but by how earnestly he had served the rebellion against English rule. The average citizen's primary political attachment was to his native state. Loyalty to country had not yet had time to become an inborn sentiment in either east or west. The westerner's attitude toward the nation was further tempered by his compulsion to consider first the safety of his home and family. A convention of Kentucky, or Franklin, or Cumberland, composed of delegates of his own election, appeared to him more responsive to his needs than could be a distant Congress or a novel Constitution. This instinct to think first of his own welfare and that of his children and his neighbors was as natural as the singleness of purpose with which he defended his stockade against Indian assault. Events finally demonstrated that any westerner—Sevier, Robertson, Clark, Morgan, perhaps even Wilkinson—would have preferred maintaining ties with his fellow countrymen in the east. But the west was under such pressures of necessity that these relations had to prove of mutual and reciprocal advantage. Simple, unwavering loyalty, as defined in later years, was a luxury westerners could not then afford. Realization that the west's interests were distinct from those of the east had progressed until a fairly general middle-of-the-road opinion, widely and openly discussed in 1788, held that it was no more than sensible to threaten to secede or

to turn to Spain or England even if for no other purpose than to
force the east to give more consideration to the west. The records
are too scanty and the evidence too confused to determine which of
the many Kentuckians who in 1788 were venturing near that perilous line were actually prepared to cross it.

One fact stands out. At neither 1788 convention was a resolution
proposing secession introduced or the question formally and publicly
considered. Wilkinson's influence in Kentucky was then at its zenith.
He was the dominant figure in both conventions and in both served
as chairman of the committee of the whole in which most business
was transacted. He had publicly opposed ratification and to many
trusted followers had privately advocated secession to be followed by
association with Spain. But he did not press his program in open
session upon either convention. Various explanations have been advanced to account for his restraint: (1) His trading privileges were
more profitable so long as they remained exclusive, and he had
therefore no wish to accelerate a move toward Spain that would
require him to share them sooner than necessary with fellow Kentuckians. (2) He had been made aware by private polls that if put
to the test of a recorded vote he could not gain the convention's support for his Spanish program. (3) He had been hoodwinking the
Spaniards for money and still remained at heart a loyal American.
His own contemporary testimony sheds little light on his actual
motives. His voluminous reports to Miro on his manipulation of the
conventions merely strove to give the impression that, given time
and sufficient money, he was certain soon to succeed in bringing
about Kentucky's secession.

The principal recorded action of the Sixth Convention was the
unanimous adoption of a resolution drafted by Wilkinson recommending that the people of Kentucky elect delegates to another
convention to meet in November with renewed authority to deal
with the independence question. The most significant statement of
the resolution was in its phrase, "do earnestly recommend to the
good people . . . that they delegate to their said representatives full
powers . . . to do and accomplish whatsoever, on a consideration of

the state of the district, may in their opinion promote its interests." By his adroit wording of the resolution Wilkinson had continued to reassure both his Spanish patrons and those dissident Kentuckians who were becoming suspicious of his Spanish sympathies. The former he could remind of the next convention's power to "accomplish *whatsoever*" was needed to promote Kentucky's interests and the latter he could remind that independence for Kentucky was contemplated so that it might the sooner become a *"member* of the United States of America."

For months before the July convention there had been much angry though vague talk of the possibility that continued refusal of admission might drive Kentucky to the extreme of declaring itself independent of the United States as well as Virginia. After the convention this talk for the first time took the turn to an uneasy discussion of the possible advantages, after independence, of an association with Spain or Great Britain. Along with the public's discussion there was growing speculation on how many prominent Kentuckians might already be secretly committed to such a course. During the interval between the conventions two events gave immediacy to the discussion.

The first was the arrival of Brown's letter detailing Gardoqui's offer which was, as Brown had intended, discreetly shown to many important Kentuckians.[11] In his letter Brown had expressed no personal opinion of the Spanish proposal but the care he had taken to give it circulation indicated his conclusion that it merited consideration. Brown himself arrived in Kentucky, the Continental Congress having ceased to exist with its final adjournment October 21st, in time to attend the November convention. Whatever his attitude in private conversations, he began publicly to advocate immediate independence from Virginia as the most effective step possible toward

[11] There was another item in the letter bound to have an effect on current opinion in Kentucky. Brown had written: "I fear, should not the present treaty at Muskingum prove successful, that we shall have an Indian war on all our borders. I do not expect that the present congress will in that case be able to take any effectual measures for our defence. There is not a dollar in the federal treasury which can be appropriated for that purpose."

gaining greater consideration from the new congress when it assembled.

The second was the active entry of another foreign power into
the contest for Kentucky's favor. Dr. John Connolly arrived in
Louisville while the election of delegates was under way and began
interviewing prominent Kentuckians with a view to convincing
them that Great Britain was a more appropriate protector than
Spain.[12] In a letter to Washington of February 12, 1789, Colonel
Thomas Marshall, after detailing his suspicions of Wilkinson's and
Brown's allegedly pro-Spanish activities, informed him of Connolly's offer to assist Kentucky in opening the Mississippi, quoting
him as stating: "Lord Dorchester was cordially disposed to give us
powerful assistance, that his Lordship had (I think he said) four
thousand British troops in Canada, beside two regiments in Detroit,
and could furnish us with arms, ammunition, clothing and money;
that with his assistance, we might possess ourselves of New Orleans,
fortify the Balize at the mouth of the river, and keep possession in
spite of the utmost efforts of Spain to the contrary." Among the first
Kentuckians Connolly contacted was Wilkinson, who listened to
him with apparent sympathy and interest as a prelude to the establishment of secret relations with British authorities in Canada which
he maintained for years. Wilkinson took care meanwhile to keep
his Spanish welcome warm by immediately informing Miro of Connolly's design. As a result of Connolly's visit, Dorchester was able
to report to his government April 11, 1789, that a Kentucky committee of correspondence had been organized. With the report went
a memorial, written in Wilkinson's familiar style, welcoming any
move against Spain and remarking on the range of common interests between the Americans in the west and the English in
Canada. It was probably true that most westerners, moved by consideration of language and religion, would have been better able to

[12] St. Clair's intelligence system was already so well developed that he learned
promptly that Connolly had reached Detroit, that his instructions from Dorchester
had been accompanied by an advance of 200 pounds and that he had departed for
Louisville, enabling St. Clair to order Major John Wyllys, commander of the Fort
Steuben garrison, to keep Connolly under surveillance while he was in Kentucky.

stomach a consort with England than one with Spain. England's long standing alliance with the west's Indian enemy remained, however, an unsuperable barrier.

At its Seventh Convention, assembling November 3, 1788, in an atmosphere of tense excitement after an agitated election of delegates, Kentucky faced at last its moment of truth. Wilkinson's personal domination of the convention's proceedings was even more evident than at the July session. Its every decision and resolution was reached under his guidance after receiving his public if not his private approval. Yet neither the secession nor the Spanish cause was advanced, though this fortunate development became apparent only after maneuvers so devious and confusing that they provided new fuel for the future fires of controversy over the true sentiments of the convention's principal delegates.

At the outset the convention reiterated the stock demands made at every former convention for separation from Virginia and admission as a state. Brown then proposed immediate independence from Virginia, with or without Virginia's consent or congressional approval, as a means to force later recognition and admission. Wilkinson successfully moved that this be tabled and read to the convention the greater part of his Memorial to the King of Spain, thus turning the delegates' attention from the present disadvantages of nonadmission to the future advantages of a Spanish connection. He then called upon Brown to inform the convention of Gardoqui's proposal to him. The obviously startled Brown, apparently unprepared for this public revelation and possibly unwilling to serve as Wilkinson's cat's-paw, stammered that it had been a private and confidential communication. Every major delegate had been given an earlier opportunity to read the letter, however, and realized what Wilkinson was bringing to the convention's attention and why he was doing it. Surely the moment had now come, if it was ever to come, for Wilkinson to press for secession and a formal overture to Spain. Instead he allowed the convention to come to an end without accomplishing a nearer approach to his Spanish program than a flamboyantly worded resolution demanding navigation of the Mississippi, another stating "that this convention highly approve" his Spanish Memorial, and with the calling of another newly instructed convention the following August under a resolution stating that "the discordant opinions which at present divide the good people" represented by this convention rendered it doubtful whether it could "adopt any plan which will embrace the opinions of all, or even secure the support of a majority."

If Wilkinson had hoped to accomplish more he had at any rate again taken care to have all couched in language enabling him to impress upon his Spanish masters the diligence with which he was working in their interest and the many difficulties inherent in his task.[13] On the surface of its formal record the Seventh Convention by its votes on these several resolutions appeared to have evaded coming to any decision. Actually the people of Kentucky had come to a supremely important one. By the unanimous vote of their recently elected and newly instructed representatives they had chosen to reserve final judgment until the new government of the United States under the Constitution had begun to demonstrate whether it might prove able to function more successfully than had the old one under the Confederation. A decision more vital to the future of the United States could not have been taken. The west had not yet been won but neither had it in this most critical of all the nation's years been lost. The union would meanwhile remain still intact until the new national government had had time to prove itself.

Memorable as had been 1788's succession of sensational events—the narrowness of the margin by which the Constitution had been ratified, the expressed readiness of every western leader to rebel, the evolution of the Spanish conspiracy, the manifestation of Great

13 St. Clair, though not present, was equipped with well developed facilities for collecting Kentucky information. In a letter of December 13, 1788, to Secretary for Foreign Affairs John Jay he made the flat statement: "It is certain, sir, that in the last Convention a proposal was made that the district of Kentucky shall set up for itself, not only as independent of Virginia, but of the United States also, and was rejected by a small majority only." Presumably St. Clair was referring to a private poll of delegate sentiment which may have convinced Wilkinson that a formal secession proposal could not be carried.

Britain's Mississippi design, the hesitation of the Kentucky conventions to vote secession, and the appalling increase in Indian hostility coupled with the imminence of a general Indian war—another
event had a more significant bearing on the west's future and therefore on the nation's. There was so pronounced an acceleration in the
movement westward of new settlers that the year came to be known
at the time as the Year of the Great Migration. On June 15th Harmar reported that his officers' official census of Ohio River travel
had counted during the spring "308 boats, 6,320 souls, 2,824 horses,
515 cattle, 600 sheep, 9 hogs and 150 wagons." He added, "the emigration is almost incredible." There had been a proportionate increase in the movement over the Wilderness Road. A new and more
direct road was being opened to Nashville, facilitating the migration
to Cumberland. Indian attacks, stimulated by the increase in opportunity, had likewise multiplied, taking a savage toll on all three
routes, but such numbers were in transit that the great majority
reached their destination.[14]

A striking feature of this Great Migration of 1788 was the first
crossing of the Ohio, an event in the westward movement almost as
significant as the first crossing of the mountains. It constituted not
only a direct challenge to the allied Indian nations of the northwest
whose military power had been manifest since the victories of Pontiac but a challenge as well to Britain's imperial designs in the
northwest based on British support of the Indians and British military presence in the Lake posts. Almost as striking, the initiative in
this first crossing of the Ohio was taken not by the Virginians or
North Carolinians who had spearheaded every former thrust into
the wilderness but by New Englanders who had always before been
indifferent or opposed to the westward movement.

The New England advance, unlike any of its turbulent predecessors, was planned, organized, managed, and premeditatedly legal.
These provident and practical newcomers were even armed with

---

[14] As one example, the party with which Andrew Jackson was traveling west
escaped Indian attack by a night march taken at his suggestion. The party immediately following was annihilated.

a sense of history. They christened the boat carrying their first company of settlers *Mayflower* as a mark of their realization that they were engaged in another momentous beginning on a wild, strange shore, and their first town *Marietta,* in honor of the soon to be martyred Marie Antoinette of France, as a mark of their gratitude for French aid during the Revolution. There were 48 persons in this first settlement, founded April 7th at the mouth of the Muskingum just across that stream from the protection of Fort Harmar. From the outset the New Englanders conducted their affairs with a becoming regard for classical precedent, legal formality, and religious observance. The field before the stockade was called *Campus Martius* and the main street of the settlement *Sacra Via.* The clergyman was considered as important an official as the governor or the sheriff, and all official occasions were accompanied by prayers. The institution of self-government was regarded with special solemnity and when on September 2nd the first court was held the historic moment was celebrated with processions and pageantry.

This second landing of the *Mayflower* was followed before the end of the year by another crossing of the Ohio, this one a much less orderly settlement of the site of the present Cincinnati under the auspices of Territorial Judge John Cleve Symmes, heading a group of New Jersey speculators which had undertaken the purchase of a tract from the Ohio Company.[15]

Important as were these first lodgments north of the Ohio they were made by only a handful of settlers compared to the main rush of the 1788 migration headed for Kentucky and Cumberland. Unlike earlier westward surges most were families without former frontier experience. All must have gained some advance idea of the hazards they were accepting. Still they persisted and their very unpreparedness for the shocks they sustained provided further testimony to the inherent fortitude of the pioneer temperament. Many of this new generation of settlers were also men of some substance.

---

[15] This settlement was originally named Losantiville, signifying the town (ville) opposite (anti) the mouth (os) of the Licking (L) by John Filson, the first historian of Kentucky. He was killed by Indians in October while surveying nearby.

The day of the more primitive frontier family, trudging over the mountains with a sack of seed corn and all else they possessed on their backs, had passed. Every partial count of the 1788 migration mentioned the number of cattle and horses and wagons. There was further evidence of how many men of property were beginning to come west in the contemporary estimate that of the population of Kentucky in 1788 nearly 20 per cent were slaves. This characteristic of the post-Revolutionary westward movement is historically as significant as the unique character of the earlier movement, led by men in buckskin almost as well suited to the wilderness as the Indians they were defying. A whole people was now on the move. The readiness of substantial citizens already successfully established in a familiar and congenial environment to pull up roots and venture into distant and totally different surroundings on the chance of finding wider opportunities remains probably the trait that most distinguishes Americans. The experience of no other country offers a parallel. Upon this readiness has most depended the phenomenal momentum of the country's development.

A chief effect of the westward surge of nonfrontier people in the late 1780's was a further dislodgment of the original frontier people. The majority of these later comers were armed with land titles or the money to buy them while the earlier of their predecessors had come before such legal devices were available. Evictions were general but whether dispossessed or not the real frontier people tended to move on. They had crossed the mountains and then kept on to Kentucky or Cumberland in a quest for that greater personal freedom which could only be enjoyed were they to gain what they termed "elbow room." They had accepted the perils of a wild environment because every danger was accompanied by the reward of escape from the interfering demands of ordinary society. With the increase in population during the 1780's the reappearance of these demands renewed the unease of the earlier and more primitive settlers who had known frontier conditions since the days of their grandfathers and who had learned to prefer isolation and freedom to comfort and safety. They resumed their probing advance outward and onward into the wilderness, sifting into disputed Indian territory across the Ohio or the Tennessee or southwestward and westward into Spanish territory in a new pulse of the westward movement that would soon carry them as far as western Missouri and eastern Texas. They were continuing to perform their historic function as the irresistible vanguard of national expansion, continuing to serve, as they had for a generation, as the sharp, tough teeth of the saw that was cutting the path of empire.

Another principal consequence of the west's population increase was its effect on the frontier's attitude toward the east. By the late 1780's, 250,000 people had found residence west of the mountains in the westward extensions of Pennsylvania, Virginia, and North Carolina. These represented a scant six per cent of the nation's total population. But they were so separated from the vast majority of their fellow countrymen by distance, by the mountain barrier, and by economic, social, and political differences that there was among them very little disposition to feel that they were necessarily subject to the will of that majority, along with a deepening realization of how many needs and interests they shared only with each other. The combined impulses of a quarter million headstrong, opinionated, and violent-tempered people most of whom as individuals had long been accustomed to independent action constituted a formidable force. The west had become well aware that it was no longer obliged to beg the east's consideration. The time had come either to demand it or to renounce it. The danger that the west might seek its own destiny by the establishment of a separate and independent nation in the Mississippi Valley had by no means passed with the collapse of Franklin and the continued restraint shown by the several Kentucky conventions, while numbers had given its people a mounting sense of self-sufficiency.

The unforeseen rapidity of the west's population increase had also augmented the external danger by requiring Spain, France, and Great Britain to realize that unless their long-term designs on the Mississippi Valley were to be abandoned they must be promptly activated. At the close of 1788 the over-all western pattern of threatened secession, annexation, and war, not only with Indians but possibly also with foreign powers, presented mortal dangers to the infant republic whose former government under the Confederation had passed out of existence and whose new government under the Constitution was as yet untried. Again and again during the next fifteen years the issue would appear to be in doubt. They were dangers only eventually to be countered by the inspired leadership and statesmanship of Washington and Jefferson.

XIII

&

Washington

A little after noon on April 14, 1789, Charles Thomson, veteran Secretary of the Continental Congress, standing in the dining room at Mount Vernon, delivered to Washington the certificate of his election as first President of the United States. On April 16th Washington started north to assume his enormous responsibility, entering the moment in his diary as, "About ten o'clock I bade adieu to Mount Vernon, to private life, and to domestic felicity, and with a mind oppressed with more anxious and painful sensations than I have words to express, set out for New York."[1]

The public acclaim with which he was greeted at every step of his journey soon relieved his worst forebodings. All was in welcome contrast to his lonely mountain expedition less than five years before when he had so nearly despaired of his country's survival as a united nation. The cheering throngs swarming about him in Alexandria, Baltimore, Philadelphia, Trenton, and New Brunswick were testifying unmistakably not only to the people's acceptance of him as their leader but to their acceptance of the national government that he personified. The wild enthusiasm of his New

---

[1] The February 3–September 30, 1789, portion of Washington's diary has been lost. The quotation is from Jared Sparks, *Writings of Washington*. Boston, 1836.

York reception completed his reassurance. On May 9, 1789, he was happily writing Philip Schuyler: "That invisible hand which has so often interposed to save our Country from impending destruction, seems in no instance to have been more remarkably excited than in that of disposing the people of this extensive Continent to adopt, in a peaceable manner, a Constitution, which if well administered, bids fair to make America a happy nation."

Beyond the foreground adulation, however, loomed problems of excruciating complexity. The most pressing of these was posed by the west. Washington, himself almost a westerner, had not become guardian in chief of his country in order to preside over the loss of that immense and infinitely valuable region. Yet the threat of so grievous a loss was fearfully apparent from the moment he took office and remained his primary concern throughout both his terms. With the perspective of his wide experience as commander and statesman he could see that the danger in the west was a three-headed monster of a nature with which it was peculiarly difficult for a new and weak nation successfully to cope. The triple peril was composed of the continuing brush war with the Indians, complicated by the possibility that the extreme dissatisfaction of the American inhabitants might lead to a civil war, and further complicated by the developing undeclared war being waged upon the United States by foreign powers. He was confident that the first two threats could be managed, with any luck. The brush war could be controlled, given time, as the overwhelmingly superior power of the United States could eventually be brought to bear. The civil war could be avoided, given time, by more judicious attention, the moment that became practicable, to the needs of the west. But the demands of the undeclared war were immediate. The longer it lasted, the greater the likelihood that some incident might provoke an unlimited war which the United States, without the French support which had underwritten victory in the Revolution, could not hope to win. Yet the United States, with an empty treasury[2] and no more than a

[2] Washington himself, in order to put his affairs in a shape to permit him to leave Mount Vernon, was obliged to seek a loan of 600 pounds, a recourse, he wrote, "I never expected to be driven to—that is, to borrow money on interest."

token military establishment, was compelled to continue to tempo-rize. Even though Spain and Great Britain were in military occupa-tion of large portions of American territory, including positions on the Great Lakes and the lower Mississippi which gave them strangle-holds on the west, the new American government's resources were too limited to contemplate making any attempt in the foreseeable future to eject either by force. Meanwhile, both were taking advan-tage of Indian hostility and western disaffection to advance their rival designs on the Mississippi Valley. As a result all three chal-lenges were inseparable, with each inflaming the other two. Never during the worst hours of the Revolution had Washington been confronted by a situation more perplexing or vexatious or that would to any other man have seemed more discouraging.

He had had enough frontier experience to understand the frontier temperament and to realize the lengths to which western resent-ment might be driven. In 1784 he had voiced the opinion that "the touch of a feather might turn them away." Since then he had been in frequent correspondence and consultation with many westerners. In recent months he had received the notable letters from George Morgan and Thomas Marshall reporting in detail on the unrest in Kentucky. He was continuing to receive reports from Marshall by way of a correspondence conducted, at his own suggestion, in cipher. He was spared a certain knowledge, however, of the extent of the secret relations between many western leaders and Spain or of how deeply committed were several of the most important to foreign intrigues. These individual involvements had not been exorcised by the ratification of the Constitution or Washington's accession to the presidency. The day after he was notified of his election James White arrived in New Orleans to acquaint Miro with all the de-tailed intricacies of the frontier's anomalous attitude toward Spain. While Franklin collapsed, Sevier had on February 17th taken his oath of allegiance to North Carolina, but the southwestern frontier was still rebellious. As late as September 2, 1789, Robertson was writ-ing Miro:

We have just held a convention which has agreed that our members shall insist on being Separated from North Carolina. Unprotected, we are to be obedient to the new Congress of the United States; but we cannot but wish for a more interesting connection. The United States afford us no protection. The district of Miro is daily plundered and the inhabitants murdered by the Creeks, and Cherokees, unprovoked. For my own part, I conceive highly of the advantages of your Government.[3]

Before the end of the year Wilkinson had made a second journey to New Orleans, composed a second Spanish memorial, and had returned to Kentucky with two mule loads of silver. Morgan had established his Spanish colony at New Madrid and gone on to New Orleans to confer with Miro. Clark, after Gardoqui's rebuff, was taking an opposite tack, inviting even more hazardous consequences, by undertaking to raise an irregular army of Kentuckians to attack Natchez and New Orleans.

Though unaware of the full extent of these foreign and domestic intrigues, Washington's judgment that it was not yet too late to compose the national government's differences with the west was being nevertheless justified by events before the end of 1789. Wilkinson, Sevier, Robertson, White, Morgan, and Clark were all in the course of being disillusioned by the hesitations and vacillations in Spanish policy, dictated by Madrid, which had made it impossible for Miro or Gardoqui to meet their overtures with a sufficiently concrete response to give any promise of real advantage to either party. A new definition of imperial policy from Spain's Council of Ministers, received by Miro in March 1789, expressly directed him to refrain from any overt action calculated to foment insurrection in the American west, to reduce American frontier animosity by lowering the tariff on American goods to 15 per cent and in certain cases to 6 per cent, and to facilitate the migration of American settlers into Spanish territory. Spain's long-held fears of an armed

[3] In a letter of July 7, 1789, to his confidential associate, Daniel Smith, Robertson had indicated that his Spanish approach was a desperate last resort from which he would be happy to withdraw were Cumberland to be granted adequate protection by the United States.

invasion by American frontiersmen had prompted this resort to appeasement, and the same uneasy care to avoid offense remained Spanish policy until after American defeats in the Indian war two years later.

One result of Madrid's decision was to strip Wilkinson of the exclusive trading and colonizing privileges he had sought and to relegate him to the role of Spain's secret agent in Kentucky. The immense fortune that had seemed at his fingertips had again eluded him, and he was compelled to look to the American government for employment. He remained meanwhile in the Spanish service, being furnished a steadily increasing amount of secret-service funds to be used for the subversion of his fellow Kentuckians.

Other political tensions in the west and southwest had begun to relax in 1789 even before the new central government had undertaken any steps which might affect frontier conditions. Franklin became a romantic memory. North Carolina ratified. The Eighth Kentucky Convention, of which Wilkinson was not even a member, loudly protested Virginia's land and militia laws but then peaceably adjourned after another patient reiteration of the demand for recognition and admission. During Washington's first months in office the danger that the west might attempt to secede thus had lessened, but as a direct consequence of the continued delay in any final political adjustment the greater danger that the west's general intransigence might provide an opening for foreign intervention had increased.

This danger was enormously aggravated by Indian hostilities, presenting the policy dilemma which necessarily became Washington's first and principal concern. Upon Indian behavior and his government's reaction to it hinged every other development in the west, including the explosive threat that at any moment the United States could be involved in a war with Spain or Great Britain or both. He was better able than anyone else in the national government to comprehend the peculiar complexities of wilderness warfare. His early military experience had included five years of campaigning in a war in which Indian participation had been the major element.

Upon assuming the presidency he was briefed on the current Indian situation[4] by Henry Knox since 1785 Secretary of War for the Continental Congress and slated to continue in that post in Washington's administration. Through all of his five years in office his most important duty had been the conduct of Indian affairs. He had been Washington's commander of artillery in the Continental Army, long his personal and trusted friend, and the two had maintained a constant correspondence since the Revolution. To no one, after Hamilton, was Washington prepared to listen with more attention. Knox prefaced his report with a penetrating observation on the political and moral issues involved:

> Most of the nations of Indians within the limits of the United States are, at present, discontented, and some of them turbulent . . . An inquiry would arise whether . . . the United States have a clear right, consistently with the principles of justice and the laws of nature, to proceed to the destruction or the expulsion of the savages. The Indians being the prior occupants, possess the right of the soil. It cannot be taken from them unless by their free consent, or by the right of conquest in case of a just war.

His report to the President then came to grips with the realities involved in a resort to war, just or otherwise. To subjugate the Miami, the only northern Indian nation openly and actively belligerent, he estimated, would require an army of 2500, compared to Harmar's existing force of less than 600 of which only 400 were available for a field campaign. To raise the additional 1900, he continued, would "require the sum of $200,000, a sum far exceeding the ability of the United States to advance." In the south, any attempt to subjugate the Creek, he had advised Congress the year before, would require another army of 2800 which when added to the northern requirement reached a total altogether out of the question. He could therefore only recommend that the United States con-

---

[4] The immediate pressures on the southwestern frontier had been somewhat relieved January 9, 1789, by an attack by Sevier and his volunteers on an Indian encampment on Flint Creek near Jonesborough. The ensuing battle in the snow developed into the bloodiest engagement of the southern Indian wars. Sevier reported having buried 145 Cherokee and his own loss as 5 killed and 16 wounded.

tinue to attempt to negotiate the best treaties possible with any Indians who could be persuaded to confer, in the face of the fact that all treaties so far negotiated had failed to satisfy either Indians or settlers or appreciably to diminish border hostilities. This compulsion to treat instead of fight, he implied, must be expected to prevail until, in the north, the British could be persuaded to turn over the Lake posts, and, in the south, Spain could be persuaded to cease arming the Indians and McGillivray be persuaded to adopt a more amenable attitude toward the United States.

Washington had on many former occasions been obliged to practice patience and he had more need than ever for patience now. There appeared no escape from the harsh conclusion that for some time to come the frontier people must be left unaided, whatever their sufferings and no matter how much the failure of the new national government to come to their rescue might impede a final solution of the western problem. His first use of the treaty powers of the Senate was to ask its ratification of the former treaties made under the authority of the Continental Congress with the northern Indians. This was little more than a gesture since the majority of the Indians concerned had repudiated all of them and there was as little prospect that new treaties seeking an Indian renunciation of the Ohio boundary would prove more effective. Meanwhile, Indian attacks on the Kentucky, Virginia, and Pennsylvania frontiers and on Ohio River traffic were continuing to increase. Miami, Shawnee, and visiting Cherokee were particularly active but groups of anti-pacifist warriors from every northern nation frequently participated.[5] According to William Littell's contemporary estimate, more Kentuckians were killed by Indians in 1789 than in any former year.

There appeared to Washington and his advisors, however, a faintly brighter opportunity for achieving something by diplomacy

[5] On the day Washington's arrival was being cheered in New York, Indian raiders were attacking a settlement as far east as the Monongahela in an area which had been originally settled 20 years before. In his letter of condolence to Governor Beverly Tucker of Virginia on May 16, 1789, Washington wrote: "The Governor of the Western Territory, who is here, will soon return to the frontiers, and he will, in conjunction with the commanding officer of the troops, take such measures with the . . . refractory tribes as the occasion may require, and the public situation admit."

in the south. McGillivray's supremacy made it possible to deal with one literate and rational man instead of, as in the north, with a hundred lesser chiefs from nearly as many nations. If his territorial dispute with the Georgians could be resolved, there was just a chance that he might be weaned from his Spanish alliance and his three-year-old war against the American southwestern frontier brought to an end. In the Presidency's first collaboration with the Senate's constitutional role in the conduct of foreign affairs, Washington gained that body's advice and consent to the appointment of a peace commission to negotiate with the Creek chieftain. It was composed of figures of no less national reputation than Benjamin Lincoln, the Revolutionary general who had accepted Cornwallis' sword and more recently had suppressed Shays' Rebellion, Cyrus Griffin, last president of the Continental Congress, and David Humphreys, a member of Washington's household soon to become Minister to Portugal and then Minister to Spain.

Distinguished as were the commissioners, they failed to impress McGillivray. Having ascertained that they were not empowered to offer important concessions, he abruptly broke off negotiations and abandoned the conference at Rock Landing on the Oconee without even the courtesy of leave-taking. His insulting defiance was emphasized by his subsequent destruction of the Doughty expedition. Major John Doughty, the most competent of Harmar's officers, was in command of the first employment of federal troops on the southern frontier. He had ascended the Tennessee from the Ohio with a small expedition to guard the establishment of a trading post requested by the Chickasaw, alone among Indian nations in electing to become allies of the United States. Given advance information of the project by Doughty's friend, Wilkinson, and irritated by this American intrusion into his sphere of influence in which it was his policy to maintain Panton's trading monopoly, McGillivray dispatched a band of Creek and Chickamauga warriors to intercept it. Of Doughty's little force of 15 regulars, 6 were killed and 5 wounded and he was forced to seek ignominious sanctuary with the Spanish commandant at New Madrid.

The exasperated commissioners returned to New York to recommend the raising of an army of 4250 and the erection of 6 border forts as the only recourse if McGillivray were to be brought to terms. Congress had no disposition to undertake any such effort and as yet no resources upon which to draw even were it disposed to act. The nearly total lack of military force continued to lie at the heart of Washington's problem in casting about for some way to cope either with the Indians or their Spanish and British sponsors. According to Knox's report to Congress of August 8, 1789, the entire federal establishment consisted of 76 men in two companies stationed at West Point and at the arsenal at Springfield, Massachusetts, and of 596 men stationed in various posts along the Ohio and Wabash. On December 31, 1789, he further reported his estimate that the army could be increased to 5000 at an annual cost of $1,152,836, to 1600 at a cost of $196,507, and to 840 at a cost of $126,956. Congress continued to balk at any except the lowest figure. Aside from the deterrent of cost the post-Revolutionary aversion to a "standing army" was still a strong political prejudice. Before adjourning September 29th, Congress went only so far as to accept theoretical responsibility for the national defense to the extent of recognizing the military establishment inherited from the Confederation as the Army of the United States. Washington's hand was at the same time somewhat strengthened by authorizing him to call upon the militia of the states in important emergencies. The year 1789 closed with but one other perceptible improvement in the nation's military posture, the establishment of a new regular army post on the Ohio, Fort Washington, at the site of the present Cincinnati. During the first nine months of the new national government's conduct of affairs, no distracted frontier family had been given reason to feel safer than under the old one, no Indian nation had been given pause, and the west appeared as open as before to every foreign design.

Washington's first message to Congress, January 8, 1790, was devoted almost exclusively to the frontier's sufferings under Indian attack and to the desperate need to rebuild the nation's military establishment. "To be prepared for war," he sternly reminded Congress, "is one of the most effectual means of preserving peace." Congress, largely composed of members whose primary concern was for the mercantile, shipping, fishing, and financial interests of the east, paid little heed to his admonition.

With Washington's firm hand at the helm ensuring popular confidence, the authority of the national government was in 1790 nevertheless beginning to gain internal recognition in the west as well as the east. In January and February, St. Clair made a tour of that portion of the Northwest Territory not controlled by Indians or British, setting up county governments under the provisions of the Ordinance of 1787, a process which gave the old French communities at Vincennes, Kaskaskia, and Cahokia some semblance of the law and order they had not enjoyed since the first intrusion of American settlers upon their former peace and quiet. On July 26th the last Kentucky Convention met to discuss the organization of a state government with the comforting assurance that Virginia was in full agreement and that the new Congress was committed to admission. Meanwhile, on February 25, 1790, North Carolina at last, and this time without reservations, had ceded that state's western lands to the United States, completing the process initiated north of the Ohio by New York and Virginia during the Revolution. As a consequence Congress was able on May 20th to establish the Southwest Territory as a companion piece to the Northwest Territory. The long-troubled Holston and Cumberland thus became a national responsibility and were afforded the same theoretical protection of the central government that had been extended the national territory north of the Ohio by the Ordinance of 1787. Henceforth it was the federal power of the United States which was in direct confrontation with the intrusions of Spanish and British power on both the southwestern and northwestern frontiers.

Washington's administrative appointments in the newly established Territory were shrewdly devoted to the healing of many old wounds. Blount was made its Governor and Superintendent of Indian Affairs for the southwest, and Sevier and Robertson brigadier generals of its militia. Whether Washington was fully aware of the recent relations of the three with Spain and was therefore calculatingly striving to restore their interest in their country's service is not clear. At any rate, the process of rewarding with federal preferment the more prominent leaders of the west's disaffection was continued in Kentucky where Wilkinson's associate, Harry Innes, was appointed federal judge and Wilkinson himself, the following year, commissioned a lieutenant commandant in the Army of the United States.[6]

This momentary improvement in defense conditions on the southwest frontier was climaxed by what appeared on the surface a sensational triumph. Determined to make a further effort to negotiate with McGillivray, Washington persuaded Marinus Willett, the outstanding Revolutionary hero of New York's border wars, to become his unofficial emissary to the Creek chief. McGillivray was gratified to have his favor sought by so noted a soldier who was also Washington's personal representative and by Willett's earnest suggestion that he pay a state visit to the American president. The two hit it off from the outset, each soon acquiring a respect for the other's intentions. McGillivray was made more receptive by the recurrent weakening of Spanish support and by the new anxiety in Miro's pleas that he avoid carrying his resistance to settler encroachment to the point of provoking a war with the United States. The sagacious Creek had decided that Spanish appreciation of the value of maintaining Creek independence as a buffer between Spanish and American territory might be reinvigorated were he suddenly to appear to be seeking an arrangement with the Americans. Washington had received little recent good news and was therefore the more pleased by the word July 1st from Willett that he was on his way north accompanied by a delegation of 30 Creek "chiefs and kings," headed by McGillivray himself. Washington hastily dispatched a warning to Willett to be on guard against a Spanish secret agent, Carlos Howard, armed with $50,000 in available bride funds,

6 James O'Fallon, in the midst of his Yazoo dispute with the national government, wrote Washington in September offering to spy on Wilkinson in the national interest.

who was known to be likewise en route to New York with presumed instructions to interfere with the negotiations.

McGillivray's own conception of his place in history had been strikingly expressed in his letter of April 8, 1787, to James White: "I aspire to the honest ambition of meriting the appellation of preserver of my country, equally with those chiefs among you, whom, from acting on such principles, you have exalted to the highest pitch of glory." Even so he was astounded by the warmth of his New York welcome. As the alarmed Spanish agent, Josef de Viar, reported to his government, McGillivray and his entourage "were received hardly less highly than royal persons." New York had not been so excited since the arrival of Washington at the end of his inaugural journey. Salutes were fired, bells rung, cheering crowds thronged the streets. The Tammany Society entertained the visitors with an elaborate night-long dinner at the City Tavern, attended by a host of officials including even congressmen from the traditional Creek enemy, Georgia, in the course of which the guests of honor performed a wildly applauded dance and McGillivray was enrolled as a member of the Society. The main delegation was quartered, appropriately enough, at the Indian Queen Hotel, but McGillivray was Knox's house guest where his chronic ill health was in sad contrast to the hearty appetites of his 280-pound host and his 250-pound hostess. Washington received him repeatedly, stood beside him at a military review staged in his honor, and personally escorted him on a visit to the merchantman, *America,* a rival object of current public interest by reason of its having just returned from a trading voyage to Canton, China.[7]

Pleased as was McGillivray with the generosity of his reception and disturbed as he was upon reaching New York to learn of the apparent imminence of a war between Spain and Great Britain

---

[7] That same August, Captain Robert Gray in *Columbia* returned to Boston by way of Cape of Good Hope after a trading venture to the Northwest coast and China, thus becoming the first American captain and American ship to circumnavigate the globe. In 1792 on his next voyage he identified and named the Columbia River. The American public was more familiar with accounts of the farthest shores of the Pacific than with the reports on the interior of their own continent.

which could leave the Creek isolated, he nevertheless drove a hard diplomatic bargain. In the Treaty of New York, signed August 13, 1790, first by Knox, then by the 30 Creek delegates, and finally by Washington, in the presence of an attentive congregation of officials and congressmen, McGillivray relinquished Creek claims to the narrow strip on the Georgia border between the Oconee and the Ogeechee so stubbornly occupied by settlers and acknowledged the sovereignty of the United States over that portion of the Creek country which might prove to lie on the American side when the Spanish-American boundary was finally determined. But he declined to renounce either his Spanish connections or the trade monopoly enjoyed by his friend and partner, Panton, and he extracted Washington's assurances that the federal government would oppose such land-company operations in the southwest as the Yazoo project. In conformance with secret articles in the treaty he was commissioned brigadier general, appointed United States Agent to the Creek, and granted an annual salary of $1500.

In submitting the treaty to the Senate for ratification, Washington described it as the "main foundation of the future peace and prosperity of the southwestern frontier of the United States." Actually, McGillivray had merely recognized previously existing conditions and far from weakening his position had materially strengthened it. The thoroughly alarmed Spanish authorities renewed their protestations of support, and Madrid hastily authorized Miro to pay him $2000 a year and to double this amount, if necessary, "since he is at the same time being courted by the United States and the English." The diminution of Indian hostilities on the southwestern frontier lasted but a few months. The most favorable result of the treaty was the impression made on public and congressional opinion. The prestige of the national government was dramatically enhanced by this demonstration that Washington's administration was capable of coping with the diplomatic maneuvers of foreign powers.

The momentary improvement in the south, however, was more than balanced by a drastic deterioration in the situation in the north. Indian refusal to admit the legitimacy of the Treaty of Fort Harmar had become general and adamant. Indian depredations were becoming unbearable. Harmar's weak garrisons were being further weakened by hunger and desertion. St. Clair made one more effort to draw the Indians into renewed negotiations. American emissaries could not be employed since they could not safely venture into the Indian country. As a last resort, St. Clair persuaded Antoine Gamelin, a respected French trader of Vincennes, to make an attempt to reopen diplomatic relations. From April 5th to May 8th Gamelin traveled from one Indian town to another, visiting the Miami, the Shawnee, and the Kickapoo and gathering evidence on the sentiments of the Delaware, the Potawatomi, the Ottawa, and the Chippewa. He reported upon his return that the Indians were convinced that the Americans harbored only aggressive intentions and that they would consent to further discussions only if the Americans came to Detroit to conduct the conversations in the presence of the British commander there. The Miami gave gruesome point to their scorn of this final American peace overture by burning an American captive after Gamelin's conference with them.

All through the early summer St. Clair was bombarded with reports of Indians attacks. "Every day, almost, brings an account of some murder or robbery," he wrote Knox. The raids ranged from Marietta, where the New Englanders were becoming imbued with a thoroughly western aversion to Indians, to Carpenter's Station, within 12 miles of Danville, Kentucky's provisional capital, to the vicinity of Kaskaskia, where French inhabitants who had for three generations lived at peace with the Indians were being made to suffer by their association with Americans. Attacks were most prevalent on river traffic, including two on Harmar's supply convoys in which a total of 11 were killed or wounded and 8 taken captive. In another on the Wabash, Francis Vigo, the widely esteemed Italian trader who had in 1779 brought Clark information on Lieutenant Governor Hamilton's occupation of Vincennes, was despoiled by Indians under the initial impression that they had intercepted St. Clair.

After having been authorized by Congress to call up state militia in case of necessity, Washington had on October 6, 1789, in turn authorized St. Clair to call out western militia in the event such a recourse seemed imperative. This delegation of authority was made necessary by the many weeks required for the passage of communications between the seat of government in New York and the far reaches of the west. Washington had accompanied his militia authorization, however, with the injunction that an offensive campaign against the Indians "ought to be avoided by all means consistently with the security of the frontier inhabitants, the security of the troops, and the national dignity." Aware of his responsibility in making so weighty a decision, St. Clair was nevertheless convinced by the result of the Gamelin embassy that a solid counteroffensive offered the one hope of putting an end to Indian attacks on the long-suffering settlements. Hurrying from Kaskaskia to a conference with Harmar at Fort Washington, on July 15, 1790, he issued a call for 1500 Kentucky and Pennsylvania militia to man an expedition to be commanded by Harmar and spearheaded by his regulars. Having with the fervent approbation of Kentucky got the organization of this project under way, he hurried on to New York to confer with Washington and Knox.

Washington, who had served with Braddock and Forbes[8] and had himself for years commanded Virginia's frontier defense, was equipped with a painfully acquired understanding of the extreme hazards invariably associated with any military expedition into the Indian country. But in this instance the greater hazards of involvement in a foreign war overhung every wilderness peril. The Nootka controversy[9] between Great Britain and Spain had developed to a point leading every foreign office in Europe to consider war between them inevitable. In such a crisis the British were bound to consider an American expedition into the Indian country either as a direct move against the Lake posts or a preparation for making American

8 Major General Edward Braddock had in 1754 been utterly routed by Indians. Major General John Forbes had in 1758 lost most of a Highlander regiment to an Indian surprise attack.

9 See p. 148 n.

support available to Spain.[10] The threat of involvement in the north was compounded in the south by the preparations of O'Fallon and Clark to mount an expedition of Kentucky frontiersmen against New Orleans with the loudly announced expectation of receiving the British military assistance from Canada promised by Connolly in 1788. If Clark's preparations developed to the assault stage or if British forces advanced across American territory against Spanish positions on the Mississippi, war with Spain was inevitable. If, on the other hand, the British passage was resisted or if British forces resisted an American advance into the Indian country, then war with Great Britain appeared as unavoidable.

Washington called one of his rare cabinet meetings to ask his department heads for their opinions in writing on this bristling array of threats and problems. He made similar requests for the opinions of Chief Justice Jay and Vice President Adams. The advice he received was hopelessly conflicting. Jay felt that under the country's present circumstances any alternative was more acceptable than war. Adams would refuse permission for the crossing of American territory by British forces but would hope to avoid war by refraining from any resort to force to prevent such a crossing. Secretary of War Knox urged the President to wait and see what developed before attempting to come to any decision. Hamilton and Jefferson were more forceful and definite than the others but as usual they contradicted each other. Secretary of the Treasury Hamilton admitted that a British land and sea assault upon Spanish possessions in the Mississippi Valley, even if there were no violation of American territory, must result in a loss of the American west to Great Britain. Westerners who had been on the verge of turning to alien and Catholic Spain to gain freedom of the Mississippi could not be expected to hesitate to turn to familiar English cousins to gain not only that freedom but freedom from Indian attack. Since a British military incursion could not in any event be successfully resisted,

---

[10] Dorchester was informing his government that this was his interpretation of the American preparations and urgently requesting an immediate reinforcement of 4000 soldiers to meet the prospective attack.

he advocated making the best of so unfavorable a situation by entering into an alliance with England against Spain in the expectation of gaining a cession of East Florida to the United States as a partial compensation for the loss of the west. Jefferson, who had returned from France in March to become Washington's first Secretary of State, was much more perturbed by the dangers of British encirclement. British control of the shores of the Great Lakes, the Mississippi, and the Gulf represented, in his view, a totally unacceptable curb upon the future development of the United States. He advocated armed resistance to any British intrusion and if necessary an alliance with Spain against England in the hope of being able to extract as a reward the cession of both Floridas and New Orleans. The extraordinary dangers envisaged by every advisor accentuated the special risk inherent at so critical a moment in the Harmar campaign.

Having listened carefully to all these warnings, Washington nevertheless refused to recognize any such limitation on the nation's freedom of action and determined to proceed as though only American issues were involved. What was to him the most unacceptable of all was that the killing of American citizens by savages should be permitted to proceed one moment beyond that moment when his government appeared to be able to make at least an effort to put a stop to the practice. He directed St. Clair to go ahead with the Harmar expedition but to attempt to reduce the English war risk by getting off an official communication to the British commander at Detroit assuring him that the campaign was devoted solely to the punishment of marauding Indians. On August 26th he dealt with the Spanish war risk by issuing a proclamation denouncing the O'Fallon-Clark project and demanding "all officers of the United States, as well civil as military, and all other citizens and inhabitants thereof, to govern themselves according to the treaties and act aforesaid, as they will answer the contrary at their peril."

These precautions proved sufficient. Disconcerted by the proclamation, O'Fallon and Clark waited for Britain to move. British authorities in Canada, conscious of their own military weaknesses on their western frontier, were relieved by St. Clair's disavowal of aggressive intentions. British and Spanish moves in the west were suspended while awaiting the outbreak of war. Harmar alone did not wait. Before the end of the year there came the announcements from Madrid and London that Spain had bowed to the English ultimatum and that war between those powers had been for the moment averted. Washington had not had that comforting assurance, however, when he had faced up to his difficult decision.

A peculiarly aggravating feature of decisions in those days of retarded communication was the prolonged waiting to learn the consequences. Weeks and months passed without word from or of Harmar. Washington, in Mt. Vernon for a brief vacation during the congressional recess, became increasingly disturbed by the lack of news and then troubled by premonitions of disaster. Stories of Harmar's drinking had lowered his never very high opinion of that general's military capacities. In a letter of November 19th to Knox he referred to the possibility that the expedition had come to some "disgraceful termination." Upon his return to Philadelphia, once more the nation's capital, he delivered his second message to Congress on December 8th, still without direct word from Harmar. What had meanwhile occurred in the west was worse than any of Washington's fears.

XIV

༞

War in the West

In the familiar American stereotype of Indian warfare the appearance of regulars galloping to the rescue invariably provides a happy ending. In 1790 the first deployment of regulars in a field campaign in American history provided, instead, a most unhappy beginning. Washington had decided that in the face of whatever international hazard the national government was obliged to make some effort to relieve the sufferings of the country's western inhabitants. A passive defense of the endless frontier line by stationary troops was impossible no matter how many might be raised for the purpose. The one alternative, therefore, was to strike so painful a blow at the Indians' homeland as to instill in them respect for the authority of the United States.

The point selected for attack was the group of Miami towns clustered about the portage between the Maumee, the St. Joseph, and the Wabash rivers. This long noted area, the site of the present Fort Wayne, was a hub of wilderness communications. From it radiated trails and waterways to Lake Erie and Lake Michigan, to the lower Ohio and the Mississippi by way of the Wabash, and to the middle Ohio by way of the St. Mary's and the Great

Miami. This nine-mile portage and the fourteen-mile portage at Niagara were the only land links in the tremendous water route stretching more than 2500 miles through the center of the continent from the mouth of the St. Lawrence to the mouth of the Mississippi. Its location made it a trading center from the earliest days of the French occupation. Fort Miami, built to guard the portage, had been destroyed by Pontiac in 1763. Hamilton had used the portage in his descent upon Vincennes in 1778. It had always been a position of more strategic importance than any other between the Ohio and the Lakes. This importance was underlined in 1790 by the location here of the principal towns of the Miami, since the Revolution the most recalcitrant and belligerent of all Indians.

Knox's final instructions of September 14, 1790, to St. Clair and Harmar were detailed and explicit. While acknowledging that the establishment of a permanent fort at the portage would prove of immense usefulness in maintaining control over the Indians, he ruled such an effort beyond the present resources of the United States. The essential purpose of the expedition, he directed, was "to exhibit to the Wabash Indians our power to punish them for their positive depredations, for their conniving at the depredations of others, and for their refusing to treat with the United States when invited thereto" and to demonstrate this power "by a sudden stroke, by which their towns and crops may be destroyed."

To reduce the risk that authorities in Canada might consider the British position so threatened by Harmar's advance as to lead them to oppose it, St. Clair on September 19, 1790, wrote Major Patrick Murray, Detroit commander:

> I am commanded by the President of the United States to give you the fullest assurance of the pacific disposition entertained toward Great Britain and all her possessions, and to inform you, explicitly, that the expedition about to be undertaken is not intended against the post you have the honor to command, nor any other place at present in the possession of the troops of his Britannic Majesty, but is on foot with the sole design of humbling and chastising some of the savage tribes whose depredations are becoming intolerable, and whose cruelties of

late become an outrage not on the people of America only, but on humanity.

Harmar began gathering his army at Fort Washington, with September 15th the date set for the militia to assemble. Nothing went right. He had no little reason for that resort to alcoholic comfort which his detractors asserted was his custom. The contractors failed to produce supplies either in the amounts required or at the times scheduled. Pennsylvania furnished but a fraction of its militia quota. The quality of the more numerous Kentucky militia was disappointing. The original self-reliance of communities which had formerly taken for granted their ability to hold their lodgments in the wilderness had been diluted by the more recent migrations. There were among Harmar's militia levies relatively few of the hardy and pugnacious frontiersmen of the sort who had proved their mettle by their defense of the border during the Revolution. Most seasoned borderers remained behind to guard their constantly threatened homes on Kentucky's outer frontier lines. The greater proportion were more recently arrived easterners who had had little experience with either the wilderness or the Indians. Many came to the muster at Fort Washington with broken or useless guns or without any weapon. There was a strong disposition, reminiscent of the border in 1754, to feel that war was not a responsibility of citizens and that professional soldiers should attend to the more serious fighting. Bitter jealousies developed between regular and militia officers. Every one of the First Regiment's officers, aside from Harmar himself, was nominally outranked by the swarm of county colonels. Having dealt as well as he could with all of these difficulties, Harmar marched on September 30th with a force consisting of 320 regulars and 1133 militiamen, of which nearly a third were mounted.

In all former such organized invasions of the Indian country the greatest danger apprehended had been from Indian surprise attack as an unwieldy and slow-moving white army pressed deeper into

WAR IN THE WEST
1790-94

Ft. Mackinac

Lake Huron

Lake Michigan

Niagara

Detroit

Lake Erie

Maumee Rapids
Fallen Timbers
Fort Miami

Auglaize

Harmar's Defeats
Fort Wayne   Fort Defiance

Fort Mc Intosh

Allegheny R.

Legionville

Scott &
Wilkinson Raids

Ft. Recovery
(Site of St. Clair's Defeat)
Fort Greenville
Fort Jefferson
Fort St. Clair
Ft. Hamilton

Maumee R.

Great Miami R.
Little Miami R.
Scioto R.

Muskingum R.

Pittsburgh
Wheeling

Marietta

Fort
Harmar

Cincinnati
(Ft. Washington)

Monongahela R.

Mississippi R.

Missouri R.
St. Louis

Cahokia

Kaskaskia

Wabash R.

Vincennes
(Ft. Knox)   Ft. Steuben

Ohio R.

Louisville

Gallipolis

Limestone

Licking R.

Kentucky R.

Kanawha R.

Fort Massac

New Madrid

Cumberland R.

Tennessee R.

Cumberland R.

Holston R.

HAGSTROM CO., N.Y.

the wilderness. It was Harmar's one stroke of good fortune that his
was subjected to no such hazard. British intelligence in Canada,
largely dependent on Indian and trader hearsay, was notoriously
inefficient. Reports reaching Detroit placed Harmar's numbers as
high as 8000 and were hastily circulated, without verification,
among the Indians thought to be so fearfully menaced. St. Clair's
message to Murray had lent added weight to the assumption that
the Americans must be so strong that they were quite willing that
the Indians be given advance notice that they were coming. These
exaggerated warnings led the Indians to abandon any attempt to
resist an invasion ostensibly so formidable. After a laborious two-

week march, Harmar approached his objective, increasingly puzzled by the lack of opposition. The Miami, unsupported by their allies, had withdrawn into the forest, and he was able to occupy the area without the firing of a shot. Their five largest towns were burned and some twenty thousand bushels of corn destroyed. There had still been no fighting. The only evidence that there might be Indians in the surrounding woods had been the theft of so many of the army's horses that Harmar's further movements were hampered.

There was keen disappointment in all American ranks that they had made so great an effort and come so far without having succeeded in bringing the Indians to battle. Colonel John Hardin, the most experienced and respected of Harmar's militia officers, who had served with Morgan's Rifles and on the Pittsburgh frontier during the Revolution, gained permission to make a reconnaissance in force on the chance of forcing an engagement upon the elusive enemy. The Indians had meanwhile been studying the invaders and had come to the conclusion that they presented by no means so fearsome a threat as they had been led to suppose. They had the further advantage of being led by a hitherto unknown Miami war chief, Little Turtle, who was for the next four years to demonstrate capacities as an Indian commander second only to those manifested in the past by Brant and Pontiac. He managed to reassemble a small force of the scattered Miami and awaited his opportunity. When Hardin had advanced several miles, Little Turtle struck him with a surprise attack by whooping horsemen supported by encircling warriors on foot firing from the forest's cover. The sudden ear-splitting din of war cries, war whistles, and gunshots proved too much for the inexperienced militia. At the first impact they broke and fled back to the main army's camp. The small detachment of regulars with Hardin, standing its ground, lost 22 out of 30. Of the fleeing militia 70 were pulled down by the pursuing Miami.

In spite of his dissatisfaction with this misadventure Harmar felt compelled by his rapidly worsening supply and transport situation to begin his withdrawal without further delay. At the first evening encampment at the end of an eight-mile march the still bellicose

Hardin persuaded Harmar to permit him to return to attack the Indians who could be expected to have begun reoccupying their ruined towns. The next day, October 22nd, Hardin set out with a striking force of 340 militia and 60 regulars. Again he found the encounter he sought. Again the militia proved useless. Again the regulars stood alone and were cut to pieces. Harmar thereupon resumed his homeward march. The Indians who had in neither engagement numbered more than a hundred did not pursue.

Harmar, though he had lost 183, including 79 hard to replace regulars, considered that in burning the Miami towns and granaries he had relieved the frontier by permanently discouraging Indian belligerence. St. Clair reported to Knox that the operation had been "an entire success" and a "terrible stroke" from which the Indians would be long recovering. Actually the Indians had instead gained the impression that they had won a great victory. The American army on the Ohio had for years remained in Indian estimation an unknown and therefore threatening quantity. Its cannon and uniforms and drums and trumpets were devices of which Indians with their respect for all indications of military proficiency had taken anxious note. Now at last they had met that army in combat. On fields where the Indians were outnumbered five to one they had driven the Americans in panic-stricken flight, had killed them easily and by the score, and had themselves suffered insignificant losses.

In December the nations of the Ohio–Great Lakes region met in general council at the falls of the Maumee to assess the Harmar campaign's effect on their situation. Alexander McKee, who as Deputy Indian Superintendent was in immediate and active control of Britain's Indian affairs in the west, took a prominent part in the proceedings. In Quebec and London official British policy with respect to the Indians and the Lake posts was outwardly still as amorphous as during Brant's 1786 visit to England. In his public pronouncements Dorchester was still urging the Indians to make their peace with the United States, warning them not to expect British troops to march into American territory to their assistance, and yet at the same time reminding them that they had every justification for insisting on their territorial rights which he reaffirmed had in no way been abridged by the peace treaty between the United States and Great Britain. But McKee, in his personal representation of British policy at the Maumee council, indulged in no such hair-splitting. He reminded his Indian hearers that they would never be safe until they had driven the American intruders back across the Ohio and assured them that they might be certain of every sort of military support short of direct intervention by the British regular army. The few delegates still advocating renewed negotiations with the United States were silenced by the majority's clamor for war.

Instead of waiting as was their custom for spring, the Indians in their exultation over Harmar's reverses launched a series of attacks the first week of January on the thin fringe of settlement north of the Ohio. All outlying settlers were driven to the sanctuary of stockades, hounded by the same bitter necessity so familiar on the border since 1754. Among Indian successes was the first destruction of a New England settlement, Big Bottom, near Marietta, where 11 men, 1 woman, and 2 children were killed and 3 men taken. An attack on Dunlap's Station near Cincinnati attracted special frontier attention by the peculiar horror of an accompanying atrocity. When the station, with the aid of a detail of 18 soldiers from Fort Washington, successfully resisted the assault of 300 Miami led by Simon Girty, the Indians burned a white captive, Abner Hunt, so near the walls that the appalled defenders were obliged for many hours to watch his writhing and listen to his screams. Other parties struck across the river at the borders of Kentucky, Virginia, and Pennsylvania. The range and intensity of these operations were making it distressingly apparent that the military result of Harmar's campaign had been to stimulate rather than to discourage Indian belligerence. The impact of this development was described in a January 2, 1791, letter of Rufus Putnam at Marietta to Washington as:

> Thus, sir, the war, which was partial before the campaign of last year, is, in all probability, become general. I think there is no reason to suppose that we are the only people on whom the savages will wreak their vengeance, or that the number of hostile Indians have not

increased since the late expedition. Our situation is truly critical . . .
The garrison at Fort Harmar, consisting at this time of little more
than twenty men, can afford no protection to our settlements, and the
whole number of men, in all our settlements, capable of bearing arms,
including all civil and military officers, do not exceed two hundred
and eighty-seven, and these, many of them, badly armed. We are in
the utmost danger of being swallowed up.

Now for the first time it was New England settlers who were
writing of the frontier's perils to their relatives and friends in the
east. New England members of Congress became immediately more
conscious than they formerly had been of federal responsibility for
defense of the west and of the need for a stronger federal army. On
March 3rd Congress, with a sudden surge of new regard for what
Washington had termed "the national dignity," voted to increase
the army by one regiment of regulars and two regiments of six-
month levies and to authorize Washington to call into service as
large a number of militia as he deemed necessary. Eastern public
opinion, which so long had been inclined to hold that the frontier
people's troubles with Indians had been a natural result of their own
unprovoked aggressions, had been given a more combative turn by
the revelation that the first military enterprise undertaken by the
United States had met humiliation at the hands of a pack of savages.
There was general approval in the north as well as the south of the
new and more militant preparations. St. Clair was recommissioned
major general, his Revolutionary rank in the Continental Army, and
while continuing as governor placed in personal command of the
new effort. Nothing was to be spared to make his invading force so
powerful that this time there could be no question that Indian resistance would be crushed.

After consultations with Washington, Knox, and congressional
committees, St. Clair started west in April to undertake the organization of his campaign. Congress had meanwhile directed one more
effort at negotiation. Colonel John Proctor, Revolutionary veteran
and Philadelphia politician, was dispatched to the Iroquois to engage
their protection and sponsorship in order to make possible the ex-

tension of his embassy to include a visit to the belligerent western nations. The Iroquois were thought to be receptive to this resort to their good offices. They had been more than reasonable at the treaties of Fort Stanwix and Fort Harmar. The previous December a gregarious Iroquois delegation had paid a festive visit to Philadelphia, and Cornplanter had delivered an address to Congress in an atmosphere of mutual good fellowship. But the Iroquois had been disturbed by St. Clair's ill-advised request that they furnish him a corps of warriors to serve against their fellow Indians, the Miami, and by the recent territorial demands of New York and Pennsylvania. Proctor was rebuffed by the Iroquois, denied permission to continue his journey westward by the British commander at Niagara, and returned to Philadelphia in June to report the failure of his mission.

Knox had also endeavored in May, through Governor Clinton of New York, to enlist Brant's assistance in reopening negotiations with the western Indians. Dorchester had at almost the same moment besought him to use his influence with them in the British interest. Brant's own only consideration was the Indian interest. The policy he urged upon his fellow Indians never varied. Perpetually he counseled them to unite and to reflect. In the early summer of 1791 he rushed west to address councils at Sandusky and Detroit. He deplored the rising war spirit among the western Indian nations. He implored them to tighten their confederation so that they might the more effectively negotiate with the United States. He warned them against being overimpressed by the reverses they had inflicted on Harmar. He reminded them that a war with the United States was not, however many battles they won, a war that they could ever finally win. So desperately expeditious was his journey and his mission that by August 17, 1791, he was back in Quebec reporting to Dorchester that he had succeeded in persuading "the Confederated Western Indians" to consider peace with the United States on the basis of a compromise boundary, if it were hereafter to be "inviolably observed," running up the Ohio to the Muskingum, up that river to its headwaters, and east from there to the already recognized borders between Pennsylvania, New York, and the Iroquois.

This belated Indian consent to negotiate was already too late, however, for the war in the west had already been resumed. Kentucky, with its rapidly increasing population, was stirring with new energies. The references to Kentucky's importance in Washington's message to Congress, the February 4, 1791, vote of Congress for Kentucky's admission, and the appropriation of federal money for Kentucky's defense had aroused public enthusiasm. There was interest in Clark's still projected New Orleans expedition[1] but a greater interest in striking back at their Indian tormentors. Kentucky's self-esteem had been wounded by the misconduct of Kentucky militia in the Harmar campaign and its people were demanding an opportunity to restore their martial prestige. Washington had vested responsibility for raising Kentucky's militia for the Indian war in a committee consisting of Brigadier General Charles Scott, John Brown, Harry Innes, Isaac Shelby, and Benjamin Logan, and a preliminary fund of $10,000 had been made available for the purpose. Handicapped by delays in the organization of his main army, St. Clair gave the impatient Kentuckians permission to embark independently on preliminary operations.

Toward the end of May, Scott, who had lost one son in a 1787 Indian raid and another in the Harmar campaign, marched against the upper Wabash towns with a militia force of nearly 1000. He met no opposition, burned several towns, and killed or captured a few nonbelligerent Wea and Piankashaw who had failed to escape in time, but was prevented by supply difficulties from pressing his advantage. Wilkinson had been his second in command and late in July, now himself a brigadier general of militia, led an expedition of 500 mounted militiamen against several more distant Wabash

---

[1] On March 19, 1791, Washington had issued a second proclamation denouncing the Yazoo project, declaring "whereas it hath been represented to me that James O'Fallon is levying an armed force in that part of the State of Virginia which is called Kentucky . . . it is my earnest desire that those who have incautiously associated themselves with the said James O'Fallon may be warned of their danger."

towns. He likewise met no opposition and killed or captured 42 Indian men, women, and children his horsemen had succeeded in overtaking.

Neither expedition had accomplished any significant military purpose other than to provide the militia with a needed training exercise. Wilkinson's conduct of his operation was regarded so highly, however, that he was offered a commission as lieutenant commandant in the regular army which, having been driven close to bankruptcy by the failure of his private enterprises, he was glad to accept. He promptly petitioned Miro for an increase in his Spanish secret-service payments on the grounds that his new rank in the Army of the United States placed him in a position where his services might prove of even greater value to Spain.

Brant had scarcely started back to report to the Iroquois at Niagara and to Dorchester at Quebec on his efforts to promote a more temperate Indian attitude in the west when the effect of his mission was destroyed by the Scott and Wilkinson expeditions. The most pacifist or cautious Indian was convinced that the Americans were determined upon continued aggressions. Brant's and McKee's otherwise conflicting advice had meanwhile coincided insofar as both had been urging the Indian need to unite. Under the pressures of the self-evident emergency the Indian confederation gained de facto authority. In council, minorities were for the first time accepting the will of the majority. Military coherence accompanied political coherence. By his successes against Harmar, coupled with his forceful personality and his readiness to accept responsibility, Little Turtle was gaining recognition as the outstanding Indian commander upon whom every nation might most surely rely in the developing war. He had refrained from premature interference with the militia expeditions of Scott and Wilkinson, correctly judging these to be no more than large-scale raids which could have no more significant bearing on the war than to arouse his Indian followers to the gravity of their danger. His attention remained fixed on St. Clair's preparations. The crisis he awaited was the northward march of the Army of the United States and he husbanded Indian capabilities for that hour of decision.

St. Clair's preparations were being embarrassed by every sort of delay that can compromise a military operation. The War Department supply system depended upon arrangements made with private contractors. All of them failed to fulfill their commitments. Recruiting had been equally mismanaged. St. Clair had asked for 1000 Kentucky militia though he would have been satisfied, on account of his supply difficulties, with 750. But only 300 had appeared before he marched from Fort Washington September 17th. He would have been more disturbed by this militia deficiency had not the nature of his campaign forced him to place his chief reliance on the regular army. His major objective was the establishment of permanent forts in the Indian country which could only be garrisoned by the permanent military establishment. But he was having as much trouble with his regulars as with the militia. Recruiting officers had filled his Second Regiment with the combings of eastern slums and jails. The arrival of his two regiments of six-month levies had been so delayed that the enlistments of many were expiring during the opening days of his campaign. He was most of all handicapped by the lack of assistant commanders with combined military and wilderness experience. Harmar had demanded a court of inquiry and when exonerated by it in September resigned from the service. The famous Kentucky militia commanders, Scott, Wilkinson, Logan, and Hardin, whose reputation might have inspired the army with more confidence, remained at home. In their view this was to be primarily a performance staged by the regulars with the militia consigned to a minor role. St. Clair's great dependence was necessarily, therefore, on his second in command, Major General Richard Butler, the senior officer in the regular army after Harmar's resignation. Butler came of a noted frontier family, had had long wilderness experience as an Indian trader, and was a veteran soldier whose Revolutionary service had included significant participation in both the Saratoga and Yorktown campaigns.

St. Clair's basic campaign plan, approved by Washington and Knox, involved the construction of forts at thirty- or forty-mile intervals during the northward march so that at its conclusion there would exist a chain of centers of American military power extending from the Ohio into the heart of the Indian country. After the construction of Fort Hamilton, at the present Hamilton, Ohio, the army moved forward to commence, October 12th, the construction of Fort Jefferson, near the present Greenville, Ohio. The march was again resumed October 24th.

Slow as had been the expedition's progress, it had only been achieved by a constant struggle against agonizing difficulties. The contractors had been so criminally remiss that the army was perpetually hungry. The season was so late that forage for the horses which earlier had been plentiful was frostbitten. As winter neared, the weather which had been bad became steadily worse, with freezing storms of rain, hail, sleet, snow. Conventional military order was impossible to maintain among untrained troops commanded by company officers of little more training. Resort to floggings and hangings failed to improve discipline. As the six-month enlistment periods began to expire, men insisted upon discharge. Desertions, particularly from the militia, multiplied until they were occurring by groups of thirty and sixty. St. Clair was finally forced to send his best corps, the First Regiment, back along his line of march to guard his supply convoys from pillaging by gangs of starving deserters. He himself became so ill from a recurrence of the gout that he required transportation by litter.

His army which had numbered 2300 regulars and 300 militia when he had marched from Fort Washington had been reduced to 1400 when it camped just before dark, November 3rd, on frozen and snow-covered ground beside a headwater creek of the Wabash in what is now Mercer County, Ohio. It was a chilled and hungry army which had for days been depressed by privations and oppressed by premonitions of disaster. The story of Harmar's saturnine prediction had been endlessly retold about its campfires. In urging his aide-de-camp, Major Ebenezer Denny, now St. Clair's adjutant, not to resign from the army, Harmar had said, "You must go on the campaign; some will escape, and you may be among the number." St. Clair and his officers might better have been dwelling on the parting advice given him by Washington the previous April: "As an old soldier, as one whose early life was particularly engaged in Indian warfare, I feel myself competent to counsel. General St. Clair, in three words, beware of surprise . . . again and again, General, *beware of surprise.*"

St. Clair's illness invested Butler with chief responsibility for heeding this advice. On each day's march he had guarded against surprise attack by maintaining an advance and flank screen of scouts and rangers. Furnishing additional protection, Piomingo, the noted Chickasaw chief, joined the army October 27th with a band of his warriors to aid the Chickasaw's new American allies against their ancient enemies, the northern Indians. But these Chickasaw auxiliaries, who might have been of unique value to the army's screen, were dispatched October 29th on a distant raid into the Indian country with directions to bring back prisoners with possible information on Indian intentions. They did not return from this excursion until long after the battle.

Day after day the presence of Indians had been detected in the forest through which the army was hacking its road and continuing its advance. They had always disappeared when patrols were sent out to intercept them. The November 3rd encampment, 98 miles from the Ohio, was made more hurried than usual by the imminence of darkness. The site selected was a clearing where at an earlier time there had been an Indian town. The available high ground above the marshy creek bottom was too restricted for the entire army and the militia was therefore encamped on another rise 450 yards away across the stream from the main camp. During the night sentinels reported the presence of Indians in the surrounding forest in apparently greater numbers than on former nights. A patrol in some force confirmed this suspicion. The sick commander in chief was not notified, however, and no unusual defense dispositions were ordered.[2] A half hour before sunrise the troops were paraded as usual and then dismissed for breakfast. It was at that instant that the blow fell.

Little Turtle had again been awaiting his opportunity with the sure judgment of the born commander. The long delays which had so weakened the effectiveness of St. Clair's campaign had strengthened by as much the force at his disposal. Indian ammunition which had been insufficient at the time of the Scott and Wilkinson expeditions had been amply replenished by urgent shipments from British magazines in Detroit and Sandusky. The Miami, the nation directly threatened by St. Clair's advance, had been joined by bands of warrior from every other nation in the northwest. By November Little Turtle's total force had increased to nearly 1500. It was a more united Indian army than had taken the field since the days of Pontiac. Indian confidence in his leadership was further supported by the presence of distinguished white sympathizers. Not only Alexander McKee and Matthew Elliott of the Indian Department but Captain Joseph Bunbury and Lieutenant Prideaux Selby of the British Army were at his side as observers and counselors. Simon Girty assumed active command of the Wyandot contingent. Some scores of English and French traders, dressed and painted as Indians, joined him as volunteers. Tecumseh, in command of his advance scouting parties, kept him constantly informed of every detail of St. Clair's strength, progress, and dispositions. All of these developments had bestowed upon him the priceless command advantage of being able to choose the time and place for battle. Since the Americans appeared to be taking measures to guard against being ambushed on the march, he elected a form of surprise that they were obviously not expecting. Many white armies had been discomfited by attack while stretched out in the long thin column required by passage through the forest, but never before had one

[2] Butler's failure to inform his superior of the apparent Indian concentration later became the subject of a bitter dispute between supporters of the two generals. The March 27, 1792, report of the Congressional Committee of Inquiry approved St. Clair's conduct, considered the contractors' failures the primary cause of the defeat, and included no reference to Butler's neglect.

been assaulted while assembled in its camp. During the hours before dawn of November 4, 1791, he moved his warriors swiftly into position.[3]

In that cold, gray light, the favorite hour for Indian attack on the most obscure settler's cabin, the numbed and scarcely awakened soldiers were as stunned by the sudden pandemonium as ever had been a helpless family. The first blast of rifle fire and war whoops from the encircling forest threw the American camp into immediate disorder. The most seasoned veterans may be demoralized if taken sufficiently by surprise. St. Clair's half-trained troops never recovered from that first shock. The militia, conscious of their isolation in their detached bivouac, instantly bolted across the stream to the imagined safety of the main camp. Their frenzied influx disrupted the defense formations being hastily improvised by the regulars. St. Clair struggled from his sickbed to take personal command. Eventually he was able to mount a number of limited bayonet charges in a desperate endeavor to loosen the Indian encirclement. The Indians briefly gave way at any point directly assailed but flanked each such advance, forcing its retirement. The cannon thundered uselessly until they were silenced by the death of their gun crews, the special target of Indian rifle fire. Senior officers engaged in attempting to order defense dispositions were likewise special targets. Major General Butler was killed and four colonels and four majors were killed or wounded. St. Clair's clothing was six times pierced, though he escaped injury. The whole army was jammed together in a milling mass in the open while hundreds fell under the incessant rain of bullets from an invisible enemy. The pall of smoke from long-continued gunfire so obscured vision that the attackers were able to make brazen dashes well within the defense perimeter and continually to tighten their coil about the camp.

After three hours during which his troops suffered as horribly and as helplessly as had Braddock's red coats 36 years before, St. Clair was forced to realize that if any portion of his army were to be

---

[3] Neither of the battles in 1790 and 1791 between the Army of the United States and the confederated Indians has ever been dignified by historians with a name. They have instead been commonly cited as "Harmar's defeat" and "St. Clair's disaster."

saved an escape must be attempted. By a well directed bayonet charge that began as a feint the Indian line was penetrated. Through the gap poured the remnant of the army in a frantic retreat down the recently opened road by which it had advanced from Fort Jefferson. There was a vivid and bitter eye witness account of that flight in St. Clair's report of November 9, 1791, to Knox:

> The retreat in those circumstances was, you may be sure, a very precipitate one; it was, in fact, a flight. The camp and the artillery was abandoned, but that was unavoidable; for not a horse was left alive to have drawn them off had it otherwise been practicable. But the most disgraceful part of the business is that the greatest part of the men threw away their arms and accouterments, even after the pursuit, which continued about four miles, had ceased. I found the road strewed with them for many miles, but was not able to remedy it; for, having had all my horses killed, and being mounted on one that could not be pricked out of a walk, I could not go forward myself, and the orders I sent forward, either to halt the front, or to prevent the men parting with their arms, were unattended to. The route continued to Fort Jefferson, twenty-nine miles, which was reached a little after sun-setting.

St. Clair's army had suffered casualties totaling 913, of which 68 had been officers. This was by far the greatest loss ever inflicted by Indians on an organized white force.[4] It must have been much greater had the Indians persisted in their pursuit of the disorganized fugitives. Instead they returned to collect the loot of the battlefield and to torment prisoners and wounded. Among the victims were a number of the American army's women camp followers into whose bodies heavy wooden stakes were forced. The Indians took particular satisfaction in the capture of the cannon. Unwilling to undertake the labor of making a road over which they might be transported, they buried the pieces in pits in the expectation of finding a future use for

---

[4] In other noted engagements Braddock's loss at Turtle Creek was 714 of 1200 present on the field, Grant's at Fort Duquesne 300 of 800, Bouquet's at Bushy Run 115 of 480, Herkimer's at Oriskany 400 of 700, Butler's at Wyoming 302 of 450, compared to St. Clair's 913 of 1400.

them. Then, satiated with victory, they returned to their towns to celebrate their triumph.

News of St. Clair's defeat swept the frontier with such a chill of dismay as had not been known since 1782. It was a fear soon justified. Emboldened by their successive victories over the Army of the United States, the Indians resumed with renewed rapacity their assaults on their most hated enemy, the settler. Midwinter raids struck the frontier from the Allegheny to the Savannah. Everywhere outlying families were driven to the refuge of stockades. Many raiding parties penetrated even the most populous centers of Kentucky which had for years been safe from molestation.[5] Residents of the outskirts of Lexington, Danville, or Harrodsburg had nearly as much occasion for dread that winter as the most isolated inhabitants of the most exposed border. Large bodies of Kentucky militia were mustered under Scott and Logan but the Indian raiding parties were so many and so elusive that the brunt of defense fell upon local community leaders such as Simon Kenton whose volunteer bands of seasoned Indian fighting frontiersmen of the stamp of Jacob Wetzel stood always ready to seek the Indian in the forest. Tecumseh led a number of these 1791–92 raids into Kentucky. Twice there were encounters between these two redoubtable champions of their respective races, Tecumseh and Kenton, in which first one and then the other won the advantage.

St. Clair reorganized the remnant of his army at Fort Washington about the nucleus of the First Regiment. With the aid of contingents of Kentucky militia he maintained his hold on Fort Hamilton and Fort Jefferson. He was able to reinforce the Fort Harmar garrison to afford more protection to the threatened New England settlements

---

[5] One of these, an attack on the cabin of John Merrill in Nelson County on Christmas Eve, 1791, gained much contemporary attention. Merrill was wounded by the first Indian fire but managed to bar the door. The Indians hacked away a section of the door and began crawling through the aperture into the cabin. Resolved to defend her injured husband, her brood of children, and her home, Mrs. Merrill caught up an ax with which she successively dispatched each Indian as he entered until she had disposed of four. Other Indians were attempting to come down the chimney. Mrs. Merrill threw the contents of a featherbed on the coals. Two more Indians, overcome by the fumes, fell to the hearth where the wounded Merrill brained them with a log of firewood. The surviving attackers abandoned the assault.

on the Muskingum but could not spare aid for the recently arrived, bewildered and terror-stricken French inhabitants of Gallipolis. As far east as western Pennsylvania and northwestern Virginia, border districts that had been settled for a generation were gripped by alarm. On December 11, 1791, the inhabitants of Pittsburgh were petitioning Governor Mifflin of Pennsylvania:

> During the late war there was a garrison at this place, though, even then, there was not such a combination of the savage nations, nor so much to be dreaded from them. At present, we have neither garrison, arms, nor ammunition to defend the place. If the enemy should be disposed to pursue the blow they have given, which it is morally certain they will, they would, in our situation, find it easy to destroy us; and, should this place be lost, the whole country is open to them, and must be abandoned.

A companion memorial came from the inhabitants of the counties of Westmoreland, Washington, Fayette, and Allegheny:

> Your excellency is well aware of the great extent of our frontier; and when you consider the high degree of spirit which the savages, animated by two successive victories, entertain, you may more easily conceive, than we can describe, the fears which pervade the breasts of those men, women and children, who are more immediately subject to their barbarities and depredations.

Representatives of Virginia's Ohio County were appealing to their state government:

> The alarming intelligence lately received, of the defeat of the army in the western country, fills our minds with dreadful fears and apprehensions, concerning the safety of our fellow-citizens in the country we represent . . . In the course of the last year, upwards of fifty of our people were killed, and a great part of our country plundered . . . The success of the Indians in their late engagement with General St. Clair, will, no doubt, render them more daring and bold in their future incursions and attacks upon our defenceless inhabitants.

Similar representations revealed the state of mind along the nearly two thousand miles of border. In the east as well the public was deeply disturbed. The effort of the new national government to solve the western problem by relieving the frontier and compelling Indian recognition of American sovereignty had so far proved a humiliating failure. The challenge appeared more nearly unanswerable than when Washington had taken office. It was instead developing into a struggle which was to become progressively more difficult until the last year of his second term, a strain matching the seven-year travail that preceded victory in the Revolution.

XV

⁊

Washington 2

Major Ebenezer Denny, toiling up the Ohio and over the mountains to deliver the bad news, reached the President's house in Philadelphia with St. Clair's dispatch the evening of December 9, 1791.
Having himself been present on the field he was in a position to add
his personal account of that morning of confusion and terror. On the
12th Washington transmitted a full and detailed report to Congress,
making no effort to minimize the extent of the disaster. Fortified by
the memory of his own many experiences with defeat, he earnestly
reminded Congress, however, that the battle on the Wabash, while
a grievous repulse, must be regarded as only an episode in a war in
which the United States was committed to persevere and was certain
eventually to win. But the mood of Congress and the eastern public
had radically changed since the wave of easy confidence that had
marked the authorization of St. Clair's expedition in the spring.
The war in the west had become unpopular even before it was
known to have turned out so badly.

Captain Charles Stevenson of the British army, in New York on
an observation mission, was gleefully reporting January 7, 1792:

> You cannot conceive the terror the last victory of the Savages has
> spread over the country. All the Ambition of Congress who made the

war to impress the Savages with their Military prowess is disappointed. The whole country abuse the Senate for it and I am much afraid that notwithstanding the desire of Congress to retrieve their Military fame that the people will compell them to make peace.

The exultant young officer was not greatly exaggerating the public's reaction. The news of St. Clair's defeat had been preceded by other reports from the west almost as disillusioning. The Ohio land companies organized in 1787 with such widely acclaimed prospects were foundering amid allegations of speculation, misrepresentation, and corruption. Their bankruptcies had seriously embarrassed financial stability in the east. One of their leading founders, William Duer, was in jail, charged with embezzlement. The misfortunes of the distressed French colony at Gallipolis had stirred wide indignation. Even the relatively respectable New Ohio Company, under the sponsorship of shepherds as reputable as Rufus Putnam and Manasseh Cutler, had proved unable to meet its obligations to the government. Western sympathizers as devoted as Washington and Jefferson were joining the chorus of criticism. Washington was declaring that unless "the spirit of speculation in lands" were checked "this country will be constantly embroiled with, and appear faithless in the eyes of not only the Indians but the neighboring powers also," and Jefferson was lamenting "the credit and fate of the nation seem to hang on the desperate throws and plunges of gambling scoundrels." Public opinion had swung back to the long-familiar position from which it regarded the west's troubles as due to the unprincipled machinations of land speculators and shameless aggressions of settlers. There was little disposition to accept further national sacrifices to save the west from the deserved consequences of its own sins.

By patience and perseverance, Washington nevertheless persuaded Congress of the necessity of a second enlargement of the defense establishment. A new national army of 5000 to be known as the American Legion, organized according to a plan long favored by Knox, was voted March 5th, though a reluctant Congress and a dubious public continued to regard this third essay at creating a federal military force with no enthusiasm. A first necessity was the selection of a sufficiently trustworthy commander to undertake operations in an area so distant and subject to international complications so critical. St. Clair had resigned his commission as major general while continuing to serve as Governor of the Northwest Territory. Westerners would have preferred Wilkinson, Scott, or Clark as the new military commander, but Washington wanted one who might be expected to think first of the country instead of first of the west. His own preference was Richard Henry Lee of Virginia but this was made impracticable by the vanity of other Revolutionary veterans who outranked him. After long and harassed consideration, while rival candidates competed for congressional support, Washington on April 3rd chose Anthony Wayne, a Revolutionary major general commonly known by the nickname "Mad Anthony" he had won at Stony Point. Since the Revolution Wayne had failed in business, had been elected to Congress by Georgia, had been unseated by the House on charges that his election had been irregular, and had increasingly suffered from a periodic illness resembling gout which was said to have encouraged his inclination to drink immoderately. The appointment was violently criticized, especially in Virginia, and Washington himself was none too confident of its wisdom.

Wayne's new army could not with the best of management be ready for the field until the late autumn at the earliest. Washington was relieved by the necessary delay even though it prolonged by another year the frontier's exposure to Indian inroads. Aside from the American public's growing disapproval of the wilderness war, international developments were adding to its risks. Every other European power's condemnation of the French Revolution appeared to be leading inevitably toward a general European war which must almost as certainly become a world war in which the Mississippi Valley could become a theater. This seemed to Washington and his cabinet most distinctly not an appropriate moment to accentuate that risk by any headlong display of American aggressiveness. Nearer events lent added weight to this view. Within recent months the North American policies of both Spain and Great Britain had become unmistakably more hostile to the interests of the United States in the west.

Hector de Carondelet, who had succeeded Miro December 30, 1791, was manifesting none of the discretion of his predecessor. Miro's efforts to retard American advance in the southwest by conspiratorial relations with frontier leaders, by restrictions on the navigation of the Mississippi, and by controlled colonization had proved an obvious failure. In Carondelet's estimation a bolder course was indicated. He was wholly unacquainted with Indian affairs or frontier conditions and the confidence in Indian military prowess given him by St. Clair's defeat had been encouraged by the far from disinterested counsel of Bowles and Panton. His imagination was fired by the prospect of raising an army of militant savages, a corps of North American sepoys, as it were, to guard this most exposed border of Spain's world empire. Early in 1792 he was attempting to form a military confederation of the four southwestern Indian nations, offering them Spain's territorial guarantee against the United States, promising them an unlimited arms supply to encourage their attacks on the frontier, and insisting that McGillivray denounce the Treaty of New York. At his instigation Spain's agents in Philadelphia,[1] Josef de Vaudenes and Josef de Viar, were permitted to warn Jefferson that any further American encroachment on the territory of Spain or Spain's Indian allies must result in war with Spain.

On the northwestern border the foreign threat had likewise been made more apparent by the appearance in local charge of British policy of an equally aggressive personality. John Graves Simcoe, who had arrived in Quebec on November 11, 1791, to assume his duties as the first Lieutenant Governor of the newly established Province of Upper Canada, had absorbed a violent antipathy to everything American in the course of his active military service in the Revolution which had begun at Boston in 1775 and continued until he became a prisoner at Yorktown. His new post gave him immediate

---

[1] After Gardoqui's departure in 1789 Spain did not afford Washington's administration the courtesy of maintaining even a chargé d'affaires in the American capital.

authority over the northwest border area in which British retention
of the Lake posts and British support of the Indians brought British
intentions into head-on collision with American aspirations. With
Dorchester taking a two-year leave of absence in England, Simcoe
was in a position offering him every opportunity to nurse his anti-
American sentiments.[2] That these might be given considerable rein
was indicated by the April 6, 1792, report to Washington by Gouverneur Morris, his semiofficial representative in London, that Henry
Dundas, Secretary of State charged with colonial affairs, had voiced
his government's persistence in the opinion that the 1768 readjust-
ment of the Proclamation Line, the Ohio River, remained the legal
boundary between Indian and American territory.

There was further evidence of the steady stiffening of British
policy in the attitude of the recently arrived first British minister to
the United States, George Hammond. The astute young diplomat
was outwardly reasonable, unassuming and friendly while earnestly
disclaiming any British interest in inciting Indian hostility. But he
suavely declined to discuss a date for British evacuation of the Lake
posts. Instead he suggested an American request for British mediation of the dispute between the Indians and the United States and
the recognition of an Indian buffer state northwest of the Ohio with
its integrity guaranteed by both powers. He did not strongly persist
in these proposals after they had been coldly repulsed but he had
clearly revealed the growing British disposition to recapture advantages in the northwest that they had too easily relinquished in the
treaty ending the Revolution. Hammond reported candidly to London that he had encountered no American either in or out of government who was not fully determined sooner or later to have the posts
but he had also been made aware of how delayed might be the

---

[2] These were probably as pronounced as his American critics of the time asserted
them to be. He had written Sir Joseph Banks, January 8, 1791, that he would "die
by more than Indian torture to restore my King and his Family to their Just inheritance," and to Henry Dundas, August 26, 1791, that he had accepted his Canadian
post "in the hope of being instrumental in the *Reunion of the Empire.*" On August
20, 1792, he wrote Alured Clarke, "There is no person, perhaps, who thinks less of
the talents or integrity of Mr. Washington than I do."

danger point by his knowledge, gained through the Indian capture of St. Clair's papers, of Knox's secret letter of instructions to St. Clair, July 14, 1791, in which Knox had said:

We must by all means avoid involving the United States with Great Britain . . . a war with that power in the present state of affairs, would retard our power, growth and happyness beyond almost the power of calculation.

Confronted by this 1792 accumulation of foreign threats and domestic difficulties, Washington reluctantly concluded that there could be no escape from practicing the utmost restraint. Before renewing the war another and greater effort to make peace must be undertaken. He realized that there could be no more unfavorable occasion to sue for peace than on the morrow of a military disaster but he could detect no alternative. The federal governors, St. Clair and Blount, were instructed and the border-state governors begged to take every possible measure to keep the frontier people from embarking upon offensive operations against their Indian tormentors. Knox was directed, meanwhile, to strive by any means available to reopen negotiations with the Ohio Indians. The administration felt obliged to persist in this course even after repeated rebuffs and frustrations had demonstrated that as a national policy it amounted to frantic appeasement.

As a first move in this uncomfortable undertaking, on January 2, 1792, the Iroquois[3] were invited to a conference at Philadelphia at which it was hoped that they might be persuaded to mediate between the United States and the western Indians. Some 50 leading Iroquois, with customary Indian readiness to enjoy the prolonged festivities of a major conference, came cheerfully to Philadelphia, March 13th, where they were fed, feted, and granted a $1500 increase in their annuities. Washington, addressing them March 23rd, assured them that "if the Western Indians should entertain the opinion that we want to wrest their lands from them, they are laboring under an

---

[3] Five of the original Six Nations were still residing in extreme western New York. Brant and his Mohawk had removed at the end of the Revolution to the Grand River in Canada.

error." In their enjoyment of the government's hospitality the Iroquois lingered in Philadelphia more than a month, finally leaving April 30th with a promise to send a delegation west to acquaint their belligerent brethren with the peaceful intentions of the United States. They had little heart for their mission, however, and dawdled most of the summer before embarking upon it.

Having got the Iroquois intercession under way, Knox as a second step on January 9, 1792, enlisted the services of Peter Pond and William Steedman, traders then preparing to enter the Indian country by way of Lake Erie. Pond, a Connecticut veteran of the French and Indian war, had become the most celebrated and successful of the earlier English-speaking traders in the far northwest. During and after the Revolution he had extended his operations from Detroit and then Mackinac to the extreme distance of Great Slave Lake. Altercations with competitors, involving in two instances the death of rivals, had become so violent, however, that he had been obliged to transfer his activities to the United States. In the hope of taking advantage of Pond's long and intimate experience with Indians, Knox directed him and Steedman to conceal their role as representatives of the United States "until the proper time." His instructions continued:

> When at Detroit assume the character of traders with the Indians —a business Mr. Pond is well acquainted with. Mix with the Miami and the Wabash Indians. Find their views and intentions, through such channels as your discretion shall direct. Learn the opinions of the more distant Indians. Insinuate upon all favorable occasions, the humane disposition of the United States; and if you can by any means ripen their judgment, so as to break forth openly, and declare the readiness of the United States to receive, with open arms, the Indians, notwithstanding all that has passed, *do it.*

Knox's hope to make use of the traders' Indian contacts was disappointed at the outset of their journey. They were refused permission to proceed west by the British commander at Niagara.

A more direct and responsible effort to reopen negotiations was

mounted at Fort Washington. In this major American peace overture, Captain Alexander Trueman of the regular army and Colonel
John Hardin of Kentucky were appointed formal and accredited
plenipotentiaries of the United States. Their extraordinarily hazardous mission, for which they volunteered, committed them to traveling northward through the wilderness until they had gained contact
with the Indians. They carried a peace message to the Indian confederation which read, in part:

> The President of the United States entertains the opinion that the
> war which exists is founded in error and mistake on your parts. That
> you believe the United States want to deprive you of your lands, and
> drive you out of the country. Be assured this is not so . . . reflect
> how abundantly more it will be for your interest to be at peace with
> the United States, and to receive all the benefit thereof, than to con-
> tinue a war, which, however flattering it may be to you for a mo-
> ment, must, in the end, prove ruinous . . . Do not suffer the advantages
> you have gained to mislead your judgment, and to influence you to
> continue the war.

Trueman and Hardin left Fort Washington May 22nd, the one
bound for the Indian towns on the Maumee, the other for those at
Sandusky. Both were murdered en route before they could deliver
their message. It was generally believed at the time that the killings
were instigated by the more belligerent faction in the Indian confederation in collusion with English traders in order to assure the war's
continuation. It was later learned that Hardin was axed by a casually
encountered Indian hunter and his half-grown son after Hardin
had permitted himself to be tied to a tree to demonstrate how completely peaceful were his intentions. The circumstances of Trueman's
death remained less clear though he was apparently killed on sight
by an accidentally encountered war party. The diplomatic result was
the same as had the murders been planned. The peace envoy's papers
were delivered by their assailants to the British commander at Detroit who forwarded them to Simcoe.

Attaching yet other negotiating strings to his bow, Knox had
meanwhile enlisted the services of Hendrick, a chief of the remnant

of the Mohican nation which had come to be called the Stockbridge Indians. Hendrick, with instructions similar to those of the other emissaries, set out for the west from his home in the Iroquois country. Being an Indian he was not assassinated en route but he was not permitted to attend the main Indian council on the Maumee and was obliged to leave his edition of the peace message with McKee in Detroit. Even Brant, anxious as he was to reopen negotiations, referred to him contemptuously as "the yanky Indian."

Responsibility for another major overture was delegated to Brigadier General Rufus Putnam, newly appointed commander of one of Wayne's sublegions, who was commissioned to make, with the aid of John Heckewelder, the Moravian missionary, the same sort of attempt as had Trueman and Hardin to establish direct contact with the Indians. He was instructed "to make it clearly apparent that we want not a foot of their land" and to invite their principal chiefs to a peace conference with Washington in Philadelphia. By the time he had reached Fort Washington, Putnam had learned the fate of the two earlier envoys and abandoned any thought of repeating their venture into the wilderness. He went instead to Vincennes where on September 23rd he concluded a treaty with a number of lesser nations occupying the area to the west and northwest of the belligerent Miami and Shawnee. The treaty had no bearing on the restoration of a general peace and was in any event promptly repudiated by both the Indian confederation and the United States Senate.

Among all these strenuous efforts to find a basis for reopening negotiations with the western Indians, Knox had placed the most hope in his projected enlistment of Brant's mediation. After asking Brant's old friend and mission associate, Alexander Kirkland, to prepare the way, Knox wrote Brant February 25, 1791:

> I can assure you that the President of the United States will be highly gratified by receiving and conversing with a chief of such eminence as you are, on a subject so interesting and important to the human race. This invitation is given to you from the fairest motives. The President of the United States is conscious of the purest disposition to promote, generally, the welfare of the Indians.

Brant replied March 27th that "to accomplish such desirable ends as civilization and peace-making, no exercise on my part shall be wanting." He explained that he would have to wait for the approval of the western Indians to give him "such powers as will give energy to what I do." During the interval Colonel Andrew Gordon, British commander at Niagara, and Joseph Chew of the Indian Department entreated him to decline the invitation. But early in June he set out for Philadelphia with a safe-conduct escort provided by Israel Chapin, American agent to the Iroquois. In passing down the Mohawk Valley which Brant had ravaged so often during the Revolution, the party was obliged to take some care to avoid assault by embittered inhabitants. John Wells, whose father had been killed by Brant's Indians at Cherry Valley, followed to Albany with the announced intention of shooting Brant but was dissuaded by mutual friends. There was evidence of how speedily most easterners had forgotten the frontier excesses of the Revolution in the New York newspaper notice:

> On Monday last arrived in this city, from his settlement on Grand River, on a visit to some of his friends in this quarter, Captain Joseph Brant of the British army, the famous Mohawk chief who so eminently distinguished himself during the late war as the military leader of the Six Nations. We are informed that he intends to visit the city of Philadelphia, and pay his respects to the President of the United States.

Brant safely reached Philadelphia to have his first audience with Washington June 21st. In continuing conversations Washington and Knox repeatedly emphasized the moderation of the American position in pressing their request that Brant use his good offices in gaining for them the attention of the western Indians. He was, meanwhile, reminded of the British attitude while being entertained by the British minister. The American position was summarized in a written statement Knox handed Brant June 27, 1792. In substance, the United States insisted on the legality of the Fort Harmar land cession though there was included an offer of certain readjustments in the boundaries and some additional compensation. Of special interest to Brant was the suggestion "that the United States will make arrangements to teach the Indians, if agreeable to them, to rise their own bread and Cattle as the White people do." But the point that most struck home to Brant was that "your own observation of our numbers will have convinced you that in a long and continued contest with the United States the Indians must be utterly ruined." Brant later affirmed that he had also been secretly offered a township of land, a thousand guineas, and double the annuity paid him by Great Britain. These offers he asserted he had refused but he did agree before he left Philadelphia July 1st to seek Indian consideration of the American peace proposal.

This most promising of the Washington-Knox peace efforts encountered the same obstacles as had the others. After a sociable pause in New York, where he was entertained by some of the city's first families and saved by police from assault by another visiting frontiersman, Brant fell ill en route home and as a result was prevented from reaching the western Indian council before it had adjourned. While still at Niagara he received sufficiently detailed reports of its preliminary proceedings to transmit to Knox the unwelcome news that the confederation remained resolutely opposed to the Fort Harmar cession.

During these dogged attempts of the troubled administration to evade a renewed resort to war, Wayne was struggling with the organization of an army against the day that he might have to fight one. The elements with which he had to work were the dispirited regulars surviving from the St. Clair and Harmar campaigns, now garrisoning the forts on the middle Ohio, and the new levies authorized by Congress, now being painfully recruited in the east. The state of morale among the veterans was evidenced by the standing reward of $40 for the head of a deserter paid civilian scouts skilled in forest tracking. The recruits were an even less prepossessing lot than had been furnished St. Clair. The pay of $3 a month was not an impressive incentive to attract any sensible man to a service committed to all the privations and horrors known to mark wilderness warfare.

In coping with his fearful task Wayne was compelled to rely heavily upon the popularity and experience of his second in command, Wilkinson. Upon St. Clair's resignation Wilkinson had become the senior regular officer in the west and March 5th he was commissioned brigadier general to command one of the four sublegions provided in the table of organization of the new army. He was in immediate charge of Fort Washington and its system of outposts to the north which guarded the main invasion route to Kentucky which was also the route Wayne would take if eventually he assumed the offensive. In February Wilkinson had led a much advertised though unopposed expedition to the scene of St. Clair's defeat where his soldiers interred as many of the bodies of the fallen as could be found under the deep snow. On May 12th he dispatched Reuben Reynolds, a sergeant in his confidence, to the Indian country and Canada on the ostensible mission of gathering information on British and Indian intentions. Reynolds proved able to circulate with astonishing freedom among Indian towns as distant as Mackinac, was furnished an English passport at Detroit, was interviewed by Simcoe, visited Montreal, and returned to the United States by way of Vermont. While thus cultivating his British relations Wilkinson had not lost interest in his Spanish connections. With due regard for his rapid rise in rank he was on February 1, 1792, granted a permanent Spanish pension of $2000 a year dating from January 1, 1789. Wayne, becoming suspicious, arrested Reynolds when he had reached Pittsburgh on his return journey but it was many months before Wayne began actively to question Wilkinson's loyalty.[4]

Wayne reached Pittsburgh in June 1792. Over the mountains behind him were trudging the first contingents of the Legion. Their encounter with those wooded heights as a foretaste of the wilderness

[4] As further evidence of how adroitly Wilkinson was able to beguile most of his contemporaries, Washington was writing Knox, August 13, 1792: "General Wilkinson has displayed great zeal and ability for public weal since he came into the Service. His conduct carries strong marks of attention, activity and spirit, and I wish him to know the favorable light in which it is viewed."

ahead persuaded many already dubious marchers that their enlistment had been ill-advised. Some of the weary and footsore companies lost more than half their number by desertion before the passage was completed.

Wayne and his rabble were coming to an historic frontier. This storied region about the Forks of the Ohio had never known peace. For nearly forty years it had been swept by the ebb and flow of invasion—by Frenchmen, by Englishmen, by Americans, and repeatedly by Indians. In this arena had appeared commanders as noted as George Washington, Edward Braddock, John Forbes, Henry Bouquet. Its defense had been served by frontier leaders of the stature of Andrew Lewis, George Rogers Clark, Archibald Lochry, William Crawford. Among Indians who had fought to hold this east-west gateway had been chiefs as memorable as Pontiac, Guyasuta, Custaloga, Cornstalk. Innumerable nameless settlers, soldiers, and warriors had here performed feats never to be forgotten by their neighbors, comrades, or companions. The dangers that had confronted the first white men to come here loomed now more starkly than ever. The attack now momentarily expected was by an Indian enemy more united and better armed than ever before. There could be little wonder that inhabitants imbued with such memories and traditions should regard the arrival of this fat and sickly general and his scarecrow army with a mingling of contempt and pity.

Longer acquaintance failed to improve the impression. The men appeared as unprepared for the rigors and perils of the wilderness as any who could conceivably have been assembled from a city's alleys. Most of their officers seemed chiefly concerned with drinking, gambling, duelling, and pursuing their sergeants' wives. A midnight false alarm that Pittsburgh was under Indian attack threw these misnamed legionnaires into a hopeless panic. There was as yet no suggestion of that attribute which was to fit this absurd army for one of the most notable triumphs ever won by American arms: Its commander was a soldier who was irascibly resolved to pound on these miserable recruits until they, too, became soldiers.

The frontier Wayne had come to defend was in the gravest need of defense. Indians everywhere, south as well as north, had been exhilarated by Little Turtle's victories over Harmar and St. Clair. They realized as well as did the oldest settler that the only successful defense of the endless line of exposed outer settlement lay in a counterinvasion of the Indian country by an organized army of sufficient strength to carry the war to the Indian centers of population. Their former fears of such massive retaliation had been dispelled by the twice demonstrated impotence of the American regular army. The multitude of peace overtures emanating from Philadelphia added to Indian complacency. Nothing had so far developed in Wayne's preparations to reawaken their concern. At Pittsburgh he was in any event many hundreds of miles from the most seriously threatened frontiers of Kentucky, Cumberland, and the Holston. He could have afforded those tortured borders as much protection had he remained east of the mountains. By midsummer it had become apparent that he could not be ready to mount an invasion for another year. Even had he been ready the peace policy of the national government would have held him inactive. Defense of the frontier, as had been the case since the first crossing of the mountains, still depended on the people who lived on it.

In the north the great Indian onslaught expected in the early spring of 1792 did not materialize. The Miami and Shawnee were occupied with gathering their towns into a new grouping along the middle Maumee where their nearness to each other assisted their mutual defense and their nearness to the British base at Detroit made their supply more secure. The new position possessed the further advantages of forcing an American invading army to make a longer march through the wilderness and at the end of so dangerous an advance to make so near an approach to Detroit as to increase Indian hopes that the British army might be compelled to intervene. By late spring many warriors were free, however, to attempt fresh ventures. During the ceremonies attending the inauguration of Kentucky's state government, June 1, 1792, a number of inhabitants were killed almost within sight of the stand from which Kentucky's first governor, Isaac Shelby, was speaking. As an insulting adjunct to raids on settlements, Indians infested the military road connecting Forts Washington, Hamilton, St. Clair, and Jefferson, watching for opportunities to ambush a convoy or pounce on a straggler. In an attack of June 5th on a detachment gathering hay outside Fort Jefferson 16 soldiers were killed. Wilkinson remained strictly enjoined, nevertheless, to make no offensive move, even locally, and to strive to prevent Kentuckians from attempting retaliatory excursions north of the Ohio.

In the south Indian aggressions became bolder, more numerous, and more destructive in 1792. Their raids commenced as early as the first week in February. Cumberland and the Wilderness Road, as usual, bore the brunt, but the southern borders of Kentucky and Holston were not spared. There came a brief respite when the Indian cause received a stunning blow in the death of Dragging Canoe, the most bellicose war chief the southern Indians ever produced, apparently from the excesses of a night-long scalp dance staged to celebrate a recent success. His son, assuming the name Dragging Canoe, and other young men, most notably John Watts, Old Tassel's nephew, strove to exercise his military leadership, but the loss had been one that proved difficult to replace.

Excited by Spanish promises of arms and by the visits of delegations of northern Indians preaching the gospel of Indian military superiority, the Chickamauga, reinforced by bands of Creek volunteers, resumed the aggressive. From April through June a storm of raids swept the southern frontier. Governor Blount, faithful to his admonitions from Philadelphia, sternly directed frontier militia to remain on the defensive under whatever provocation and under no circumstances to press a pursuit of retiring raiders across the Tennessee. As one of the national government's continuing efforts to persuade the Indians to listen to reason, Blount paid a personally dangerous visit to Coyatee in the Cherokee country where nearly 2000 Cherokee and Chickamauga assembled to listen with outward attention to his peace proposals which centered around his pressing invitation that they send delegations of chiefs to confer with Washington and Congress in the American capital. Blount had gained his audience by the promise of elaborate entertainment. The festivities continued for some days while the rounds of eating, drinking, making speeches, and firing salutes were accompanied by many Indian protestations of peaceful intentions. An incident of the proceedings was the ceremonial acceptance by the Cherokee chief, Bloody Fellow, of the more pacific name, Clear Sky. Actually Blount's listeners were much more interested in what they had been hearing from Carondelet. The sole significant consequence of the conference was the approval by the Cherokee as resident American interpreter of Blount's candidate, James Carey, later to be associated with the 1797 Florida conspiracy which resulted in Blount's expulsion from the United States Senate. Scarcely had the convivial gathering broken up before most of the Indian participants had scattered again to resume their attacks on the frontier. The succeeding acceleration of hostilities culminated June 26th in one of the rare captures of a stockade. In the destruction of Ziegler's Station, near Nashville, 5 of the inhabitants were killed, 5 wounded, and 12 carried into captivity.

Carondelet continued to press the advantage he conceived the Indian cause to be gaining everywhere. Having succeeded in disposing of Bowles,[5] he summoned McGillivray to New Orleans. McGillivray, conforming to the immemorial Creek policy of playing one white power against another, came willingly. He suspected that Spain was becoming, at least for the moment, the stronger of the two, and assured Carondelet, "It never was my Inclination to be on good terms with the Americans." By the Treaty of New Orleans, July 6, 1792, McGillivray agreed to make war upon the United States until he had regained all territory recognized as Creek in British times. Spain promised an adequate arms supply and affirmed Spain's guarantee of that boundary. As a mark of Spain's esteem, McGillivray's annuity was raised to $3500 a year.

Of the four southwestern Indian nations only the Chickasaw remained cool to Carondelet's confederation design. John Watts, encouraged by the prospect that his Chickamauga were about to re-

[5] See p. 124.

ceive strong Creek and Cherokee reinforcement, began advocating a new military doctrine. In his ambitious view, Indians should substitute for their indiscriminate raiding the full-scale invasion for which they now had adequate arms and numbers. Indians need no longer be satisfied to punish the frontier, he asserted, for the time had now come when they could destroy it.

Washington's summer vacation at Mount Vernon was haunted by successive packets of bad news, ranging from the murder of his peace envoys to the increasingly obvious support offered the Indians by Great Britain and Spain. His judgment told him he must continue to resist the impulse to strike back but he could give vent to his anger in private. He wrote Knox August 19, 1792, "The conduct of Spain in this business is so unprovoked, so misterious, and so hostile in appearance that . . . the mind can scarcely realize a procedure so base and inhuman." Further dwelling on the affronts to which his government and his country were being subjected by Spain and Great Britain caused him to burst forth in another letter to Knox three days later in which he declared that the influence being exerted by those two powers on the Indians "admits no doubt in my mind . . . that it may be a concerted plan . . . to check the growth of this rising country . . . diabolical as it may seem." There still seemed to him, notwithstanding provocations so mortifying, no opportunity as yet for any departure from the appeasement policy. The peace offers to both northern and southern Indians were kept open. Blount, St. Clair, Wayne, and Wilkinson, in their respective posts of federal authority in the west, were directed to continue to prevent so far as they were able any retaliatory action by the inhabitants of the frontier which was being so viciously assailed. In October, Knox again wrote the governors of Virginia, South Carolina, and Georgia to reiterate his statement that "it is the desire of the President of the United States that no expedition be made against the Indian towns at present." He urged the governors to withhold any offensive action until Congress, soon to assemble, should have an opportunity to consider American resumption of the war.

The Indian invasion of the southwestern frontier advocated by

BORDER WAR IN THE
SOUTHWEST, 1784-94

------ Approximate limit of settlement

Watts and approved by Carondelet was attempted in late September. A defense accustomed to hit-and-run raids was suddenly confronted by marching armies numbering hundreds of warriors. McGillivray was confined to his bed by an illness contracted during his return from New Orleans, and the Indian preparations had lacked the benefit of his counsel. Watts had become the generally recognized field commander of the allied forces. The immediate objective was the capture of Nashville as a first step in compelling the evacuation of the entire Cumberland. Three converging columns were involved in the invasion. One, under Doublehead, became entangled in a confused night engagement in a canebrake with a militia detachment under Lieutenant William Snoddy in which the Indians were demoralized by the unexpected loss of 13 killed while nevertheless failing to complete the destruction of the much smaller white force. The second, under Middlestriker, ambushed and routed, with the capture of its commander, Captain Samuel Handy Handley,[6] a militia force en route to assist in the defense of Nashville. The main Indian army, under Watts, variously estimated at 300 to 700 warriors, about half of them mounted, drove straight for Nashville but became embroiled en route in command disputes among the chiefs of the Chickamauga, Creek, and Cherokee contingents. Instead of keeping on to its objective, as Watts wished, a diversionary assault was made on Buchanan's Station,[7] a small stockade four miles outside Nashville. Its defenders numbered only 15 but their marksmanship was expert. Watts was wounded, it was thought at the moment mortally, and the senior Creek chief and four other prominent chiefs killed, early in the assault. Disheartened by the fall of their leaders and having lost any hope of surprising Nashville, the Indian invading force broke up, its members returning with relief to the so much simpler practice of raiding. It had again been demonstrated that for all the daring, skill, and initiative that marked Indian conduct of such lesser tactical maneuvers as raids, skirmishes, and ambushes, Indian political and military organization was inadequate to maintain and control the number of warriors required for a sustained field operation except on those rare occasions when the personality of an extraordinary commander had excited exceptional enthusiasm.

[6] Handley was three times tied to the stake in preparation for burning. He was saved once by having been rendered unconscious by preliminary torment, again by the sudden breaking of a rainstorm, and the third time by the intercession of Watts. He lived to be exchanged three months later. In the interim his hair had turned white.

[7] The 1792 assaults on Ziegler's and Buchanan's stations produced anecdotes casting light on the attitudes and conditions of the times. Under cover of the flames, smoke, and confusion accompanying the capture of her station, Mrs. Jacob Ziegler, stuffing a rag into her baby's mouth to still its crying, made a successful escape by crawling from the burning stockade into the woods. Mrs. John Buchanan's active participation in the successful defense of the other elicited her husband's approving comment: "Mrs. Buchanan had killed buffalo and deer and cannot now plead innocence of aim and intent to kill an Indian."

Washington's address to the reconvened Congress, November 6, 1792, was chiefly devoted to the Indian problem. He emphasized his deepening concern "that reiterated endeavors, toward affecting a pacification, have hitherto issued only in new and outrageous proofs of persevering hostility." Another of these outrageous proofs was occurring at the very hour his message was being delivered. On that same November 6th a pack train, guarded by 120 mounted Kentucky militia, engaged in transporting supplies to the forts north of the Ohio, was attacked, pillaged, and the escort driven into the shelter of Fort St. Clair with a loss of 11 killed. The regular garrison, mindful of orders to remain always on the defensive, offered the militia no assistance other than to accept their wounded and replace their ammunition. Every report Washington received from the west confirmed the conclusion that the appeasement effort had so far served only to make Indian defiance more belligerent and more flagrant.

The sufferings of the frontier had been in no way lightened by the presence of Wayne's troops drilling in Pittsburgh, or of the garrisons holding the Ohio forts, or of the three companies of regulars mounting a token guard over the southwestern frontier. Insistence on purely defensive tactics had increased western impatience and scorn. James Seagrove, United States agent to the Creek, wrote Washington July 27, 1792, that frontier people "now consider the troops and servants of the United States nearly as great enemies as they do the Indians." Yet Washington and his advisors remained too conscious of the enormous foreign and domestic risks involved to consider a resumption of the war in any other light than as a last resort. With the full approval of Congress he remained determined to postpone considering any offensive action until he had learned the outcome of the great council of the western Indians which was known to have assembled. There lingered a hope that the intercession of the Iroquois might yet evoke a negotiable response.

The Indian council assembling in August at Au Glaize,[8] a group

8 At the time often called Grand Glaize, The Glaize, or simply, Glaize.

of towns clustered about the confluence of the Auglaize and Maumee rivers in what is now Defiance County, Ohio, was attended by 28 nations, including the Miami, Shawnee, Wyandot, Delaware, Cherokee, Creek, Ottawa, Potawatomi, and Chippewa. Indian confidence had been so inflated by reflection on their victories over American armies and on American appeals for peace that it was the inclination of most delegates to proceed without any ado to the reaffirmation of their bonds of union, to the issuance of a joint blast of defiance, and to a summons to all Indians to redouble their attacks on the American frontier. By another of those adroit manipulations of Indian opinion of which he had become a master, McKee persuaded the delegates instead to await the arrival of the Iroquois delegation with its heralded report on American intentions. McKee's task was the nearly impossible one of giving some appearance of sense and coherence to Britain's imperial policy in the northwest. In conforming to this policy, he was expected to strive to maintain the Indian barrier to American expansion by encouraging Indian insistence on the Ohio boundary and yet, at the same time, to strive to keep open the door to further negotiations in order to postpone the evil moment when Britain might be forced into a war with the United States to defend her Indian allies.

The laggard Iroquois delegation at last arrived September 11th with the tin dispatch box containing the papers, copies of former treaties, maps, and other records defining the American position which at once became the center of much mocking attention. After many days of private conversations and public entertainment the full council formally convened September 30th. The official minutes of its deliberations, furnished McKee for the information of Simcoe, detailed many spirited exchanges over the differences between the Iroquois and western Indian points of view. Western Indians addressing the Iroquois declared:

> You know when we last met at the Foot of the Rapids 4 years ago it was unanimously agreed upon by all Nations to be strong & to defend our Country but we have never seen you since that time; We suppose you have been constantly trying to do us some good . . .

You have told us, you have been listening these 2 years last past to the United States and that during that time, you heared nothing but what tended to the welfare of the people of our Colour; How can this be? for whilst you say you were considerng for the good of your Western Brethren, two powerful Armies were sent by the Americans to destroy us; Has their sweet Speeches so much intoxicated you and blinded you, that your sight could not reach so far as where we are now sitting?

To these unfraternal charges the Iroquois replied:

You have talked to us a little too roughly, you have thrown us on our backs . . . Washington asked us what was the cause of the uneasiness of the Western Nations, we told him it was in regard to their Lands . . . He did not say that he would give up the Lands, but that he would satisfy the Indians for them. That he wanted nothing so much as the friendship of all his Brothers the Indians . . . You remember, when our Father [the King of England] & the Americans quarrelled, the Americans desired us Red People to sit still, as we had no business in their dispute, but our Father put the Hatchet into our hands to strike the Americans, and both him and us were unsuccessful. From that moment our lands were torn to pieces and the Americans triumphed as the greatest people in this great Island. These are matters for you to consider well, before you give us your sentiments fully; We have now delivered ours from our heart, and whatever you may determine on, with regard to a Boundary line, as we have now united ourselves to you, we shall join you heartily in representing to the United States.

After a week of heated debate, during which the differences between the majority and the Iroquois were somewhat reconciled, the final determination of the council was announced to the Iroquois for delivery to the government of the United States:

We are not proud spirited, nor do we attribute our great good fortune these last 2 years, to our own strength alone, but to the great Spirit who governs all things on this Earth & who looks on us with as much or perhaps more compassion than those of a fairer complexion. You know very well the boundary that was made between us and the English & Americans when they were as one people. It was the Ohio River, now Brothers of the 6 Nations, as you were sent here by the Americans to tell us what they say, we now tell you Brothers to go the same road you came and inform them, that the boundary line then fixed on is what we now want and that is the determination of all the Nations present, yours as well as ours . . . we do not want compensation, we want restitution of our Country . . . if the Americans want to make peace with us . . . we will meet them next Spring at lower Sandusky, where all the parties who formerly settled the Boundary line must be present.

As its final action the council on October 9th sent a deputation to McKee to request him to inform Simcoe of its decision and to request that at any future conference with the United States the British government be officially represented. In appearing to follow its own bent the council had at the same time acceded to British wishes. Its decision represented another of McKee's many successes in meeting the infinitely perplexing demands of Britain's anomalous Indian policy. By accompanying their renewed defiance, their demand for the Ohio, and their insistence on British participation with a grudging consent to negotiate, they had struck what was in the British official view just the right note.

Brant, delayed by his illness, did not reach the Maumee until October 13th when it was too late to participate in the proceedings of the General Council but he was gratified by its reaffirmation of Indian union and relieved by its offer to resume negotiations. At a rump council of Shawnee and Delaware called October 28th to receive him he re-emphasized the need for Indian union and the imperative necessity of refusing to negotiate with the United States except as a union. "General Washington is very cunning," he warned, "he will try to fool us if he can." In private conversations, however, he must have endeavored to prepare his listeners for the probable need for some boundary concessions for on January 28, 1793, Simcoe was grumbling in a letter to Hammond: "This Cunning and self interested savage *chooses* not to understand the difference between a fair Peace, and one upon any terms. I have much to complain of his behavior of late."

Thanks to a wilderness express from Simcoe, Hammond was privileged to impart to the anxiously awaiting American administration the first information on the outcome of the Indian council. Taking his customary advantage of the personal rivalry between Hamilton and Jefferson, he first told his story in private to Hamilton and then more formally to Jefferson. The definitive Indian reply was delivered to the United States by the Iroquois November 16, 1792, in a council at Buffalo Creek attended by a delegation of six British officers and officials headed by John Butler, the veteran Indian administrator and former Tory commander. The substance of the Indian pronouncement and the manner of its delivery could scarcely have been more galling. There was no slightest disposition in either administration or congressional circles to accept either of the two principal Indian demands, the Ohio boundary and British mediation. On the other hand, the alternate disadvantages of war were still as obvious as ever. The offered opportunity to postpone a resort to force by agreeing to new talks was therefore grasped.

After consultations with congressional leaders, instructions for the prospective American peace commissioners were drafted and submitted to the Senate. There was still so little readiness to come to grips with the mounting crisis that the phrase in the instructions most widely approved was the admonition to the as yet unnamed commissioners, "You must be well aware of the extreme dislike of the great majority of the citizens of the United States to an Indian war, *in almost any event.*"

On December 12, 1792, Knox got off his answer to "the Western Indians" and "all the other tribes in alliance with them, to the southward of the Lakes and north of the Ohio, and east of the Mississippi," accepting the Indian suggestion of a conference "when the leaves shall be fully out the next Spring." "The President of the United States," he declared, "embraces your proposal, and he will send Commissioners to meet you." Knox added a proposal for an armistice as a condition to this acceptance:

> We shall prevent any of our parties going into the Indian Country, so that you may with your women and children, rest in full

security. And we desire and shall expect, that you call in all your Warriors, and prevent their going out again; it will be in vain to expect peace while they continue their depredations on the frontiers.

Despite a quest so earnest the path to peace continued to sprout new thorns. Knox had inadvertently referred to the Maumee Rapids[9] instead of Sandusky as the site for the conference. Immediately suspecting an American attempt to gain some advantage, the Indians hurled back an extravagantly insolent reply, addressed to "General Washington President of the Congress of the United States of America" and accusing him of speaking "with a double tongue" and holding "good in one hand and evil in the other." Meanwhile, Simcoe had brusquely rejected Knox's proposal that the United States furnish provisions for the conference, an all-important prestige factor in every assembly of Indians. The British and Indian attitudes had by now made it insultingly clear that, in order to hold a conference on the soil of the United States with Indians inhabiting the territory of the United States, the United States must accept total British supervision of the transaction. Even the approach to the conference of the representatives of the United States must be by permission and in the custody of British officers.

Washington called a cabinet meeting February 25, 1793, to consider whether or not in view of conditions so humiliating the attempt to reach a peaceful settlement should be pursued further. There were, as always, many differences of opinion, particularly between Hamilton and Jefferson, but on the main question the judgment was unanimous that in spite of circumstance so distasteful the government should proceed with the treaty. On February 28th Knox therefore meekly wrote the Indians that the representatives of the United States would meet with them at Sandusky June 1, 1793, adding the pious hope "that the Great Spirit might infuse into the hearts of all concerned, a sincere desire for peace and friendship, so necessary to the happiness of human nature."

9 Most contemporary mention of the Maumee referred to it as the Miami, the Miamis, or the Miami of the Lakes. This river flowing into Lake Erie is not to be confused with the Great Miami or the Little Miami, both flowing into the Ohio.

Wayne had meanwhile removed his Legion from the distractions of Pittsburgh to the rigors of a winter camp at Logstown, 23 miles down river, where he intensified the severities of his training regime. The news from Philadelphia meant that it would be another six months at the earliest before he would be obliged to lead his army into action. The delay was providential. Shaping such men into the kind of soldiers he knew that such a campaign would require was a task demanding time.

XVI

※

Brant 2

Not many men in history have been required to realize that the survival of their people had become a personal responsibility. Upon Brant had long rested that burden and in 1793 its weight had become more crushing than any man could sustain. Of all the Indians gathered in that year's climactic council at which for the last time Indians were privileged to deliberate upon their own fate, he alone was equipped with the knowledge and vision correctly to estimate the implacable consequences of their decision. No other Indian had had his breadth of experience with the world beyond the wilderness. He had traveled widely, twice crossed the Atlantic, and been honored and feted in London, Paris, New York, and Philadelphia. No other Indian had had his political experience. He had attended as many conferences in white capitals as in his native forest and was as well acquainted with the highest figures in the British and American governments as with his fellow chieftains. No other Indian had had his military experience. His familiarity with martial affairs had commenced at the age of thirteen at the Battle of Lake George in 1755, had continued with major command responsibilities in the Niagara, Oriskany, Cobleskill, Andrustown, Cherry Valley, Min-

isink, Newtown, Ohio, Kentucky, Harpersfield, Canajoharie, and
Schoharie campaigns, as well as innumerable intervening engagements, skirmishes, and raids, and had included repeated and protracted opportunities to observe in detail the operations of professional white armies. He was, therefore, in a position to appreciate as
could no other Indian the gravity of the council's decision. Upon it
depended more than victory or defeat in a war. Upon it depended
the final fate of a race.

In spite of the confidence engendered by the Indian aggressions
and victories of the past three years, the Indian world in 1793 was
checkered with areas of developing weakness. In the central Indian citadel on the Maumee the Shawnee, Miami, Delaware, and
Wyandot were determined upon the war for the Ohio boundary for
which they were certain they were ready. For the fully successful
prosecution of that war, however, they required the whole-hearted
support of the Lake Indians, the Indians of Canada, and the Iroquois. But the Lake Indians were absorbed in the profits of the fur
trade, the Canadian Indians lived at a distance which kept their
interest theoretical, and the dangerous proximity of the American
frontier to the residue of the Iroquois homeland made caution the
Iroquois' first impulse. American reluctance to make war was
matched only by Indian unreadiness to wage one.

In the south the Indian cause suffered at the outset of 1793 a blow
from which there could be no recovery. On February 17th McGillivray died in his bed of the last of his many illnesses. From late
February through March a visiting delegation of northern Indians
trooped from one council fire to another among the Creek and
Cherokee, feverishly advocating a concerted attack on the southern
frontier to coincide with the northern Indians' approaching collision with Wayne. The southern Indians agreed with all the enthusiasm with which Indians always greeted proposals that red men
unite for the purpose of attacking white men, but in the absence of
strong leadership took no concrete steps to prepare for the enterprise. The one tangible result of the ardent conferences was to stir
some scores of restless southern warriors to journey northward to

enlist with Little Turtle and some hundreds of others to raid the nearer settlements with greater gusto.

Whatever chance there might have been for concerted action in the south had in any event been lost by the untimely outbreak in February of the Chickasaw-Creek War. As usual in Indian inter-tribal conflicts it aroused more interest and venom than often attended their differences with their white enemies. The circumstances leading to it had been particularly provoking to the Chickasaw's Indian neighbors. The Chickasaw had stubbornly clung to their strange and never to be rewarded American attachment. They had furnished St. Clair a corps of warriors and were assembling the same support for Wayne. Creek condemnation of so objectionable a departure from the Indian norm had at length reached a stage of violence much applauded by frontier whites. A Chickasaw war party permitted to pass directly through Nashville en route to an assault on the Creek was wildly cheered by inhabitants who had never before found occasion to approve anything Indian. Carondelet and Panton were making frantic efforts to mediate the dispute while Wayne was shipping the Chickasaw 500 guns, 2000 pounds of powder, 4000 pounds of lead, and 4000 flints.

These stresses of Indian disunity in the south had not, however, brought relief to the individual settler. Robertson was writing Daniel Smith July 20, 1793: "Bad as were the times when you left this country, they are much more gloomy at present. Indians are plenty in all quarters . . . they do, of late, penetrate further into our settlements than before." Similar raids were tormenting the Holston. One was long remembered for an affecting circumstance. After an assault on the cabin of William Casteel, he, his wife, and their five children were mutilated, scalped, and left for dead. Neighbors were burying the bodies in a family grave when a spark of life was detected in ten-year-old Elizabeth. She recovered and lived out her life in the vicinity of her childhood home.

Blount had continued by admonitions and proclamations to impress upon the southern frontier the need to refrain from retaliation lest the national government's peace program be jeopardized. But in early June Captain John Beard, infuriated by a particularly destructive raid near Knoxville, disobeyed his standing orders to remain north of the Tennessee and fell upon Coyatee, the Cherokee town in which was gathering at the moment a delegation of chiefs to make the peace pilgrimage to Philadelphia so long promoted by Blount. Eight of the unsuspecting and unresisting inhabitants and a resident white trader were killed. Major Thomas King and Daniel Carmichael, in Coyatee to escort the Indian emissaries on their peace mission, narrowly escaped death during the indiscriminate killing. Among the wounded was Hanging Maw,[1] a chief long known as a peace advocate, his wife, and a daughter of the renowned Nancy Ward, famous throughout her long life for her friendliness toward whites. Blount ordered Beard's court-martial but so intense was public feeling in his favor that, like all such white offenders in frontier history, he was never punished. The peace-seeking majority of the Cherokee, as had been the case so often before, was so exercised by the Coyatee outrage that most younger warriors rushed to offer their services to the Chickamauga.

On the Ohio frontier that spring of 1793 Wayne's preparations were proceeding at what at the time seemed a snail's pace but with what was eventually to prove inexorable purpose. Having drilled his unlikely troops mercilessly throughout the long winter at the Logstown camp he had called Legionville, he moved his army down river on the swell of one of the highest floods of contemporary memory to reach Fort Washington April 30th. He was not yet certain that Wilkinson was at the bottom of the virulent controversies constantly erupting among his officers but he was beginning to be fairly sure. Wayne undertook at once the strengthening and provisioning of the chain of existing forts extending northward and the opening of a road beyond the northernmost, Fort Jefferson. This technical violation of the armistice did not escape immediate Indian attention and denunciation.

North of the border all attention was fixed on the meeting with

---

[1] Among his various white contacts had been service with Washington in the French and Indian War.

the representatives of the United States scheduled for Sandusky in June. At every former diplomatic contact with the United States the Indians had been summoned to an American fort where the treaty terms offered had been those that can be dictated by a conqueror. The prospective negotiation was to be a confrontation of equals at which if there were to be an advantage due victors it would be an Indian advantage. In February, Simcoe made a midwinter journey to Detroit, his first visit to that capital of the British-Indian wilderness, to give his personal supervision to the Indian preparations. Brant accompanied him, anxious to be present at consultations so important to the Indian future, but part way down the snowbound Thames was called back by an urgent appeal from the Iroquois, perpetually involved in the pressures of American encroachment on their remaining lands. Simcoe reached Detroit February 18, 1793, where he was able to instruct McKee in person and in detail on the manner in which McKee might most usefully devote his enormous influence over the western Indians to serve the requirements of British policy during the coming negotiations. Nine days after Simcoe's arrival the western Indians got off a peremptory invitation demanding the attendance of the Iroquois and the Seven Nations of Canada at a new general council at Maumee Rapids "before We go to meet the Commissioners of the United States at Sandusky, that We may be well prepared and all of one mind to speak to them."

The Iroquois were surprised by the unexpected summons but, no less than Brant, were ready to subscribe to any attempt to strengthen Indian union. Their delegation, headed by Brant and accompanied by Deputy Indian Superintendent John Butler,[2] set out for the west May 5th. Brant had conferred at length with Simcoe on the British position, the various implications of which he probably understood more clearly than did the Lieutenant Governor. British policy was based on a desire to maintain the Indian barrier in order to prevent an American approach to the Lake posts, control of which depended on continued British domination of the whole region of the Great Lakes and the upper Mississippi. Brant's policy was based on a

2 Butler soon became too ill to take an active part in the mission.

desire to guard Indian living space against American encroachment as long as possible and by every means possible short of resort to a war which he was convinced the Indians must lose. The distinction was defined accurately enough in Simcoe's letter of April 1, 1793, to Alured Clarke, acting governor general during Dorchester's English leave: "The independence of the Indians is his [Brant's] primary object; his views are extensive, and he speaks most contemptuously of the Superintendent [Sir John Johnson] and his Deputies [John Butler and Alexander McKee] and, indeed, of everybody, but I conceive his attachment next to the Indians, is decisively to the British Nation."

Since the defeat of the British-Indian alliance in the Revolution, Brant's sole hope for Indian survival as a people lay in their dispossession being sufficiently delayed to enable them in the meantime to learn to substitute pastoral and agricultural pursuits for hunting and trapping as a means of subsistence. He had made a start in this direction with his Mohawk on Grand River.[3] Even under presumably benevolent British auspices Brant had found the task of achieving such a transition beset with difficulties. In a February 25, 1793, letter to McKee he had reported on the upshot of one Mohawk land rights dispute with Simcoe:

> It hurt my pride and feelings Extremely . . . I cannot hardly reconcile myself to Live on such situation I never . . . expected that my attachment to the English should any time shake I am totally dispirited.

Brant's greater anxieties with respect to the immediate future of all Indians were multiplied by every development following his arrival at the Maumee Rapids. It soon became apparent that the

---

[3] This resettlement project was described in the journal of Simcoe's Detroit journey kept by his aide, Major E. B. Littlehales: "On our arrival at the Mohawk Village, the Indians hoisted their flags and trophies of war, and fired a feu de joie in compliment of His Excellency, the representative of the King, their Father . . . Here is a well built wooden church with a steeple, a school house, and an excellent house of Captain Brant's . . . We heard Divine Service performed by an Indian. The devout behaviour of the women, the melody of their voices, and the excellent time they kept in singing Hymns is worthy of observation."

invitation of the western Indians had been a device to separate the Iroquois from their American contacts as a first step in a scheme designed to reduce the influence of Brant and the Iroquois with the confederation and to frustrate the negotiations with the Americans. When the Iroquois delegation reached the Rapids there was a studied absence of that ceremonial recognition of their arrival stipulated by Indian protocol. Most of the more important western confederated nations lived nearby but neither had any of their delegations assembled nor was there any intention evident of soon holding a general council. McKee had taken residence in his trading post at the Rapids and was keeping open house to streams of western Indian callers, but the Iroquois who had been summoned from a distance continued to be totally ignored by their Indian hosts.

"During this time," Brant recorded in his journal, "many evil reports were circulated against me by the Shawnoes,[4] saying I was a Traitor & that I only came here to receive Money and that they would have nothing to do with me." The fuming Iroquois, long accustomed to hold the center of the stage at every Indian gathering, were with difficulty persuaded by Brant to remain. After three weeks of these cat-and-mouse tactics Brant insisted June 15th on meeting with as many Shawnee, Delaware, Miami, and Wyandot chiefs as could be buttonholed. To them he remonstrated:

> Seeing the business we are invited here to assist in is at a Stand, I have thought it advisable that we should meet together to know the reason . . . We have had various meetings with the Americans, but none of such importance as this Will be, it therefore Stands us in need to give it the most serious Attention, and requires the greatest Prudence & Unanimity amongst ourselves for upon the event of it Depends the future ease and happiness of ourselves & our Posterity.

Several of his hearers smugly protested that there had been no intention to insult Brant or the Iroquois. Brant's journal continues:

[4] McKee had been closely associated with the Shawnee since his first residence in the nation more than 40 years before. Both he and his father had married Shawnee women and one of his sons was an important Shawnee chief.

Notwithstanding this Friendly Council we were kept at the Same Distance as before and evil reports still Continued against Me. The Shawnoes, Delawares and Miamis, held Private Councils many nights, to which none of the Six Nations were invited. From 15th June to the 1st July no Public Business was transacted.

In this weird competition to control Indian opinion between the dedicated Indian leader and the equally dedicated British administrator, McKee had the great advantage of counseling procrastination while Brant was urging action. No advice could be more welcome to Indians than a suggestion that any decision be postponed. Of the hundreds of delegates who had by now gathered at the Rapids, only the more sophisticated Brant and the Iroquois were concerned by the long delay in the council's formal opening. The others were enjoying the free provisions, entertainment, and rum provided by McKee and relaxing in the pleasant prospect of a long, sociable, and interesting summer. The June 1st date set for the meeting with the American commissioners had long since passed. Even the preparatory Indian council at the Rapids had not yet been convened. By arrangement between Simcoe and McKee the American commissioners were being detained at Niagara. McKee's program, sanctioned by his superiors, was to delay their meeting with the Indians as long as possible and then, when the majority of Indians had become sufficiently accustomed to the idea, to attempt to prevent it altogether.

Not until July 1st did McKee disclose his actual program. In a private conversation with Brant he proposed that the council send an official delegation to meet the American commissioners at Niagara for the purpose of (a) confronting them with a declaration protesting Wayne's breach of the armistice and (b) demanding whether or not they had their government's authority to accept the Ohio boundary, inasmuch as any negotiations were useless if they had not that authority. Brant consented with a number of reservations that were at the moment overlooked and the hastily convened council approved the undertaking. Confident that so defiant and insulting a pronouncement must terminate negotiations forthwith,

McKee made the mistake of agreeing to Brant's becoming a member of the delegation. Most of the deputies were principal chiefs representing the council's war faction but, when faced with the demands of a formal conference with British and American officials, they yielded to Brant's command of English and familiarity with white diplomacy by recognizing him as the delegation's spokesman.

After much anxious consideration, Washington had selected his peace commissioners February 19th, and the appointments had been confirmed by the Senate March 1st. Their national reputations demonstrated the importance attached to their embassy. Benjamin Lincoln had been a major general in the Continental Army. Timothy Pickering had been Postmaster General and was the next year to become Secretary of War. Beverly Randolph had been Governor of Virginia. Their secret instructions empowered them to give up most of the land claimed under the Treaty of Fort Harmar if this proved absolutely necessary and to insist only upon the retention of land north of the Ohio already settled or allocated for settlement. Among cabinet members only Jefferson had objected to this American retreat and his exception was on constitutional grounds.

The commissioners reached Niagara May 17th where they were received with outward courtesy by Simcoe.[5] They were detained at this British post on American soil for more than a month. Simcoe's explanation was that they must await word from McKee that the Indians were ready to receive them. He had had to attach even more critical importance to the prospective American-Indian negotiations since he had learned May 4th that France had declared war on England. He, in common with every other British official, could only assume that the existing French-American alliance might presently lead to the United States entering the war on the French side. The commissioners had no recourse other than to acquiesce patiently in the delay, inasmuch as they could only proceed westward by

[5] Simcoe's private opinion was not so urbane. In a June 14, 1793, letter to Alured Clarke he remarked of the commissioners: "These Gentlemen have much of that low Craft which distinguishes, and is held for Wisdom by People who like the Subjects of the United States, naturally self-opinionated, have a very trifling share of Education."

British transportation, in British custody, and under British protection. Mindful of the fate of their predecessors, Trueman and Hardin, they accepted the protection as a necessity and earnestly requested that their escort include officers of the British army in addition to the assigned officials of the Indian Department. They whiled away the time by sightseeing visits to Niagara Falls and neighboring Iroquois towns and by attending the King's Birthday ball at which they were much impressed by the social graces of several of the daughters of Sir William Johnson and Molly Brant.[6] Finally yielding to their protests that the summer was passing, Simcoe consented to their starting west, directing the officers conducting them to hold them at the mouth of the Detroit River and to deny them permission to visit Detroit or attend the Indian council at the Rapids.

After being further delayed some days at Fort Erie by contrary winds, the commissioners were astonished by the appearance of Brant and his delegation of 50 chiefs. Brant brusquely insisted that they return to Niagara in order that the Indian message might be delivered in Simcoe's presence.[7]

In the ensuing three-day conference between the representatives of the Indians and the representatives of the United States over which the British Lieutenant Governor presided, the commissioners answered the first question posed by the Maumee council with a disclaimer. They insisted that Washington had ordered a complete cessation of hostilities, exhibited copies of conforming proclamations issued by Wayne and the governors of the states adjoining the Ohio, and pointed out that as peace commissioners they would scarcely be venturing into the Indian country unless they had been made certain the armistice would be observed. To clinch the matter they agreed to get off an express to Washington urging him to order Wayne to show greater restraint. To the second and decisive question they were enabled to give as outwardly satisfactory an answer by the

[6] Johnson and Molly had had eight children surviving infancy of whom six were girls.

[7] With the delegation had come a July 1, 1793, dispatch from McKee to Simcoe, stating flatly: "the Indians have made a resolution not to make peace on any other terms" than the Ohio boundary.

care with which Brant had phrased it. Instead of asking if they had authority to accept the Ohio boundary, as he had been instructed by the council, he asked if they were "authorized to establish a Boundary between" the Indians and the United States. Taking equally careful advantage of this opening they replied, "explicitly that we have that authority." Brant's fellow delegates, who had permitted him to do the talking, were somewhat bemused by the proceedings but conceived that they had fulfilled their mission. The commissioners, having by a combination of diplomatic humility and agility apparently thwarted the design to stave off negotiations, again started west, reaching the mouth of the Detroit River July 21st where they were quartered in the house of Matthew Elliott of the British Indian Department. Here, as Simcoe had foreseen, they were no nearer establishing contact with the Indians than had they remained comfortably at home.

Brant and the returning Indian delegation reached the Rapids that same day with their report on the Niagara conference, and on July 23rd the Indian general council at last convened with the serious intention of dealing with the decisive question of war or peace. By now the five major groups of nations represented at the council had divided into two sharply opposing camps. The war faction bitterly denounced Brant for his failure to turn back the American commissioners at Niagara. The Iroquois approved heartily of his stratagem and, after some reflection on the alternative consequences, the Lake Indians also came to his support. The principal delegations speaking for the war faction, the Shawnee, Delaware, Miami, and Wyandot, received at least the vocal support of the delegations from the distant Creek, Cherokee, and Seven Nations of Canada.

The vital issue in dispute was the definition of the boundary to be demanded of the peace-seeking Americans. There was some legalistic justification for the Ohio line. It rested on a principle established by the King's Proclamation of 1763 which had been reaffirmed in the 1768 Treaty of Fort Stanwix with England and the 1775 Treaty of Pittsburgh with American representatives speaking for Virginia, Pennsylvania, and the Continental Congress. Those had been the last treaties to which Indians had assented except under duress. The Indians had, meanwhile, been constantly advised by their British patrons at every general council since 1783 that their rights under those older treaties had not been abridged by the peace treaty between the United States and Great Britain. Brant argued passionately for the more realistic view that some such concession as the Muskingum line must be made were war to be avoided. He kept forcefully reiterating the assertion made in his March 23, 1793, letter to McKee, "This is the best time to obtain a good Peace, and if lost, may not be easily regained." McKee later insisted that he himself had not once offered advice on the boundary question in open council but all through the summer he had daily conducted private conversations with delegates and his admitted personal encouragement of the war faction's stand kept him at constant odds with Brant. Simcoe's formal instructions to McKee to work for peace if one could be achieved without compromising essential Indian and British interests had amounted to an official approval of his course. McKee's conduct of Indian affairs which during this critical period led inevitably to war received the later commendation of his superiors and was rewarded by his continued promotion and preferment.

By July 26th Indian union was clearly disintegrating with each of the opposing parties accusing the other of destroying the confederation. In this struggle to dominate the will of the council the militant party enjoyed that advantage always possessed by aggressors of being able if balked to resolve the issue by taking the field, thereby committing the interests of all other Indians as well to the hazards of war. They enjoyed the further advantage that the council's sole means of communication with the American commissioners was by way of those British officials who were in attendance at the council and those who were in charge of the commissioners.

On July 26th Captain Johnny, principal chief of the Shawnee, ended the acrimonious debate with the blunt announcement, "We are . . . here to form another Message to the Commissioners, we must Strike a Boundary line, that line must be the one agreed upon at the Treaty of Fort Stanwix." Brant declined to sign the message or to write it in English. This secretarial function was performed by Lieutenant Prideaux Selby of the British army, one of the many British observers at the Rapids. The message, reiterating the demand Brant had evaded delivering at Niagara, was dispatched July 28th.

The American commissioners had been restlessly waiting in Elliott's house across Lake Erie from the mouth of the Maumee, increasingly conscious of how helpless was their situation with every means of communications with the Indian council subject to British control. Their suspense was ended by the arrival July 29th of a delegation of 20 chiefs in charge of Elliott. The message from the council, nominally delivered by a Wyandot chief, Carry-One-About, was interpreted by Simon Girty, the entire diplomatic contact thus being under the supervision of the two former Tory partisans who had escaped from Pittsburgh with McKee in 1778 and had ever since devoted their services in the Indian Department to the promotion of Indian hostility to the United States. The gist of the council's message was in the abrupt statement:

> Brothers: You know very well that the boundary-line, which was run by the white people and us, at the Treaty of Fort Stanwix, was the river Ohio . . . If you seriously design to make a firm and lasting peace, you will immediately remove all your people from our side of that river.

Any further attempt at seeking some basis for negotiations appeared useless, but the commissioners had endured too much to give up without one last effort. They were encouraged in this persistence by Elliott who was safely able under the circumstances to maintain the fiction that the Indian Department favored a peaceful settlement. In reply the commissioners drafted a candid statement of the American position, the most essential passages in which were:

> It is impossible to make the river Ohio the boundary between your people and the people of the United States . . . It is now impracticable to remove our people from northern side of the Ohio . . . The United States wish to have confirmed all the lands ceded them by the Treaty of Fort Harmar . . . and in consideration thereof, the

United States would give such a large sum, in money or goods, as was never given at one time, for any quantity of Indian lands, since the white people first set foot on this island.

The American proposal when received by the council served no other purpose than to inflame the conflict in Indian opinion beyond any hope of reconciliation. Realizing he was faced with what seemed his last chance to avert Indian disaster, Brant, speaking for the Iroquois view which was also his own, made an eloquent final appeal:

> It is well known that for these many years past, we have exerted ourselves for the Confederacy and no part of their situation has escaped our Notice . . . Weighing in our Minds our Force, Resources, and every local advantage we Possess, we declare our sentiments from the bottom of our hearts that the Boundary of the Muskingum if adopted in General Council, is for the interest of us all and far preferable to an uncertain War . . . I therefore beg of you not to be rash and consider the Consequences of a War in which we are not unanimous.

The effect of his appeal was undermined by the sensational reply of the chief of the Seven Nations of Canada whose residence deep in British territory persuaded other Indians that his judgment of British intentions might rival Brant's:

> My opinion when I left home was that we were to defend the Old Boundary which is the Ohio, and in this opinion I was confirmed by the English as I passed their Posts, you may think I speak very free, as I live at a Great Distance, but whatever you determine upon I will abide by, my words must be true as I have only one mouth.

By now the Indian confederation which Brant had labored so long to activate and develop was irretrievably compromised. Each successive speaker charged the Iroquois with having taken a position which amounted to having withdrawn from it. This Brant did not attempt to deny. The confederation as a political entity had shrunk to the hard core of the western Indian advocates of an American war who were determined to persist in this course even though it must be waged with help from other Indian nations limited to volunteers. After a midnight conference of the Shawnee, Miami, Wyandot, and Delaware with McKee, Captain Johnny announced to the council the decision of this rump confederation:

> We now are to explain our final Resolution with respect to this Business, our opinion is that the line made in 1768, and which is the Ohio from its Source, is our just Boundary, we will therefore transmit our Sentiments to the Commissioners, who, if they will not relinquish our Lands, may return.

A vote was taken by passing a ceremonial wampum belt from delegation to delegation. The western Indians and the Seven Nations voted to fight for the Ohio, the Iroquois only if the compromise of the Muskingum had first been sought. At this point Brant's journal records:

> Buckongehalis, the Chief of the Delaware . . . pointing to Col. McKee, said that is the Person who advises us to insist on the Ohio River for the line.

Brant's last statement in council indicated how clearly he perceived the swiftly gathering shadows:

> Since the Council is now over and you are come to a final resolution, we hope success will attend you, at this time it is not in our Power to assist you, we must first remove our People from amongst the Americans.

The last entry in his journal noted:

> When the Council was over a War feast was prepared, and the Chiefs of the Shawanoes singing the War Song encouraging the Warriors of all the Nations to be active in defending their Country, saying their Father the English would assist them and Pointed to Col. McKee.

The definitive Indian reply received by the American commissioners August 16, 1793, included language not without a certain dignity:

Money, to us, is of no value, & to most of us unknown, and as no
consideration whatever can induce us to sell the lands on which we
get sustenance for our women and children; we hope we may be
allowed to point out a mode by which your settlers may be easily
removed, and peace thereby obtained . . . We know that these
settlers are poor, or they would never have ventured to live in a
country which have been in continual trouble ever since they crossed
the Ohio; divide therefore this large sum of money which you have
offered to us, among these people, give to each also a portion of what
you say you would give us annually over and above this very large
sum of money, and we are persuaded they would most readily accept
of it in lieu of the lands you sold to them, if you add also the great
sums you must expend in raising and paying Armies, with a view to
force us to yield you our Country, you will certainly have more than
sufficient for the purposes of repaying these settlers for all their
labour and improvements. You have talked to us about concessions.
It appears strange that you should expect any from us, who have only
been defending our just Rights against your invasion; We want Peace;
Restore to us our Country and we shall be Enemies no longer . . .
our only demand, is the peaceable possession of a small part of our
once great Country. Look back and view the lands from whence we
have been driven to this spot, we can retreat no further . . . we have
therefore resolved, to leave our bones in this small space.

The commissioners returned a curt expression of their regret that
peace had not resulted and immediately took ship homeward to
announce the failure of their foredoomed mission. Brant, too, had
failed and in a far larger sense. To Americans the frustration had
been but a temporary setback. For Indians it forecast total catastrophe. Brant, sailing homeward, was forced to realize that in his lifelong struggle to promote unity among Indians as the sole hope of
prolonging their existence as a free people he had been as fatally
confounded by his fellow Indians as had Pontiac.

XVII

༄

Washington 3

The resolution with which western Indians and British officials had advocated war at the Maumee council was not matched by the resolution with which they contemplated the military crisis that had thereby been precipitated. All through September and October every Indian town and British post was swept by exaggerated rumors of Wayne's strength, progress, and intentions. Breathless runners from Indian scouting parties sent out to observe his movements returned almost daily with reports adding new dimensions to the apparent threat. McKee, at his headquarters at the Rapids, entered reports in his journal that Wayne's army was "infinitely more numerous than St. Clair's," that the "American Army was coming on very rapidly," that its objective was definitely Detroit, and that "General Washington has offered . . . three hundred dollars for my scalp." Urgent appeals were dispatched to the Lake Indians to assemble to aid in the defense of Detroit and of their imperiled neighbors on the Maumee. Dorchester, just returned to Quebec, wrote Simcoe October 7, 1793, advising him that the imminent American invasion by a force so much stronger than the small British border garrisons might require the abandonment of all Upper Canada. Simcoe became so agitated by this suggestion that he protested over Dorchester's head directly to Dundas.

The actual military situation had little relation to this tempest of alarm. Wayne's offensive, already delayed through two campaign seasons by his government's appeasement policy, was being further delayed for another year by other restraints over which he had as little control. The moment the returning American commissioners had reached Fort Erie August 23rd, they had got off an express via Major Isaac Craig, commanding at Pittsburgh, to inform Washington at Mount Vernon and Wayne at Fort Washington of the failure of their mission and the consequent end of the armistice. But after having had 16 months in which to assemble and organize his army and after having for weeks expected momentarily word that the truce had expired, Wayne, to his boundless mortification, was still unable to take the field.

Through most of the summer his army had been prostrated by an influenza epidemic. In the spring Kentucky had at his call furnished 1500 militia under Brigadier General Charles Scott, his old friend and Revolutionary companion in arms who had been with him at the storming of Stony Point. Dissatisfied with the inaction prescribed by the armistice and irritated by the nondelivery of their federal pay,[1] most had since straggled homeward. By September there remained with the army only 360 of these vitally important auxiliaries while his regular force had been reduced by sickness and desertion to 2600 effectives. Even more critical was the inadequacy of his supply procurement system. Preoccupied with training and disciplinary problems, he had delegated this responsibility to Wilkinson, his second in command. It had appeared a sensible arrangement in view of Wilkinson's experience as quartermaster during the Revolution and his long acquaintance with mercantile and agricultural affairs in the west. There had not been, however, in spite of

[1] Some of the war department's failure to fill Wayne's needs on schedule had been due to the flight of government personnel from Philadelphia during the 1793 yellow-fever epidemic. For a time Knox was the only major federal official at his desk at the seat of government.

Wayne's increasingly violent strictures, a sufficient accumulation of supplies to enable the army to undertake a campaign.

This had revealed a basic difficulty that threatened to become the most serious of all. Wayne's friends were becoming each week more certain that the supply failure had been calculated and was primarily due to Wilkinson's desire to embarrass his superior. Wilkinson had long made no secret of the fact that he considered himself infinitely better fitted than Wayne for the chief command. To hasten the moment when this might be more generally recognized he had embarked upon the same sort of campaign of interference, disparagement, and misrepresentation that had accomplished the downfall of Clark in 1786. His friends spread a story that the nonpayment of the Kentucky militia had been due to Wayne's embezzlement of funds. Scurrilous articles reflecting on Wayne's character and intelligence were inserted in western newspapers. Letters were circulated censuring Wayne's conduct and ridiculing his ability. Among charges published and circulated were that "such feeble & improvident arrangements, and such guardless & disorderly conduct was never before witnessed in any military corps" and that "the whole operation presents us a tissue of improvidence, disarray, precipitancy, Error & Ignorance, of thoughtless temerity, unseasonable cautions, and shameful omissions" and characterizing Wayne as "a liar, a drunkard, a Fool . . . a Coward . . . and a Hypocrite." The veteran general's choleric temperament, ill health, occasional intemperance, and furious impatience kept him an inviting target for abuse.

Wayne, intermittently exhausted by fits of rage, drinking bouts, and recurring ailments, nevertheless permitted nothing to swerve him from his determination to hammer his army into that state of disciplined readiness his professional judgment considered necessary. On October 5th he wrote Knox, "I pray you not to permit present appearances to cause too much anxiety either in the mind of the President, or yourself, on account of this army." On the 7th he marched from Fort Washington. Due to the lateness of the season and the lack of supplies, it could be only a token advance to the end of the six miles of road beyond Fort Jefferson which he had built in the spring before Knox had brought the work to a halt by his reiterated insistence on a closer observance of the armistice. Here Wayne went into winter quarters in a fortified camp he called Camp Greenville[2] and the moment his defenses were secure resumed his remorseless drilling.

The need for the discipline upon which he insisted was emphasized October 17th by an Indian attack on one of his convoys in which the train was destroyed and its 90-man escort routed with a loss of 16 killed, including two much mourned young officers. On Christmas Eve he rose from a sickbed to lead a winter march to St. Clair's haunted battlefield where his Legionnaires pitched their tents among the frost-encrusted heaps of bones that had escaped Wilkinson's hasty interment. Here a new advance post, Fort Recovery, was built and garrisoned. A persistent search discovered the hiding place of the lost cannon, buried by the Indians after their capture two years before. They were refitted and mounted on the walls. Wayne was now poised for the war's culminating campaign the next year. His chain of forts extended like a gigantic spear 98 miles into the Indian country, its point thrust toward the central Indian stronghold on the Maumee.

Wayne's inability to mount an offensive in 1793 was a bitter disappointment to the long-suffering frontier but to Washington with his wider view of the other threats confronting the nation the delay had its compensatory aspects. Since his first day in office his anxiety to defend the frontier had been more than balanced by a stronger anxiety to avoid involvement in a foreign war for which the struggling young republic was fatally unprepared. The risks of such an involvement had suddenly increased in 1793 until they towered on every horizon. The news from France continued to rock the world. Louis XVI was beheaded January 21st and within a matter of days France's war with Austria and Prussia had widened to include England, Spain, and Holland. The blasts of the great conflict

---

[2] Wayne named the camp Greeneville in honor of his Revolutionary comrade Nathanael Greene, but most historians since have conformed to the spelling adopted by the city of Greenville, Ohio, which later rose on the site.

in Europe reverberated almost as ominously in North America. England and Spain, enemies through the centuries, were now allies. A frontier incident on the Maumee or the Yazoo that led to war with either could henceforth mean war with both. The constant and embittered fighting between American frontiersmen and the Indian allies of Britain and Spain made such an incident seem sooner or later inevitable. Wayne's organized invasion of the Indian country could only be viewed as a nearly certain precipitant. This inherent and perpetual danger was in 1793 enormously aggravated by the anxiety of France to provoke a war between the United States and France's two principal enemies. In this aim France had a double motive. The fanatically aggressive French republic was bent on recovering the North American empire that had been lost by the French monarchy. And it was fully realized in Paris that no shrewder blow could be struck at France's bitterest enemy, England, than to involve the great maritime state in a conflict with her maritime former colonies.

Washington's resolve to keep his country out of this new world war was beset within the country's borders by the explosions of political controversy ignited by the French Revolution. Most Americans had applauded the transition of an ancient monarchy into a sister republic. Memories of French aid in the American Revolution were still fresh. That war's legacy of anti-British sentiment, kept vigorous by British retention of the Lake posts, encouragement of Indian attacks, and interference with American trade, was still strong. It was widely held that observance of the memorable alliance with France by which independence had been won was a course demanded by national honor. The excesses following the King's execution disconcerted many Americans but stirred the more ardent pro-French enthusiasts to even more violent expressions of sympathy. Increasingly sharp and bitter differences developed. The cleavage in public opinion tended to follow the lines apparent during the great debate over ratification of the Constitution. The Federalist advocates of a strong central government hailed Washington's peace policy as a sensible regard for the nation's security while their democratic opponents, then called Republicans, denounced it as a sordid service to British interests.[3]

Washington had been unanimously re-elected February 13, 1793, but by spring he was being subjected to the perpetual criticism and intermittent vilification which has been the normal lot of every president since. A rash of "democratic societies" had erupted, modeled in part on the American pre-Revolutionary committees of correspondence and in other aspects on the French pre-revolutionary Jacobin clubs. Their primary function was to give louder voice to their members' pro-French and anti-English sentiments and wider currency to their denunciations of the administration's course. The most responsible public figures were adding their contribution to this torrent of censure. Madison was writing, "It is mortifying that the President should have anything to apprehend from the success of liberty in another country, since he owes his preeminence to the success of it in his own." Monroe, correctly considering Washington's dispatch of the peace commissioners to the Indians as a basic element in his peace program, wrote Jefferson, "I trust our humiliation has attained its lowest point, when we are capable of placing ourselves in a situation so degrading and shameful." Jefferson, though still a member of Washington's cabinet, made no secret of his definition of the issue: "The old Tories joined by our merchants, who trade on British capital, and the idle rich, are with the kings. All other descriptions with the French."

Nowhere was public reaction to Washington's peace policy more active and violent than in the west. There the democratic societies were less concerned with words than with preparations for action. The frontier's scorn of neutrality was the embittered revulsion of a people who well realized that for them there had been no peace and still was no peace. In 1788 westerners had tacitly chosen to postpone judgment on federal union until the new federal government had

[3] As one illustration of the bitterness marking this political dispute Jefferson was writing James Monroe May 5, 1793: "All the old spirit of 1776, is rekindling . . . In the meantime H. [Hamilton] is panic-struck if we refuse our breach to every kick which Gr. Brit. may chuse to give it. He is for proclaiming at once the most abject principles, such as would invite & merit habitual insults."

had an opportunity to prove itself. The more centralized powers embodied in the Constitution had so far produced no advantage discernible in the west other than the belated and grudging admission of Kentucky. Five more years had passed and the Indians were still holding their ground, the Mississippi was still closed, the Spanish were still at Natchez, the British were still on the Lakes, the smoke of burning cabins still streaked the sky, and every border family remained still in daily and deadly danger. Contempt for the national government's performance was given a new vigor and volatility in 1793 by the wave of ideological sympathy with the French Revolution which was accompanied by a feverish resort to liberty poles, red caps, libertarian slogans, and all the trappings of radical upheaval. This spirit of revolt found contrasting outlets in the two great centers of western population, Kentucky and transmountain Pennsylvania.

In western Pennsylvania it developed into a direct attack on the federal government with the local democratic societies becoming centers of resistance to federal taxation. The popular movement on the Monongahela progressed through the stage of harassing tax collectors and burning the stills of inhabitants who paid the tax to an organized and armed insurrection marked by the destruction of federal property, assaults on federal troops, seizures of the mails, and so complete a defiance of the national government's authority that Washington late in 1794 was obliged to call up an army of eastern militia five times more numerous than Wayne's regular army then engaged in the Indian campaign.

In Kentucky the outlet found for western dissatisfaction, though a less direct rejection of national authority, threatened for a time even more alarming consequences. There the democratic societies' protestations of sympathy for revolutionary France led naturally and inevitably to a revival of the long-familiar proposal to take the Mississippi from the west's great enemy, Spain, now also become the enemy of republican France. As in so many former crises attention turned to Clark, in frontier estimation still the greatest westerner. In 1786 and 1790 his similar projects had been frustrated by the national government's interference. This time the more aggressive support of his fellow westerners could be expected to preclude that interference. Clark was receptive. His final petition for reimbursement of his personal expenditures during his Revolutionary conquests, reiterating his declaration, "I have given the United States half the territory they possess, and for them to suffer me to remain in poverty, in consequence of it, will not redound much to their honor hereafter," had been denied in November by Virginia. He had always been ignored by the federal government. Agonized as he had been by his repeated repudiations by his state and his country, particularly by the instances of their preferment of his despised rival, Wilkinson, he even so did not feel that his long-harbored Mississippi design was fundamentally disloyal to either. He considered driving Spain from the Mississippi no more than a passing service to France while remaining convinced that it was an imperative and permanent service to the west. It was to the west that his services had always been dedicated.

For this last of his many campaigns his basic plan was as daring and at the same time as reasoned as in the case of his greatest successes. In taking Vincennes he had led a mixed force of American Frenchmen and American frontiersmen. The French inhabitants of the shores of the Mississippi outnumbered the present Spanish garrisons by 10 to 1. The essence of his plan was a sweep of the river by an expedition of Kentuckians operating in conjunction with an uprising of these French residents. After consultation with his brother-in-law, James O'Fallon, with whom he had been associated in the earlier Yazoo project, he got off a letter in December 1792 to O'Fallon's old friend, Thomas Paine, announcing his intention and requesting the co-operation of a coincidental French naval demonstration in the Gulf. Paine had been elected member of the Convention from Calais upon his escape from England after writing *The Rights of Man* and, in company with a number of other American expatriates in Paris, was in a position to take a helpful interest in such American schemes as Clark's. The widening disclosure of Clark's intentions, as Kentucky discussions continued, gained him the approval of most Kentuckians. Washington's concern lest the United States become involved in a new foreign war was not shared in the west. In the west the last foreign war had not yet ended.

Fortified in his intentions by word from his correspondents in Paris that France proposed to send a minister to the United States armed with instructions to promote just such enterprises as he had in mind, Clark wrote his famous letter of February 2, 1793. The document is made the more interesting by the revealing light cast upon Clark's personality, upon conditions in the west at the time, and upon the range of difficulties confronting Washington:

> I can raise abundance of men in this western country—men as well Americans as French who have repeatedly fought, obtained laurels, and never yet met with a repuls under my command, men whose courage, fidelity to their country and confidence in my arrangements, which never yet failed them of success, took the Illinois and Pos St. Vincennes from the Britons, saved St. Louis and the rest of Louisiana for the Spaniards, from that nation, humbled the whole Northern and Southern tribes of Indians, (those in particular who are now so hostile and triumphant) to the very dust, preserved Kentucky, Cumberland, and the whole territory northwest of the Ohio to the United States, and protected the western frontiers of Virginia and Pennsylvania from British and Indian depredations . . . Out of Kentucky, Cumberland, the settlement on Holston, the Wabash and the Illinois I can (by my name alone) raise 1500 brave men—and the French at St. Louis and throughout the rest of Louisiana, together with the American Spanish subjects at the Natchez would, I am sure of it (for they all know me) flock to my Standard . . . With the first 1500 alone I can take the whole of Louisiana for France. If France will be hearty and secret in this business—my success borders on certainty.

Upon learning of the momentous widening of the war in Europe, Washington rushed from Mount Vernon back to Philadelphia, more resolved than ever to keep his country out of it. His first business was to instruct the American peace commissioners, then on the eve of setting forth on their dismal pilgrimage to Niagara and the Indian country. Despite indignant April letters from Governor Henry Lee of Virginia and Governor Isaac Shelby of Kentucky, demanding authority to retaliate against continuing Indian outrages,[4] he continued sternly to insist on observation of the armistice. After two stormy cabinet meetings in which only Hamilton and Knox supported his views and Jefferson's and Hamilton's disagreements were even more heated than usual, Washington took the step he had in any event determined to take. His neutrality proclamation, signed April 22, 1793, called upon all citizens to refrain from hostile acts and stated, "the duty and interest of the United States require that they should with sincerity and good faith adopt and pursue a conduct friendly and impartial toward the belligerent Powers." He was not disturbed by the immediate roar of disapproval from the country's pro-French majority. The first President's considered judgment was a rock not easily shaken. That same day he received word that the heralded new French minister had arrived in faraway Charleston.

That Gallicly effervescent emissary, Citizen Edmond Genêt, driven off course by contrary winds during a laborious 48-day passage, had disembarked, April 8, 1793, 600 miles from his Philadelphia destination. He was fresh from a tour of duty at the court of Russia and his varied background included a sister who had been Marie Antoinette's companion and friend. Novel to him as was the new world scene upon which he had entered, he began at once to make himself completely at home while proceeding with immense enthusiasm to carry out his instructions to engage the United States in the war on the side of France. He won the confidence of Governor William Moultrie of South Carolina, commissioned American

---

[4] Among the hundreds of settlers killed in 1793 was Governor Shelby's brother, Evan. In John Haywood's *Civil and Political History of Tennessee,* Knoxville, 1823, a survey of the region's Indian wars based on contemporary records and recollections, 29 pages were devoted to 1793 depredations and 109 distinct attacks listed for the Holston-Cumberland frontier alone. Washington was fully aware of and deeply moved by the border people's plight. In his May 6, 1793, reply to Lee he wrote, "It gives me inexpressible pain to receive such frequent and distressing accounts from the Western frontiers."

privateers to prey on English commerce, and undertook the organization of expeditions of Georgia frontiersmen, backed by South Carolina land-company interests, to launch attacks on Spanish posts in Florida and Louisiana.

Having lighted these insurrectionary fires in the south, he set off northward to present himself officially to the government to which he was accredited. His journey across the Carolinas and Virginia was more like the triumphal progress of a proconsul on his way from frontier victories to claim a capital's laurels than it was like the circumspect approach of a foreign ambassador. Everywhere he received the acclaim of democratic societies, of throngs of sympathizers with the French Revolution, and of local Republican politicians. All was climaxed by the fervor of his reception in Philadelphia. Cheering thousands waving tricolored cockades lined the streets. Processions, demonstrations, and salvos of artillery salutes persuaded him that he was regarded as a public hero of Messianic proportions. His formal reception by Washington was frigid but he had been so enthralled by the displays of American sympathies with France and the indications that the administration's neutrality policy lacked public support that he was led to the fatal mistake of undertaking to appeal to the American people over the heads of their government. In thus committing himself to a collision course with Washington he was inviting a contest which presently proved to be beyond his capacities.

Upon his arrival in Philadelphia, May 16, 1793, Genêt found Clark's February 2nd letter awaiting him. It offered what appeared to him a heaven-sent opportunity to make sure of provoking a Spanish-American war. His choice of André Michaux, the eminent French naturalist, as his agent to contact and encourage Clark was a selection in which advantage and disadvantage were curiously mixed. Michaux had had no military or diplomatic experience but he was accustomed to wilderness travel, his scientific reputation provided a cloak of innocence while assuring him a respectful hearing in French communities in the west, and he was an ardent republican. The savant dutifully accepted his conspiratorial mission and journeyed west accompanied by two French artillery officers. He carried with him authority to appoint Clark "Major General in the Armies of France and Commander-in-Chief of the French Revolutionary Legion on the Mississippi River" and letters of introduction to Governor Shelby of Kentucky from Congressman John Brown and Secretary of State Jefferson.

Having had no reply to his February 2nd letter, Clark had lost hope of French support. His enthusiasm was revived by the startling call to action brought to him September 17th at Louisville by Michaux. Genêt's master plan envisaged not only Clark's Kentucky expedition but supporting invasions from the Georgia, Holston, and Cumberland frontiers. Michaux was authorized to promote coincidental French insurrections in Spanish territory and to negotiate French treaties with Indian nations. Intense interest in the project was kindled throughout Kentucky. Democratic societies took the lead by encouraging enlistments, getting off memorials to Philadelphia denouncing neutrality and raising funds to underwrite expenses pending the arrival of the money promised by Genêt. Clark contributed $4680 from his own meager resources. Frontier leaders of the stature of Benjamin Logan and John Montgomery rallied to his standard. He devoted himself to his preparations with a considerable resurgence of his onetime energy.

Stirred by Spain's indignant protests, born of urgent warnings sent to Carondelet by Wilkinson and Harry Innes, Washington's administration strove to put out the fire. Even the bright glow of Jefferson's republican sympathies had been cooled by Genêt's indiscretions and particularly by his disposition to take his case to the American people. Referring to the President's views, Jefferson wrote Shelby urging that Clark's preparations be suppressed before they constituted an act of war against a friendly nation. Knox wrote Shelby authorizing him to use force if necessary. St. Clair issued a proclamation calling upon the French inhabitants of the Northwest Territory to keep the peace and to arrest Genêt's agents. Washington was with some difficulty dissuaded from expelling Genêt, but a demand was dispatched to his government that he be recalled. The first major casualty in this fierce contest between Federalists and Republicans, France's censors and France's champions, the national government and the west, was Jefferson. Realizing how much his usefulness had been impaired by his many disagreements with the President's judgment, he resigned December 31, 1793.

It was in faraway Paris that the mounting pressures in the American west were eventually somewhat relieved. Preoccupied with military reverses in Europe, internal insurrections, and the excesses of the Reign of Terror, the revolutionary masters of France were unable to pursue their peripheral commitments in North America. The new French minister, Joseph Fauchet, finally arrived February 21, 1794, and on March 6th reluctantly withdrew French support from all of Genêt's enterprises. Clark, already handicapped by Genêt's inability to furnish the financial support he had promised, nevertheless continued his preparations. Shelby, impressed by most Kentuckians' approval of the anti-Spanish, pro-French project, had repeatedly declined to interfere. As chief executive of the only western state and as such a principal spokesman for the western point of view, he had clearly defined that view in writing Jefferson that he knew of no law to forbid any American to move anywhere in the United States or to restrict his actions after he had crossed the country's borders and in his January 13, 1794, letter to Washington:

> I shall upon all occasions be averse to the exercise of any power which I do not consider myself as being clearly and explicitly vested with, much less would I assume a power to exercise it against men whom I consider as friends and brethren, in favor of a man whom I view as an enemy and a tyrant.

With Kentucky's complete approval Clark, on January 25, 1794, began to publish his proposals in newspapers, calling for volunteers each of whom was promised 2000 acres of Spanish land and all "lawful Plunder to be equally divided agreeable to the custom of War."

After Fauchet's repudiation of Genêt[5] and Shelby's refusal to intervene, the administration redoubled its attempts to break up the expedition. Though the House in March refused to join the Senate in voting penalties against filibustering expeditions, on March 24th Washington issued a proclamation calling upon Clark and his adherents to desist, on March 31st Knox ordered Wayne to rebuild Fort Massac on the lower Ohio and to establish a garrison there to prevent Clark's descent of the river, and in June Congress at last yielded to Washington's prodding by making it a crime for a citizen to engage in hostile acts against any foreign power with which the United States was at peace.

There was still no assurance that Clark could be deterred. Loss of official French support had served to make the undertaking seem more than ever the essentially Kentucky enterprise that he had from the first considered it. Flatboats were under construction at Louisville. Clark's lieutenant, Colonel John Montgomery, descended the Cumberland to the Ohio at the head of a contingent of Cumberland frontiersmen and French volunteers. He there built a stockade and began to interrupt river traffic destined for Spanish territory. Meanwhile on the Georgia frontier, Elijah Clarke, forced to postpone his Genêt-inspired invasion of Spanish Florida by the withering of French support, instead crossed the Oconee with his volunteer force, in defiance of Georgia and the United States as well as of the Creek and Spain, to seize a strip of Creek land, defining his occupation as the establishment of an independent republic.

For years Spanish commanders in Florida and Louisiana had been obsessed by their apprehension of large-scale aggressions by American frontiersmen. George Rogers Clark's preparations to attack Spanish territory and Elijah Clarke's intrusion into Creek territory appeared to confirm their worst fears. The stationing of Wayne's garrison at Fort Massac only added to their alarm. It was regarded as a subterfuge indicating that the United States proposed when the

[5] Fauchet had brought with him instructions to return Genêt under arrest to France for trial, but Genêt claimed sanctuary in the United States, married Cornelia Clinton, daughter of Governor George Clinton of New York, and lived out his life in this country.

which was immediately broken by themselves as soon as Peace was signed, would have been mended, or a new one drawn in an amicable manner; here also I have been disappointed. Children: Since my return, I find no appearance of a Line remains; and from the manner in which the People of the States push on, and act, and talk on this side, and from what I learn of their conduct towards the Sea, I shall not be surprized if we are at war with them in the course of the present year; and if so, a Line must be drawn by the Warriors . . . I shall acknowledge no Lands to be theirs which have been encroached on by them since the year 1783; they then broke the Peace, and as they kept it not on their part; it doth not bind on ours . . . therefore all their approaches towards us since that time . . . I consider as an Infringement on the King's Rights; and when a Line is drawn between us, be it in Peace or War . . . those people must all be gone who do not obtain leave to become the King's subjects . . . Children: What further can I say to you? You are Witness that on our parts we have acted in the most peaceable manner, and borne the Language and Conduct of the People of the United States with Patience; but I believe our Patience is almost exhausted.

The full impact of Dorchester's address could only be judged, then or now, with reference to the effect on his listeners. These were Indians who during the Revolution had fought the United States in complete and active association with British troops. Since 1783 they had been repeatedly warned by Dorchester that while they enjoyed British sympathy in their continuing war with the United States they could not expect the British army to intervene in their behalf. Now he was suddenly announcing a totally different policy. The energy with which he expressed antipathy to the United States and urged them to persist in their fight for the Ohio boundary could only represent in their minds an unmistakable assurance that Great Britain would enter the war at their side. Insofar as the highest ranking British official in North America could speak for his government he had proclaimed British determination to assert dominion over the northwest. Upon his declaration that American settlers remaining north of the Ohio must become British subjects Indians could place no other construction than that Great Britain proposed to champion Indian rights to the point of annexing the Indian country.

Whatever doubt there may have been of the meaning of Dorchester's words was swiftly removed by the testimony of his actions. On February 17th he ordered Simcoe to establish and garrison a British fort at the Maumee Rapids. This favorite council site had gained recognition as a kind of Indian capital. Here, too, stood McKee's private trading post and official headquarters, toward which for nearly a generation Indians had looked for the gifts, munitions, trade goods, and guidance that marked British patronage. Simcoe began construction of the fort April 10, 1794, naming it Fort Miami in a strained grasp at the military and diplomatic technicality that the establishment represented no more than the reoccupation of a long-maintained British position.[6] On April 14th he reiterated and re-emphasized British intentions by reading Dorchester's address to a great assembly of western Indians at Au Glaize. The jubilant Indians were by now fully convinced of the authenticity of these assurances by which the Lieutenant Governor and the Governor General were confirming what McKee had been telling them for years. With their own eyes they could see that British troops, British guns, and the British flag had become a principal feature of the defenses of the central Indian stronghold on the Maumee upon which Wayne must advance were the Americans so foolhardy as to persist in the war.

The more sophisticated Iroquois were likewise becoming convinced. After years of discreet accommodation to American demands and attempts to persuade the western Indians to make similar accommodations, the Iroquois attitude had suddenly hardened. Brant, so long sceptical of British sincerity, had been lifted from the depths of his discouragement. He could realize that with the new British

---

[6] The original Fort Miami, at the present Fort Wayne, Indiana, had never been rebuilt as an army post after its destruction by Pontiac in 1763. The later trading post on the site, serving the Miami Indians, had moved with the Miami as they moved and could be said to be situated in 1794 at the Rapids. This reasoning failed to disguise the fact that the British army had advanced into American territory to take a position where it might more effectively defend Britain's Indian allies with whom the United States was at war.

assurance of support there had opened one last opportunity to establish an Indian union capable of protecting Indian interests. He was writing McKee May 8, 1794, "all proposals . . . to promote peace between the Indians and the yankys must now come to an end." Devoting his energies to the military preparations of the Iroquois, he exhorted the Seven Nations of Canada to honor their promise to share in the confederation's defense.

He did not at the time appear to have much misjudged the sudden new earnestness of British official intentions. Simcoe's April 11, 1794, letter to Carondelet comforted his Spanish counterpart with accounts of British military moves and the assertion that war with the United States was "very probable." Dorchester was taking eager advantage of his government's permission to raise a corps of 1500 provincials, was diligently strengthening British forts and naval forces on the Lakes, and in his April 14, 1794, letter to Simcoe referring to war with the United States as "inevitable."

Every development of the spring increased the excitement among the formerly cautious Iroquois. Aroused by a most unfortunately timed Pennsylvania occupation of Iroquois land near the present Erie, Pennsylvania, Iroquois councils were united for the first time since the Revolution. Brant, addressing the United States through Israel Chapin, American agent to the Iroquois, at the Buffalo Creek conference, April 21, 1794, declared, "We are of the same opinion with the people of the United States; you consider yourselves as independent people; we, as the original inhabitants of this country, and sovereigns of the soil, look upon ourselves as equally independent, and free as any nation or nations." The Iroquois nursed their indignation until by July 4, 1794, the Buffalo Creek council was serving on the United States an ultimatum couched in terms harsh with insolence and menace:

> General Washington, attend. What gives us room for the making of so many speeches, is, because you relate all the former deceptions that have been used . . . Brother: We are determined now, as we were before that the line shall remain. We have fully considered on the boundary we have marked out . . . If you do not comply with

our request, we shall determine on something else, as . . . we are determined to be a free people. You know, General Washington, that we, the Six Nations, have always been able to defend ourselves.

Washington's long struggle to keep his country out of war had been made to appear a disastrous failure by the stunning truculence of the British challenge and the new surge of Indian defiance. The disadvantages of war had meanwhile multiplied. There could no longer be even the slightest doubt that it must become a two-front war with the United States engaged simultaneously with both Great Britain and Spain. France had been rendered useless as an ally by continental commitments in Europe. Even the immediate Indian enemy had become stronger. The formerly amicable Iroquois were bristling as menacingly as their embattled brothers on the Maumee. Their belligerence was given added importance by their influence over other Indians and their occupation of the most strategic location on the continent.[7]

The maintenance of peace was threatened almost as fearfully by the wave of pugnacity sweeping the people of the United States. It had become obvious that the impulse of the Georgia, Cumberland, Holston, and Kentucky frontiers to attack Spanish Indians and Spanish territory could not possibly be much longer restrained. The inhabitants of western Pennsylvania, selecting their own government as their enemy, were arming and drilling for civil war. The state government of Pennsylvania, while deploring the rebellion within its borders, was nevertheless dispatching militia under the command of Captain Ebenezer Denny to occupy Iroquois land in the Erie Triangle. The usually more sedate people of the seaboard, the great majority of the country's population, were in the grip of impulses as aggressive as those of the frontier they had so often deprecated. Already stirred to an emotional pitch by the pro-French controversy, anti-English sentiment was fired to a frenzy by the

[7] As an illustration of the significance of their situation, Simcoe in a March 14, 1794, letter to Dorchester proposed that at the commencement of hostilities between Great Britain and the United States he lead an attack, in conjunction with Brant's Iroquois, upon Wayne's communications by way of an advance from Niagara upon Pittsburgh and then down the Ohio upon Cincinnati.

British seizure of American shipping in the West Indies and by the news of Dorchester's address. Congress, particularly the House, responded to the surge of popular rage and was with the greatest difficulty restrained by the administration from steps leading irretrievably to war. In early March, Congress voted large increases in the military and naval establishment and imposed a 30-day embargo. On March 31st the House voted an army of 80,000 militia and 25,000 regulars and on April 25th a nonintercourse resolution which escaped Senate concurrence only by the breaking of a tie vote by Vice President Adams.

Washington's resolve remained nevertheless unshaken. He had not forgotten the terrible strains of the Revolution. He knew the young nation was not yet ready for the strains of another war to be this time waged with only its own limited resources. How sound was his judgment was demonstrated when the war with Great Britain did come 18 years later in 1812. By then three western states, Kentucky, Tennessee, and Ohio, had been admitted, nearly a million and a half Americans lived west of the mountains, the threat of the west's secession had faded, the country's population had passed seven million with a far more than comparable increase in its wealth, the federal government had compelled general respect and acceptance by functioning successfully through six administrations, and still the war was marked by an all but fatal series of military disasters and national humiliations.

With the threats of war becoming more menacing every day and in every quarter, Washington continued to hold to his course with the same calm pertinacity with which he had dealt with so many past crises. The Governor of Georgia was directed to remove Elijah Clarke and authorized to resort to the use of South Carolina militia or federal troops if he found Georgia militia unreliable. The Governor of Pennsylvania was persuaded to halt his militia at Le Boeuf, the already historic spot where the young Washington 40 years before had delivered Virginia's warning to the French during his celebrated winter journey. Any attempt to suppress the western Pennsylvania rebellion by federal arms was postponed until commissioners representing the United States and the legal government of Pennsylvania had had ample opportunity to seek a solution of the dispute by negotiation. To deal with the sudden Iroquois intransigence, Knox was instructed, "to leave no means unassayed to keep the Six Nations well disposed . . . and to buy Capt Brant off at almost any price." And, finally, to cope with the gravest of the many threats, Great Britain's challenge, Chief Justice John Jay was recruited from the bench to proceed to London as minister extraordinary to make one last effort to seek some basis upon which the tensions between the two countries might be eased.[8]

Jay's appointment aroused a new storm of public protest which erupted most violently of all in the west. Whatever he managed to achieve could in any event have no effect for during the many months required to get across the Atlantic, conduct the negotiations, and get word of the result back to Philadelphia and Quebec the actual events of the intervening summer campaign could meanwhile have committed both governments to a contrary course of action.[9] Eight days after his May 12, 1794, sailing from New York there came news of the British invasion at Fort Miami. There was inflicted upon Washington the sudden necessity to make the most oppressive decision any president can make. He accepted it with the same resolution with which he had formerly clung to his determination to keep the peace. The dangers surrounding war with Great Britain had not been reduced, but he was as susceptible to one demand as was Lincoln in his later torment. At whatever cost the union must be preserved. Washington had considered the Lake posts not worth a war inasmuch as the natural growth of the United States must in time inevitably lead to their possession. But that growth could be

[8] The term *cold war* had not, of course, then been invented. But the parallel between the nature of the problems which had absorbed Washington for the last five years and the complexities confronting us today is unmistakable. Both periods have imposed upon the President the fateful duty of balancing the demands of national security and national survival.

[9] Definitive official word of Jay's Treaty first reached Secretary of State Edmond Randolph March 7, 1795, and Simcoe did not receive his official copy of the terms, together with his government's instructions written November 20, 1794, until October 1795.

cut off by the west's secession which appeared a certain consequence were the national government's hesitation to deal with the west's Indian enemy to be prolonged for even one more year. If the British persisted in their announced intention of defending the Indians, then war with Great Britain must forthwith be faced. Wayne was instructed to proceed with his invasion of the Indian country and, if British forces attempted to interfere, to attack them with the same vigor with which he proposed to attack the Indians.

Congress adjourned June 9th. Washington left for Mount Vernon June 17th. In accepting the presidency he had committed himself to personal responsibility for the fate of his country. He was now required to endure the suspense while his country's future depended upon distant actions and decisions over which he could have no control and of which he could not even know until weeks and months after they had occurred.

XVIII

ତ୍ତ

Revolt in the West

The summer of 1794, while Washington awaited the portentous news from Wayne and Jay, was made more fearfully anxious by a final demonstration of how clear and present had been the separation danger in the west. Twenty years of antipathy to the east, aggravated by dissatisfaction with a central government which most westerners believed solely devoted to eastern interests, finally reached the stage of armed rebellion not on the farther and wilder frontier but in the western portion of Pennsylvania. The gravity of the challenge was compounded by the circumstance that these were westerners who were also citizens of an eastern state.[1] Pennsylvania was, moreover, the anchor state of the federal union with a long-exercised moderating influence which had often been successfully exerted to compose sectional differences. That it should be citizens of Pennsylvania who had been first to take arms against the national government emphasized how deep-seated was the disposition of people living beyond the mountains to consider themselves more committed to the demands of their special situation than to their status as Virginians or Pennsylvanians or Americans.

[1] Inhabitants of Virginia's Ohio County took some part in the rebellion.

That the long gathering storm should erupt in this nearest and oldest section of the west was not in itself surprising. This was a population accustomed to violence in thought as well as deed. The evolution of the Pennsylvania border had from the outset presented a case history of frontier intransigence. The first settlers on the Monongahela had come in defiance of land companies, their provincial governments, and the King's proclamation. They had remained in the face of all efforts by the English army and their Indian enemies to expel them. The land to which each had clung had been held only by his own will and determination during the long period in which no legal titles could be established. Land disputes between individuals had been inflamed by the conflicting territorial claims of Pennsylvania and Virginia to the area. Duplicate courts, sheriffs, militia commanders, and tax gatherers had confused every function of government. Disrespect for higher authority had become a conditioned reflex of a people driven to the realization that their survival depended entirely upon their own resourcefulness. There had been no improvement after the Continental Congress had become that higher authority. During all the years of the Revolution the border inhabitants had battled for their lives while their central government remained unable to furnish effective aid. Frontier resentment had become embittered and chronic. The impact of seven more years of Indian depredations on people who had recently suffered east of the mountains the horrors of Pontiac's War and the French War had aroused passions of hatred exemplified by the applauded exploits of Lewis Wetzel and the mass murder of the Moravians.

Peace had neither quieted these passions nor inspired new faith in the national government. The United States had proved for year after dreary year unable to open the Mississippi, to remove British bases from the Lakes, or to reduce the Indian danger. Its every governmental posture, either under the Confederation or the Constitution, had indicated a sustained disregard for the west. When federal troops whose only former action had been the eviction of settlers had at last taken the field against Indians, they had suffered humiliating defeats. When, therefore, as a climax to this unrelieved record of inability to help or defend the west the national government had levied a tax on the west's one valuable export, frontier rage could have flamed no more furiously had there been federal agents beating upon every cabin door.

Secretary of the Treasury Hamilton had realized when the new national government took office under the Constitution the imperative necessity of establishing the nation's credit. Among the revenue-raising measures to which he resorted had been the March 3, 1791, enactment of an excise tax of seven cents a gallon on spirits. In the east this amounted to an eighth of the value, but in the west to more than a quarter. Whisky was one of the few western products that could be transported eastward over the mountains at a profit. A horse could pack no more than four bushels of rye but after its conversion into whisky could carry the equivalent of 24 bushels. Westerners were convinced that if the east was not making another attempt to retard the west's development it was certainly taking a calculated and unjustifiable advantage. They conceived that there was a principle involved as real as taxation without representation, and every other resentment became merged in this basic rejection of federal authority.

On the frontier direct action was always a first impulse. Physical resistance to the federal impost was instant and vigorous. Mass meetings were held, committees of correspondence organized, protests and memorials drafted. Violence was not at first publicly recommended but was from the first practiced. A principal response was a popular and spontaneous program of intimidation. Roving gangs of night riders, commonly known as "Tom the Tinker's Boys," destroyed the stills of whisky makers who paid the tax. Federal officials were whipped, tarred and feathered, robbed and burned with heated irons. Inhabitants who admitted federal sympathies were threatened. A people accustomed to bear arms was up in arms.

Federal authorities were startled and puzzled by the unexpected vigor of this frontier defiance. Repression by force was not at first contemplated and was in any event for a time impossible. The national government's limited military resources were entirely devoted to Wayne's slow buildup. Washington was embarked upon the policy of appeasement upon which he considered the nation's security depended. The threat of possible war with England, Spain, or France, added to the demands of the continuing Indian war, left little room to deal with an internal rebellion. During 1792 and 1793 no serious efforts were made to collect the tax or to punish those who had harassed federal officials. The national government's patience and forebearance produced some relaxation of tensions west of the mountains.

These tensions were renewed and redoubled, however, by the political controversy aroused by Washington's 1793 neutrality proclamation. Republican sympathy with France and aversion to England were magnified in the Republican west. The frontier embraced the doctrine of equal rights for all men with a fervor matched only by the vehemence of the suspicion that other men were constantly scheming to abridge those rights. It was the average westerner's first impulse to ascribe his difficulties to the machinations of eastern merchants, bankers, and speculators and to regard the Federalist program as a calculated preparation for the restoration of "tyranny." The spread of the democratic societies to the Monongahela in late 1793 provided an outlet for extremist agitation. A series of mass meetings led to the organization of "associations" pledged to mutual resistance to every manifestation of the national government's authority. The movement drew more of its inspiration from the contemporary extravagances of the French Revolution than from the earlier attitudes of the American Revolution. The incipient insurrection took on more and more of the aspects of a class war. Liberty poles were erected, tricolored badges flaunted, Jacobin slogans shouted. A few more responsible citizens, including distillers and merchants with contracts to supply Wayne's army, counseled moderation but were howled down by the mass of impoverished settlers who had nothing to lose.

The most important of these moderates was John Neville, long considered the leading citizen of western Pennsylvania. He had served with Washington in Braddock's campaign, had commanded at Fort Pitt at the outbreak of the Revolution, and during the war had risen to colonel of the 4th Virginia continental regiment. Though personally opposed to the whisky tax he had accepted the post of excise inspector in the hope that he might exert a moderating influence on both parties to the dispute. Instead, his former great popularity was replaced by public denunciation, he was widely accused of having been "bought" by the administration, and his residence became the first battleground of the rebellion.

The federal government had been warily reluctant to take action but could not indefinitely overlook the increasingly blatant defiance of federal authority. The excise act had been amended to permit accusations of noncompliance to be brought in the nearest state court, but a number of earlier warrants had been issued requiring the attendance of delinquents at the federal court in Philadelphia. This provision that westerners be transported over the mountain to stand trial in the hostile east stirred a stronger resentment than had the original tax. In an attempt to serve one of these warrants on a farmer-distiller, Neville and United States Marshal David Lenox were fired upon and driven from the premises. A hastily assembled body of local militia followed Neville to his home, Bower Hill, the most imposing residence in the region, with the demand that all warrants and tax records be destroyed. Neville armed his servants and Negroes and resisted. Six of the assailants were wounded, one mortally.

Neville appealed to the nearest civil authorities for protection but was informed that all peace officers, like the militia, sympathized with the attackers. His son-in-law, Major Abraham Kirkpatrick, brought a file of 11 regulars from the tiny Pittsburgh garrison to defend the Neville house. During the night Neville himself slipped away into hiding but Kirkpatrick remained to guard the property. The next day the investing force had been reinforced by militiamen from nearby districts until it numbered more than five hundred men. With the usual frontier regard for the democratic processes of local self-government a committee was elected to supervise the operation. It was clearly recognized by all concerned that an attack upon this detachment of federal troops constituted rebellion against the United States. The responsibility was accepted and the prospect welcomed.

Kirkpatrick refused to surrender. In the ensuing gunfire a number of defenders and besiegers were wounded and the rebel field commander, James McFarlane, a militia major, was killed. Outbuildings were set afire, endangering the main house. Realizing further resistance was hopeless, Kirkpatrick capitulated. Only the captured marshal was seriously mistreated. Neville's entire property was looted and burned. The exultant insurgents dispatched a deputation of two, one a justice of the peace, to Pittsburgh to demand that Neville resign, that all tax processes and warrants be delivered up, and that all attempts to enforce the tax be renounced. Denied any assurance of protection by local authorities, Neville and the other federal officials and federal sympathizers began fleeing down the Ohio.

The insurrection's leaders, of whom the most noted and radical was the lawyer and politician, David Bradford, were determined upon steps so drastic as to remove any hope of reconciliation with the national government. United States mail was seized in transit and examined to discover the identity of federal sympathizers. All such were marked for punishment or expulsion. Special elections were held in every community to register a popular verdict on the rebellion, but since the voting was not secret the hesitant were obliged by threats to cast votes satisfying the more militant. A general muster of all western Pennsylvania militia was summoned at Braddock's Field August 1st. Five thousand men armed and equipped for active service were easily moved by their rabble-rousing leaders to undertake a march upon Pittsburgh, generally regarded as a hotbed of federal sympathies. The advance upon the town was accompanied by many women eager to share in the prospective loot. The quick-thinking townspeople averted the threatened disaster by desperate hospitality. Instead of erecting barricades they awaited the marchers behind tables piled with food and whisky. The mercurial temper of the invaders who had vowed the town's destruction melted into a mood of fraternization. The anxious citizens professed attachment to the rebellion. Pittsburgh was spared. Only a few sheds and barns were burned and an occasional home looted.

The organized attack on United States troops and the seizures of United States mails had made it impossible for the administration to continue to ignore the situation. On August 4th Justice James Wilson of the Supreme Court certified the western counties to be in a state of insurrection. Secretary of the Treasury Hamilton assumed the added duties of Secretary of War upon Knox's taking leave of absence and was therefore charged with both the revenue and military responsibilities involved. He believed the rebellion offered a fortunate opportunity to strengthen the union by demonstrating the national government's determination to meet the challenge.

Washington was as aware as Hamilton of the need to reassert federal authority if the principle of federal union was to be maintained. In his proclamation of August 7, 1794, he referred to the western outbreak as "acts which I am advised amount to treason, being acts of levying war against the United States," and declared "the very existence of government, and the fundamental principles of social order, are materially involved in the issue." But he remained as painfully aware of wider and greater dangers to the union. Wayne had disappeared into the wilderness where, even though he succeeded in defeating the Indians, he could be precipitating a war with England. Jay had disappeared beyond the sea and could by now have discovered that the British home government was as bent upon aggression in the west as it had been made to seem by the hostile actions of Dorchester and Simcoe. On the other western frontier Spain was building forts, arming river fleets, and attacking Clark's vanguard. The situation represented a conjunction of external and internal threats in which any number of apparently imminent developments could be expected to spread the flames of revolt throughout the west. Instead, therefore, of moving immediately to suppress the Monongahela rebellion, Washington, on the urgent recommendation of Governor Mifflin of Pennsylvania, first attempted a negotiation by a combined team of federal and state plenipotentiaries. United States commissioners William Bradford, Attorney General, James Ross, United States Senator, and Jasper Yeates, of the Pennsylvania Supreme Court, and state commissioners, Chief Justice Thomas McKeon of the Pennsylvania Supreme Court and Representative William Irvine, were instructed to investigate and placate. All were conversant with the issues and prejudices involved. Ross was a resident of western Pennsylvania and Irvine had been commander at Pittsburgh during the closing years of the Revolution.

The negotiators' difficult task was made more difficult by every attendant circumstance. They were as unable to approach the rebels on the Monongahela with any assurance of personal safety as the peace commissioners had been unable to approach the Indians on the Maumee the year before. The insurrectionist mass meetings were so dominated by the more radical faction that any attending who were inclined to temporize were terrified into conformance. After some weeks of confused and inconclusive parleys the commissioners returned to report their failure September 24th. The next day Washington called for troops.

The response was heartening. Stirred by sectional antipathies, as well as by a surge of loyalty to the national government, the militia of Pennsylvania, Virginia, Maryland, and New Jersey eagerly assembled. By October 9th Washington had completed at Carlisle the organization of a federal army of more than 13,000 men. Henry Lee of Virginia was appointed field commander with Edward Hand, first continental commander at Fort Pitt during the Revolution, as his adjutant. Hamilton accompanied the army as civil authority, representing his twin responsibility for the treasury and war departments.

Marching west over Forbes' Road along the same route as when he had commanded the First Division in the campaign of 1758, Washington himself had need to proceed no further than Bedford. Confronted by so determined a display of federal power, the rebellion had collapsed. The collapse had been accelerated by one of those coincidences in the early history of the republic that Washington was accustomed to term providential. After 20 years of bitter dissatisfaction and disaffection the first armed revolt in the west had been delayed until the occasion for it had passed. Every major western grievance was already in the process of relief by a series of distant events having nothing directly to do with the Mononga-hela insurrection.

XIX

Ɛ

Fallen Timbers

More than two years had passed since Wayne had been appointed to command the Army of the United States with his government's directive that he compel the western Indian confederacy to acknowledge the sovereignty of the United States. His vaunted Legion had yet to venture from the entrenched security of fortified camps and posts. These years of inaction in the midst of a war represented a period comparable to the lapse of time between Lexington and Saratoga or between Lincoln's first call for volunteers and Gettysburg. The stagnation had neither been of Wayne's seeking nor to his liking. He was far from a calm, a patient, or a cautious man. No commander could have been more galled by delays so protracted. Every attendant circumstance, moreover, had made the long wait more maddening. He had been perpetually plagued by the administration's appeasement policy, by hunger, sickness, and desertion among his troops, by outrageous quarrels among his officers, by the lack of supplies, by the frontier's scorn, by constant public criticism, by Wilkinson's machinations, and by his own prejudices and ills.

Nevertheless, he had not permitted the months and years of frustration to undermine the primary purpose to which he remained dedicated. His professional experience had fixed in his mind the principle that only the most rigid discipline could sufficiently prepare any army for the special hazards of a wilderness campaign. Unpromising as was his material, he had drilled his recruits and had kept on drilling them, winter and summer, spring and fall. Next in importance in his estimation was the military principle that appearance was essential to a soldier's self-respect and esprit de corps. He lavished much care on matching the horses of his cavalry squadrons. Complete uniforms were not to be had but he improvised standards and emblems and white, red, yellow, and green plumes to distinguish his four sublegions. Most of all, however, he kept at the drilling. He demanded soldiers who would instinctively obey orders under whatever stresses of confusion or surprise. In his considered judgment the one certain way to beat Indians was to go for them with the bayonet.

By early summer of 1794 he was satisfied that his army at last was ready. Setting a date to march was dependent only on the accumulation of supplies which, after all the ferocities of his feuds with Wilkinson and the contractors, remained still insufficient to maintain an expedition in the field for more than a few days. Exasperating as was this familiar problem, its solution would serve only to bring him up against as awesome an array of greater difficulties as may ever have afflicted a commander on the eve of a campaign. The sole element in his situation that offered the slightest promise of success was his own confidence in himself and in his army. Every other aspect forecast catastrophe.

There was, first off, the very nature of his campaign. In all military operations there is an element of risk, but, as had been so often demonstrated, in none was that element so pronounced as in an undertaking to lead an organized regular army into the wilderness against active Indian opposition. Of the last eight commanders who had attempted the venture, five had encountered bloody reverses, two had met total disaster, and the other, Major General John Sullivan in 1779, though successful tactically, had utterly failed to compel Indian submission.

Next there was the status of his base, the factor upon which any army in the field is most dependent. Wayne's base, the adjoining Kentucky and Pennsylvania frontiers, could scarcely have been less dependable. Kentucky's extreme dissatisfaction with the national government had been accentuated by contempt for the long armistice and by popular sympathy with Clark's preparations which, in turn, presented the threat that at almost any moment a war with Spain might be precipitated in Wayne's rear. In western Pennsylvania the outright rebellion against the national government had by midsummer completely cut Wayne's line of communications with the east.

After considering these difficulties in his rear, he had then to consider the strength of the Indian enemy with which he proposed to seek battle in the depths of the Indian country. Harmar had had to deal with only a portion of the Miami. St. Clair had been crushed by the western confederates. But the 1794 Indian force upon which Wayne now contemplated advancing had been augmented by such support as no former Indian alliance had ever enjoyed. Indians from Canada and the farthest Lakes and packs of volunteers from the most distant south were swarming to the rendezvous on the Maumee. Every report reaching Wayne in the early summer obliged him to take into account the near certainty that by the time he marched the Indian forces would have also received the redoubtable reinforcement of Brant and his Iroquois.

Upon this alarming increase in Indian strength was superimposed another prospect of vastly more threatening import. Dorchester's address, the construction of Fort Miami, and the unconcealed preoccupation of British regular officers with the transportation, supply, organization, and supervision of the Indian forces left no room for doubt in Wayne's mind that he was marching to an encounter with the British as well as the Indian army. But no consideration of these many extraordinary hazards, either those in his rear or those in his front, moved him to any perceptible inclination to hesitate.

There may have been other commanders to embark upon a campaign while faced with difficulties matching the variety of Wayne's, but surely none has ever been burdened with such a second in command. Wilkinson, the necessary confidant of every command council, was contributing his acquaintance with Wayne's problems and his inspired talent for making mischief to his never flagging effort to insure Wayne's failure. Wayne despised and mistrusted him, but, on account of Wilkinson's popularity in Kentucky and his apparent favor with Knox and Washington, had not insisted upon his removal. Convinced as he was of Wilkinson's personal malevolence, he had not yet begun to suspect the incredible complexity of his principal lieutenant's foreign intrigues.

Wilkinson was in 1794 receiving more Spanish money than ever before and demanding much more.[1] He was assuring Carondelet that it had been entirely due to his exertions that Clark's expedition had been delayed. Next he was warning Carondelet that Wayne's defeat, which he asserted was inevitable, would surely result in Kentucky's turning toward a union with Britain. To make certain of his being able to avert a development so injurious to Spanish interests he estimated would require his being furnished an additional fund of $200,000.

At the same time Wilkinson was dipping more deeply into Spanish coffers, he was maintaining his British contacts. By employing the services of such ostensible deserters as Robert Newman, the curiously garrulous Kentucky schoolmaster, he was appearing to keep McKee and Simcoe informed of Wayne's movements and intentions.

And finally, in a bizarre accompaniment to these relations with the expedition's foreign ill-wishers and for all his professed certainty

[1] Of the $16,000 Carondelet reported sending Wilkinson in 1794 only $5100 appears to have reached him. One shipment of 6000 silver dollars concealed in kegs was dispatched up the Mississippi by galley in the care of Wilkinson's agent, Henry Owens. After the turn into the Ohio his Spanish military escort was obliged to withdraw, and Owens was killed by his Spanish barge crew, aware by now of the secret cargo's value. Several of the assailants were apprehended in Kentucky and brought into Judge Harry Innes' federal district court. Appalled by the disclosures that must result from a trial, Innes ruled that the prisoners were suspected spies who required examination by the army and hurried them to Wilkinson at Fort Washington. Equally disconcerted, Wilkinson as hastily shipped them off to the Spanish authorities at New Madrid. They were intercepted en route by the alert Major Thomas Doyle, commanding at Fort Massac, and returned to Kentucky. This time Innes maintained his composure and dismissed the charges for want of evidence. None of the money was ever recovered but Wilkinson once more escaped contemporary exposure.

that the expedition was destined to defeat, he persisted with un-diminished energy in his endeavor to displace Wayne as its com-mander. In June of 1794 he got off a series of letters by special messengers to Knox, reiterating and elaborating all the charges against Wayne that had been circulated or published and earnestly advising Wayne's removal from command. Knox sent the letters on to Washington at Mount Vernon who discounted the more extrava-gant charges and forebore to interfere. Knox wrote Wayne, "you may rest assured that . . . I shall sincerely endeavor to guard you from all misrepresentation," but Wilkinson was neither reprimanded nor removed from Wayne's staff, Wayne was not warned of his subordinate's subversion, and the commanding general of an army in the field was permitted to march on into battle with a second in command whose personal disloyalty to him had been completely disclosed to the War Department and the President.[2]

While Wayne was grappling with his multiple disadvantages, his opponent, Little Turtle, was being even more embarrassed by the multiplicity of his apparent advantages. Indian enthusiasm for war had never been so rampant nor had Indian unity ever appeared so firm. Indian confidence bred of their victories over Harmar and St. Clair had been inordinately magnified by the spring's assurances that they might henceforth count on the British army as an active ally. McKee's May 7th summons brought hundreds of Lake Indians streaming south to the Maumee. By mid-June the central encamp-ment at Au Glaize teemed with 2000 warriors. So considerable a mobilization, of which Indians, unassisted, must have been incapa-ble, had been made possible by British transport, British provision-ing, and the supervision of British officers. Some scores of ex-Tories

[2] Among other incongruities surrounding Wayne's fateful march none was more inexplicable than Knox's untimely leave of absence. After so many years of pains-taking public service, he chose the moment that the nation was confronted by re-bellion on the Pennsylvania frontier and gripped by the suspense following the dis-appearance of Wayne's army into the wilderness to take a several month vacation to attend to personal business in Maine. Upon his departure from Philadelphia, August 8, 1794, Hamilton, always more intrigued by military than by financial af-fairs, assumed the responsibilities of the War Department along with those of the Treasury.

and English and French traders joined the Indian army, dressing and painting to appear as Indians. The most notable of these white warriors was William Caldwell, the veteran Ranger commander whose Revolutionary war record had been marked by victories at Wyoming, Cherry Valley, Sandusky, and Blue Licks. Brant and his Iroquois were no longer expected but they were known to be gathering their forces to resist Pennsylvania encroachment at Le Bouef, a distraction of the American war effort which was considered even more useful to the general Indian cause. The lesson of former wars had made Indian leaders as aware as were British commanders of the supreme importance of holding the Niagara link in the St. Lawrence–Great Lakes supply route to the west.

There were, at any rate, already too many Indians at Au Glaize. The slow accumulation of supplies which had so agonized Wayne was now proving of unforeseen service to him. The Indians had expected him to march by the first of June and when he did not their war plan was discomposed. Little Turtle had his own supply problem. The limitations of wilderness transport made it impossible for the British supply system to keep so large an assembly of Indians fed for more than a few days. Little Turtle had hoped to wait to attack Wayne until after the American army had advanced from its fortified cover into the wilderness. But he could not wait long, for hunger must soon dissipate his force. As an alternative plan, it was determined to advance to meet Wayne and, if he remained within his fortifications, to circle on south to attack his line of communications. This was a shrewd move, throughly approved by Little Turtle's British military advisors. Indian infestation of Wayne's long supply route, stretching nearly a hundred miles from fort to fort back to the Ohio, could be expected to pin him down indefinitely and possibly even to force his capitulation.

After a final council of war June 16th in which every speaker voiced a boastful impatience to come to grips with the laggard Americans, the Indian horde plunged southward through the Ohio wilderness. Due to the scarcity of rations the army separated into a number of divisions to facilitate hunting en route. According to the anonymous "Diary of an Officer in the Indian Country" included in British official reports of the campaign, hunters supplying the camp to which he was attached brought in 40 deer and 5 bear one day and on another day 200 deer and 200 turkeys. There were frequent skirmishes with Wayne's scouting patrols of Chickasaw warriors and Kentucky frontiersmen as each commander sought to learn his opponent's movements and intentions.

The Indian force had spread so widely through the forest, however, that it had become impossible for Little Turtle and his British advisors to maintain sufficient staff control to make efficient use of such information as was collected or to bring so portentous an aggregation of Indian power to a point of decisive application. He had intended to strike Wayne's communications near the Ohio and at a point between Wayne's army at Greenville and his militia reinforcement known to be assembling in Kentucky. The less experienced and therefore more impetuous contingent of Lake Indians insisted instead upon veering off to the northernmost of Wayne's posts, Fort Recovery, upon receiving word of the arrival there of a large convoy. Little Turtle, with the more war-wise Miami-Shawnee core of his army, was obliged to conform. The convoy of 300 pack horses, under the command of Major William MacMahon and guarded by 90 riflemen, was emerging from the fort to return to Greenville when the Indians fell upon it. The result demonstrated how successful might have been Little Turtle's intention to cut Wayne's main supply route. MacMahon was killed, the escort overwhelmed, the convoy pillaged, and a troop of Legion cavalry sallying from the fort to the rescue driven back through the gates.

Elated by this success on the very ground where they had destroyed St. Clair, the overconfident Indians disregarded their leaders' protests and flung themselves into a violent assault on the fort itself. The hail of rifle fire was so intense that many defenders were killed by bullets entering the loopholes. The Indians had counted on disinterring the buried cannon, and it was only after they were already committed to the attack that they realized these were now firing from the walls upon them. A day and a night of vigorous but vain assault served only once more to demonstrate the validity of the military axiom that a staunchly defended fort could not be taken without artillery. After suffering losses far greater than in the defeat of St. Clair, the disheartened Indians collected their dead and withdrew.

The first flush of Indian enthusiasm for war had been chilled by this premature excursion and its bloody repulse. Most of the Lake Indians, arguing that they had already done as much as they had promised in a quarrel which was after all not directly their own, began to drift northward. Little Turtle still had sufficient numbers to threaten Wayne's communications but, in the hope of keeping his army intact, followed with his Maumee allies. At Au Glaize hundreds of Lake Indians kept on homeward. It was only by the most energetic exertions that McKee and his assistants were able to persuade a portion of them to wait. The mercurial Indian temperament had so soon plummeted from the heights of bravado to the depths of discouragement. Depression reawakened doubt of British intentions. Little Turtle went to Detroit to demand point-blank of Lieutenant Colonel R. G. England, British commander in the west, just what military assistance he proposed to furnish. England reported to Simcoe July 22, 1794, "I of course talked him over for two or three days, and dismissed him seemingly contented." It was at this low ebb in Indian morale that Wayne marched.

Scott's Kentucky militia, 1600 mounted riflemen, arrived at Greenville July 26th in response to Wayne's summons. Observation of his army in recent months had converted the frontier's former contempt into an increasingly less grudging respect. In 1794 Kentuckians were for the first time pleased to be serving with regulars. Wayne marched from Greenville July 28th. From the outset his brooding months of preparation began to show results. Every move had been prepared, every eventuality foreseen.

His arrangements to prevent surprise, the great danger that had in the past brought disaster to so many such marches, made surprise impossible. Each night his encampment was fortified by trenches and breastworks. On the march the security of his army was guarded by a screen of more than 200 Chickasaw and white scouts.[3] His advance was slow but its very deliberation made it seem irresistible. There was no lapse in judgment, no opportunity offered of which Indians might seize advantage. Little Turtle was so disagreeably impressed by Wayne's vigilance that he was reported to have said in council: "The Americans are now led by a chief who never sleeps. He is like the black snake, the night and day are alike to him."

The Indians had expected Wayne to advance upon the Miami portage, as had Harmar and St. Clair, but instead he drove straight for the center of Indian population at Au Glaize. Caught off balance, they gathered their women and children and as much of their property as they could carry and withdrew to the Rapids without offering even token resistance. McKee was surprised and mortified by this sudden maneuver but in Indian estimation it possessed one striking advantage: Were Wayne to continue to advance upon them the decisive battle would be fought literally under the guns of the British fort and the British army's participation in it made thereby certain.

At Au Glaize, site of so many great Indian congresses, ringed by Indian towns and cornfields, the very heart of the Indian country, Wayne paused to erect Fort Defiance. While laying waste their towns and fields, he increased Indian perturbation with a renewed offer to negotiate. They might still escape the battle that they were certain to lose, he arrogantly pointed out, were they sensibly and immediately to submit. Placing an unerring finger upon their chief cause for disquiet, he warned them, "Be no longer deceived or led astray by the false promises and language of the bad white men at the foot of the rapids; *they have neither power nor inclination to protect you.*"

---

[3] His chief of scouts was William Wells, a Kentuckian who had been captured at the age of 12 and who during his long captivity had been adopted by the Miami, had married Little Turtle's daughter, and had fought on the Indian side against Harmar and St. Clair before yielding to the impulse to return to his own people. During the preceding winter Simon Kenton had contributed to Wayne's need for scouts a long-remembered ranger company of fellow frontiersmen of his own selection which had patrolled so aggressively along the Maumee that the Indian country was repeatedly agitated by rumors that Wayne was making a winter invasion.

Little Turtle grasped at the opportunity to gain time by accepting, ostensibly, Wayne's offer to negotiate. McKee approved. He was still endeavoring to retrieve more of the homeward bound Lake Indians in order to build up Indian strength at the Rapids. Wayne's diplomatic gesture, however, had brought into the open the growing Indian suspicion of British sincerity. The doubt was largely removed by Colonel England's next move. On August 9th he dispatched strong reinforcements of men and artillery to Fort Miami. Once more persuaded of the firmness of British intentions, Indian martial spirit revived and their councils were again loud with confidence that they could deal with Wayne as successfully as they had with Harmar and St. Clair.

In response to the evasive Indian request for a ten-day suspension of operations to give them time properly to consider his offer to negotiate, Wayne began a deliberate march down the Maumee, burning abandoned towns and fields as he advanced. On August 17th he camped at the head of the rapids on a low wooded ridge locally known as Presque Isle where he constructed Fort Deposit to shelter his baggage and supply train. He was now less than five miles from the British fort. The long-threatened collision between American power and British power, which Washington had for six years sought to postpone, appeared now inevitable.

The commander of Fort Miami, Major William Campbell, was frantically engaged with the aid of a corps of French laborers from Detroit in strengthening his defensive works. To gain him more time, Little Turtle, at the earnest insistence of his British advisors, moved forward to interpose his Indian army between Wayne and the British post. The Indians were the more easily persuaded to accept this responsibility by their realization that the position available to them was one of unique advantage. A onetime tornado had tumbled a two-mile wide belt of forest into one of those jack-straw swaths of splintered trunks and entangled branches termed on the frontier "fallen timbers." An arena more ideally adapted to a full exploitation of Indian skills in forest combat could hardly have been imagined. There was even the circumstance that the belt of fallen timbers slanted at an angle from the river, forcing Wayne's further advance into a corridor in which he would be exposed to the sort of Indian flanking attack which had proved fatal to white opponents at Turtle Creek, at Niagara, and at Wyoming. To hold this natural fortress Little Turtle had a force of some 1500 warriors stiffened by cadres of traders, ex-Tory partisans, and French volunteers. They took position in the edges of the tornado's track, improved its defensive values by planting patterns of sharpened stakes to impede Wayne's cavalry, and lay grimly and confidently in wait.

Wayne, however, gave a final brutal twist to the war of nerves he had been levying on Indian morale. For two days he remained silent and motionless in his fortified camp. The delay imposed the kind of strain that the Indian temperament was least able to sustain. Warriors who had the first day been ready to pounce with wild abandon on an awaited enemy were drained of that initial keen edge of excitement by the long uncertainty. By the second night most were further weakened by hunger as a consequence of the Indian custom of fasting before battle. When a heavy rainstorm broke at dawn on the third day some 500 seized advantage of the apparent opportunity to slip back to their camps about Fort Miami to get food. They had scarcely straggled off when the storm began to clear and Wayne emerged.

The Legion in 1794 had 2634 men fit for service on its rolls but, after detaching garrisons for the forts guarding his 240-mile supply line, Wayne had available for the battle August 20th no more than 1500 regulars and 1500 mounted militia. His various personal ailments, including particularly his swollen leg, were more distressing than usual that morning but he was determined to take personal command on this day to which he had looked forward so long. The leg was tightly bound from ankle to hip with bands of flannel. It required three men to hoist his bulk into the saddle. To the protests of aides that, if he were killed there would be no one to give the army orders, he testily replied that the orders would under all circumstances remain the same—"charge the damn rascals with the bayonet."

The sun had broken through the clouds and the weather had turned hot and steamy. The advance was in a broad column, through open cornfields dotted by clumps of trees, along the corridor between the river on the right and the angle of the Indian line to the left, directly into what the Indians had conceived to be their waiting trap. Wayne had placed the mounted Kentucky militia in the van and on the left. In the center marched the solid mass of the Legion infantry. The Legion cavalry was held in reserve.

Offered the opportunity for which they had waited, the Indians launched their attack, a blast of fire from the edges of the fallen timbers followed by an immediate wild charge. The militia gave way and the Indian pursuit was pressed for nearly a mile. This was the moment that they had anticipated, the sudden shock of surprise and terror which had spelled doom to so many white armies. But this was a different kind of army. There had not been surprise. The fat, bellowing general on horseback was making dispositions which he and his lieutenants had long planned to meet a situation which he had long foreseen.

The Legion's ranks opened to permit the mounted riflemen to pass through without confusion, then wheeled into attack formation. Scott's Kentucky horsemen regrouped and swung to the left in an encircling movement around the Indian right flank. The Legion cavalry began to clear the riverbank on the Indian left. The Legion infantry moved upon the main Indian position in the center. The eager Indian pursuit, met in the open by this totally unexpected development, recoiled. The regulars' advance was deliberate, at a walk, without firing, the first rank with fixed bayonets, the second with pieces atrail.[4]

Regaining the cover of the fallen timbers the Indians crouched and resumed their fire upon the American advance. But the plumed legionnaires took their losses and kept on coming, their muskets still cold, until in that classic climax toward which the professional sol-

[4] Once battle was joined, Wilkinson participated with notable gallantry. In reporting the victory to Knox, Wayne especially commended Wilkinson "whose brave example inspired the troops."

dier's training is directed they were able to close with the enemy at the bayonet's point. Indian indiscipline was no match for American discipline. No Indian warrior had sufficient confidence that his fellows would stand fast to be moved himself to hold his ground. When the first line was broken there developed no later point where a new line could be established. The inexorable advance of the Legion infantry moved steadily on through the two-mile wide belt of fallen timbers to drive the Indians into the open beyond before the encircling cavalry had completed their flanking movements.

It had not been a hard-fought battle or a costly victory. The American loss, during all that audacious advance, had been 44 killed and 87 wounded while the Indian loss had not been above 50. But it had been a humiliating and decisive Indian defeat in which Indian opinion had been stripped of every former conception of military superiority.

Emerging from the tangle of fallen timbers, the army was in the presence of the British fort, where British gunners stood with lighted matches at their pieces and the British flag flew overhead. Wayne was able then to witness a spectacle that richly rewarded him for all his months of trial. The fleeing Indians sought admission and succor at the fort, but the gates were closed against them and red-coated soldiers prodded them away with bayonets. It was an unmistakable demonstration of British anxiety to give Wayne no excuse for pressing his pursuit to the point of making an attack on the British position. The Indians fled on down the river, howling imprecations.

Wayne realized in that instant how complete had been his victory. Those gates closing upon the Indians had closed also upon British dominion in the northwest. The monumental British bluff which for thirteen years had encouraged Indian belligerence had been called. It had been made clear that the British commander had been as carefully instructed as had Wayne to attack the other only as a last resort, that the British government had no greater wish for war than had his own government, and that Great Britain was actually as little inclined in 1794 as in 1783 to make any decisive contribution to the Indian cause.

To make certain that the full import of this revelation had not been lost on the Indians, Wayne began most thoroughly to devastate Indian towns and cornfields up and down the river and to within a pistol shot of the fort. McKee's headquarters, across the river from the fort, was destroyed with special glee. In the fort the British garrison watched the destruction with a fuming helplessness that the Indians were never able thereafter to forget.

The next day, relieved by the realization that he was after all not to be directly attacked, Campbell ministered to his military dignity by addressing Wayne a note of pained remonstrance. The ensuing dialogue possesses intrinsic interest inasmuch as it was a colloquy between field commanders in the depths of the wilderness, each of whom was separated by weeks of communication time from his government and either of whom could at any moment by a single slight miscalculation have precipitated a war of incalculable consequences to both countries.

Campbell initiated the exchange with some caution:

An Army of the United States of America said to be under your Command, having taken Post on the banks of the Miamis, for upwards of the last twenty four hours, almost within reach of the Guns of this Fort, being a Post belonging to His Majesty, the King of Great Britain, occupied by His Majesty's Troops, and which I have the honor to Command, it becomes my duty to inform myself as speedily as possible in what light I am to view your making such near approachs to this Garrison. I have no hesitation on my part to say, that I know of no War existing between Great Britain and America.

Wayne retorted:

Without questioning the Authority or the propriety Sir, of your interrogatory, I think I may without breach of decorum observe to you, that were you entitled to an Answer, the most full and satisfactory one was announced to you, from the Muzzels of my small Arms yesterday morning in the Action against the hoard of Savages in the vicinity of your Post, which terminated Gloriously to the American Arms—but had it continued until the Indians &c were drove under the influence of the Post and Guns you mention—they would not have much impeded the progress of the Victorious Army under my command, as no such Post was Established at the Commencement of the present War, between the Indians and the United States.

Wayne's bluster had failed to conceal his circumspection or to deny Cambell room for some gasconade of his own:

Although your letter of yesterday's date fully authorizes me to any Act of hostility, against the Army of the United States of America, in the Neighborhood under your Command Yet still anxious to prevent that dreadful decision, which perhaps is not intended to be appealed to, by either of Our countries, I have foreborne for these two days past to resent those Insults you have offered to the British Flag flying at this Fort, by approaching it within pistol shot of my Works, not only singly, but in numbers with Arms in their hands. Neither is it my wish to wage War with Individuals, but should you after this continue to approach my post, in the threatening manner you are at this moment doing, my indispensable Duty to my King and Country, and the honor of my profession will Oblige me to have recourse to those Measures, which thousands of either Nation may hereafter have Cause to regret, and which I solemnly appeal to God, I have used my utmost endeavors to avert.

In this infinitely dangerous game of words played by commanders equally avid to sustain the demands of honor, Wayne advanced to the very brink of the abyss:

. . . the hostile Act that you are now in commission of i.e. by recently taking post far within the well known and acknowledged limits of the United States, and erecting a Fortification in the Heart of the settlements of the Indian Tribes, now at war with the United States . . . appears to be an Act of the highest aggression, and destructive to the peace and interest of the Union:—hence it becomes my duty to desire, and I do hereby desire and demand in the name of the President of the United States that you immediately desist from any further Act of Hostility or aggression:—by forbearing to fortify and by withdrawing the troops, Artillery and Stores under

your orders and directions forthwith, and removing to the nearest
post occupied by his Britannick Majesty's Troops at the peace of 1783:
—and which you will be permitted to do, unmolested by the troops
under my command.

Campbell had, as Wayne had no doubt intended, now been offered
ground upon which he could take his stand:

> . . . being placed here in the Command of a British Post, and acting
> in a Military Capacity only, I cannot enter into any discussion either
> on the right, or impropriety of my occupying my present position,
> those are matters that I conceive will be best left to the Ambassadors
> of Our different Nations. Having said this much, Sir, permit me to
> inform you, that I certainly will not abandon this Post, at the Sum-
> mons of Any power whatever.

Campbell had had the last word. But Wayne could afford to be
more than content. He had the military force to compel the fort's
surrender but, with a soundness of judgment that no one, including
Washington, had suspected that he possessed, he realized that to do
so was to substitute for a war that he had already won a greater war
of most uncertain issue. His major objective, of far larger importance
than any physical defeat of the Indians, had been to break up the
British-Indian alliance. In this he had completely succeeded.

Having accomplished the total devastation of this center of British
influence, he marched back up the Maumee to build Fort Wayne at
the Miami portage, the strategic key to the northwest. He had now
established a system of forts and supply routes which dominated the
entire country of the western Indians and had only to wait for the
fruits of his victory to fall. He had not long to wait. Brant and
Simcoe rushed west to support McKee in one last frantic effort to
restore Indian confidence. Their most fervent appeals gained no
hearing. Indian disillusionment was complete and permanent. They
had been abandoned by France in 1763 and by England in 1783. This
was the third time that they had been flagrantly betrayed by a European ally and they had had enough. They could not be fooled again.
Every belligerent western nation embarked upon negotiations with

Wayne and on February 22, 1795, he was able to proclaim the end of hostilities.

His proclamation, criticized at the time as premature, was prophetic. This *was* the end. Indian attacks on the frontier ceased, in the south as well as in the north. Indian hostility was never again to prove a significant factor in the continued advancement of the American frontier. Fallen Timbers had brought to a decisive conclusion the last Indian war with any most distant bearing on any strategic or international situation. The Indian problem was never thereafter a concern, internally or externally, of national policy. Every later Indian campaign was in the nature of a police action undertaken to chastise and regulate the lawlessness of homeless bands foredoomed to submission or extinction.

The consequence of Fallen Timbers of far greater importance than the suppression of the Indian menace was the victory's effect on frontier opinion. For twenty years the frontier people had lived in constant dread and danger. Their national government's impotence to protect them had been the well spring from which had flowed the main currents of western disaffection, secessionism, and foreign intrigue. Now that fearful pressure had been suddenly, miraculously, and totally relieved. The national government was triumphant. Throughout the west a dawning pride and respect replaced the old scorn and contempt. Clark's New Orleans project withered. The western Pennsylvania rebels submitted, without the firing of a single shot, to the display of federal force.[5] Carondelet's new Kentucky conspiracy attracted no attention outside the circle of those Kentuckians who were accepting Spanish money. No later separation movement was to gain public support in the west. Fallen Timbers signified union of east and west as clearly as did Gettysburg the union of north and south.

[5] Washington learned of Wayne's victory September 30th and on October 9th completed the organization of the army mobilized to suppress the rebellion. Meanwhile, on October 2nd at Parkinson's Ferry, delegates representing Pennsylvania transmountain townships had voted unanimously to offer no resistance.

XX

༂

Reality Recognized

The year 1795 was made memorable for the west by a sudden blaze of triumph. After the desperate twenty-year-long struggle the west's three chief antagonists, the Indians, Great Britain, and Spain alike admitted defeat. Every objective for which the frontier people had striven—elimination of the Indian menace, the use of the Mississippi, access to the Great Lakes—had been won. The most impoverished settler might henceforth expect a market. The most isolated cabin was henceforth secure. The westerner might henceforth consider himself in every respect an American.

This was likewise a triumph for Washington and his policy of resolute moderation. He had avoided the fearful perils of foreign war and yet had gained for the west and for his country every advantage that might have been won by even the most successful war. Entering upon the last year of his presidency and nearing the end of his life, he could realize with the deepest satisfaction that he had succeeded in preserving the union of which he had been the most effective advocate and in saving the west which he had been the first to claim on his winter journey in 1754.

The good news broke upon the west in a series of waves. First, and to the ordinary settler most important, a peaceful spring brought proof that Wayne's midwinter proclamation had not been premature. The Indians had indeed capitulated. The most strenuous British efforts were failing to recapture their savage protégés' allegiance. The Indians persisted in good faith in their negotiations with Wayne and in midsummer assembled in his camp to sign on August 3, 1795, the definitive Treaty of Greenville. Practically every important western Indian leader, including Little Turtle, contributed his name and influence to the peacemaking. By the treaty all Indian claim was relinquished to the south, central, and eastern portions of what is now the state of Ohio, as well as to isolated tracts sufficient for military control, together with access routes, of every strategic point in the northwest, including the Miami portage, Au Glaize, the Maumee Rapids, the mouth of the Maumee, Detroit, Mackinac, and the site of the present Chicago. The renowned Proclamation Line which had been a bone of contention in so many conferences and so many wars over a period of 34 years had at last passed into history.

This had not been just another treaty negotiated by manipulation of Indian minorities and factions or by connivance with nations presuming to alienate the lands of their neighbors. It had been a treaty genuinely negotiated with fully accredited representatives of nations whose interests were directly involved and who clearly recognized that peaceful submission was the inescapable consequence of an irretrievably lost war. By it the twelve principal Indian nations of the northwest formally acknowledged the sovereignty of the United States. It marked the end for all time to organized Indian resistance to the frontier's advance. It opened most of Ohio to immediate settlement and carried the implication that as soon as further settlement needs developed Indiana, Illinois, Michigan, and Wisconsin would become likewise open. Of overwhelmingly greatest moment to the individual settler was his sudden realization that the most striking feature of his existence, the daily fear of an assault upon his cabin, had become a phantom of the past.

Deprived of the support of Great Britain and their western allies, the Iroquois were forced to the conclusion that they, too, must submit by accepting whatever accommodation was required of them by

the United States or by the states of New York and Pennsylvania.
They, like all Indians east of the Mississippi, had become, in effect,
the wards of the federal government.[1]

The full significance of the Treaty of Greenville was accentuated
as news of Jay's secret British treaty, ratified by the Senate June 24,
1795, began to reach the west. Jay's arrival in England the previous
June had been welcomed by the British government as an unexpectedly peaceful overture at a moment America's entry into the war
at the side of her old friend and ally, France, had been regarded as
certain. The same ship that had brought Jay had brought word of
Dorchester's incendiary address to the Indians. Embarrassed by
French military successes on the continent, the ministry had no wish
to become additionally involved in a peculiarly awkward war in the
distant center of the North American wilderness. Dorchester was
reproved, directed to maintain the "status quo" by remaining strictly
on the defensive, and warned that it might become advisable to give
up the Lake posts.[2] A withdrawal in the American northwest at the
periphery of imperial commitment appeared to a government already concerned for the safety of Gibraltar, Egypt, and India to be
the simplest and cheapest concession by which American neutrality
might be courted. Negotiations dragged on into November without
Jay's being able to gain any other.

In the United States his treaty was violently denounced by eastern
commercial interests who had not been relieved by it of British
shipping restrictions and by Republicans who were animated by
sympathy for France, hostility to England, and an inherent inclination to disapprove all acts of the Federalist administration. There
was likewise political criticism in the overwhelmingly Republican
west, even though no westerner could fail to recognize the enormous

[1] Brant, whose life work had ended in total failure, ascribed the Indian downfall
to the vacillations of British policy. The year was further embittered for him by the
death of his son, Isaac. The twenty-year-old youth, an habitual drunkard who had in
alcoholic furies twice killed companions, attacked his father with a knife and in the
ensuing struggle received a cut from which he died three days later. Brant was held
blameless by both legal and public opinions.

[2] The rebuke could not reach Dorchester until long after Wayne's campaign. His
defense was that inasmuch as war with the United States had appeared inevitable he
had considered it imperative to reinvigorate Indian resistance by any means at hand.

advantage gained the west by the treaty. The conquest of Detroit had been a western dream since 1778 and it was fully realized that its delivery would make impossible any later reorganization of Indian resistance to the northwestward advance of settlement, yet Jay was pilloried for his earlier appeasement of Spain and his new treaty was pronounced a pusillanimous surrender to England. In the west there was seldom popular sympathy for any policy that fell short of continuous and total aggressiveness.

The sudden collapse of Indian and British opposition in 1795 was accompanied for a time by the appearance of an intensified Spanish opposition. Carondelet's fanatical determination to turn back the advance of the American frontier reached a hysterical climax. He was reporting to his government that his new Kentucky conspiracy had been made "infallible" by his having advanced far greater sums of money which had gained him the positive assurance of the more active co-operation of his Kentucky agents. Wilkinson pocketed the money, assured Carondelet that all was going very well, but at the same time warned him that he was obliged to move with care since he was already suspected by Wayne and Washington. Carondelet was forced to be content with resort to Wilkinson's associates, Harry Innes and Benjamin Sebastian, as go-betweens. He was, meanwhile, further bolstering Spain's claim to the disputed territory south and west of the Tennessee by building Fort San Fernando at Chickasaw Bluffs, strengthening his border garrisons, adding to his river fleet, and appealing desperately to Havana and Madrid for reinforcements.

What he could not know was that his government had already come to the same conclusion as had the British government: To undertake in the midst of a European war opposition by military force to the expansion of American settlement in the Mississippi Valley was an effort too distant, too dangerous, and too doubtful to justify the risk. By the Treaty of Basle in July, Spain had abandoned her British ally by making peace with France, and had no desire to find American hostility combined with British hostility to enlarge the threat to her vulnerable New World possessions. On August 14, 1795, the Council of State decided to cease disputing American demands in the southwest and on October 27, 1795, Washington's emissary, Thomas Pinckney, was able to conclude the Treaty of San Lorenzo by which Spain abandoned claim to all territory east of the Mississippi to a point south of Natchez and granted freedom of navigation of the Mississippi together with the right of deposit at New Orleans.[3] The two most fevered excitements of western discontent, trade restriction and Spanish-sponsored Indian aggression, had been relieved. The west's commerce could now flow normally to the sea, and prospective American occupation of the southern Indian country eliminated the Indian peril on the southwestern border as completely as it had been eliminated in the northwest at Greenville.

Similar reasoning had led the governments of Great Britain and Spain to their nearly simultaneous decisions to relinquish their long-harbored designs on the Mississippi Valley. Each had at last been made to recognize the implacable realities of the westward movement of American settlers. The recognition was expedited by the pressures of the war in Europe. Neither Britain nor Spain could afford hazardous dispersals of their military effort in a theater so distant from the main battleground. Both governments were astonishingly ill informed of actual conditions in the wild, wide expanses of interior North America, an ignorance accentuated by the endless delays of eighteenth-century communications, but in both there were men in power with the perspicacity to evaluate correctly the inexorable progress of events during the past twenty years. All had centered about the impulsive and seemingly irrational movement of American settlers across the mountains. Unlike former colonists known to history, they had come without the support of their homeland and they had expected or required none. They were there of their own volition and they were there to stay. During the Revolution the most aggressive exertions of the English-Indian alliance had failed to dislodge even the handful ensconced in their few small stockades in Kentucky. The efforts of the Spanish-supplied southern Indians had likewise failed to dispossess the most outlying fringe of Cumberland's undermanned settlements. By the middle of the 1790's that

---

[3] The precise line yielded by Spain in the treaty ran down the middle of the Mississippi channel to the 31st parallel, thence east to the Apalachicola River, thence to the headwaters of the St. Mary's River, thence to the Atlantic.

first trickle of intruders into the central valley had swelled to a torrential quarter of a million. Most were absorbed in the problems of maintaining a family on a primitive stump-dotted farm, but any overt threat could be expected to draw thousands of expert riflemen to the defense of their borders. Any attempt to subjugate such a people by military force applied at the end of a communications line stretching across an ocean and on into a wilderness had been by 1795 wisely judged by both Britain and Spain a totally untenable project.

For some time after the population of the American west had become too numerous to invite aggression by force, Britain and Spain had continued to regard the Mississippi Valley with interest. There had lingered the hope, stimulated by the treasonable overtures of most frontier leaders and fostered by the overconfident reports of British and Spanish officials in North America, that the dissatisfied American west might secede from the United States and seek relief from its adversities by accepting the protection of one or the other of its grasping foreign neighbors. But the innate common sense of the westerners, ably supported by the firmness of Washington's adminis-tration and his ability eventually to mount Wayne's expedition, had at first gradually and then finally quenched this hope. The west had been proved too strong to invade and too shrewd to subvert. Britain and Spain had been left with no other recourse than to bow out of what had become so unequal a contest. Both had done so. This 1795 admission of American superiority in the west was the longest stride so far in the stubborn westward march of the frontier people.

Had European cabinet ministers had any doubts regarding their circumspect judgment of the hornets' nest in the west, those doubts must have been removed in the next few months. In immediate response to news of Wayne's victory and the Jay and Pinckney trea-ties the greatest of all migrations set in. The ark of empire which had been borne westward on flatboat and pack saddle and the backs of people was now mounted on wheels. The Wilderness Road be-came a wagon road in 1796. Other roads were opened to Cumber-land and into the interior of Ohio. New Englanders streamed into western New York. The fringe of Ohio's population along the river which had been too scant to count in the 1790 census began to mount by 10,000 a year as settlement pushed northward along the Muskingum, the Scioto, and the Miami. Kentucky's population raced toward the 200,000 mark. In one two-month period in 1795, 26,000 were counted crossing the Cumberland. The combined population of Cumberland and the southern Holston had passed 77,000, making possible the 1796 admission of the two districts as the state of Tennessee.

All the prospective benefits to the west of the Jay and Pinckney treaties were not, however, immediately forthcoming. There were delays in the British evacuation of the Lake posts, some due to British procrastination, some to American administrative difficulties. Detroit, the base from which in the past so many hundreds of Indian attacks had been launched against the frontier, was occupied July 11, 1796, by an American force under Captain Moses Porter. Wayne arrived August 13th and took residence in McKee's house. Mackinac, the fur-trade and Indian supply center, was occupied by Major Henry Burbeck October 2, 1796. While continuing his inspection of the new line of American border defenses and pressing with furious vigor his denunciations of Wilkinson, Wayne died December 15, 1796, on the upper floor of the fort at Presqu' Isle.

Wilkinson succeeded to command of the army, a rank which required him to preside over the transfer to the United States of the southwest, the Spanish claim to which had been relinquished by Pinckney's treaty. Washington's suspicions of Wilkinson had been by now thoroughly aroused but he retained him in command on the theory that his Spanish associations might simplify and expedite the transfer. This proved an unfounded hope as Spain continued on a succession of varying pretexts to obstruct implementation of the treaty.

Spain's renewed recalcitrance was more than just another example of the old rule that in the west nothing ever proceeded as expected. It heralded a new danger of the most menacing proportions. The flush of victory in the west was being darkened by a monstrous shadow which appeared for a time the most sinister threat that the frontier had yet faced.

XXI

༇

Jefferson

Since their first crossing of the mountains the frontier people's bid for possession of the Mississippi Valley had been challenged by a succession of celebrated opponents: the Indian leaders, Cornstalk, Blackfish, Dragging Canoe, McGillivray, Brant, and Little Turtle; the English governors, Henry Hamilton, Frederick Haldiman, John Graves Simcoe, and Lord Dorchester; and the Spanish governors, Bernardo de Galvez, Esteban Miro, and Hector Carondelet. Now, after a quarter century of conflict in which again and again disaster had been escaped by a hairsbreadth, there came the final and decisive challenge from an immeasurably more portentous antagonist whose power was beginning to shake the world, Napoleon. In this supreme crisis the west which in former emergencies had been served so signally by Clark, Wayne, and Washington found a new and sufficient champion in Jefferson. The contest determining the destiny of a continent became a personal duel of wits and will between the greatest autocrat of his time, whose conquests were achieved by the march of armies, and the greatest democrat of his time, whose more enduring conquests were achieved by the impact of ideas.

The sudden French reach for the west was no new thing. The

interest of France in the Mississippi Valley had never diminished. France had been first to claim possession, and from the moment possession had been lost had remained determined to regain it. A residue of French inhabitants scattered from Niagara and Mackinac to Mobile and New Orleans still considered themselves Frenchmen. In the cession splitting the Valley between England and Spain in 1763 after defeat in the Seven Years' War, France had proceeded on the theory that the division would facilitate eventual repossession. In the military and diplomatic ministries of every succeeding French government perpetually revised plans for that repossession had been considered principal items of unfinished business. Throughout the 1779–1782 diplomatic maneuverings which led to recognition of American independence, France had insisted that England cede the region west of the mountains to Spain, regarding Spain's possession as an interim depository for French interests. The sudden intrusion of American settlers had been unforeseen but came to be accepted as not so much a deterrent as a possible advantage. They could be expected, in association with their neighbors, the long-established French communities, to recognize in a return of French dominion a relief from the trials imposed upon them by the hostility of their Indian, British, and Spanish enemies.

This deep-seated urge to regain France's lost empire in North America survived the fall of the monarchy. The new revolutionary government dedicated its new energies to the cause.[1] A dynamic republic felt impelled to restore to France what had slipped from the grasp of a decadent monarchy. Citizen Genêt was repudiated not because he had exceeded his instructions but because he had failed to execute them. Through all the tumult of the French Revolution's internal and external conflicts not one of the succession of the republic's leaders lost sight of the North American objective. At Basle,

[1] The new French threat was early recognized in the United States. On February 23, 1793, Colonel William S. Smith, son-in-law of Vice President Adams and former aide-de-camp to Washington, informed Washington upon returning from Paris that France proposed to recover the West Indies and was considering support of Francisco de Miranda's projected attack upon Spain's American colonies.

Spain was pressed to retrocede Louisiana.[2] Acutely aware of the value of a French bulwark between the American frontier and Mexico, Spain was more than willing and hesitated only to bargain for better terms. France was thenceforth assured that it was about to become once more a North American power.

The Directoire, upon taking office in 1795, picked up the gage. Pierre Adet, French minister to the United States, kept his government constantly informed on conditions in the west. In March 1796 he dispatched General Victor Collot on a personal tour of the west to conduct an up-to-the-minute investigation and survey. His espionage mission was immediately suspected by both American and Spanish authorities and he was once even arrested, but Collot nevertheless persisted in his inquisitive journey down the Ohio and the Mississippi, noting the disposition of American and French inhabitants, inspecting military sites, measuring the currents and depths of rivers, estimating distances, and gathering comprehensive data which he incorporated in a report for the information of his government and any future commander of an invading army. He recommended that France without further delay gain possession of Louisiana, whether by negotiation or by force, as the sole means sufficiently to limit a growth of the United States which must otherwise permit the two English-speaking nations to dominate the Atlantic.

Rumors sweeping the west that Spain had already retroceded Louisiana were given credence by Collot's tour, by Spain's refusal to evacuate the border territory, by renewed contacts between George Rogers Clark and his expatriate correspondents in Paris, and by obvious manifestations of British alarm which included apparent preparations for a British attack on New Orleans, launched down the Mississippi from the Great Lakes. It had been clearly recognized in the west that Spain's weak grasp on the mouth of the Mississippi

[2] In the diplomatic and geographical language of the time *Louisiana* meant the area north and east of the present Texas, extending indefinitely westward from the Mississippi; *East Florida* referred to the peninsula of Florida and *West Florida* to a strip extending along the Gulf coast from the northwestern shoulder of the peninsula to the Mississippi. New Orleans was considered the common capital of Louisiana and West Florida.

could be easily broken whenever necessity demanded, but it was now as clearly recognized that establishment of French power at New Orleans could constitute a permanent and impassable barrier. Among many westerners this stirred a new impulse to attack Spanish possessions while there was still time. In the Federalist national government it aroused an even more chilling apprehension. Were French control of the Mississippi established it was considered certain that the latent secessionism of the Republican west would lead inevitably to the transfer of its allegiance to France. So soon after the triumphs of 1795 did the west appear tossed in political crosscurrents as confused and diverse as in 1788. The United States boundary commissioner, Andrew Ellicott, engaged in a frustrating attempt to hasten Spanish compliance with the Pinckney agreement, reported to his government from Natchez in 1797 that he had detected unmistakable evidence of three major plots: (1) another revival of the pro-Spanish conspiracy of Wilkinson and his associates, (2) a scheme concocted by American westerners to promote a revolution of American and French residents in Spanish Florida and Louisiana, and (3) a projected expedition of American frontiersmen to invade Spanish possessions in the name of either Great Britain or the United States.

The first overt action to emerge from this ferment was the dramatic disclosure of William Blount's conspiracy. Tennessee, upon admission as a state, had elected the former governor of the Southwest Territory to the United States Senate. Blount was a politician of national note, had been a member of the Continental Congress and the Constitutional Convention and by his advocacy of ratification had stood out as the only prominent western leader who could be considered a Federalist. He was also still as interested in the long cherished Muscle Shoals and Yazoo land-company schemes as he had been in 1785. In 1795 the Georgia legislature renewed the Muscle Shoals grant under more favorable terms. There could, however, be no rapid rise in land values south of the Tennessee as long as the area was denied a commercial outlet on the Gulf. Were France to replace Spain at Mobile and Pensacola, this door could be permanently closed. Action anticipating the French move was indicated. Spain's October 7, 1796, declaration of war on England appeared to Blount to offer the opportunity, and John Chisholm, an ex-Tory resident of the southern Indian country, supplied the final spark. Chisholm came to Philadelphia to propose to Blount and Robert Liston, British minister to the United States, that Cherokee and Creek Indians be offered a major role in any invasion of Spanish territory.

Liston was sufficiently interested to send Chisholm on to London to explain this Indian phase to his government. Blount assumed responsibility for American preparations. In substance his plan envisaged an assault by an expedition of Tennessee-Kentucky frontiersmen and Natchez ex-Tories on New Orleans and an attack by Cherokee, Creek, and Florida ex-Tories on Pensacola in conjunction with British naval operations in the Gulf, and an attack by a British-Indian expedition from Canada on New Madrid. In his exuberance he wrote an indiscreetly revealing letter to James Carey, his Tennessee protégé whom he had appointed Cherokee interpreter in 1792. The jubilant Carey celebrated with an even more indiscreet drinking bout as a result of which the letter came to the attention of the administration. President John Adams and his Federalist advisors consulted for a number of anxious months on how most appropriately to regard this adventure of a fellow Federalist before coming to the conclusion that a war upon Spain and France in alliance with Great Britain was for the moment an ill-advised step in view of the current temper of the American people. This conclusion had meanwhile been supported by Great Britain's hasty disclaimer of any intention of taking liberties with American neutrality. On July 3, 1797, the Carey letter was laid before the Senate which hit upon the simplest solution to the problem by immediately expelling Blount, thus avoiding whatever further disclosures might have resulted during impeachment proceedings.

The Blount imbroglio worsened Spanish-American relations, already embittered by Spain's long delay in complying with the Pinckney treaty. Even the grudging evacuation of Natchez, March 31, 1798, did little to relieve the tension. For the French threat looming behind Spanish obnoxiousness was becoming each day more ominous. The Directoire, incensed by the Jay Treaty and by American evasion of the old French alliance, was assuming an increasingly anti-American posture. French violations of American shipping rights had become more onerous than British. The administration resumed the naval building program that had been permitted to lapse at the end of the recent Algerian war. The vigor of Republican opposition frustrated the Federalist inclination to declare war on France, but publication of the sensational XYZ letters gave the administration a freer hand. The forever famous new frigates *Constitution, Constellation,* and *United States* put to sea. The ensuing naval engagements of the still undeclared war demonstrated American seamanship and gratified American pride.

The belligerent excitement brought Hamilton back from private life to emulate the filibustering projects of his lesser predecessors in that inviting field, Sevier, Clark, Bowles, and Blount. As befitted his stature as a proven statesman his design was on a more grandiose scale than any formerly contemplated. In his seasoned estimation the opportunity to take possession of the southwest before France was established there was one which if not promptly seized might forever pass. Returning in 1799 to temporary active service with his Revolutionary rank of major general, as senior officer of the army he summoned Wilkinson from Natchez to his New York headquarters where the two held long and earnest consultations. Wilkinson was enchanted with a project having so many ramifications which only he was in a position fully to appreciate. Hamilton proposed the enlistment of an overwhelmingly large provisional army of westerners to drive Spain altogether from the Mississippi Valley and the shores of the Gulf. He did not rule out Mexico as a possible later objective. He had the year before been in correspondence with his Revolutionary companion in arms, the peripatetic Venezuelan patriot, Francesco Miranda, who was at the moment in London seeking British support for projected descents upon all Spanish possessions in the New World.

But Hamilton was giving full attention as well to more practical details. To stimulate frontier interest Sevier was slated to be a brigadier general in the provisional army. The assistance of Panton was sought to assure the co-operation of the southern Indians. Eastern political support was solicited by the argument that the west was bound to be so enthralled by the conquest of New Orleans that it would turn to the Federalist party. The Hamilton-Wilkinson project, propitious as it appeared for a time, was nevertheless strangled in its comparative infancy by failure to meet either basic requirement upon which its development depended, western participation and presidential approval. In the stubbornly Republican west there was no enthusiasm for any venture under Federalist sponsorship. And though for many weeks he had refrained from interfering, Adams, when no longer able to evade contemplation of a president's awful responsibility in committing his country to war, suddenly and obstinately said no. The one positive result of the episode was another elevation in rank for Wilkinson. On Hamilton's recommendation he had been promoted to major general.

The French threat continued to mount until it appeared the most devastating of the many storms that had beaten on the west. There was new manifestation in Napoleon's invasion of Egypt in 1798 of the fierce energies generated in France by the Revolution. It had been made all too apparent that a France capable of undertaking an advance upon her former possessions in India was as capable of reaching for her former possessions in North America. In 1799 Napoleon returned to become First Consul, magnifying the dangerous might of the most powerful nation in the world by imposing upon its government the centralized authority of an absolute ruler whose ambitions were limitless. After the Treaty of Luneville, February 9, 1801, he was at war only with England, posing the new and no less alarming threat that England, with command of the sea, might attempt to forestall him in Louisiana. This danger presently passed when England instead also sought peace but the same shift in power politics augmented the French danger. With Nelson no longer denying the seas to him, Napoleon was now free to undertake whatever imperial adventure most suited him. There was unmistakable evidence that his attention was fixed on the western hemisphere in his immediate dispatch of an army of 25,000 under command of his brother-in-law, General Charles Leclerc, to put down a popular uprising in Santo Domingo.[3] He made no secret of his belief that Santo Domingo was the key to Louisiana. He was already on the march to the Mississippi.

Responsibility for coping with this swiftly and fearfully developing menace fell upon the third president, the intellectually dogmatic democrat, Thomas Jefferson. In assuming office March 4, 1801, he was the first president to be inaugurated in the new capital, Washington. The national and international scene that he was obliged to contemplate was as dismal as the vista of stumps and mud in his immediate foreground. To meet the dangers that impended he could not act or speak with the full authority due the acknowledged leader of a united people. His taking office was clouded by the uncertainties shrouding the first transfer in American history of political power from one party to its rival. The country had been more fiercely divided during the closing years of Adams' administration than it was ever to be again until 1861. Jefferson's own elevation to the presidency had been by a margin so excruciatingly narrow as to accentuate these divisions. Tied with Aaron Burr in the electoral college, he had owed his preference by the House of Representatives to the influence of his old antagonist, Hamilton.

Among the many demands upon him, none pressed so heavily as the exploding crisis on the Mississippi. For this contest he did not appear particularly fitted. It presented a problem that was primarily military. Almost alone among American leaders of his time he had had no military experience and had taken democratic pride in the fact. It presented also an essentially western problem. He had had no direct contacts with the west. He had never been west of the mountains. He was an easterner who had spent his life in the study, in legislative halls, and in administrative offices. His

---

[3] As further evidence of how serious were Napoleon's New World intentions, he permitted his favorite sister, Pauline, to accompany her husband on the expedition.

great interests, aside from an intense and all-encompassing scientific curiosity, had been in democratic doctrine, constitutional law, and diplomacy.

Yet there were within him unsuspected resources upon which he and his country could rely. If not a soldier, he was endowed with a soldier's chief requisite, courage. If not outwardly a westerner, he was one at heart. His warmest sympathies had been aroused by the west's democratic tendencies. He was as confident as had been Washington of the west's future development and progress. From his boyhood friend and tutor, Thomas Walker, the great explorer, he had gathered a fascinated acquaintance with the physical aspects of the immense and distant land still so little known and to this he had since added all he could learn from every source available to him. His imagination had already transported him across it all the way to the Western Ocean. As events were soon to demonstrate, to no man's hands could the west's future have been more fittingly trusted.

In so extreme an emergency much depended on the capacities of the American minister to France. With trans-Atlantic communication a matter of months an ambassador had often to make the most significant decisions on his own initiative and responsibility. Jefferson selected the New York aristocrat, Robert Livingston, for the Paris assignment. The president's instructions were necessarily vague since there was no certainty in Washington that Spain's cession to France had yet been consummated. Livingston was directed to seek an opportunity to suggest an offer of the Floridas, or at least of West Florida and New Orleans, to the United States as the only reasonable response to the growing pressure of American settlement. Jefferson and his Secretary of State, James Madison, had given no thought to Louisiana. It was upon the mouth of the Mississippi and the nearer Gulf coast that their interest, and that of the west, was centered. It had been Louisiana and New Orleans, however, that Spain had ceded to France in the secret Treaty of San Ildefonso, October 1, 1800, with the transfer more precisely defined in a second secret agreement between Lucien Bonaparte and Godoy,

March 21, 1801. Spain had insisted and was to continue to insist upon retaining the Floridas.

Before Livingston had reached Paris, December 3, 1801, Rufus King, United States minister to England, had reported the imminence of peace between England and France, a development which would forthwith enable Napoleon to proceed with his Mississippi venture. This intensely disturbing news was followed by a February 18, 1802, report from King enclosing a copy of the March 21st Bonaparte-Godoy agreement. There could no longer be any doubt of Napoleon's intent and had there been any it would have been dispelled by Livingston's April 24, 1802, report that General Jean Bernadotte was assembling an expedition of five to seven thousand men to occupy New Orleans.

But Jefferson had not needed to wait for Livingston's warning that Napoleon's military preparations were already under way to make up his mind. He had fully recognized the tremendous consequences at issue and had had no other impulse than to defy Napoleon's challenge. The intellectual democrat who liked to emphasize the simplicity of his republican principles by receiving gold-braided foreign ambassadors in frayed dressing gown and carpet slippers was animated by a spirit as fierce as any warlord's. His April 18, 1802, letter to Livingston, entrusted for transmittal to the eminent Franco-American, Du Pont de Nemours, with instructions to make certain its contents were impressed upon the government of France, rang with phrases as defiant as battle cries:

There is on the globe one single spot, the possessor of which is our natural and habitual enemy. It is New Orleans, through which the produce of three eighths of our territory must pass to market, and from its fertility it will ere long yield more than half of our whole produce and contain more than half our inhabitants. France placing herself in that door assumes to us the attitude of defiance. The day that France takes possession of New Orleans, fixes the sentence which is to restrain her forever . . . It seals the union of two nations, who, in conjunction, can maintain exclusive possession of the ocean. From that moment, we must marry ourselves to the British fleet and nation.

In challenging France and at the same time turning so readily to the prospect of an alliance with England, he had stolen the loudest Federalist thunder. Since the days of the Genêt controversy it had been Hamilton and his Federalists who had advocated an accommodation with England, and Jefferson and his Republicans who had extolled American friendship for France. But in this foreign crisis politics had for Jefferson stopped at the water's edge. He had made the great discovery made by most presidents since that he must first of all and above all regard himself as the chief defender of his country.

With Jefferson's defiance in one hand Livingston was instructed to advance in the other a request that France set a price on the sale of West Florida and New Orleans to the United States. Livingston reported that he could gain no serious attention for the offer and that in any event it had become clear that West Florida was still held by Spain and therefore technically not at Napoleon's disposal.

Thereafter events began gathering an ever more dangerous momentum. Napoleon had withheld Bernadotte's sailing only in order to assemble a larger Louisiana expedition under the command of General Claude Victor. Livingston continued through November and December to press upon Joseph Bonaparte, whose partial attention he had gained, various proposals involving the purchase of West Florida and New Orleans by the United States, making reiterated use of Jefferson's declaration that any other course would drive the United States into alliance with Great Britain. Early in the winter Napoleon learned of the ruin of his Santo Domingo army by yellow fever, with its commanding general among the dead. Undeterred either by the Santo Domingo disaster or by Jefferson's warnings, he increased his projected Louisiana army to 20,000 and on December 19th ordered Victor to sail.[4] An unseasonably early

---

[4] Napoleon's instructions to Victor, prepared November 26, 1802, included: "The inhabitants of Kentucky, especially, must engage the attention of the captain-general. The rapid current of the Ohio and the rivers whose shores they inhabit, and which empty into the Mississippi, permit them so much the more easily to attempt an expedition against New Orleans. The slight preparation which it would be necessary for them to make, and the modesty of their needs, would accelerate the execution of

accumulation of sea ice held Victor in Dunkirk, thereby delaying a French initiative that must have led certainly to war.

Meanwhile, a development in the harbor of New Orleans had invited an American initiative which fell short of war by as narrow a margin as the escape contrived by the advent of ice in the harbor of Dunkirk. With a display of ineptitude astonishing even when considered in the light of Spain's long record of colonial ineptitude, Juan Morales, Louisiana Intendant, by what authorization appears still a mystery, proclaimed on October 18, 1802, the closing of the American right of deposit at New Orleans. The news reached Nashville by express rider November 18, 1802, and New York by sea November 22nd. The instant roar of American rage was as loud in the east as in the west. The east had at last become aware that navigation of the Mississippi was of as much commercial importance on one side of the mountains as on the other and that it was in fact a national necessity upon which depended the preservation of the union. Immediately responsive to the public's intense excitement, Congress on December 17th called upon the Secretary of State for a report on what measures were being taken to counter this aggression by France and Spain.

No one was more aware of the importance of the Mississippi than Jefferson. But he was also President of the United States. Upon his conscience rested personal responsibility for making decisions upon which depended the security of his country. In keeping with the tradition already established by his predecessors, Washington and Adams, he conceived it his first duty to spare the young nation the incalculable risks of a foreign war. The first three presidents had forged the doctrine that resort to war, in a president's estimation, must always remain a last resort after every other means to guard

---

such an expedition. A powder-horn, a pouch of bullets, their provisions of cold meal, form their equipment. Great readiness, add those persons who have lived among them, is lent by their custom of living in the forests and enduring fatigues. Beyond a doubt such neighbors merit being watched . . . The intention of the First Consul is to give Louisiana a degree of strength which will permit him to abandon it without fear in time of war, so that its enemies may be forced to the greatest sacrifices merely in attempting an attack upon it."

the nation's essential interests have been demonstrated to be insufficient.

Jefferson considered the agitation in the east a political eruption with which the passage of time could assist him to cope. It was only in the west that unauthorized and precipitate armed action might develop which might lead irreversibly to total hostilities. He moved swiftly and surely to reassure the west. On January 11, 1803, he appointed James Monroe minister extraordinary and plenipotentiary to France and Spain with directions to proceed at once to Europe to impress American determination upon both governments. On January 18th he wrote the governor of Kentucky assuring him that the national government proposed to spare no effort to gain free use of the Mississippi.[5] There had been telling testimony to the firmness of his intentions in his selection of ambassador to conduct the all-important mission. Monroe was a violent Republican, had large western land interests, and had been a confirmed advocate of all western causes since the first outbreak of the Mississippi controversy in 1786. Though he now knew that Napoleon's Louisiana expedition had been assembled and might well be on the high seas, Jefferson did not yield an inch. He authorized Monroe to offer a maximum of $9,375,000 for West Florida and New Orleans while in his February 1, 1803, letter to Du Pont, intended for the information of Napoleon, he bluntly restated the alternative:

> For our circumstances are so imperious as to admit of no delay as to our course; and the use of the Mississippi so indispensable, that we cannot hesitate one moment to hazard our existence for its maintenance.

The public clamor for war continued. The Federalists were not above seeking political advantage in the crisis by renewing their effort to detach the west from its Republic sympathies. The west's indignation was courted by reminders that the west's interests were

[5] As further evidence of the trend of Jefferson's thinking, that same January 18, 1803, he sent a secret and confidential message to Congress advising American exploration of the Missouri River and the route to the Western Ocean.

being ignored by a Republican president. Federalist newspapers were filled with inflammatory articles. The Federalist leaders, Morris and Hamilton, accused Jefferson of appeasement and denounced the Monroe mission as an admission of weakness. The disappointed Republican, Burr, who had missed by but one vote being invested with the power to decide now held by Jefferson, added his voice to the chorus. The pro war movement came to a head with the introduction by Pennsylvania Senator James Ross of a resolution authorizing the President to call 50,000 Georgia, South Carolina, Ohio, Kentucky, Tennessee, and Mississippi Territory militia to act with the regular army of the United States in undertaking the seizure of New Orleans. After long and acrimonious debate the Ross resolution was defeated February 25, 1803, by a vote of 15 to 11. Every western senator voted no, even though this was a project of which the west had dreamed for a generation. The Federalist appeal to the west had failed. Jefferson's tactics, including particularly his appointment of Monroe, had prevailed. Having at last a Republican national government, the instinctively Republican west remained, even under the strain of this temptation, more disposed to trust that government than its Federalist opponents.

Monroe reached Paris April 13, 1803, intensely conscious of the importance of his mission. Jefferson had appropriately described it as one upon the issue of which "depends the future destinies of the republic." Monroe could have no way of knowing, any more than could Livingston, as the two anxiously conferred, that the stupendous question was already settled. Napoleon had been committed to his decision a month before when on March 12, 1803, he had made his historic remark to the British ambassador: "I find, my lord, your nation wants war again." Having determined to resume his conquests in Europe, he was forced to the same conclusion as had been Great Britain and Spain in 1795. Distance made war in North America unreasonably expensive in men and money while the rewards to be gained there did not match those to be sought in Europe. The defense of Louisiana on the far shore of an ocean which his prospective British enemy must dominate appeared an unacceptable burden. New Orleans, the one spot in the whole area of present strategic or commercial value, must be regarded as subject to capture by either the United States or Britain. Jefferson had convinced him that the United States was certain to make the attempt. On the terrible chessboard of war which he now contemplated, Louisiana had become a pawn which, since it must be sacrificed, might better be yielded to the United States than to his principal enemy, England.

The evening of the day of Monroe's arrival, while Monroe was studying the papers detailing Livingston's previous negotiations, Livingston was taken for a stroll in the garden by his old friend of Philadelphia days, François de Barbé-Marbois, now Napoleon's minister of finance. Barbé-Marbois suddenly proposed the sale of the whole of Louisiana, including New Orleans, to the United States. Livingston was at once thunderstruck and fascinated. Nothing in either his or Monroe's instructions authorized them to consider an unforeseen transaction of such proportions. Though personally at odds, with each assuming the other was seeking chief credit for their mutual endeavor, the two had the courage and vision to pursue the negotiation. With a diplomatic competence reminiscent of the proficiency demonstrated by the American peace commissioners in 1782, they shrewdly haggled for better terms without permitting the fabulous opportunity to escape them. After a state dinner with Napoleon May 2, 1803, they signed the treaty, dated April 30th, providing for the purchase of Louisiana by the United States for $11,250,000 plus American payment of American claims pending against France, the cash to be produced by the English banking firm of Baring and Hope upon acceptance of American bonds. By those unauthorized strokes of their pens the two ambassadors had not only thrown open the New Orleans door to the west's future but had opened to the dominion of the United States a boundless land that extended westward into regions no white man yet knew.

The event, the most memorable in American history after the

ratification of the Constitution, Yorktown, the Declaration of Independence, and the first crossing of the mountains, had been attended by extraordinary ironies and anomalies. Livingston and
Monroe had been commissioned to buy Florida and had instead
bought Louisiana. Jefferson, whose democratic principles had been
dedicated to the sternest limitations upon the national government's
powers, had found himself committed to an arbitrary expansion of
executive authority which he considered to the day of his death a
flagrant violation of the Constitution. The Federalists who had for
years been whipping the country on to war with France in order to
win the west had found all the rewards of their labors dropping
without a war into the lap of a Republican president. And British
bankers had paid Napoleon to deliver to the United States a vast
territory which he was in any event certain to lose and which could
otherwise have fallen to England.

Momentous as was the Louisiana Purchase as a diplomatic and
political achievement and significant as was the ratification of the
treaty by the Senate October 20, 1803, and the occupation of New
Orleans for the United States December 20, 1803, by the American
commissioners, Wilkinson and William Claiborne, these formal
transactions were in essence no more than a progressive recognition
of an existing situation. The phenomenal extension of American
settlement which had in the past quarter century taken possession of
the entire Ohio basin was beginning as inexorably to take possession
of the entire Mississippi Valley. With the end of the Indian wars in
1795 the outer and more aggressive fringe of settlement, composed
largely of the original frontier people, had begun at once to press
not only northward toward the Great Lakes but southward toward
the Gulf and westward across the Mississippi.

Spain had as a policy discouraged the founding of organized
American colonies, such as those projected by Wilkinson and Clark
and undertaken by Morgan, but had intermittently and cautiously
sanctioned the migration of individuals. In 1796, fearing an English
invasion of Louisiana, Spain had for a period openly invited settlement. A contemporary British foreign office report estimated that

2000 American families had taken advantage of the opportunity. Alarmed Spanish authorities soon attempted to halt the influx but it was already too late, if it had not always been too late.

The composition of the American population in the west made regulation or control of its movements impossible by any exertion of authority, whether domestic or foreign. The west was being occupied, as it had been from the beginning, not according to any program of public planning or organized co-operation or corporate promotion but by the independent initiative of individual families. Its people formed a society as dispersed and amorphous as it was vigorous and willful, which considered itself subject only to its own option, even its own caprice. There were in the structure of this society few of the political and social elements through which people are ordinarily governed. All but a minute fraction of the west's population still resided in small, separate one-family farms that had been only recently torn from the wilderness. Its most important cities were scarcely villages. In 1800 the population of Pittsburgh numbered 1565, Lexington 1797, Nashville 355. The impulsive movements of a people so self-sufficient who were scattered so widely could be neither restrained nor channeled. The immense extent of Louisiana made the exclusion problem insoluble. As Godoy put it in 1797, "You can't lock up an open field." By 1803 American settlers were pressing well up the Missouri and from the lower Mississippi as far west as the Sabine. When Spain made the formal transfer of Louisiana to France at New Orleans November 30, 1803, Louisiana was no longer Spain's to bestow.

There was another clue to the actual situation in the identity of many of these early trans-Mississippi intruders. Daniel Boone, a Kentucky founder, and Moses Austin, later to become a Texas founder, were among those established on the Missouri by 1797. Among their neighbors were families with names long famous in frontier history, Bryan, Callaway, Lynn, Hubbard, Spencer. This was a unique stock. They were people accustomed to following their own bent. Their continuing to follow it could not have been prevented had Victor's army sailed before the ice formed at Dunkirk. In his sagacious decision to sell Louisiana while he still had something to sell, Napoleon had more than the British fleet to guide his judgment. He had also to consider that the frontier people were already in possession.

XXII

❧

A New Power

The frontier people had now completed the third of their historic missions. Their first had been their crossing of the mountains into the interior wilderness, in the face of hazards both known and unknowable, in defiance of the united opposition of every political and military force that in any way bore upon their venture, and at the last moment before the great opportunity must otherwise have been lost forever. Their second had been the incredible maintenance of their exposed position during the border war of the Revolution which subjected them to years of such miseries and horrors as no other people have ever been obliged to endure. Their third had been to attach the west so firmly to the United States that there could be no question of Americans having become one nation occupying the major portion of the continent. Their endurance, energy, and initiative had extended the dominion of their country over an area that matched the proportions of all Europe. They had thrust the American boundary westward to the farther limit of lands so far known, a limit that was continuing to recede and that already stretched westward from the Atlantic a distance equal to that from London to Constantinople. In the brief span of twenty years they had raised the United States from the status of a new nation to that of a new power.

The full dimensions of this last achievement may only be perceived after reflection on the dangers with which they had coped while attaining it. England's concession of the west to the United States at the end of the Revolution had been at the time universally considered a temporary expedient. In the light of the realities of international politics and what were assumed to be the realities of border conditions, the cession had been regarded by none of the great powers concerned, Great Britain, Spain, or France, as a permanent disposition of the Mississippi Valley. It had at first been taken scarcely more seriously by more than a few members of the Continental Congress which had been in any event powerless to support the American position in the west.

Most observers had been of the opinion that Indian belligerency would prove in itself sufficient to check the further development of American settlement which had appeared from the beginning a venture so irrational that it could not conceivably be expected to persist. To this basic deterrent Great Britain and Spain had added the burdens of the Lake posts and Mississippi closure situations. There had seemed every reason to believe that the western American's life had been made so nearly insupportable that he must either withdraw or turn to one or the other of his oppressors to seek surcease from his afflictions. The ensuing test of his endurance had been prolonged. The Indian menace, which fell most heavily on the family which was the economic and political unit upon which frontier society altogether depended, had provided a thirteen-year-long harassment that made any kind of normal existence impossible. Every circumstance had conspired to discourage any impulse that might move the individual westerner to set a high value on his nominal connection to his own national government. It had been the unanimous advice of his principal leaders that he accept instead the persistently proffered protection of foreign powers. His quandary had not been simplified by the eight-year-long refusal of Congress to recognize Kentucky's demand for statehood. These combined

assaults upon his mind as well as upon his body had imposed grave
and terrible pressures. The frontiersman's refusal to yield to them
has since been taken for granted as a natural and normal reaction.
It had, instead, been a protracted and desperate struggle in which
the issue had been often in suspense and had only been finally resolved by the same acceptance of risk, the same willingness to endure
privation, and the same readiness to die that had marked his first
crossing of the mountains or the defense of his Revolutionary stockades.

It had been a struggle waged in the west and won in the west,
by westerners. During its later stages there had been much emi-
nently wise support from Washington and Jefferson, but by then
the first gleams of victory had been beginning to appear in the
western sky. It had remained throughout a conflict fought on the
frontier with every major turning point, except the last at Fallen
Timbers, the consequence of frontier action or decision. Even after
the establishment of the presidency had given the national government a more significant role, the inescapable dictates of geography
had continued to force upon the west principal responsibility for
the course of events. It is difficult now to realize what a distance
then separated Nashville, Louisville, or Cincinnati from New
York, Philadelphia, or Washington. Positions had been taken,
alternatives chosen, decisions made weeks before word of them
could reach the national government and many more weeks before
its response could be known west of the mountains. When Washington addressed Congress December 8, 1790, he had still not heard
of Harmar's defeat 48 days earlier. St. Clair was writing Knox that
same year: "Of what is passing in your quarter, or in the European
world, we know as little as the man in the moon. For pity sake,
send some newspapers."

The key to the great achievement had been not so much the
indomitability of the original frontier people as the example they
had set for others perhaps not so fitted for the ordeal. In their crossing of the mountains, their maintenance of the Revolutionary stockades, and their defense of the most exposed outer fringes of the

frontier during the Indian wars after the Revolution, their thinning ranks had been intermittently strengthened by those among the later comers who were by disposition prepared to accept an existence so demanding. It had been these hardy inhabitants of the outer frontier who had, first by opening the way and then by guarding the safer central areas of settlement, made possible the ensuing westward surge numbered in hundreds of thousands. It was this extraordinary influx that had proved the eventually deciding factor in assuring the United States undisputed possession of the Mississippi Valley. It had been the example set by the frontier people's original initiative and their proven ability to sustain it that had stirred countless more prudent eastern families who without it would never have been moved to accept so obvious a risk, to venture where it had already been demonstrated other families had ventured. It was, moreover, an example which strikingly contributed to the development in the entire American people of the most essentially American of all their characteristics. In all the years that followed nothing more distinguished the American people from other peoples than the average American's instant impulse to take advantage of any opportunity, however startling appeared the departure from all that he had formerly known. It was an example that helped free the American imagination not only for the eccentricities of the westward movement but for every sort of novel enterprise from the digging of canals and the building of railroads to the inventing of better mouse traps.

Another key to the achievement had been the edifice of fully functioning self-government erected by the frontier people upon the foundation of the frontier's natural self-reliance and self-sufficiency. From the days of the Boonesborough Convention the least prepossessing settlement had insisted upon its inherent right to govern itself. This universally held frontier view was never more cogently stated than by John Emerson, an otherwise totally obscure settler. Upon being ejected by Harmar's soldiers from his unauthorized holding on the west bank of the Ohio, he protested March 12, 1785:

I do certify that all mankind, agreeable to every constitution formed in America, have an undoubted right to pass into every vacant country, and there to form their constitution, and that from the confederation of the whole United States, Congress is not empowered to forbid them.

It had been this insistence upon self-government far more than any tug of loyalty to the United States that had led the frontier people to reject the overtures of Spain and Great Britain. They had elected a way of life that they refused to compromise, least of all by submission to another power. They had as instinctively refused to submit to the United States and had instead forced the implementation of the doctrine of the successive admission of new, free, and equal states which, until they took their stand, had been no more than an intellectual theory. The significance of this contribution to the development of the republic can never be sufficiently recognized.

The most amazing aspect of their whole amazing achievement was the incredible speed with which a wilderness was transformed into a civilized, populous, and prosperous commonwealth. One of the favorite anecdotes of frontier days concerned the instances in which babies were born during the wild excitement and hideous tumult of an Indian assault on a family cabin. One often mentioned example was the birth of James Robertson's son Felix on the day of a 1780 attack on his Freelands station. A child born under such circumstances in 1794 would have entered a blood-stained and fear-haunted environment not so far removed from the primitive savageries of the stone age. By the time he could talk he would have found that the Indian danger which, while his mother was carrying him, had dominated every phase of his family's daily life had receded to what already seemed so far in the past that it had become no more than a subject for occasional reminiscence. He had scarcely learned to read before the Louisiana Purchase had removed the foreign threat to the American west as completely as had been the Indian threat. By the time he was old enough to think of having a child of his own there were steamboats on rivers that had known only flatboats and keelboats, and the $8.00 per hundred-weight cost of freight sent overland from Philadelphia to Cincinnati had fallen to $1.00 when sent instead by sea and the Mississippi. His father's world of corn patch and cabin, buffalo herds and thirty-foot cane, Indians and wolf packs had, before his own children were born, become a world of fields and fences, roads and bridges, schools and churches, mills and banks, towns and cities.

The vigor which had marked the initial invasion of the wilderness by Americans was equally manifest in the extraordinary and uninterrupted development of the west after 1795. The great complex of waterways extending from the Great Lakes to the Gulf provided unparalleled advantages to migration and commerce. By 1820 Ohio and Kentucky were exceeded in population only by New York, Pennsylvania, Virginia, and North Carolina. Five of the original seaboard states had fewer inhabitants than Tennessee. More people lived west of the mountains than had inhabited all thirteen colonies the year Boonesborough was founded 45 years before. The west which so recently had seemed isolated and neglected and thwarted, which had seemed hopelessly separated from the east by differences and prejudices as massive as the intervening mountains, had increased in numbers, substance, and political stature until it was able to take a dominant place in the nation's councils. In 1828 Andrew Jackson, as representative, unregenerate, and self-willed a westerner as could have been singled out, was elected President of the United States.

Meanwhile, most of the original frontier people, still in search of that larger freedom which they had sought from the beginning, had long since resumed their self-perpetuating quest. Some had pushed the frontier northwestward across Ohio and Indiana into southern Michigan and northern Illinois.[1] Others had pressed southward

[1] Abraham Lincoln's family had played a representative part in this migratory movement. His maternal grandfather, Abraham Hanks, after starting for Boonesborough in 1775, had been temporarily turned back by an Indian scare, and his paternal grandfather, Abraham Lincoln, had been killed by Indians in Kentucky in 1784. The Lincoln family made successive moves northwestward across Kentucky and Indiana into central Illinois.

into the Creek and Choctaw country of Alabama and Mississippi. Those most committed to their quest had pushed westward to the Missouri and the Sabine.

Here they were confronted by the frontier people's fourth and final mission. They had come far but a greater distance still stretched before them. They had already opened the way to Kentucky, Tennessee, and Missouri, to Ohio, Indiana, and Illinois, to Alabama, Mississippi, Louisiana, and Arkansas. All these they had added to the country which they had come fully to realize was their country. Beyond the horizon lay other notable regions to be possessed. Texas and Oregon and California still awaited them. There also awaited many strange new difficulties, as strange and in a different way as formidable as the dangers they had encountered when they had first crossed the eastern mountains. For they had come to the western edge of the great forest which clothed all of the continent which they had so far penetrated. They had not realized how much they had depended upon that forest until they had come to the end of it. So far in their adaptation to the demands of survival in a wilderness they had enjoyed the advantages of wood always at hand for fuel, shelter, fences, and implements and abundant water always available, from a spring in the dooryard to mighty rivers capable of transporting a whole community with all of its property. But now there loomed before them a land as alien in all its aspects as the surface of another planet—treeless plains, arid deserts, tremendous mountains, and, most forbidding of all, distances so vast that travel across them must be measured not in days but in months. Even the rivers ran the wrong way.

Behind them lay all the tedium, toil, and terror of perpetual privation, foreign intrigue, political controversy, and forty years of Indian war. Ahead of them waited new demands for which their experience had not prepared them and the extent of which no man could foresee. This final challenge they were to prove also able to meet.

BIBLIOGRAPHY

Bibliography

Among published material available in most larger libraries to the reader inclined to pursue the subject, the following have been found useful in the preparation of this work:

Abernethy, Thomas Perkins. *From Frontier to Plantation in Tennessee*. Chapel Hill, 1932.

Abernethy, Thomas Perkins. *Western Lands and the American Revolution*. New York, 1937.

Adair, James. *History of the American Indians*. London, 1775. Reprint (Samuel Cole Williams, ed). Johnson City, 1930.

Alvord, Clarence W. *The Illinois Country, 1673–1818*. Springfield, 1920.

Alvord, Clarence W. *The Mississippi Valley in British Politics*. 2 vols. Cleveland, 1917.

Ambler, Charles H. *George Washington and the West*. Chapel Hill, 1936.

American State Papers. Washington, 1832–61.

Annals of St. Louis. Frederick L. Billon, ed. 2 vols. St. Louis, 1886–88.

Annals of the West. James H. Perkins and J. M. Peck, eds. St. Louis, 1850.

Bailey, Kenneth P. *The Ohio Company of Virginia*. Glendale, 1939.

Bakeless, John. *Background to Glory*. Philadelphia and New York, 1957.

Baldwin, Leland D. *The Keelboat Age on Western Waters*. Pittsburgh, 1941.

Bartram, William. *Travels*. Philadelphia, 1791. Reprint (Mark Van Doren, ed.). New York, 1940.

Bemis, Samuel F. *Pinckney's Treaty*. Baltimore, 1926.

Billington, Ray Allen. *Westward Expansion*. New York, 1949.

Bond, Beverly W. *The Foundations of Ohio*. Columbus, 1941.

Boyd, Thomas A. *Mad Anthony Wayne*. New York, 1928.

Brown, John Mason. *The Political Beginnings of Kentucky*. Louisville, 1889.

Brown, John P. *Old Frontiers*. Kingsport, 1938.

Buck, Solon J. and Elizabeth H. *The Planting of Civilization in Western Pennsylvania*. Pittsburgh, 1939.

Burt, A. L. *The United States, Great Britain and British North America*. New Haven, 1940.

Butler, Mann. *A History of the Commonwealth of Kentucky*. Louisville, 1834.

Butterfield, Consul Wilshire. *History of the Girtys*. Cincinnati, 1890.

Callahan, North. *Henry Knox*. New York, 1958.

Caughey, John W. *Bernado de Galvez in Louisiana 1776–1783*. Berkeley, 1934.

Caughey, John W. *McGillivray of the Creeks*. Norman, 1938.

Chalmers, Harvey and Monture, Ethel Brant. *Joseph Brant, Mohawk*. East Lansing, 1955.

Cist, Charles. *Cincinnati Miscellany*. 2 vols. Cincinnati, 1840.

Clark, George Rogers. *Papers*. James Alton James, ed. 2 vols. Springfield, 1912 and 1926.

Collins, Richard H. *History of Kentucky*. 2 vols. Covington, 1877.

Continental Congress. *Journals*. 23 vols. Washington, 1904–15.

Cotterill, Robert S. *History of Pioneer Kentucky*. Cincinnati, 1917.

Cotterill, R. S. *The Southern Indians*. Norman, 1954.

Dangerfield, George. *Chancellor Robert Livingston*. New York, 1960.

Darling, Arthur P. *Our Rising Empire*. New Haven, 1940.

Dillin, John G. *The Kentucky Rifle*. Washington, 1924.

Doddridge, Joseph. *Notes on the Settlement and Indian Wars of Virginia and Pennsylvania*. Wellsburg, 1824. Reprint (Alfred Williams, ed.). Albany, 1876.

Downes, Randolph C. *Council Fires on the Upper Ohio*. Pittsburgh, 1940.

Downes, Randolph C. *Frontier Ohio*. Columbus, 1941.

Drake, Daniel. *Pioneer Life in Kentucky*. Cincinnati, 1870. Reprint (Emmet Field Horine, ed.). New York, 1948.

Driver, Carl S. *John Sevier*. Chapel Hill, 1932.

Dunbar, Seymour. *History of Travel in America*. 4 vols. Indianapolis, 1915.

Filson, John. *The Discovery, Settlement and Present State of Kentucky*. Wilmington, 1784. Reprint (Willard Rouse Jillson, ed.). Louisville, 1929.

Gayarre, C. E. A. *History of Louisiana*. 4 vols. New Orleans, 1903.

Gitmore, James R. *Rearguard of the Revolution*. New York, 1887.

Hamilton, Peter J. *Colonial Mobile*. Boston, 1910.

Haywood, John. *Civil and Political History of Tennessee.* Nashville, 1823. Reprint. Nashville, 1891.

Henderson, Archibald. *Conquest of the Old Southwest.* New York, 1920.

Hornaday, William T. *Extermination of the American Bison.* Washington, 1889.

Houck, Louis. *History of Missouri.* 3 vols. Chicago, 1908.

Hulbert, Archer Butler. *Historic Highways of America.* 16 vols. Cleveland, 1902–05.

Imlay, Gilbert. *A Topographical Description of the Western Territory of North America.* London, 1792. Reprint. 2 vols. New York, 1793.

Jacobs, James R. *Tarnished Warrior.* New York, 1938.

James, James Alton. *Life of George Rogers Clark.* Chicago, 1928.

Jefferson, Thomas. *Writings.* Paul L. Ford, ed. 10 vols. New York, 1892–99.

Jefferson, Thomas. *Notes on Virginia.* Paris, 1785. Reprint (Paul L. Ford, ed.). Brooklyn, 1894.

Jillson, Willard Rouse. *Pioneer Kentucky.* Frankfort, 1934.

Kellogg, Louise Phelps. *The British Regime in Wisconsin and the Northwest.* Madison, 1935.

Kenton, Edna. *Simon Kenton.* New York, 1930.

Kincaid, Robert L. *The Wilderness Road.* Indianapolis, 1947.

Kinnaird, Lawrence. *Spain in the Mississippi Valley 1765–1794.* 3 vols. Washington, 1946–49.

Lewis, George E. *The Indiana Company.* Glendale, 1941.

Littell, William. *Political Transactions in and Concerning Kentucky.* Frankfort, 1806. Reprint. Louisville, 1926. (Containing introduction by Temple Bodley and text of the first Wilkinson Memorial.)

McKnight, Charles. *Our Western Border.* Philadelphia, 1875.

Marshall, Humphrey. *History of Kentucky.* 2 vols. Frankfort, 1824.

Monette, J. W. *History of the Discovery and Settlement of the Mississippi Valley.* 2 vols. New York, 1846.

Mooney, James. *Myths of the Cherokee.* Washington, 1900.

Morgan, Lewis H. *League of the Iroquois.* 2 vols. Rochester, 1851. Reprint. 2 vols. in 1. (Herbert M. Lloyd, ed.). New York, 1904.

Paxon, Frederick. *History of the American Frontier.* New York, 1924.

Phelan, James. *History of Tennessee.* Boston and New York, 1888.

Pickett, Albert James. *History of Alabama.* 2 vols. Birmingham, 1900.

Ramsey, J. G. M. *Annals of Tennessee.* Charleston, 1853. Reprint. Kingsport, 1926.

Riegal, Robert E. *America Moves West.* New York, 1930.

Robertson, James Alexander. *Louisiana Under Spain, France and the United States.* 2 vols. Cleveland, 1911.

Robertson, James Rood. *Petitions of the Early Inhabitants of Kentucky.* Louisville, 1926.

Roosevelt, Theodore. *The Winning of the West.* 6 vols. New York, 1889–96.

Royce, Charles C. *Indian Land Cessions.* Washington, 1900.

Russell, Nelson V. *The British Regime in Michigan and the Old Northwest.* Northfield, 1939.

St. Clair, Arthur. *Papers.* William H. Smith, ed. 2 vols. Cincinnati, 1882.

Savelle, Max. *George Morgan, Colony Builder.* New York, 1932.

Shaler, N. S. *Kentucky.* Boston, 1885.

Simcoe, John Graves. *Papers.* E. A. Cruikshank, ed. 5 vols. Toronto, 1923–31.

Stevens, Wayne E. *The Northwest Fur Trade 1763–1800.* Urbana, 1926.

Stone, William L. *Life of Joseph Brant.* 2 vols. New York, 1838.

Speed, Thomas. *The Political Club, Danville, Kentucky, 1786–1790.* Louisville, 1891.

Swanton, John R. *Early History of the Creek Indians.* Washington, 1922.

Toulmin, Harry. *The Western Country in 1793.* San Marino, 1948.

Thwaites, Reuben Gold (ed.). *Early Western Travels.* 32 vols. Cleveland, 1904–07.

Thwaites, Reuben Gold. *Daniel Boone.* New York, 1928.

Turner, Frederick Jackson. *The Frontier in American History.* New York, 1920.

Turner, Frederick Jackson. *The Significance of Sections in American History.* New York, 1932.

Vail, R. W. G. *Voice of the Old Frontier.* New York, 1949.

Washington, George. *Diaries.* John C. Fitzpatrick, ed. 4 vols. New York, 1925.

Washington, George. *Writings.* John C. Fitzpatrick, ed. 39 vols. Washington, 1931–44.

Whitaker, Arthur Preston. *The Spanish-American Frontier.* Boston and New York, 1927.

Whitaker, Arthur Preston. *The Mississippi Question 1795–1803.* New York, 1934.

Wildes, Harry E. *Anthony Wayne.* New York, 1941.

Williams, Samuel Cole. *History of the Lost State of Franklin.* New York, 1933.

Williams, Samuel Cole (ed.). *Early Travels in the Tennessee Country.* Johnson City, 1928.

Winsor, Justin. *Narrative and Critical History of America.* 8 vols. Boston and New York, 1889.

Winsor, Justin. *The Westward Movement.* Boston and New York, 1897.

Withers, Alexander Scott. *Chronicles of Border Warfare.* Clarksburg, 1831. Reprint (Reuben Gold Thwaites, ed.). Cincinnati, 1895.

INDEX

Index

DATE DUE